Exegetical Guide to the Greek New Testament

Colossians and Philemon

Exegetical Guide to the Greek New Testament

Edited by Murray J. Harris

This ambitious new series seeks to bring together classroom, study, and pulpit by providing the student or pastor with the information needed to understand and expound the Greek text of the New Testament. The *Exegetical Guide to the Greek New Testament* closes the gap between grammatical analysis and exegesis, leading the reader into an in-depth understanding of the New Testament Greek text by guiding him or her through the processes of thorough exegesis flowing into sermon construction.

Each of the twenty projected *EGGNT* volumes will provide the following for the biblical book or books on which they are written: a brief introduction on authorship, date, occasion, and purpose, an analytical outline of the book, a list of recommended commentaries, extensive exegetical notes, a translation and an expanded paraphrase of the whole book, a comprehensive exegetical outline, and a glossary of grammatical and rhetorical terms.

The rich exegetical notes make up the heart and bulk of the guide. Covering the text paragraph by paragraph, they provide the following: (1) the **Greek text;** (2) a **structural analysis;** (3) a comprehensive discussion of each phrase in turn, treating significant **textual variants** and **vocabulary,** giving detailed **grammatical analysis** (including parsing), exploring the options in **disputed points of exegesis,** and providing, in effect, an **index to the standard reference works**—grammars, word-study books, and the BAGD lexicon; (4) a **translation** and an **expanded paraphrase,** both incorporating the results of the exegetical discussion; (5) a list (for most paragraphs) of **exegetical and biblical-theological topics** arising in the text and suggested for further study, with detailed bibliography given for each topic; and (6) **homiletical suggestions,** designed to help the pastor move from the Greek text to preaching that reflects careful exegesis of the text.

This resource is so complete that any given person will likely use only selected parts according to his or her needs. Indeed, the *EGGNT* will prove helpful for a wide readership: students tackling New Testament studies, teachers seeking an aid for their students in reading the Greek New Testament, and preachers who wish to use the Greek text in their sermon preparation but whose knowledge of Greek has receded. No other available work in New Testament literature provides a comparable combination of serious exegetical work and homiletical intent.

Colossians & Philemon

Murray J. Harris

Professor of New Testament Exegesis and Theology
Trinity Evangelical Divinity School
Deerfield, Illinois, USA

WILLIAM B. EERDMANS PUBLISHING COMPANY
GRAND RAPIDS, MICHIGAN

Copyright © 1991 by Murray J. Harris
First Published 1991 by William B. Eerdmans Publishing Co.
255 Jefferson Ave. S.E., Grand Rapids, MI 49503
All rights reserved

Printed in the United States of America

Library of Congress Cataloging-in-Publication Data

Harris, Murray J.
    Colossians & Philemon / Murray J. Harris
        p.   cm. — (Exegetical guide to the Greek New Testament)
    Includes bibliographical references.
    ISBN 0-8028-0375-X
    1. Bible. N.T. Colossians—Commentaries. 2. Bible.
N.T. Philemon—Commentaries. I. Bible. N.T. Colossians. Greek. 1991.
II. Bible. N.T. Colossians. English. Harris. 1991. III. Bible. N.T.
Philemon. Greek. 1991. IV. Bible. N.T. Philemon. English. Harris. 1991.
V. Title. VI. Title: Colossians and Philemon. VII. Series:
Harris, Murray J. Exegetical guide to the Greek New Testament.
BS2715.3.H36   1991
227'.7048—dc20   90-47018
                                                                      CIP

Books of Colossians and Philemon are from the Greek New Testament, edited by Kurt
Aland, Matthew Black, Carlo M. Martini, Bruce M. Metzger, and Allen Wikgren, Third
edition (corrected) © 1966, 1968, 1975, 1983.
Used by permission.

This *Guide* is dedicated to those who have read the
Greek New Testament with me in New Zealand,
England, and the United States of America.

Contents

COLOSSIANS

PHILEMON

CONTENTS

General Introduction

Who is the* Exegetical Guide *for?

In recent years many helps have been produced to ease the task of the person seeking to learn New Testament Greek. But even after the student has painstakingly worked his or her way through an introductory grammar with its isolated examples drawn at random from the Greek New Testament, there remains the formidable task of grappling with the Greek text itself, where difficult verbal forms, new vocabulary, and grammatical irregularities jostle for the student's attention and threaten to overwhelm. To help at this stage there have arisen further helps, such as intermediate grammars, which contain more numerous examples of each construction, and grammatical analyses, which focus on vocabulary and parsing. But the grammars, for all their value, still leave the student stranded at a distance from the Greek text itself, and the analyses, though welcome, are often hampered by their necessary brevity and cannot bridge the gulf between analysis on the one side and translation and exegesis on the other.

The *Exegetical Guide (EGGNT)* aims to close that gap between stranded student (or former student) and daunting text and to bridge that gulf between morphological analysis and exegesis. Each volume of the *Guide* seeks to provide in a single volume all the necessary information for basic understanding of the Greek text, and to afford suggestions for more detailed study. The individual volumes are not full-scale commentaries. But they should prove helpful to those who need some aid in understanding the Greek New Testament and in particular to several groups of persons: students preparing for examinations in New Testament studies, ministers and pastors who are hard-pressed for time yet eager to maintain the momentum in the study of Greek that they gained in their theological training and who wish to use the Greek text as the basis for their sermon preparation, and teachers seeking to help students gain confidence in reading the Greek New Testament.

A wide variety of people, then, should find useful material in the *Guide*—even those who struggled with an introductory Greek course or whose knowledge of Greek has receded into the forgotten past. But in deciding what to include in the *Guide,* several assumptions had to be made. The *Guide* assumes that the reader:

1. has completed an introductory New Testament Greek course (such as J. W. Wenham's *Elements of New Testament Greek* [Cambridge: Cambridge University, 1965]);
2. has learned the meanings of words occurring in the New Testament more frequently than 25 times (see B. M. Metzger, *Lexical Aids for Students of New Testament Greek* [Princeton: the author, 1970[2]] 7-23, or R. E. Van Voorst, *Building Your New Testament Greek Vocabulary* [Grand Rapids: Eerdmans, 1990] 15-60, 78-82);
3. has been introduced to the textual criticism of the New Testament (see, e.g., J. H. Greenlee, *Introduction to New Testament Textual Criticism* [Grand Rapids: Eerdmans, 1964]); and
4. possesses a copy of *The Greek New Testament,* third edition, ed. K. Aland, M. Black, C. M. Martini, B. M. Metzger, and A. Wikgren (New York: United Bible Societies, 1975).

What Does the Exegetical Guide *Do for the Reader?*

Each *EGGNT* volume begins with a brief introduction to the particular New Testament book (including matters such as authorship, date, occasion, and purpose), an outline of its contents, and a list of recommended commentaries. At the end of each volume is a translation and an expanded paraphrase of the whole biblical book, a comprehensive exegetical outline of the book, and a glossary of grammatical and rhetorical terms.[1]

The major part of each volume is given over to paragraph-by-paragraph exegetical treatment of the text of the New Testament book. The treatment of each paragraph includes:

1. the Greek text of the passage from the third edition of the United Bible Societies' *Greek New Testament* (UBS),

---

1. To keep the Glossary relatively brief, references to the grammars are not listed for the point in question; their own indexes should be adequate to discover their treatment of the issue. However, if an example of the usage occurs or is thought by some to occur in the particular New Testament book under discussion, or if references to the grammars are given in the discussion of a particular passage, then the relevant passage is cited in the Glossary.

2. a structural analysis of the passage,

3. a discussion of each phrase of the passage in turn, with discussion of vocabulary and significant textual variants and detailed grammatical analysis, including parsing,

4. a translation and an expanded paraphrase, both incorporating the results of the exegetical discussion,

5. a list of suggested topics for further study with bibliography for each topic, and

6. a series of homiletical suggestions designed to help the preacher or teacher move from the Greek text to a sermon outline that reflects careful exegesis of the text.

More needs to be said about each of these parts of the exegetical discussion.

1. The Greek text of the UBS third edition is virtually the same as that of the twenty-sixth edition (1979) of the Nestle-Aland *Novum Testamentum Graece* (Stuttgart: Deutsche Bibelstiftung). The UBS edition is preferred over the Nestle-Aland edition because of its clearer Greek script and more attractive format, its inclusion of punctuation variants, its more extensive textual apparatus, albeit on fewer variants, and the availability of a *Textual Commentary* related to the UBS edition (see below).

In the few places where the *Guide* follows an alternative reading rather than that of the UBS text, reasons for the preference are given.

Single square brackets ([ ]) in the UBS text "enclose words which are regarded as having dubious textual validity" (UBS, xli). These brackets are not reproduced in the *Guide* since the UBS (and Nestle-Aland) editors themselves assume that the bracketed material is part of the original text. This assumption is clear since (a) the textual data relating to these readings are infrequently cited, and (b) when the data are cited these bracketed readings are always treated as part of the text, being cited first in the textual apparatus (see, e.g., Col. 1:20; 3:6).

2. The *Guide's* structural analysis of each passage is not "sentence diagramming," since it does not focus exclusively on the syntactical relationships of words and phrases. Rather, it is a simple exercise in literary physiology—showing how the grammatical and conceptual parts of a paragraph are arranged and related. The analysis seeks to isolate emphases and delineate recurring patterns so that the reader can better appreciate the biblical writer's train of thought and principal message. Quite naturally, therefore, the first "homiletical suggestion" (or sermon outline: see 6. below) is closely related to this structural analysis.

3. In the phrase-by-phrase discussion, when more than one solution is given for a particular exegetical problem, the author's own preference, reflected in the translation and expanded paraphrase, is indicated by an asterisk (*).[2] (When no preference is expressed, the options are judged to be evenly balanced, or it is assumed that there is intentional ambiguity in the text [e.g., ἐν ὑμῖν, Col. 3:16].) In this way, readers who do

---

2. When textual evidence is cited or discussed, an asterisk after the symbol for a manuscript indicates the reading of the original hand of that manuscript as opposed to subsequent correctors of the manuscript.

not wish to examine all of the possible options may at least readily discover the view of this particular writer. A diagonal line (/) is sometimes used to indicate options in exegesis or grammar.

When a particular verbal form may be parsed in two ways, only the parsing appropriate in the specific context is given (e.g., Col. 3:19), but where there is difference of opinion among grammarians or commentators, both possibilities are given and the matter is discussed (e.g., Col. 3:24). If the verbal form appearing in the text is the basic lexical form (e.g., ἐλπίζω, Phlm. 22), it is generally not parsed.

Where it is helpful to make clear that a particular part of a verse (in Greek, not English) is being referred to, the appropriate letter, a, b, c, or d, is added to the verse number. For example, Col. 1:12b refers to the second half (roughly based on length) of Col. 1:12, namely, εἰς τὴν μερίδα κτλ. Or, exceptionally, if four sections of a long verse, such as Col. 1:16, are referred to, 1:16c would denote the third quarter of the verse, viz. εἴτε θρόνοι . . . ἐξουσίαι. These rough divisions of a verse are usually clear from the punctuation (periods, semicolons, and commas). But nothing crucial ever hangs on the division itself, which is arbitrary.

4. Considerations of space often prevent discussion of word-order in the phrase-by-phrase exegetical discussion, even though it is an important aspect of exegesis. But where a particular word-order is deemed significant, this is reflected in the translation, or, more often, in the expanded paraphrase. A diagonal line (/) indicates alternative renderings in translations. Square brackets ([ ]) enclose material in the translation or expanded paraphrase that has been supplied.

5. An asterisk (*) in one of the "For Further Study" bibliographies draws attention to a discussion of the particular topic that is recommended as a useful introduction to the issues involved.

6. The "homiletical suggestions" are outlines representing the three basic kinds of preaching of the Bible:

a. An *expository sermon* is a verse-by-verse or consecutive exposition of an extended portion of Scripture. Colossians 1:9-14, for instance, deals with "Paul's Intercession for the Colossians." An expository sermon based on this passage might be entitled "How to Pray for Other Christians." Colossians 3:12-17, " 'Putting on' Virtues," suggests the sermon title "Smarten Up!"

b. A *textual sermon* is detailed exposition of a single verse or a small number of consecutive verses. For example, "The Sinner's IOU to God" could be a textual sermon that examines closely each phrase in Colossians 2:14. "The Normal Christian Life" would be a suitable title for a detailed study of the four participles in Colossians 1:10-12a or the four participles in 2:7.

c. A *topical sermon* is based on a theme mentioned in a particular text but also aims to give an overview of biblical teaching on that topic. Thus a topical sermon drawing on Colossians 1:4-5 might bear the title "A Harmonious Trio: Faith, Hope, and Love," or "A Perfect Business Partnership," but would also deal with other New Testament passages where these three virtues are mentioned together or at least with the three such passages in Paul's letters (1 Cor. 13:13; Col. 1:4-5; 1 Thess. 1:3).

The first homiletical suggestion given for any particular paragraph of the text is always an outline of the whole paragraph and is, in fact, more exegetical than homileti-cal. These detailed outlines of each paragraph build on the general outline proposed for the whole book and if placed side by side make up a comprehensive exegetical outline of the book (see pp. 231-237, 287-288).

All the outlines, whatever their nature, are merely "suggestions" intended to provide some of the raw materials for sermon preparation. None of them should be used without modification and specific application to the lives of the hearers. True biblical and expository preaching is aimed at more than informing the mind. It also seeks, through the Spirit of God, to sway the emotions, to direct the will, and to produce in the hearer spiritual change in keeping with Scripture. Christians not only need to hear systematic biblical exposition, verse by verse and paragraph by paragraph; we also need to have biblical truth forcefully applied by expository preachers to every aspect of our daily lives.

Few readers will find everything in any volume of the *Guide* equally suited to their particular needs. Those reading their first Greek text may be content with the assistance with vocabulary, parsing, and translation. Readers with some experience in Greek may well skip these sections and focus attention on the discussions of grammar. More advanced students may choose to pursue the topics and references to technical works under "For Further Study," while ministers or pastors may be more interested in the movement from grammatical analysis to sermon outline. Finally, teachers will appreciate having an aid for their students that frees them to concentrate their instruction on exegetical details and matters of background, criticism, or biblical theology.

References to Other Literature

While the *Guide* contains all that is needed for a basic understanding of the Greek text, standard reference works are constantly cited to indicate the source of a statement made or view expressed, to point to an authoritative treatment of the general issue being discussed, or to encourage further independent study. These references are restricted to a selected number of works in English that are in widespread use and that are regarded as generally reliable.[3]

The author hopes that the *Guide* will prompt many readers to consult (and in some cases buy) these larger specialist works, in particular the recommended commentaries on each biblical book. After readers have

---

3. The abbreviation "cf." is used to direct the reader to a similar or relevant biblical passage or to (1) support for an immediately preceding suggested translation that is not directly mentioned in the work referred to, (2) a view similar to *but not identical with* the view just expressed, or (3) a general treatment of the point under consideration in one or more of the grammars, commentaries, or dictionaries. In any reference to secondary literature lacking "cf.," what has just been said is an exact quotation from the work cited or a summary of the view expressed there.

patiently analyzed the Greek text with the help of the *Guide,* they are encouraged to engage in their own study of the text, using a concordance, and then to consult the commentaries for help with difficulties or for more detailed exegetical study.

The following are the basic research tools to which reference is made:

For Textual Criticism:

Metzger   B. M. Metzger, *A Textual Commentary on the Greek New Testament* (New York: United Bible Societies, 1971). This is a companion volume to the UBS *Greek New Testament.*

For Vocabulary:

BAGD   W. Bauer, *A Greek-English Lexicon of the New Testament and Other Early Christian Literature,* tr. and adapted by W. F. Arndt and F. W. Gingrich; second edition, rev. and augmented by F. W. Gingrich and F. W. Danker (Chicago: University of Chicago, 1979).

Grammars:

BDF   F. Blass and A. Debrunner, *A Greek Grammar of the New Testament and Other Early Christian Literature,* tr. and rev. R. W. Funk (Chicago: University of Chicago, 1961).

R   A. T. Robertson, *A Grammar of the Greek New Testament in the Light of Historical Research,* fourth edition (Nashville: Broadman, 1934).

T   *A Grammar of New Testament Greek,* by J. H. Moulton, vol. III: *Syntax* by N. Turner (Edinburgh: T. & T. Clark, 1963).

Z   M. Zerwick, *Biblical Greek Illustrated by Examples,* tr. J. Smith (Rome: Pontifical Biblical Institute, 1963).

Bible Dictionaries:

IDB   *The Interpreter's Dictionary of the Bible,* 4 vols., ed. G. A. Buttrick, *et al.* (Nashville/New York: Abingdon, 1962); Supplementary Volume, ed. K. Crim, *et al.* (Nashville: Abingdon, 1976).

ISBE   *The International Standard Bible Encyclopedia,* 4 vols., ed. G. W. Bromiley, *et al.* (Grand Rapids: Eerdmans, 1979-1988).

NBD   *New Bible Dictionary,* second edition, ed. J. D. Douglas and N. Hillyer (Wheaton: Tyndale House, 1982).

ZPEB   *The Zondervan Pictorial Encyclopedia of the Bible,* 5 vols., ed. M. C. Tenney and S. Barabas (Grand Rapids: Zondervan, 1975).

Theological Dictionaries:

NIDNTT   *The New International Dictionary of New Testament Theology,* 3 vols., ed. C. Brown (Grand Rapids: Zondervan: 1975-78).

TDNT   *Theological Dictionary of the New Testament,* 9 vols., ed. G. Kittel and G. Friedrich, tr. G. W. Bromiley (Grand Rapids: Eerdmans, 1964-74).

New Testament Introductions:

G   D. Guthrie, *New Testament Introduction,* third edition (Downers Grove: Inter-Varsity, 1970).

K   W. G. Kümmel, *Introduction to the New Testament,* revised edition, tr. H. C. Kee (Nashville: Abingdon, 1975).

L   E. Lohse, *The Formation of the New Testament,* tr. M. E. Boring (Nashville: Abingdon, 1981).

Commentaries on the Greek Text:

Three or four recommendations are listed in the introduction to each New Testament book in each volume of the *Guide.*

*   *   *

It was during a lecture visit to West Germany in 1985, when I had more time than usual to reflect on various possible writing projects, that the idea of launching the *Exegetical Guide* came to mind. Since then I have benefited greatly from conversations with many students and teachers of New Testament Greek, who have generously encouraged me in this present endeavor, assuring me that so far from duplicating anything currently available, the series would meet a need felt by many.

I am pleased to express my warm gratitude to two of my teachers: the late Professor E. M. Blaiklock of the University of Auckland, who, in his inimitable fashion, opened up to me the world of Classics, and Professor F. F. Bruce, under whose inspiring guidance I undertook biblical research at the University of Manchester. To each I am indebted for his encouragement and friendship and his example of meticulous scholarship.

To Mr. Jon Pott, Vice President and Editor-in-Chief of Wm. B. Eerdmans Publishing Company, I am grateful for his ready acceptance of my proposal for this series. In preparing this first volume for publication the

staff of Eerdmans have shown their customary skill and patience; in particular I wish to thank Dr. John W. Simpson, Jr.

Thanks are also due to various friends who read the General Introduction to the series or who used this first volume and made many useful
suggestions for improvement; to the many students in Auckland, New
Zealand, in Cambridge, England, and in Deerfield, Illinois, whom I have
had the privilege of guiding in the study of the Greek New Testament during
the last twenty years, and who have contributed so distinctively to my
understanding of the text by their penetrating questions; to Ruth Otway,
Ruth Jones, Mary Morris, and Carl J. Davis for their efficient help in typing
a difficult manuscript; and finally, and above all, to my wife, Jennifer, and
our children, Oliver and Jane, for their support and inspiration, each in a
distinctive way.

It is hoped that the twenty volumes of the *Guide,* which will cover
the whole New Testament, will appear at regular intervals during the next
two decades. In spite of care exercised, errors are bound to remain in a
technical work of this nature. The author would be grateful to have these
brought to his attention, along with any suggestions for improvement in
subsequent volumes in the series.

It is the author's keen desire that those who use the *Guide* will not
only gain proficiency in handling the Greek New Testament but also find
their thought and life shaped by the treasures contained in it.

Abbreviations

---

†   in this list of abbreviations indicates that the word or expression is discussed in the Glossary of Grammatical and Rhetorical Terms

§, §§   paragraph, paragraphs

Books of the Old Testament

Gen.	Genesis	Cant.	Song of Solomon (Canticles)
Exod.	Exodus		
Lev.	Leviticus	Isa.	Isaiah
Num.	Numbers	Jer.	Jeremiah
Deut.	Deuteronomy	Lam.	Lamentations
Jos.	Joshua	Ezek.	Ezekiel
Jdg.	Judges	Dan.	Daniel
Ruth	Ruth	Hos.	Hosea
1–2 Sam.	1–2 Samuel	Joel	Joel
1–2 Ki.	1–2 Kings	Amos	Amos
1–2 Chr.	1–2 Chronicles	Obad.	Obadiah
Ezr.	Ezra	Jon.	Jonah
Neh.	Nehemiah	Mic.	Micah
Est.	Esther	Nah.	Nahum
Job	Job	Hab.	Habakkuk
Ps(s).	Psalm(s)	Zeph.	Zephaniah
Prov.	Proverbs	Hag.	Haggai
Eccl.	Ecclesiastes	Zech.	Zechariah
		Mal.	Malachi

INVOICE DATE	INVOICE NO.		
2/13/91	990256		
ACCOUNT NO.	SHIP NO.	PAGE	
990256		1	

PURCHASE ORDER NO.

IS NEWSLETTER
SMITH - BOOK REVIEW EDITOR
1 LINDELL BOULEVARD

LOUIS   MO
                         63108 3393

TERMS		CLASS	TYPE	FEDERAL I.D.
T 3 0		11	5	38-1607583

PRICE

NT)

1/30/91

21.95

Books of the New Testament

Matt.	Matthew	1–2 Thess.	1–2 Thessalonians
Mk.	Mark	1–2 Tim.	1–2 Timothy
Lk.	Luke	Tit.	Titus
Jn.	John	Phlm.	Philemon
Acts	Acts	Heb.	Hebrews
Rom.	Romans	Jas.	James
1–2 Cor.	1–2 Corinthians	1–2 Pet.	1–2 Peter
Gal.	Galatians	1–3 Jn.	1–3 John
Eph.	Ephesians	Jude	Jude
Phil.	Philippians	Rev.	Revelation
Col.	Colossians		

† abs.	absolute(ly)
† acc.	accusative
† act.	active (voice)
† adj.	adjective, adjectival(ly)
† adv.	adverb, adverbial(ly)
† anar.	anarthrous
† aor.	aorist
† apod.	apodosis
† appos.	apposition, appositive, appositional
Aram.	Aramaic, Aramaism
† art.	(definite) article, articular
† attrib.	attributive
† aug.	augment

BAGD   W. Bauer, *A Greek-English Lexicon of the New Testament and Other Early Christian Literature,* tr. and adapted by W. F. Arndt and F. W. Gingrich; second ed. rev. and augmented by F. W. Gingrich and F. W. Danker (Chicago: University of Chicago, 1979).

References to BAGD are by page number and quadrant on the page, *a* indicating the upper half and *b* the lower half of the left-hand column, and *c* and *d* the upper and lower halves of the right-hand column. (This follows the method adopted in J. R. Alsop, *An Index to the Revised Bauer-Arndt-Gingrich Greek Lexicon* [Grand Rapids: Zondervan, 1981]).

Barclay   Translation in W. Barclay, *The Daily Study Bible. The Letters to the Philippians, Colossians and Thessalonians* (Philadelphia:

	Westminster, 1975[3]). *The Letters to Timothy, Titus and Philemon* (1975[3]).
BDF	F. Blass and A. Debrunner, *A Greek Grammar of the New Testament and Other Early Christian Literature,* tr. and rev. R. W. Funk (Chicago: University of Chicago, 1961).
BGk	Biblical Greek (i.e., LXX and NT Greek)
BT	*Bible Translator*
Burton	E. de W. Burton, *Syntax of the Moods and Tenses in New Testament Greek* (Edinburgh: Clark, 1898[3]).
c.	*circa* (Lat.), about
Cannon	G. E. Cannon, *The Use of Traditional Materials in Colossians* (Macon: Mercer University, 1983).
CBQ	*Catholic Biblical Quarterly*
cf.	*confer* (Lat.), compare
† CGk	Classical Greek
ch(s).	chapter(s)
colloq.	colloquial(ism)
† comp.	comparative, comparison
† cond.	condition(al)
Conflict	*Conflict at Colossae,* ed. by F. O. Francis and W. A. Meeks (Missoula: Scholars, 1975[2]).
† conj.	conjunction, conjunctive
† consec.	consecutive
† cstr.	construction, construe(d)
† dat.	dative
decl.	declension, decline
def.	definite
† delib.	deliberative
† dep.	deponent
dimin.	diminutive
† dir.	direct
DSS	Dead Sea Scrolls
ed(d).	edited, edition(s)
e.g.	*exempli gratia* (Lat.), for example
EGT	*The Expositor's Greek Testament,* ed. W. R. Nicoll, 5 vols. (Grand Rapids: Eerdmans, 1970 reprint of 1897-1910 ed.).
† encl.	enclitic
Eng.	English
† epex.	epexegetic
EQ	*Evangelical Quarterly*
esp.	especially

ET	English translation
et al.	*et alii* (Lat.), and others
etym.	etymology, etymologically
EVV	English versions of the Bible
ExpT	*Expository Times*
f(f).	and the following (verse[s] or page[s])
fem.	feminine
fig.	figurative(ly)
† fut.	future
G	D. Guthrie, *New Testament Introduction* (Downers Grove: InterVarsity, 1970³).
† gen.	genitive
Gk.	Greek
GNB	Good News Bible (= Today's English Version)
Goodspeed	E. J. Goodspeed, *The New Testament: An American Translation* (Chicago: University of Chicago, 1923).
Harris	"Prepositions and Theology in the Greek New Testament," NIDNTT 3.1171-1215.
Heb.	Hebrew, Hebraism
† HGk.	Hellenistic Greek
Horsley	G. H. R. Horsley, *New Documents Illustrating Early Christianity. A Review of the Greek Inscriptions and Papyri published in 1976* (= vol. 1; North Ryde, Australia: Macquarie University, 1981); *1977* (= vol. 2; 1982); *1978* (= vol. 3; 1983); *1979* (= vol. 4; 1987). These will be cited by volume.
ibid.	*ibidem* (Lat.), in the same place
IDB	*The Interpreter's Dictionary of the Bible,* 4 vols., ed. G. A. Buttrick (Nashville/New York: Abingdon, 1962); Supplementary Volume, ed. K. Crim (Nashville: Abingdon, 1976).
i.e.	*id est* (Lat.), that is
† impers.	impersonal
† impf.	imperfect (tense)
† impv.	imperative (mood), imperatival(ly)
incl.	including, inclusive
† indecl.	indeclinable
† indef.	indefinite
† indic.	indicative (mood)
indir.	indirect
inf.	infinitive
† instr.	instrument, instrumental(ly)
† interr.	interrogative

† intrans.	intransitive
ISBE	*The International Standard Bible Encyclopedia,* 4 vols., ed. G. W. Bromiley, et al. (Grand Rapids: Eerdmans, 1979-1988).
† iter.	iterative
JB	Jerusalem Bible
JBL	*Journal of Biblical Literature*
K	W. G. Kümmel, *Introduction to the New Testament,* tr. H. C. Kee (New York: Abingdon, 1975²)
KJV	King James Version (= Authorised Version)
κτλ.	καὶ τὰ λοιπά, and the rest
L	E. Lohse, *The Formation of the New Testament,* tr. M. E. Boring (Nashville: Abingdon, 1981).
Lat.	Latin
Lightfoot	J. B. Lightfoot, *Saint Paul's Epistles to the Colossians and to Philemon* (New York: Macmillan, 1879³).
lit.	literal(ly)
† locat.	locative, locatival(ly)
Lohse	E. Lohse, *Colossians and Philemon,* tr. W. R. Poehlmann and R. J. Karris (Philadelphia: Fortress, 1971).
LSJ	H. G. Liddell and R. Scott, *A Greek-English Lexicon,* new ed. H. S. Jones, et al. (Oxford: Clarendon, 1940⁹). *Supplement,* ed. E. A. Barber and others (1968).
LXX	Septuagint (= Greek Old Testament)
masc.	masculine
Metzger	B. M. Metzger, *A Textual Commentary on the Greek New Testament* (New York: United Bible Societies, 1971).
mg.	margin
† MGk.	Modern Greek
MH	J. H. Moulton and W. F. Howard, *A Grammar of New Testament Greek.* Vol. II, *Accidence and Word-Formation* (Edinburgh: Clark, 1929).
† mid.	middle
MM	J. H. Moulton and G. Milligan, *The Vocabulary of the Greek Testament Illustrated from the Papyri and Other Non-Literary Sources* (Grand Rapids: Eerdmans, 1972 reprint of 1930 ed.).
Moffatt	J. Moffatt, *The Moffatt Translation of the Bible* (London: Hodder, 1935²).
Moule	C. F. D. Moule, *The Epistles of Paul the Apostle to the Colossians and to Philemon* (Cambridge: Cambridge University, 1957).

Moule, *Idiom Book*	C. F. D. Moule, *An Idiom Book of New Testament Greek* (Cambridge: Cambridge University, 1960²).
Moulton	J. H. Moulton, *A Grammar of New Testament Greek.* Vol. I, *Prolegomena* (Edinburgh: Clark, 1908³).
mng.	meaning
ms(s).	manuscript(s)
MT	Masoretic Text
n.	note
NAB	New American Bible (1970 ed.)
NASB	New American Standard Bible
NBD	*New Bible Dictionary,* ed. J. D. Douglas and N. Hillyer (Wheaton: Tyndale House, 1982²).
n.d.	no date
NEB	New English Bible
neg.	negative, negation
neut.	neuter
NIDNTT	*The New International Dictionary of New Testament Theology,* 3 vols., ed. C. Brown (Grand Rapids: Zondervan: 1975-78).
NIV	New International Version
† nom.	nominative
NovT	*Novum Testamentum*
n.s.	new series
NT	New Testament
NTS	*New Testament Studies*
† obj.	object(ive)
† obl.	oblique
O'Brien	P. T. O'Brien, *Colossians, Philemon* (Waco: Word, 1982).
† opt.	optative
orig.	origin, original(ly)
OT	Old Testament
p(p).	page(s)
† pass.	passive
† periph.	periphrastic
pers.	person(al)
† pf.	perfect
pl.	plural
† plpf.	pluperfect
† poss.	possessive, possession
† pred.	predicate, predicative
pref.	prefix

† prep.   preposition(al)
† pres.   present
† pron.   pronoun, pronominal
† prot.   protasis
ptc.   participle, participial(ly)
R   A. T. Robertson, *A Grammar of the Greek New Testament in the Light of Historical Research* (Nashville: Broadman, 1934[4]).
rdg(s).   (textual) reading(s)
ref.   reference
† refl.   reflexive
† rel.   relative
rev.   revised, reviser, revision
Robertson,   A. T. Robertson, *Word Pictures in the New Testament.* Vol. IV,
   Pictures   *The Epistles of Paul* (Nashville: Broadman, 1931).
RSV   Revised Standard Version
RV   Revised Version
sc.   *scilicet* (Lat.), one is to understand
† Sem.   Semitic, Semitism
sg.   singular
sim.   similar(ly)
SJT   *Scottish Journal of Theology*
subj.   subject(ive)
† subjunc.   subjunctive
† subord.   subordinate, subordination
† subst.   substantive
suf.   suffix
† superl.   superlative
s.v.   *sub voce* (Lat.), under the word
T   *A Grammar of New Testament Greek,* by J. H. Moulton. Vol. III, *Syntax,* by N. Turner (Edinburgh: Clark, 1963).
TCNT   Twentieth Century New Testament
TDNT   *Theological Dictionary of the New Testament,* 9 vols., ed. G. Kittel and G. Friedrich, tr. G. W. Bromiley (Grand Rapids: Eerdmans, 1964-74).
† temp.   temporal(ly)
Thrall   M. E. Thrall, *Greek Particles in the New Testament* (Leiden: Brill, 1962).
TR   *Textus Receptus* (Lat.), Received Text
tr.   translate(d), translator, translation(s)
† trans.   transitive

Turner, *Insights*	N. Turner, *Grammatical Insights into the New Testament* (Edinburgh: Clark, 1965).
Turner, *Style*	*A Grammar of New Testament Greek,* by J. H. Moulton. Vol. IV, *Style,* by N. Turner (Edinburgh: Clark, 1976).
Turner, *Words*	N. Turner, *Christian Words* (Edinburgh: Clark, 1980).
UBS/UBS³	*The Greek New Testament,* ed. K. Aland, M. Black, C. M. Martini, B. M. Metzger, and A. Wikgren (New York: United Bible Societies, 1975³). 1st ed. 1966 (=UBS¹), 2nd ed. 1968 (=UBS²).
v(v).	verse(s)
var.	variant (form or reading)
vb.	verb
Vincent	M. R. Vincent, *Word Studies in the New Testament* (Florida: MacDonald, reprint of 1888 edition).
viz.	*videlicet* (Lat.), namely
† voc.	vocative
vol(s).	volume(s)
vs.	versus
Vulg.	Vulgate (= Bible in Latin)
Weymouth	R. F. Weymouth, *The New Testament in Modern Speech* (London: Clarke, 1909³).
WH	B. F. Westcott and F. J. A. Hort, *The New Testament in the Original Greek.* Vol. 1, *Text;* Vol. 2, *Introduction, Appendix* (London: Macmillan, 1881).
Z	M. Zerwick, *Biblical Greek Illustrated by Examples,* tr. J. Smith (Rome: Pontifical Biblical Institute, 1963).
Zerwick, *Analysis*	M. Zerwick, *Analysis Philologica Novi Testamenti Graeci* (Rome: Pontifical Biblical Institute, 1966³). (Although translated [see following entry], this original contains material not appearing in the English translation and sometimes differing from it.)
ZG	M. Zerwick and Mary Grosvenor, *A Grammatical Analysis of the Greek New Testament,* 2 vols. (Rome: Pontifical Biblical Institute, 1974, 1979).
ZPEB	*The Zondervan Pictorial Encyclopedia of the Bible,* 5 vols., ed. M. C. Tenney and S. Barabas (Grand Rapids: Zondervan, 1975).

Colossians

Introduction

AUTHORSHIP

Along with 2 Thessalonians, Ephesians, and the Pastoral epistles (1 and 2 Timothy and Titus), Colossians is sometimes taken to be "deutero-Pauline." That is, it is argued on the basis of certain allegedly non-Pauline features of vocabulary, style, and theology in these letters that they were written not by Paul himself but by a disciple of Paul, a member of a Pauline "circle" or "school," who was well versed in the apostle's theology and was now applying it afresh to particular pressing issues of a theological or pastoral nature that confronted the infant churches of the eastern Mediterranean toward the end of the first century (e.g., L 85-105).

The objections to the Pauline authorship of Colossians have been adequately answered by various scholars (see K 340-346; G 551-555). The most compelling argument in favor of the authenticity of the letter is its close connection with Philemon, an epistle whose genuineness is scarcely open to challenge. Colossians and Philemon have the following features in common:

1. The author is imprisoned (Col. 4:3, 10, 18; Phlm. 9-10, 13).
2. Among the writer's companions who send greetings are Aristarchus, Mark, Epaphras, Luke, and Demas (Col. 4:10-14; Phlm. 23-24).
3. In the opening greetings the name of Timothy is associated with Paul and he is described as ὁ ἀδελφός (Col. 1:1; Phlm. 1).
4. In Philemon 2 Archippus is named as an addressee and in Colossians 4:17 the author directs the Colossian church to charge Archippus to fulfill his ministry.
5. Philemon 12 mentions the return of Onesimus to Philemon (at Colossae),

3

while Colossians 4:9 refers to his going to Colossae in the company of Tychicus.

If Paul authored Philemon, it seems *a priori* likely that he also wrote Colossians, given these remarkable similarities of circumstance.

DATE

If, then, Colossians is Pauline, it is one of four so-called captivity epistles (sometimes also called prison or imprisonment epistles), the others being Philemon, Ephesians, and Philippians. Of these four, the first three belong together to the same time and situation. We have already cited the evidence (under Authorship above) for linking Colossians and Philemon. There are striking verbal similarities—some 32 identical words in Gk.—between Colossians and Ephesians where Paul is indicating that Tychicus is being sent as the bearer of the letters (Col. 4:7-8; 6:21-22).

Though Philippians also was written from prison (1:7, 13-14, 17), it has no personal references, apart from mention of Timothy (1:1; 2:19-23), that would link it with Ephesians, Colossians, and Philemon. They, in turn, do not reflect the sense of uncertainty about his future that Paul felt when he wrote Philippians (see, e.g., 1:19-26; 2:17, 24).

But where was Paul imprisoned or detained under "house-arrest" when he wrote these four letters? There are three possibilities:

1. *Ephesus,* during the 3 to 3 1/2 years spent there (Acts 19:10, 22; 20:31), c. Fall of A.D. 52 to Summer 55 or Spring 56.
2. *Caesarea,* where he spent two years in enforced confinement (Acts 24:23, 27), c. May A.D. 57 to September 59.
3. *Rome,* where he was under "house-arrest" for "two whole years" (Acts 28:30-31), c. February A.D. 60 to late 61 or early 62.

There have been vigorous defenses of an Ephesian or Caesarean provenance for all or some of the captivity epistles, but the traditional view which dates all four epistles during Paul's (first) Roman imprisonment mentioned in Acts 28:30-31 remains the most plausible alternative. Philippians is probably to be dated toward the end of this imprisonment, viz. late in A.D. 61; and the other three epistles at an earlier period of the confinement, viz. A.D. 60-61. See G 472-478, 515-516, 526-536, 555-558, 639; K 324-332, 346-349, 364-366.

OCCASION AND PURPOSE

Colossae was probably evangelized during Paul's residence in Ephesus, when "all the residents of Asia heard the word of the Lord" (Acts 19:10). Evidently Epaphras had been Paul's personal representative in the evangelization of the Lycus Valley region, which included Colossae, Laodicea, and Hierapolis (Col. 1:7-8; 4:12-13). When he wrote the letter, Paul had not visited the church (Col. 1:4, 8; 2:1), although he was hoping to do so (Phlm. 22); but he may have passed through Colossae on his third "missionary journey" (Acts 18:23; 19:1).

While Paul was imprisoned in Rome he was visited by Epaphras (Phlm. 23) who informed him of the spiritual state of the Colossian church (Col. 1:3-8; 2:5) and of a twofold danger confronting the Colossians: relapse into pagan ways of thinking and acting (3:5-11; the church was predominantly Gentile—1:27; 2:13) and acceptance of heretical teaching (1:23; 2:1-23). Paul's aim in writing, therefore, was to provide the Christian antidote to error in doctrine and practice. He commissioned Tychicus, accompanied by Onesimus, to carry the letter to Colossae (4:7-9), because Epaphras had chosen to remain with Paul (4:12-13; Phlm. 23).

OUTLINE

I. Introduction (1:1-14)
  A. Introductory Greeting (1:1-2)
  B. Paul's Thanksgiving for the Colossians (1:3-8)
  C. Paul's Intercession for the Colossians (1:9-14)
II. Christ's Work and Paul's Mission (1:15–2:3)
  A. The Supremacy of Christ in Creation and Redemption (1:15-20)
  B. Reconciliation and the Colossians (1:21-23)
  C. Paul's Stewardship of God's Mystery (1:24-29)
  D. Paul's Spiritual Struggle (2:1-3)
III. Error and Its Remedy (2:4–3:4)
  A. Warning against Specious Philosophy (2:4-8)
  B. Christ, the Remedy against Error (2:9-15)
  C. Warning against Mystical Legalism (2:16-19)
  D. Consequences of Death with Christ (2:20-23)
  E. Consequences of Resurrection with Christ (3:1-4)

IV. Exhortation to Holiness (3:5–4:6)
  A. "Putting off" Vices (3:5-11)
  B. "Putting on" Virtues (3:12-17)
  C. Household Relationships (3:18–4:1)
  D. Prayer and Witness (4:2-6)
V. Personal Notes (4:7-18)
  A. Paul's Two Representatives (4:7-9)
  B. Greetings and Final Instructions (4:10-18)

RECOMMENDED COMMENTARIES

Throughout this volume of the *Guide* references are made to four commentaries, written in English or translated into English and based directly on the Greek text of Colossians and Philemon. They are:

J. B. Lightfoot, *Saint Paul's Epistles to the Colossians and to Philemon* (New York: Macmillan, 1879[3]).

C. F. D. Moule, *The Epistles of Paul the Apostle to the Colossians and to Philemon* (Cambridge: Cambridge University, 1957).

E. Lohse, *Colossians and Philemon,* tr. W. R. Poehlmann and R. J. Karris (Philadelphia: Fortress, 1971).

P. T. O'Brien, *Colossians, Philemon* (Waco: Word, 1982).

Other recent commentaries on Colossians and Philemon are listed in O'Brien 309-310, and there is a comprehensive chronological list of commentators on these two letters, ancient and modern, in Lohse 210-213. For complete bibliographies of general literature (in several languages) relating to the background and exegesis of both letters, see Lohse 215-219 and O'Brien 310-318 (who also conveniently provides a relevant bibliography at the head of each section of the commentary).

I. Introduction (1:1-14)

A. INTRODUCTORY GREETING (1:1-2)

1 Παῦλος ἀπόστολος Χριστοῦ Ἰησοῦ διὰ θελήματος θεοῦ καὶ Τιμόθεος ὁ ἀδελφός
2 τοῖς ἐν Κολοσσαῖς ἁγίοις καὶ πιστοῖς ἀδελφοῖς ἐν Χριστῷ· χάρις ὑμῖν καὶ
εἰρήνη ἀπὸ θεοῦ πατρὸς ἡμῶν.

STRUCTURE

1	Παῦλος	ἀπόστολος	Χριστοῦ ... διὰ θελήματος θεοῦ
	καὶ Τιμόθεος	ὁ ἀδελφός	
2	τοῖς ...	ἁγίοις	
	καὶ	πιστοῖς ἀδελφοῖς ἐν Χριστῷ	
	χάρις	ὑμῖν	
	καὶ εἰρήνη		ἀπὸ θεοῦ

VERSE 1

Παῦλος ἀπόστολος Χριστοῦ Ἰησοῦ διὰ θελήματος θεοῦ

In epistolary salutations proper names (here Παῦλος and Τιμόθεος) are regularly anar. (cf. R 759). Ἀπόστολος is in appos. to Παῦλος and is therefore in the same case (nom.; cf. T 206; but see also Z §§ 13-14). It is anar. ("an apostle") since Paul did not claim to be "the (one and only) apostle" of Christ Jesus. "Apostle" is used in three senses in the NT: in a general, nontechnical sense, of a messenger or emissary (Phil. 2:25, Epaphroditus; 2 Cor. 8:23); in a semitechnical sense, of a Christian with a particular commission (Acts 14:14, Barnabas; Rom. 16:7, Andronicus and Junias); in a technical sense, of the

7

8

COLOSSIANS

Twelve (Matt. 10:2) and Paul (1 Cor. 9:1; 15:9). See below, For Further Study 1, "Apostleship in the NT."

The gens. Χριστοῦ Ἰησοῦ are dependent on ἀπόστολος, and express a relationship (cf. BDF § 162)—poss. ("belonging to," poss. gen.) and possibly also one of agency ("sent by," subj. gen.; cf. Gal. 1:1). In the NT names of persons are sometimes art., sometimes anar. (BDF § 260; R 791; T 165-169) but the NT epistles usually omit the art. with Χριστός when (as here, with Ἰησοῦς) it is a proper name (cf. BDF § 260[1]; R 760; T 167). On the name "Christ Jesus" (also found in 1:4; 2:6; 4:12; Phlm. 1, 9, 23), see W. Kramer, *Christ, Lord, Son of God* (London: SCM, 1966) 203-206.

The διά phrase qualifies ἀπόστολος, "an apostle . . . *by the will of God* (θεοῦ, poss. gen.)." God's will was the means by which (διά + gen.; BAGD 180c, "efficient cause") Paul was chosen and commissioned to be an apostle of Christ Jesus. The art. is often omitted in common, stereotyped prep. phrases (cf. BDF § 255).

καὶ Τιμόθεος ὁ ἀδελφός

The art. here (cf. anar. ἀπόστολος after Παῦλος above) indicates that Timothy was well-known: either "our brother" (most EVV) or possibly "my brother [in Christ]" (cf. Heb. 13:23). Timothy (Τιμόθεος, -ου, ὁ) was an ἀδελφός—both a fellow Christian (see BAGD 16b; MM 8-9; Turner, *Words* 56) and a coworker ("our colleague," NEB; see references to E. E. Ellis's articles in O'Brien 3)—but not a fellow apostle. In Colossians and in three other epistles where Timothy's name is also linked with Paul's in an opening greeting (viz., Phil., 1 and 2 Thess.), he may have served as the apostle's amanuensis—see For Further Study 2, "The Ancient Letter"; F. F. Bruce, *The Letters of Paul: An Expanded Paraphrase* (Grand Rapids: Eerdmans, 1965) 10.

VERSE 2

τοῖς ἐν Κολοσσαῖς ἁγίοις

The addressees (indicated by the dat.) are οἱ ἅγιοι, rendered variously by EVV: "the saints" (RV, RSV, NASB, JB), "the holy ones" (NAB), "God's people" (NEB, GNB), "the people of God" (Weymouth; sim. Barclay), "Christ's People" (TCNT). Here οἱ ἅγιοι stands where we find ἡ ἐκκλησία in 1 Thess. 1:1 and 2 Thess. 1:1 and the pl. αἱ ἐκκλησίαι in Gal. 1:2 (cf. Rom. 1:7; Eph. 1:1; Phil. 1:1). In 1 Cor. 1:2 κλητοῖς ἁγίοις ("called to be saints") is in appos. to τῇ ἐκκλησίᾳ κτλ. On this verbless epistolary introduction ("x to y"), see For Further Study 2, "The Ancient Letter"; but cf. Acts 15:23; 23:26; Jas. 1:1, where χαίρειν ("greetings!") is added.

Κολοσσαί, -ῶν, αἱ, Colossae. For this idiomatic pl. in nouns, see R 408. On the geography and history of Colossae, see O'Brien xxvi-xxvii; on the history and archaeology of the Lycus Valley region, see S. E. Johnson, "Laodicea and its Neighbours," *Biblical Archaeologist* 13 (1950) 1-18; C. J. Hemer, *The Letters to the Seven Churches of Asia in their Local Setting* (Sheffield: JSOT, 1986) 178-182.

καὶ πιστοῖς ἀδελφοῖς

If πιστοῖς (dat. pl. masc. of πιστός, -ή, -όν, agreeing with τοῖς . . . ἀδελφοῖς) meant simply "believing" (so BAGD 665a; Weymouth, NIV mg.; cf. NEB, "brothers in the faith"), it would be tautologous with ἁγίοις and ἀδελφοῖς. Here it means "trustworthy" or "faithful," so it is unlikely that ἐν Χριστῷ is dependent on πιστοῖς ("[the consecrated brothers] who believe in Christ"), a sense that would seem to demand τοῖς . . . ἁγίοις ἀδελφοῖς τοῖς πιστοῖς ἐν Χριστῷ (see further Moule 46; Moule, *Idiom Book* 81 n. 1, 108).

If ἁγίοις is a noun and the single art. τοῖς qualifies both ἁγίοις and ἀδελφοῖς, the meaning will be "the saints and [the] faithful brothers" (cf. T 181). In this case the ἅγιοι and the ἀδελφοί are the same persons (see Z § 184), and epex. καί introduces a description: "(the people of God at Colossae), namely/who are faithful brothers" (sim. JB, NAB). Alternatively, ἁγίοις may be an adj., and, along with πιστοῖς, may qualify τοῖς . . . ἀδελφοῖς: "the holy and faithful brothers" (NIV; sim. RV mg., Moffatt, Goodspeed; Moule 45). The former view is preferable, since whenever ἅγιοι is used in an epistolary greeting elsewhere in the NT, it clearly is a noun.

ἐν Χριστῷ

This phrase relates either to the whole expression τοῖς . . . ἀδελφοῖς, or *simply to ἀδελφοῖς (as though Paul had written τοῖς . . . ἀδελφοῖς τοῖς ἐν Χριστῷ). On the range of meaning of this Pauline formula, see Harris 1192; Lohse 10. Here, as generally in Paul, the ἐν is more likely to express incorporation ("incorporate in [the Body of] Christ"; sim. NEB) or union ("in union with [the person of] Christ"; sim. GNB) than agency ("through [the power of] Christ"). The ambiguous Eng. paraphrase "in the fellowship of Christ" perhaps catches these two predominant meanings. See For Further Study 3, "The 'In Christ' Formula."

χάρις ὑμῖν καὶ εἰρήνη

A vb. such as εἴη ("may it be", 3 sg. opt. of εἰμί) or πληθυνθείη ("may it be multiplied," 3 sg. aor. pass. opt. of πληθύνω, multiply) may be understood (cf. 1 Pet. 1:2; 2 Pet. 1:2; Jude 2, where three coordinate subjects are followed by a sg. vb.; see T 313-314). This distinctively Christian formula is related to the traditional Gk. greeting (χαῖρε or χαίρειν, "greetings!") and the customary Jewish greeting (šālôm, "peace!"). Both nouns are anar. because this expression was stereotyped (but see Lohse 6 n. 8). See For Further Study 4, "NT Benedictions." The apparently unusual position of ὑμῖν is normal in Pauline greetings.

ἀπὸ θεοῦ πατρὸς ἡμῶν

Some mss. (ℵ A C G I *Byz Lect al*) add καὶ κυρίου Ἰησοῦ Χριστοῦ after ἡμῶν. This addition is clearly a secondary variant, since (1) it conforms to normal Pauline usage (e.g., Rom. 1:7; 1 Cor. 1:3; 2 Cor. 1:2); (2) it would be difficult to account for its intentional or accidental omission if this longer rdg. were original. Cf. the textual variants in 1 Thess. 1:1. See Metzger 619, 629.

If a pers. pron. (here ἡμῶν) follows the noun on which it is dependent (here πατρός), that noun generally is art., but here this stylized formula, "from God our Father," common in Pauline salutations, accounts for anar. θεοῦ and the anar. phrase (πατρὸς ἡμῶν) that follows in appos. (BDF § 268[2]; T 206). Unless the context makes it impossible (as in, e.g., Jn 1:1; 20:28), (ὁ) θεός everywhere in the NT denotes the Father. Paul here views "God, who is our Father," as the source or origin (ἀπό + gen.) of Christian grace and peace. Cf. NAB, "May God our Father give you grace and peace" (sim. Weymouth, Goodspeed). See For Further Study 5, "The Fatherhood of God."

TRANSLATION

[1] Paul, an apostle of Christ Jesus by the will of God, and Timothy our brother, [2] to the people of God in Colossae, faithful brothers in Christ. Grace and peace to you from God our Father.

EXPANDED PARAPHRASE

[1] This letter comes from Paul, the special envoy of Christ Jesus commissioned by the will of God, and from our brother and colleague Timothy, [2] to the people of God in Colossae, who are brothers in the fellowship of Christ and faithful to God. May the grace and peace that come from God our heavenly Father be your portion.

FOR FURTHER STUDY

1. Apostleship in the NT (1:1)

Agnew, F., "On the Origin of the Term *Apostolos*," *CBQ* 38 (1976) 49-53.

Ashcraft, M., "Paul's Understanding of Apostleship," *Review and Expositor* 55 (1958) 400-412.

Barrett, C. K., *The Signs of an Apostle* (Philadelphia: Fortress, 1972).

Geldenhuys, J. N., *Supreme Authority* (London: Marshall, 1953) 46-97.

Kirk, J. A., "Apostleship since Rengstorf: Towards a Synthesis," *NTS* 21 (1974-75) 249-264.

*Moule 155-159.

Müller, D. and Brown, C., NIDNTT 1.126-137.

Nixon, R. E., ZPEB 1.216-220.

Rengstorf, K. H., TDNT 1.407-447.

Schmithals, W., *The Office of Apostle in the Early Church* (Nashville: Abingdon, 1969).

Shepherd, M. H., Jr., IDB 1.170-172.

Turner, *Words* 23-25.

2. The Ancient Letter (1:1-2)

Bahr, G., "Paul and Letter Writing in the First Century," *CBQ* 28 (1966) 465-477.

*Dahl, N. A., IDB 5.538-541.

Deissmann, G. A., *Bible Studies* (ET, Edinburgh: Clark, 1901; reprint, Peabody, MA: Hendrickson, 1988) 3-59.

Doty, W. G., *Letters in Primitive Christianity* (Philadelphia: Fortress, 1973).

Longenecker, R. N., "Ancient Amanuenses and the Pauline Epistles," *New Dimensions in New Testament Study,* ed. R. N. Longenecker and M. C. Tenney (Grand Rapids: Zondervan, 1974) 281-297.

Meecham, H. G., *Light from Ancient Letters* (London: Allen & Unwin, 1923).

Rigaux, B., *The Letters of St. Paul,* tr. and ed. S. Yonick (Chicago: Franciscan Herald, 1968) 115-146.

Seitz, O. J. F., IDB 3.113-115.

Stowers, S. K., *Letter Writing in Greco-Roman Antiquity* (Philadelphia: Westminster, 1986).

White, J. L., *The Form and Function of the Body of the Greek Letter* (Missoula, MT: Scholars, 1972).

————, *Light from Ancient Letters* (Philadelphia: Fortress, 1986).

White, W., Jr., ZPEB 3.909-911.

3. The "In Christ" Formula (1:2)

Best, E., *One Body in Christ* (London: SPCK, 1955) 1-33.

*Longenecker, R. N., *Paul, Apostle of Liberty* (New York: Harper, 1964) 160-170.

Moule, C. F. D., *The Origin of Christology* (New York: Cambridge University, 1977) 47-96.

Woodhouse, H. F., "Life in Christ and Life in the Spirit," *Anglican Theological Review* 47 (1965) 289-293.

Wedderburn, A. J. M., "Some Observations on Paul's Use of the Phrases 'in Christ' and 'with Christ,'" *Journal for the Study of the New Testament* 25 (1985) 83-97.

Wikenhauser, A., *Pauline Mysticism* (ET, New York: Herder, 1960) 21-33, 50-65.

4. NT Benedictions (1:2)

Champion, L. G., *Benedictions and Doxologies in the Epistles of Paul* (Oxford: Kemp Hall, 1934).

Dugmore, C. W., "Jewish and Christian Benedictions," *Mélanges offerts à Marcel Simon* (Paris: de Boccard, 1978) 145-152.

Jewett, R., "The Form and Function of the Homiletic Benediction," *Anglican Theological Review* 51 (1969) 18-34.

*Mullins, T. Y., "Benediction as a NT Form," *Andrews University Seminary Studies* 15 (1977) 59-64.

————, "Greeting as a New Testament Form," *JBL* 87 (1968) 418-426.

Wiles, G. P., *Paul's Intercessory Prayers* (Cambridge: Cambridge University, 1974) 108-114.

5. The Fatherhood of God (1:2)

Bruce, F. F., NIDNTT 2.655-656.

Burton, E. de W., *The Epistle to the Galatians* (Edinburgh: Clark, 1921) 384-392.

Davis, D. C., ZPEB 2.505-506.

Hamerton-Kelly, R., *God the Father: Theology and Patriarchy in the Teaching of Jesus* (Philadelphia: Fortress, 1979).

Hofius, O., NIDNTT 1.614-621.

Jeremias, J., *The Prayers of Jesus* (Naperville, IL: Allenson, 1967) 11-65.

————, *New Testament Theology: The Proclamation of Jesus* (ET, New York: Scribner's, 1971) 36-37, 61-68.

*Manson, T. W., *The Teaching of Jesus* (Cambridge: Cambridge University, 1935²) 89-115.

Schrenk, G. and Quell, G., TDNT 5.945-1022, esp. 1006-1010.

HOMILETICAL SUGGESTIONS

Introductory Greeting (1:1-2)

1. The writers: Paul (and Timothy) (v. 1)
2. The addressees: the Colossians (v. 2a)
3. The greeting: grace and peace (v. 2b)

*The People of God (*οἱ ἅγιοι, *1:1-2)*

1. Our foundation: apostles of Christ commissioned by God (ἀπόστολος Χριστοῦ Ἰησοῦ διὰ θελήματος θεοῦ, v. 1a; cf. Eph. 2:19-20)
2. Our constitution: a brotherhood (ἀδελφὸς . . . ἀδελφοί, vv. 1b, 2a).
3. Our calling: loyalty to God (πιστοί, v. 2a)
4. Our resources: grace and peace (χάρις . . . καὶ εἰρήνη, v. 2b)

B. PAUL'S THANKSGIVING FOR THE COLOSSIANS
(1:3-8)

3 Εὐχαριστοῦμεν τῷ θεῷ πατρὶ τοῦ κυρίου ἡμῶν Ἰησοῦ Χριστοῦ πάντοτε περὶ ὑμῶν προσευχόμενοι, 4 ἀκούσαντες τὴν πίστιν ὑμῶν ἐν Χριστῷ Ἰησοῦ καὶ τὴν ἀγάπην ἣν ἔχετε εἰς πάντας τοὺς ἁγίους 5 διὰ τὴν ἐλπίδα τὴν ἀποκειμένην ὑμῖν ἐν τοῖς οὐρανοῖς, ἣν προηκούσατε ἐν τῷ λόγῳ τῆς ἀληθείας τοῦ εὐαγγελίου 6 τοῦ παρόντος εἰς ὑμᾶς, καθὼς καὶ ἐν παντὶ τῷ κόσμῳ ἐστὶν καρποφορούμενον καὶ αὐξανόμενον καθὼς καὶ ἐν ὑμῖν, ἀφ' ἧς ἡμέρας ἠκούσατε καὶ ἐπέγνωτε τὴν χάριν τοῦ θεοῦ ἐν ἀληθείᾳ· 7 καθὼς ἐμάθετε ἀπὸ Ἐπαφρᾶ τοῦ ἀγαπητοῦ συνδούλου ἡμῶν, ὅς ἐστιν πιστὸς ὑπὲρ ὑμῶν διάκονος τοῦ Χριστοῦ, 8 ὁ καὶ δηλώσας ἡμῖν τὴν ὑμῶν ἀγάπην ἐν πνεύματι.

STRUCTURE

These verses, which express Paul's thanksgiving for the Colossians, form a single sentence in Gk., although most edd. of the Gk. text print a semicolon after v. 6. The basic structure of the sentence may be shown as follows. The italicized words indicate the main emphases and transition points in the sentence. Similar but not identical analyses are found in Lohse 13-14 and Cannon 143-144.

We give thanks (3a)
    when we pray (3b)
    because we have heard . . . faith . . . love (4)
        on account of the *hope* (5a)
            about which you have heard previously (5b)
                through . . . the *gospel* that has come to you (5b, 6a)
                    just as worldwide (6a)
                    just as among you (6b)
                    just as . . . from *Epaphras* (7a)
                    who informed us (8a)

Εὐχαριστοῦμεν (3a)
    προσευχόμενοι (3b)
    ἀκούσαντες τὴν πίστιν . . . τὴν ἀγάπην (4)
        διὰ τὴν *ἐλπίδα* (5a)
            ἣν προηκούσατε (5b)
                τοῦ *εὐαγγελίου* τοῦ παρόντος εἰς ὑμῳ (5b, 6a)
                    καθὼς καὶ ἐν παντὶ τῷ κόσμῳ (6a)
                    καθὼς καὶ ἐν ὑμῖν (6b)

καθὼς ... ἀπὸ ’Επαφρᾶ (7a)
ὁ ... δηλώσας ἡμῖν (8a)

VERSE 3

Εὐχαριστοῦμεν τῷ θεῷ πατρὶ τοῦ κυρίου ἡμῶν Ἰησοῦ Χριστοῦ

Εὐχαριστοῦμεν 1 pl. pres. act. ind. εὐχαριστέω, give thanks; followed by dat. (τῷ θεῷ). The subj. is either Paul and Timothy (cf. 1:1) or Paul himself (cf. 1:23-25). In spite of vigorous assertions to the contrary (e.g., W. F. Lofthouse, *ExpT* 58 [1946-47] 179-182; 64 [1952-53] 241-245), it is safe to assume that Paul sometimes used the formal "epistolary pl." (sometimes called the literary or sociative or authorial pl. or the "pl. of modesty"; not to be confused with the "pl. of majesty"; BDF § 280; R 406-407; T 28; Z § 8). On Pauline thanks-givings see O'Brien 7-9; For Further Study 6, "Pauline Thanksgivings."

Generally a noun in appos. (here πατρί) is art. (T 206). Therefore the shorter rdg. τῷ θεῷ πατρί (cf. the textual variants in 1:12; 2:2; 3:17), which has Alexandrian support (B C* 1739), is to be preferred over the rdgs. that insert τῷ or καί before πατρί. See Metzger 619; O'Brien 7n. Both τοῦ κυρίου . . . Ἰησοῦ Χριστοῦ and ἡμῶν are poss. gens., the former denoting a filial relationship.

πάντοτε

This adv. is probably to be cstr. with εὐχαριστοῦμεν ("we always give thanks," GNB, NAB; sim. Moffatt, RSV, Barclay, NIV) rather than with περὶ ὑμῶν προσευχόμενοι ("always praying for you"; sim. RV, Weymouth, NASB) for three reasons: (1) this corresponds to the customary Pauline epistolary formulae (e.g., 1 Thess. 1:2; Phil. 1:3; Eph. 1:16); (2) in NT Gk. an adv. generally follows the vb. it modifies (T 227-228); and (3) προσευχόμενοι re-stricts the mng. of πάντοτε: "always . . . when we pray" (Moffatt, RSV) = "whenever we pray" (TCNT; Lohse 15).

περὶ ὑμῶν προσευχόμενοι

Nom. pl. masc. (agreeing with the pl. subj. in εὐχαριστοῦμεν) of pres. mid. ptc. of dep. προσεύχομαι, pray. Adv. ptc. of time ("when we pray"), denoting action simultaneous with the main vb. (εὐχαριστοῦμεν). On every occasion (cf. πάντοτε) that Paul prayed for the Colossians, he gave thanks for them. Περὶ ὑμῶν could be taken with the main vb. ("we always thank God . . . for you"), especially given its position (cf. Rom. 1:8), but it probably belongs with προσευχόμενοι ("we always give thanks . . . when praying for you"). Περί ("for") here and in 4:3; Phlm. 10 means "on behalf of" rather than "concerning"; the preps. περί and ὑπέρ are often interchangeable (BDF § 229 [1]; T 270; Z § 96; see Eph. 1:16; 6:18-19).

VERSE 4

ἀκούσαντες τὴν πίστιν ὑμῶν

Nom. pl. masc. (agreeing with the pl. subj. in εὐχαριστοῦμεν) of aor. act. ptc. ἀκούω, hear. Adv. ptc. expressing cause, "because we have heard" (Weymouth, RSV, NEB, NAB, NIV; Burton § 439; R 1128). Aor. ptcs. that express antecedent action generally precede the main vb. but sometimes follow it, as here (Burton §§ 134, 136; R 860). Paul sometimes uses a ὅτι clause to express the reason for his thanksgiving (Rom. 1:8; 1 Cor. 1:4; 2 Thess. 1:3).

ἐν Χριστῷ Ἰησοῦ

After πίστις this phrase could denote the obj. of faith ("your faith, which rests in Christ Jesus"; sim. R. Bultmann, TDNT 6.204 and n. 229), but Paul, who seems to be immune from the HGk. tendency to confuse ἐν and εἰς (Z §§ 99, 106-110; T 254-257), expresses this idea in 2:5 by (τὸ στερέωμα) τῆς εἰς Χριστὸν πίστεως ὑμῶν, and in Phlm. 5 by τὴν πίστιν ἣν ἔχεις πρὸς τὸν κύριον (cf. 1 Thess. 1:8). Rather, this phrase indicates the sphere or realm in which their faith operated or was evident (Moule 46 n. 1, 49, and Moule, *Idiom Book* 81; T 263 n. 2; cf. Harris 1212): "your faith as those who are in Christ Jesus." Less probably, πίστις could mean "faithfulness" or "loyalty." On πίστις and πιστεύω in the NT, see Harris 1211-1214; E. de W. Burton, *The Epistle to the Galatians* (Edinburgh: Clark, 1921) 475-485; and for an opposing view on Paul, W. H. P. Hatch, *The Pauline Idea of Faith* (Cambridge, MA: Harvard University, 1917) who argues that "the three Pauline expressions, πίστις Χριστοῦ, πίστις ἐν Χριστῷ, and πίστις εἰς Χριστόν, are substantially identical in meaning" (46).

καὶ τὴν ἀγάπην ἣν ἔχετε εἰς πάντας τοὺς ἁγίους

Acc. sg. fem. of rel. pron. ὅς, ἥ, ὅ, referring to τὴν ἀγάπην. Tr.: "which you show (toward . . .)," a stronger expression than the ὑμῶν with τὴν πίστιν (4a). "To all God's people (without exception)," whereas τοὺς πάντας ἁγίους would convey the sense "all God's people (regarded as a whole)," the entire Christian brotherhood. The attrib. ὁ πᾶς or οἱ πάντες focuses attention on the sum total rather than the constituent parts. In the pred. position with an art. noun (as here), πᾶς means "all (without exception)." See BDF § 275; T 199-201; Z §§ 188-191.

VERSE 5

διὰ τὴν ἐλπίδα

This phrase, which specifies ground or cause (διά + acc., "on account of"), may be related to: (1) εὐχαριστοῦμεν (v. 3), "we give thanks . . . on account of the hope" (sim. Goodspeed); (2) τὴν πίστιν . . . καὶ τὴν ἀγάπην (v. 4; NEB, GNB, NAB, NIV); or (3) τὴν ἀγάπην (v. 4; JB). Against (1), note (a) that after εὐχαριστοῦμεν (which is in any case remote from διὰ τὴν ἐλπίδα) the ground of thanksgiving would normally be expressed by a ὅτι clause (e.g., Rom. 1:8) or a causal ptc. (e.g., Eph. 1:15-16) rather than by a διά phrase; (b) that v. 4 with its causal ἀκούσαντες has already stated the reason for Paul's thanksgiving and that there is no καί before διά; and (c) that this view would destroy the interrelationship of the triadic "faith— love—hope" in vv. 4-5. Alternative (3) seems arbitrarily to restrict the διά clause to its nearest antecedent. Option (2) is preferable: "both [viz. faith and love] spring from the hope stored up for you in heaven" (NEB; sim. GNB, NIV).

Unlike πίστις and ἀγάπη, ἐλπίς is here obj., not subj., in sense: in this verse hope is not an inward disposition but rather denotes, by metonymy, the obj. of hope (almost = inheritance, cf. 1 Pet. 1:4; or = "eternal life," cf. Tit. 1:2 and H. Traub, TDNT 5.532 n. 294). An objective fact produces subjective attitudes. The inheritance of Christians has the effect of stimulating in them stronger faith and deeper love. Paul is not suggesting that hope initially produces faith or love, for only the person with Christian faith can have Christian love (Gal. 5:6) or "hope." See For Further Study 7, "The Triad of Faith— Love—Hope." For this use of ἐλπίς denoting what is hoped for (BAGD 253c, 595b), see also Gal. 5:5; Tit. 2:13; Heb. 6:18; and Rom. 8:24, where both the subj. and obj. senses of ἐλπίς occur (see further Turner, *Words* 213-215). Cf. GNB, "So your faith and love are based on what you hope for."

τὴν ἀποκειμένην ὑμῖν ἐν τοῖς οὐρανοῖς

Acc. sg. fem. (agreeing with τὴν ἐλπίδα) pres. (mid./pass.) ptc. of ἀπόκειμαι, be stored up; with dat. (here ὑμῖν), be reserved for (cf. 2 Tim. 4:8). On this "present perfect" vb., see T 81-82; R 316. This art. ptc. is restrictive in mng. (cf. Burton §§ 295, 422 and see the Glossary under "Articular Participle"). It qualifies a noun (τὴν ἐλπίδα) and is equivalent to a rel. clause (cf. BDF § 412; R 764, 1106-1108; T 152), viz. ἥ ἀπόκειται, "which is stored up," as is shown by the following ἥν προηκούσατε. Ἐν τοῖς οὐρανοῖς, "in heaven" (most EVV), not "in the heavens" (RV). The pl. οὐρανοί is often used in the LXX to translate the Heb. pl. form *šāmayim*, "heaven(s)," "sky" (H. Bietenhard, NIDNTT 2.191; H. Traub, TDNT 5.509-511, 513; T 25; cf. R 408; Turner, *Words* 202-205).

ἣν προηκούσατε

2 pl. aor. act. indic. of προακούω, hear beforehand. Acc. sg. fem. of rel. pron. ὅς, ἥ, ὅ, referring to τὴν ἐλπίδα (fem. sg.). Like "hear" in Eng., ἀκούω can mean "receive news of" or "be informed about" as well as referring to the physical sensation of hearing (cf. BAGD 31d-32d). The προ- may refer to a time: (1) before the time of writing ("already," NIV); (2) "before" the Colossians heard the false teaching; (3) "before" the fulfillment of the hope; or (most probably) (4) when they first heard the gospel (v. 7) ("previously," NASB).

ἐν τῷ λόγῳ τῆς ἀληθείας τοῦ εὐαγγελίου

As a general rule, dependent nouns (here ἀληθείας and εὐαγγελίου) are art. if the governing noun has the art. and are anar. if the governing noun lacks the art. (e.g., διὰ θελήματος θεοῦ, v. 1; and note ἐν λόγῳ ἀληθείας in 2 Cor. 6:7). This is the so-called canon of Apollonius Dyscolus (see the Glossary).

        Ἐν may be locat. ("in"), temp. ("when"), or instr. ("by means of, through"). Λόγος may mean "word, message" or "proclamation, preaching." Gen. τῆς ἀληθείας may be epex./appos. ("the message, which is truth"; for this use, see BDF § 167; R 498-499; T 214-215; Z §§ 45-46), or obj. ("the proclamation of the truth"; for this use, see BDF § 163; R 499-501; T 210-212; Z § 36), but is more probably qualitative (= attrib., Heb., Sem.; "the message of truth" = the message characterized by truth, "the true message"; or "the true preaching"; for this use, see BDF § 165; R 496-497; T 212-214; Z §§ 40-41). Finally, gen. τοῦ εὐαγγελίου could be poss. ("the proclamation of the truthfulness that belongs to the gospel," i.e., the true gospel; for this use, see BDF § 162; R 495-496; T 207-208), or epex., so that either ἀλήθεια = εὐαγγέλιον or λόγος ἀληθείας = εὐαγγέλιον: either, "the proclamation of the truth, which is contained in the gospel," i.e., gospel-truth, or (as in Eph. 1:13) "the message of truth, the gospel," "the true message, that is, the gospel" (cf. BAGD 318a).

        Several possible translations emerge (here listed in descending order of probability):

(1) "through/in the message of truth, the gospel" (or, "through/in the true message which is the gospel"),
(2) "when the true gospel was proclaimed" (cf. T 252),
(3) "through/in the preaching of the truth, which is contained in the gospel," or
(4) "in the true preaching of the gospel."

        Paul's emphasis rests on (a) the Christian's hope as a crucial ingredient in the preaching of the good news (cf. vv. 23, 27); and (b) the truth of the message proclaimed to the Colossians by Epaphras (cf. ἐν ἀληθείᾳ, v. 6b), as opposed to the spurious gospel preached by certain Colossian teachers (cf. 2:8, 16-23). See For Further Study 8, "The Colossian Heresy," and 9, "The Gospel."

VERSE 6

τοῦ παρόντος εἰς ὑμᾶς

Gen. sg. neut. (agreeing with τοῦ εὐαγγελίου) of pres. act. ptc. of πάρειμι, be present, have come. An art. ptc. is equivalent to a rel. clause (see on τὴν ἀποκειμένην, 1:5). Here the ptc. is nonrestrictive or explanatory, describing something (viz. the gospel) already known (cf. Burton §§ 295, 426). The phrase is usually taken to mean "that has come to you" (BAGD 624b; NIV; sim. RSV, NASB), but it could possibly also mean "that is present among you" (Lohse 19 nn. 53, 54), although Paul is not prone to use εἰς in the sense of ἐν (see Z §§ 106-110, but note also Zerwick's earlier suggestion that, following CGk. usage, where εἰς is sometimes used with vbs. of rest [Z § 9], εἰς here bears a "pregnant" sense, implying a preceding arrival of the gospel [*Analysis* 447]; cf. E. Stauffer, TDNT 2.433).

καθὼς καὶ ἐν παντὶ τῷ κόσμῳ

Καθὼς καί, "just as also," "in the same way, too" (two occurrences in this verse). In Paul comparative clauses generally follow the principal clause (T 345). On art. πᾶς, see 1:4. "All over the world" (Goodspeed) is clearly a hyperbole emphasizing the widespread dissemination of the gospel (cf. 1:23b), esp. via the cities of the Empire, in a type of "representative universalism" (cf. Acts 2:5; Rom. 10:18). See O'Brien 13. "Heresies are at best ethnic: truth is essentially catholic" (Lightfoot 133).

ἐστὶν καρποφορούμενον

Periph. pres. (R 881; Robertson, *Pictures* 474; T 88): 3 sg. pres. indic. of εἰμί + nom. sg. neut. (agreeing with an implied τὸ εὐαγγέλιον [from v. 5b], the subj. of ἐστίν) of the pres. mid. ptc. of καρποφορέω, bear fruit. If this periph. pres. differs in emphasis from a regular pres., it does so by pointing to the continuous nature of the gospel's productivity, its ongoing action: it "continues to bear fruit" or "is constantly bearing fruit" (NASB). In v. 10 the pres. *act.* ptc. of the same vb. is found (καρποφοροῦντες). Some find no distinction in meaning (e.g., T 55), but the mid. ptc. may imply the intrinsic potency of the gospel in producing its own fruit (cf. Rom. 1:16): "bearing fruit of itself" (sim. BAGD 405b; Lightfoot 133; Zerwick, *Analysis* 447).

It is not impossible to read . . . ἔστιν, καρποφορούμενον and translate v. 6a thus: "(the gospel) that is present among you just as it is also in the whole world, where it is constantly producing fruit. . . ." On this view (cf. Zerwick, *Analysis* 447), the ptc. and the following pres. ptc. αὐξανόμενον are in apposition to the implied τὸ εὐαγγέλιον, and are not the ptc. elements of a periph. cstr.

In order to highlight the parallelism between "to/among you" and "throughout/in the whole world," a few mss. and the TR read καί before ἐστὶν καρποφορούμενον κτλ. But this removal of a somewhat awkward comparison (viz. between the arrival or presence of the gospel in Colossae and its productivity and spread throughout the world) is clearly secondary. See Metzger 619.

καὶ αὐξανόμενον καθὼς καὶ ἐν ὑμῖν

Periph. pres.: [τὸ εὐαγγέλιον] ἐστιν . . . αὐξανόμενον. Nom. sg. neut. of pres. pass. ptc. of αὐξάνω, cause to grow; (pass.) grow. "The Gospel is not like those plants which exhaust themselves in bearing fruit and wither away. The external growth keeps pace with the reproductive energy" (Lightfoot 133). On καθὼς καί, see on v. 6a. Ἐν ὑμῖν here does not mean "within you" but "among you" (most EVV), "in your midst" (NAB).

ἀφ' ἧς ἡμέρας

This is an idiomatic form of ἀφ' ἡμέρας ᾗ, "from the day on which" = "(ever) since." The dat. sg. fem. rel. pron. ᾗ is attracted into the case of its antecedent (ἡμέρας, gen.), which then is transferred to the rel. clause (cf. Zerwick, *Analysis* 447; Z §§ 17-18; R 717). The phrase is virtually a conj. ("since"; T 17; R 978).

ἠκούσατε καὶ ἐπέγνωτε

2 pl. aor. act. indic. ἀκούω, hear; learn of, be informed about. Ἐπέγνωτε, 2 pl. 2 aor. act. indic. of ἐπιγινώσκω, know, learn, perceive. Ingressive aor., "you came to know" (sim. Moffatt, Goodspeed). Some give the prep. pref. ἐπι- its full weight and render it by "completely," "fully," "thoroughly," "experientially" (cf. BAGD 291a; Lightfoot 134, 135-136), but a comparison of v. 6 with 2 Cor. 8:9 (γινώσκετε . . . τὴν χάριν κτλ.) shows that there is no necessary difference in meaning between ἐπιγινώσκειν and γινώσκειν (R. Bultmann, TDNT 1.703-704; cf. MM 236-237). Moreover, HGk. was marked by a tendency to prefer the more explicit expression and the fuller and phonetically stronger form, so that compound vbs. became more frequent and yet often meant no more than the corresponding simple vbs. had meant in CGk. (Z §§ 481-484; cf. Zerwick, *Analysis* 447).

τὴν χάριν τοῦ θεοῦ

Acc. τὴν χάριν is probably the obj. of both preceding vbs. but it is possible to supply τὸ εὐαγγέλιον (from v. 5b) as the obj. of ἠκούσατε. The gen. may be poss. ("God's grace") or subj. ("the grace that God has shown") (cf. Acts 20:24; 2 Cor. 6:1). On either view, "the grace of God" is virtually a synonym for "the gospel"; but NEB has "graciousness," NAB "gracious intention," and TCNT "loving-kindness." See For Further Study 10, "Grace."

ἐν ἀληθείᾳ

In meaning probably adv. ("in reality," "for what it truly is"; cf. BAGD 36c; Moule 51) rather than adj. with χάριν ("the true grace of God") or subst. ("in the truth," i.e., in the gospel; cf. v. 5). The contrast with the travesty of God's grace in the false teaching propounded at Colossae is implicit but nonetheless unmistakable.

VERSE 7

καθὼς ἐμάθετε

2 pl. 2 aor. act. indic. of μανθάνω, learn (through instruction; BAGD 490b). This is a summary/complexive/constative aor. (BDF § 332; Burton §§ 38-40, "historical aor."; R 831-834; T 72; Z §§ 253-255, "global aor.") that conceives of the initial learning of the gospel by the Colossians (= hearing about and coming to know God's grace, v. 6) as a single whole, although prolonged instruction by Epaphras was undoubtedly involved. Tr.: "(This was) just as you learned it," "You were taught this" (NEB), i.e. the Colossians had learned about the grace of God, the gospel, "in untravestied form" (ἐν ἀληθείᾳ, v. 6). Since the temp. meaning ("when") of καθώς is rare in the NT (only in Acts 7:17), the word here, as in v. 6, bears its usual sense of "just as," introducing a comp., but without any accompanying οὕτως, "so" (cf. 3:13; BAGD 391b, c).

ἀπὸ Ἐπαφρᾶ

Ἀπό + gen. stands for παρά + gen. after μανθάνω (T 258-259). Gk. names ending in -ᾶς, such as Ἐπαφρᾶς, have -ᾶ in the gen. (MH 119; R 254-255). Although Ἐπαφρᾶς is a shortened form of Ἐπαφρόδιτος (MH 314; BDF § 125[1]; R 172), this Epaphras, a native or inhabitant of Colossae who founded the Colossian church (1:7; 4:12; Phlm. 23), is not to be identified with the Epaphroditus of Phil. 2:25; 4:18, who was probably a native of Philippi (cf. Lightfoot 29-36).

τοῦ ἀγαπητοῦ συνδούλου ἡμῶν

Gen., in appos. to Ἐπαφρᾶ. On an art. subst. in appos. to an anar. proper noun (here Ἐπαφρᾶ) see 4:9. Epaphras, like Paul (συν-), was a bond-slave (δοῦλος) of Christ (σύνδουλος, -ου, ὁ, fellow slave). Cf. Phlm. 23, where Epaphras is described as a prisoner, along with Paul (συναιχμάλωτος), "in the service of Christ Jesus" (cf. G. Kittel, TDNT 1.196-197). On ἀγαπητός, see Turner, *Words* 266-268.

ὅς ἐστιν πιστὸς ὑπὲρ ἡμῶν διάκονος τοῦ Χριστοῦ

As in 1:2 and 4:7, πιστός here means "trustworthy, faithful" rather than "believing." Τοῦ Χριστοῦ is either a poss. gen. ("Christ's faithful servant") or, more probably, an obj. gen. ("a faithful servant of Christ," i.e. one "who is faithfully serving Christ"). Because διάκονος is anar. and Χριστοῦ is art., Robertson proposes (on the basis of the "canon of Apollonius"—see on v. 5 above) the translation "a (faithful) minister of the Christ" (R 781; sim. TCNT). But the use of the art. with proper names is notoriously irregular.

The first and second edd. of the UBS text favored the reading ὑπὲρ ἡμῶν, with a "C" rating, but the third ed. favors ὑπὲρ ὑμῶν, also with a "C" rating (see Metzger 619-620). If only transcriptional probability were considered, ὑμῶν might appear the more probable rdg., since the preceding ἡμῶν and the following ἡμῖν could have prompted a change from ὑμῶν to ἡμῶν (but, on the contrary, note the possible influence of ὑπὲρ ὑμῶν [4:12], also in ref. to Epaphras, for the opposite change). However, the variant ἡμῶν seems preferable (so also Lightfoot 134, 248-249; Moule 27 n. 1; Lohse 23 and n. 90; O'Brien 15-16; most EVV) on the basis of both (1) external evidence and (2) intrinsic probability:

(1) The witnesses supporting ὑμῶν are admittedly geographically diversified (including strong support from the versions and the Gk. and the Lat. Fathers). But the proto-Alexandrian (𝔭[46] ℵ* A B) and Western (D[gr*] G it[g] Ambrosiaster[comm]) witnesses for ἡμῶν make a formidable combination.

(2) In the context Paul is confirming the authenticity of the message and the messenger known by the Colossians. Epaphras had worked in Colossae and elsewhere in the Lycus Valley (4:12-13), as now in Rome, as Paul's representative (cf. Acts 19:10), acting on Paul's behalf (ὑπὲρ ἡμῶν) or perhaps in his place (where ὑπέρ = ἀντί; cf. Z § 91; Harris 1196-1197). Scribes often confused the plurals of first and second pers. prons.; in MGk η and υ are pronounced alike ("ee," as in feet; see MH 73, 79).

VERSE 8

ὁ καὶ δηλώσας ἡμῖν τὴν ὑμῶν ἀγάπην

Nom. sg. masc. (agreeing with ὅς, which refers to Epaphras) of the aor. act. ptc. of δηλόω, give information to someone (dat., here ἡμῖν) about something (acc., here τὴν . . . ἀγάπην; BAGD 178c). The art. ptc. ὁ . . . δηλώσας (lit. "the one who informed"), here emphasized by καί ("indeed"), is equivalent to a rel. clause, ὃς ἐδήλωσεν, "who informed" (cf. ὅς ἐστιν in v. 7b; and Burton § 142; R 764, 859). Tr.: "He it was who informed us of your love" (sim. NAB). A poss. pron. such as ὑμῶν may stand before, between (as here), or after the art. and the noun that it qualifies (R 779). Since the obj. of the Colossians' love is not specified, it might be "all God's people" (v. 6), Paul (esp. if ὑμῶν is read in v. 7b), Epaphras, Christ, or God—or all five.

It was the recent news about the Colossian church that Epaphras had brought to Paul in prison in Rome—news of their faith and love (vv. 4, 8) as well as of the danger confronting them in the false teaching—that prompted the apostle to write the present letter. But it was Tychicus, not Epaphras, who delivered the letter to Colossae (4:7-9); Epaphras remained with Paul (4:12; Phlm. 23).

ἐν πνεύματι

In Paul's letters there is often uncertainty whether πνεῦμα refers to the human spirit, to God's Spirit, or to the human spirit renewed by God's Spirit. Here, however, the sense is not "(your love) in your spirit(s)" (locat. ἐν), i.e., "your spiritual love," but "(your love) inspired by the Spirit" (instr. ἐν; sim. TCNT, Weymouth, Moffatt, GNB) or, as BAGD 677a suggests, "(your love) called forth by the Spirit." In Rom. 15:30 the same idea is expressed, after ἡ ἀγάπη, by τοῦ πνεύματος, a subj. gen., "love engendered by the Spirit" (cf. Rom. 5:5; Gal. 5:22).

TRANSLATION

[3] We always give thanks to God, the Father of our Lord Jesus Christ, when we pray for you, [4] because we have heard of your faith in Christ Jesus and of the love you show to all God's people. [5] Both stem from the hope stored up for you in heaven. You heard about this hope previously through the message of truth, the good news [6] that has come to you just as it is also constantly producing fruit and growing all over the world in the same way that it has been among you ever since you heard about and came to know the grace of God in reality. [7] You learned this from Ephaphras, our dear fellow slave, who is a faithful minister of Christ on our behalf. [8] He it was who informed us of your love in the Spirit.

EXPANDED PARAPHRASE

[3] Whenever we pray for you, without fail we give thanks to God, the Father of our Lord Jesus Christ, [4] because we have heard of your faith as those who

are in Christ Jesus and also of the love you show toward all God's people.
[5] Both of these qualities are stimulated by the hope that is reserved for you in
heaven. You came to hear about this hope previously when you heard the
message that has the stamp of truth on it—the message that is the good news
[6] that has come to you. In the same way this gospel continues to produce
throughout the whole world the same kind of harvest and increase it has been
yielding in you from the very first day that you heard about and came to
appreciate God's undeserved favor for what it truly is. [7] That was the way you
learned it from Epaphras, our dearly loved fellow slave, who has been faithfully
serving Christ as our representative. [8] It was he, in fact, who informed us of
your love—love that is produced by God's Spirit.

FOR FURTHER STUDY

6. Pauline Thanksgivings (1:3)

O'Brien, P. T., "Thanksgiving and the Gospel in Paul," *NTS* 21 (1974-75) 144-155.

————, *Introductory Thanksgivings in the Letters of Paul* (Leiden: Brill, 1977), esp.
62-104.

*————, "Thanksgiving within the Structure of Pauline Theology," *Pauline Studies,* ed.
D. A. Hagner and M. J. Harris (Grand Rapids: Eerdmans, 1980) 50-66.

Sanders, J. T., "The Transition from Opening Epistolary Thanksgiving to Body in the
Letters of the Pauline Corpus," *JBL* 81 (1962) 348-362.

Schubert, P., *Form and Function of the Pauline Thanksgivings* (Berlin: Töpelmann,
1939).

7. The Triad of Faith—Love—Hope (1:4-5)

Hunter, A. M., "Faith, Hope, Love—A Primitive Christian Triad," *ExpT* 49 (1937-38)
428-429.

*————, *Paul and his Predecessors* (Philadelphia: Westminster, 1961[2]) 33-35.

————, *Teaching and Preaching the New Testament* (Philadelphia: Westminster, 1963)
81-84.

Lohse 16 n. 28 (with BAGD 5c).

Moffatt, J., *Love in the New Testament* (London: Hodder, 1929) 185-187.

8. The Colossian Heresy (1:5)

Bandstra, A. J., "Did the Colossian Errorists Need a Mediator?" *New Dimensions in New Testament Study*, ed. R. N. Longenecker and M. C. Tenney (Grand Rapids: Zondervan, 1974) 329-343.

Bornkamm, G., "The Heresy of Colossians," *Conflict* 123-145 (ET of an article first appearing in *Theologische Literaturzeitung* 73 [1948] 11-20 as "Die Häresie des Kolosserbriefes," and reprinted in *Das Ende des Gesetzes* [Münich: Kaiser, 1952] 139-156).

Guthrie 546-550.

Hooker, M. D., "Were there False Teachers in Colossae?" *Christ and Spirit in the New Testament*, ed. S. S. Smalley and B. Lindars (Cambridge: Cambridge University, 1973) 315-331.

Lightfoot, 71-111 (reprinted in *Conflict* 13-59).

Lohse 127-131.

Lyonnet, S., "Paul's Adversaries in Colossae," *Conflict* 147-161 (ET of "L'étude du milieu littéraire et l'exégèse du Nouveau Testament," *Biblica* 37 [1956] 27-38).

*O'Brien xxx-xli, 135-156.

Stewart, J. S., "A First-Century Heresy and its Modern Counterpart," *SJT* 23 (1970) 420-436.

9. The Gospel (1:5)

*Becker, U., NIDNTT 2.107-115.

Bruce, F. F., "Galatian Problems 3. The 'Other' Gospel," *BJRL* 53 (1971) 253-271.

Burrows, M., "The Origin of the Term 'Gospel,'" *JBL* 44 (1925) 21-33.

Dodd, C. H., *The Apostolic Preaching and its Developments* (London: Hodder, 1936; reprinted, Grand Rapids: Baker, 1980).

Friedrich, G., TDNT 2.707-736.

Jackson, D. R., ZPEB 2.779-784.

Martin, R. P., ISBE 2.529-532.

Mounce, R. H., *The Essential Nature of New Testament Preaching* (Grand Rapids: Eerdmans, 1960).

Piper, O. A., IDB 2.442-448.

Reicke, B., "A Synopsis of Early Christian Preaching," *The Root of the Vine*, ed. A. Fridrichsen (London: Black, 1953) 128-160.

Worley, R. C., *Preaching and Teaching in the Earliest Church* (Philadelphia: Westminster, 1967).

10. Grace (1:6)

Conzelmann, H. and Zimmerli, W., TDNT 9.372-402.

Doughty, D. J., "The Priority of *Charis*. An Investigation of the Theological Language of Paul," *NTS* 19 (1972-73) 163-180.

Esser, H.-H., NIDNTT 2.115-124.

McDonald, H. D., ZPEB 2.799-804.

Manson, W., "Grace in the New Testament," *The Doctrine of Grace*, ed. W. T. Whitley (London: SCM, 1932) 33-60.

Mitton, C. L., IDB 2.463-468.

Moffatt, J., *Grace in the New Testament* (London: Hodder, 1931).

Smedes, L. B., ISBE 2.547-552.

Smith, C. R., *The Bible Doctrine of Grace and Related Doctrines* (London: Epworth, 1956).

Torrance, T. F., *The Doctrine of Grace in the Apostolic Fathers* (Edinburgh: Oliver & Boyd, 1948).

*Turner, *Words* 191-195.

HOMILETICAL SUGGESTIONS

Paul's Thanksgiving for the Colossians (1:3-8)

1. The reason for thanksgiving (εὐχαριστοῦμεν . . . ἀκούσαντες τὴν πίστιν . . . τὴν ἀγάπην, vv. 3-4)
2. The stimulus afforded by hope (διὰ τὴν ἐλπίδα, v. 5a)
3. The content and potency of the gospel (τὴν ἐλπίδα . . . ἣν προηκούσατε . . . τῆς ἀληθείας . . . καρποφορούμενον καὶ αὐξανόμενον . . . τὴν χάριν τοῦ θεοῦ, vv. 5b-6)
4. The ministry of Epaphras (ἐμάθετε ἀπὸ Ἐπαφρᾶ . . . συνδούλου . . . πιστὸς . . . διάκονος τοῦ Χριστοῦ, ὁ . . . δηλώσας, vv. 7-8)

A Christian Partnership (1:4-5a)

1. Love: the senior partner (1 Cor. 13:13)
   Love is superior to faith and hope (cf. Col. 3:14)
2. Hope: the creative partner (Col. 1:4-5a)
   Hope confirms and strengthens faith and love (cf. 1 Pet. 1:3-9)
3. Faith: the energetic partner (1 Thess. 1:3a)
   Faith is expressed in work (cf. Gal. 5:6b)

The Gospel (1:5b-7a)

1. Its content: hope (v. 5b), truth (v. 5b), and grace (v. 6b)
2. Its operation: fruit-bearing and growth (v. 6a)
3. Its reception: hearing (vv. 5b, 6b), apprehending (v. 6b), and learning (v. 7a)

Epaphras the Colossian (1:5b-8; 4:12-13)

1. The true exponent of the gospel (1:5b, 7a)
2. The faithful servant of Christ (1:7; 4:12a)
3. The effective representative of Paul (ὑπὲϱ ἡμῶν, 1:7b)
4. The constant warrior in prayer (4:12)
5. The tireless pastor of the Lycus Valley Christians (4:12b-13; cf. 1:28)

C. PAUL'S INTERCESSION FOR THE COLOSSIANS
(1:9-14)

9 Διὰ τοῦτο καὶ ἡμεῖς, ἀφ' ἧς ἡμέρας ἠκούσαμεν, οὐ παυόμεθα ὑπὲρ ὑμῶν προσευχόμενοι καὶ αἰτούμενοι ἵνα πληρωθῆτε τὴν ἐπίγνωσιν τοῦ θελήματος αὐτοῦ ἐν
πάσῃ σοφίᾳ καὶ συνέσει πνευματικῇ, 10 περιπατῆσαι ἀξίως τοῦ κυρίου εἰς πᾶσαν
ἀρεσκείαν, ἐν παντὶ ἔργῳ ἀγαθῷ καρποφοροῦντες καὶ αὐξανόμενοι τῇ ἐπιγνώσει
τοῦ θεοῦ, 11 ἐν πάσῃ δυνάμει δυναμούμενοι κατὰ τὸ κράτος τῆς δόξης αὐτοῦ εἰς
πᾶσαν ὑπομονὴν καὶ μακροθυμίαν, μετὰ χαρᾶς 12 εὐχαριστοῦντες τῷ πατρὶ τῷ
ἱκανώσαντι ὑμᾶς εἰς τὴν μερίδα τοῦ κλήρου τῶν ἁγίων ἐν τῷ φωτί· 13 ὃς ἐρρύσατο
ἡμᾶς ἐκ τῆς ἐξουσίας τοῦ σκότους καὶ μετέστησεν εἰς τὴν βασιλείαν τοῦ υἱοῦ τῆς
ἀγάπης αὐτοῦ, 14 ἐν ᾧ ἔχομεν τὴν ἀπολύτρωσιν, τὴν ἄφεσιν τῶν ἁμαρτιῶν·

STRUCTURE

Like vv. 3-8, these six verses form one sentence in Gk., although most edd. of
the Gk. text print a semicolon after v. 12 (as also after v. 6). Paul's prayer for
the Colossians involved thanksgiving (vv. 3-8) and intercession (vv. 9-14). The
close connection between these two aspects of prayer is indicated by: (1) the
repetition of words or phrases in the two sections ("giving thanks to the Father,"
vv. 3, 12; "we heard," vv. 4, 9; "God's people," vv. 4, 12; "producing fruit and
growing," vv. 6, 10; "ever since," vv. 6, 9); (2) the repetition of ideas in the
two sections ("we always give thanks . . . when we pray for you"—"we have
not ceased praying for you," vv. 3, 9; "you came to know"—"knowledge," vv.
6, 9-10; "hope" denoting the obj. of hope, Christian inheritance—"the inheritance of God's people," vv. 5, 12; and note the repeated use of πᾶς, "all, every
(form of)," in vv. 4, 6, 9, 10 twice, 11).

The syntactical structure of vv. 9-14 may be shown as follows:

Asking   (*nature* of the prayer)
    that you may be filled . . .   (*content* of the request)
        by having all spiritual wisdom . . .   (*means* of being filled)
        so as to lead a life . . .   (*purpose or result* of being filled)
            bearing fruit   four *characteristics* of
            growing   "a life that is worthy of
            being empowered   the Lord and that seeks to
            giving thanks to the Father   please him in everything"
                who has qualified
                he has rescued and transferred

αἰτούμενοι
 ἵνα πληρωθῆτε
  ἐν πάσῃ σοφίᾳ . . . πνευματικῇ
  περιπατῆσαι   Modifiers:
   καρποφοροῦντες   ἐν παντὶ ἔργῳ ἀγαθῷ
   αὐξανόμενοι   τῇ ἐπιγνώσει τοῦ θεοῦ
   δυναμούμενοι   ἐν πάσῃ δυνάμει
   εὐχαριστοῦντες τῷ πατρί   μετὰ χαρᾶς
    τῷ ἱκανώσαντι
    ὃς ἐρρύσατο . . . καὶ μετέστησεν

VERSE 9

Διὰ τοῦτο καὶ ἡμεῖς

Διὰ τοῦτο means "because of this," "this/that is why," and refers back to vv. 4-8, the encouraging news about the Colossians brought to Paul by Epaphras. Καί here means "also" (cf. Z § 462) and belongs with the vb.: not only did Paul offer thanksgiving to God for the Colossians (v. 3); he "also" constantly interceded for them. The news prompted intercession (v. 9) as well as thanksgiving (vv. 3-4). But Moule (52) links καί with διὰ τοῦτο: "that is *precisely* why." For the main NT uses of καί, see on 3:4.

ἀφ' ἧς ἡμέρας ἠκούσαμεν

1 pl. aor. act. indic. of ἀκούω, hear. "Ever since we heard [this]." On the construction, see on v. 6.

οὐ παυόμεθα ὑπὲρ ὑμῶν προσευχόμενοι

Παυόμεθα, 1 pl. pres. mid. indic. of παύω, (cause to) stop; (mid.) cease. Προσευχόμενοι (nom. pl. masc. of pres. mid. ptc. of dep. προσεύχομαι, pray) is a pred. ptc. (T 158-159), completing the sense of οὐ παυόμεθα: "we do not cease/we have not ceased praying for you" = "we pray for you without ceasing" (cf. BAGD 638a; NAB). This refers to prayer that is regular and frequent rather than uninterrupted. See For Further Study 11, "Prayer in Paul."

καὶ αἰτούμενοι

Nom. pl. masc. (agreeing with the subj. of παυόμεθα) of pres. mid. ptc. of αἰτέω, ask, ask for; a second pred. ptc. after οὐ παυόμεθα. This may be a case of hendiadys: "praying for you and asking" = "asking in our prayers for you" (so also Mk. 11:24, "whatever you ask in prayer"; cf. ZG 603; Z § 460). Some scholars attempt to distinguish the act. and mid. senses of αἰτέω, the act.

meaning "ask outright" or denoting the mere formality of prayer, and the mid. meaning "ask as a loan" or signifying a request made in the true spirit of prayer. But no such distinctions are consisently maintained in the NT, where αἰτέω and αἰτέομαι alternate almost arbitrarily (see BDF § 316[2]; BAGD 25d; G. Stählin, TDNT 1.192; H. Schönweiss, NIDNTT 2.856-857; Turner, *Insights* 163-164).

ἵνα πληρωθῆτε τὴν ἐπίγνωσιν τοῦ θελήματος αὐτοῦ

2 pl. aor. pass. subjunc. of πληρόω, fill. Here God is the implied agent of the action since the request is addressed to him (cf. G. Delling, TDNT 6.291). Here the ἵνα + subjunc. clause indicates the content of the petition rather than its purpose (cf. BAGD 377c and 4:3-4). "Our request is that God may fill you" (sim. Moffatt, NEB, GNB, JB, NIV). Πληρόω is usually followed by a gen. of content (e.g., Rom. 15:14, "filled with all knowledge") but here, exceptionally, an acc. denoting content is found (see Moule 52-53; T 247; R 483). Alternatively, but less probably, τὴν ἐπίγνωσιν could be an acc. of reference or respect (cf. BDF § 160; Z § 74): "that you may be filled with respect to the knowledge of God's will."

Ἐπίγνωσις (ἐπί + γνῶσις), -εως, ἡ, may mean "complete knowledge," "clear knowledge" (Weymouth), "deeper knowledge" (TCNT), or "ever-growing knowledge" (Barclay; intensive or perfective ἐπί; cf. R 600; Robertson, *Pictures* 475; sim. Lightfoot 136), but this compound noun need not signify more than γνῶσις (cf. R. Bultmann, TDNT 1.704-708). Indeed, after a detailed discussion of the issue (pp. 248-254), J. A. Robinson concludes that γνῶσις is the wider word, "knowledge" in the fullest sense and in the abstract, ἐπίγνωσις expressing knowledge directed toward (ἐπί) a particular object that, if expressed, is indicated by the obj. gen. (*St. Paul's Epistle to the Ephesians* [London: Macmillan, 1928[2]] 254), viz. τοῦ θελήματος in v. 9 and τοῦ θεοῦ in v. 10. See also the discussion of ἐπέγνωτε in 1:6 and K. Sullivan, "Epignosis in the Epistles of St. Paul," *Studiorum Paulinorum Congressus Internationalis Catholicus 1961* (Rome: Pontifical Biblical Institute, 1963) 2.405-416. See For Further Study 12, "The Will of God."

ἐν πάσῃ σοφίᾳ καὶ συνέσει πνευματικῇ

This prep. phrase may be taken in three ways:

(1) with πληρωθῆτε, ἐν being instr.: "filled . . . by having . . ." (sim. TCNT, Goodspeed, NEB, JB, NAB, NIV)
(2) with ἐπίγνωσιν, ἐν being sociative: "knowledge . . . accompanied by . . ." (Weymouth)
(3) with ἐπίγνωσιν, ἐν being epex.: "knowledge . . . which consists in . . ." (sim. GNB)

On view (1), which is preferable, πληρωθῆτε is followed by a statement, first of content, then of means: "that you may be filled *with* the knowledge of God's will *by having* spiritual wisdom and discernment (σύνεσις, -εως, ἡ) of every sort." With an anar. noun πᾶς means "every" or "all" in the sense of "every kind of" (BDF § 275[3]; R 771-772; T 199-200; Z §§ 188-191). For πᾶς with an art. noun, see on 1:4. Both adjs., πάσῃ and πνευματικῇ, should be construed with both nouns, σοφίᾳ and συνέσει. Πνευματικός here signifies "relating to the (human) spirit/spiritual matters"; or (as BAGD 679a proposes; sim. GNB; G. Schrenk, TDNT 3.58), "given by the Spirit," in comparison with the specious wisdom of the false teaching (2:23) that emanated from an unspiritual mind (2:18).

VERSE 10

περιπατῆσαι ἀξίως τοῦ κυρίου

Aor. act. inf. of περιπατέω, walk; (in a moral sense) live, behave (BAGD 649b; H. Seesemann, TDNT 5.944). This inf. is a constative aor. (see v. 7) that views the Christian's whole life and conduct as a unit, without reference to individual or repeated acts (as is expressed by τὸ περιπατεῖν in 1 Thess. 2:12), although BDF § 337(1) sees the περιπατῆσαι as highlighting the newness of the Christian's life. This inf. may express purpose (after πληρωθῆτε κτλ.), "in order that you may lead a life" (so O'Brien 18, 22; sim. R 1049, 1087; Weymouth, Moffatt, Goodspeed, NIV); or *result, "you will then lead a life" (Lightfoot 137; sim. TCNT, GNB, JB, NAB). But it is unlikely to express additional content of the request, "asking that you may be filled . . . and may lead a life." Paul's prayer, then, was in essence that the Colossians would have "all spiritual wisdom and discernment," which would mean that they were "filled with the knowledge of God's will" and thus would "lead a life worthy of the Lord."

' Αξίως (adv.), "in a manner worthy of," with gen. of the person or thing. Although God the Father is the implied agent in πληρωθῆτε and αὐτοῦ in vv. 9, 11 refers to him, τοῦ κυρίου here probably denotes the Lord Jesus (as also BAGD 460a), given the following explicit refs. to τοῦ θεοῦ (v. 10b) and τῷ πατρί (v. 12a) and Paul's customary distinction (Z § 169) between ὁ Κύριος = Christ and Κύριος = Yahweh.

εἰς πᾶσαν ἀρεσκείαν

Lit. "to every type of pleasing." On anar. πᾶς, see 1:9. Since this phrase follows "worthy of the Lord (Jesus)" as a second qualification of περιπατῆσαι, it will mean "to please him in all respects" (BAGD 105c) or "that seeks to please him in everything," with εἰς denoting purpose. In CGk ἀρεσκεία (-ας, ἡ) generally had a pejorative sense, "obsequiousness," "cringing" (cf. MH 75).

ἐν παντὶ ἔργῳ ἀγαθῷ καρποφοροῦντες

Nom. pl. masc. (agreeing with the subj. of πληρωθῆτε) of the pres. act. ptc. of καρποφορέω, bear fruit (see 1:6 for mid. use). On anar. πᾶς, see 1:9. Both adjs., παντί and ἀγαθῷ, qualify ἔργῳ: "every kind of good deed," "right action of every sort" (Weymouth). But if ἔργῳ is a generic sg. (see BDF § 139; T 22-23), the meaning will be "all kinds of good deeds" (Goodspeed; BAGD 405b) or "good deeds of every kind" (Zerwick, *Analysis* 447). Καρποφοροῦντες is the first of four pres. ptcs. in vv. 10-12 (the others are αὐξανόμενοι, δυναμούμενοι, εὐχαριστοῦντες) that modify περιπατῆσαι . . . ἀρεσκείαν and are circumstantial, describing four characteristics of "a life that is worthy of the Lord and that seeks to please him in everything." These four traits—bearing fruit, growing, being empowered, giving thanks—are portrayed as typical of the believer, not as the only marks of the Christian. Each of the four ptcs. is modified by a prep. phrase (see above on Structure). All four ptcs. are in effect coordinate, although the last two lack a connective (a case of asyndeton).

αὐξανόμενοι τῇ ἐπιγνώσει τοῦ θεοῦ

Nom. pl. masc. (agreeing with the subj. of πληρωθῆτε) of the pres. pass. ptc. of αὐξάνω, grow, cause to grow; (pass.) grow. In v. 6 this vb. denotes *extensive* growth; here, *intensive* growth (E. Schweizer, TDNT 7.1078 n. 501). Dat. τῇ ἐπιγνώσει (on the meaning of this word see on 1:9) expresses the sphere of the growth ("growing in the knowledge," locat. dat. or dat. of respect) rather than its means ("growing by the knowledge," instr. dat.). Τοῦ θεοῦ is an obj. gen., "the knowledge of God('s person)," not a subj. gen. ("the knowledge [of his will] imparted by God"). On this view, v. 10b is an instance of chiasmus (A–B–B–A): (A) a prep. phrase in the dat. (ἐν παντὶ κτλ.) modifying (B) a pres. ptc. (καρποφοροῦντες); and (B) a pres. ptc. (αὐξανόμενοι) modified by (A) a dat. phrase (τῇ ἐπιγνώσει κτλ.). But it is also possible (thus Lohse 29) to construe both modifying phrases with both ptcs.: "bearing fruit and growing in every good deed through knowing God," τῇ ἐπιγνώσει in that case being an instr. dat. expressing means.

VERSE 11

ἐν πάσῃ δυνάμει δυναμούμενοι

Nom. pl. masc. (agreeing with the subj. of πληρωθῆτε) of the pres. pass. ptc. of δυναμόω, strengthen, empower. This is the third of four circumstantial pres.

ptcs. in vv. 10-12 (see on v. 10). Ἐν is instr., lit. "(being empowered) with all power." BAGD proposes "equipped with all power" (207c) or "endowed with all strength" (208c). Πάσῃ δυνάμει may signify "power of every kind" (ZG 603; cf. 1:9) or "with full power" (cf. BAGD 631c, πᾶς denoting the "highest degree").

κατὰ τὸ κράτος τῆς δόξης αὐτοῦ

The prep. κατά may here express:
(1) conformity ("in accordance with"; "according to," RV, RSV, NASB, NIV), in which case κατὰ κτλ. points to the level of the resources available for the equipping with power;
(2) basis ("based on [his own glorious power]," JB); or
*(3) cause ("as a result of," "because of" (sim. Weymouth), and thus "through"; see BAGD 407b), in which case the ἐν phrase denotes that *with* which the Colossians are empowered and the κατά phrase, that *through* which they are empowered: God's glorious strength (κράτος, -ους, τό) imparts the power with which they are endued or empowers them with a full measure of power (cf. NAB, "By the might of his glory"; Moffatt, "May his glorious might nerve you with full power").
Gen. τῆς δόξης may be poss., "that belongs to/is characteristic of his glory (= majesty or divinity)"; or qualitative, describing τὸ κράτος as "glorious might" (BAGD 449a) or "majestic power" (BAGD 203d).

εἰς πᾶσαν ὑπομονὴν καὶ μακροθυμίαν

Εἰς indicates the goal, "for," "with a view to" (see, however, A. Oepke, TDNT 2.429). Ὑπομονή, -ῆς, ἡ, is resolute endurance under difficult circumstances, while μακροθυμία, -ας, ἡ, is patient endurance that does not retaliate (see Lightfoot 138; J. Horst, TDNT 4.384 n. 82). On anar. πᾶς, see 1:9. Tr.: "for endurance and patience of every kind."

μετὰ χαρᾶς

This phrase ("with joy") may be cstr. with what precedes (εἰς πᾶσαν κτλ.; thus WH) or with what follows (εὐχαριστοῦντες κτλ.; thus UBS). In favor of the latter construction ("joyfully giving thanks," NIV; sim. NASB, GNB; Lohse 32, 33; O'Brien 25) is the precise parallel in Phil. 1:4 and the structure of the sentence (viz. four ptcs., each modified by a phrase; see above on Structure). The Nestle-Aland[26] ed. begins a new sentence and paragraph with μετὰ χαρᾶς.

VERSE 12

εὐχαριστοῦντες τῷ πατρί

Nom. pl. masc. (agreeing with the subj. of πληρωθῆτε) of the pres. act. ptc. of εὐχαριστέω, give thanks; followed by the dat. (τῷ πατρί). This ptc. is the last of four circumstantial ptcs. that modify περιπατῆσαι κτλ. (see on v. 10) and refer to the Colossians. But it is also possible, although unlikely, that εὐχαριστοῦντες is to be taken with οὐ παυόμεθα (v. 9) and refers to Paul and Timothy (v. 1) ("we have not ceased praying . . . asking . . . giving thanks") or that the ptc. is impv. (thus Lohse 32 and n. 1; cf. BDF § 468[2]).

The unusual abs. use of ὁ πατήρ seems to have led some copyists to add the qualification τοῦ Χριστοῦ ("the Father of Christ") and others to add (τῷ) θεῷ before (καὶ)/(τῷ) πατρί ("God the Father"). See UBS and Metzger 620.

τῷ ἱκανώσαντι ὑμᾶς εἰς τὴν μερίδα

Dat. sg. masc. of the aor. act. ptc. of ἱκανόω, qualify (someone for something, τινὰ εἴς τι; here ὑμᾶς εἰς). This art. ptc. is in appos. to τῷ πατρί (T 206), lit. "the one who (has) qualified you." Εἰς states the goal of God's action ("for a share," "to have a share," "to receive our share," Weymouth), or possibly simply denotes reference ("with respect to," thus BAGD 230a). The art. with μερίς, -ίδος, ἡ ("allotted portion," "part"; "share") may be poss., "*your* share."

As well as having strong Alexandrian support (ℵ B 1739 copˢᵃ), the rdg. ὑμᾶς is to be preferred because it would readily have been altered to ἡμᾶς to conform with ἡμᾶς in v. 13a and because scribes naturally tended to make statements that were true of all Christians (v. 12b) applicable to readers and writers alike (ἡμᾶς). Similar textual issues arise in 2:13 (ὑμᾶς . . . ἡμῖν).

τοῦ κλήρου τῶν ἁγίων

Κλῆρος, -ου, ὁ, means "(apportioned) lot, inheritance." This gen., which is dependent on τὴν μερίδα, could be epex. ("the portion which consists in the lot," Lightfoot 139) but is probably partitive ("a share in the inheritance," BAGD 435c, 505c; "to share the inheritance"). On the partitive gen., see BDF § 164, 169; Moule, *Idiom Book* 42-43; R 502; T 208-210. Τῶν ἁγίων is undoubtedly poss., "the inheritance belonging to/reserved for/that awaits God's people." Some commentators argue that οἱ ἅγιοι here refers to angels (e.g., Lohse 36; also BAGD 9d), but this is improbable since (1) elsewhere in this letter οἱ ἅγιοι denotes believers (1:2, 4, 26; cf. 1:22; 3:12), and this meaning is certainly possible here, given the common Pauline concept of the believers' inheritance (see For Further Study 13, "The Concept of Inheritance in Paul"); and (2) the ideas of v. 12b are paralleled in two Lukan summaries of Pauline speeches (Acts 20:32; and esp. 26:18), where the reference is to believers, not angels.

ἐν τῷ φωτί

This prep. phrase could be cstr. with:

(1) τῷ ἱκανώσαντι—"who has qualified you . . . *by* his light (= the gospel)" (instr. ἐν); or

(2) τῶν ἁγίων—"God's people who are [τῶν] *in* the kingdom of light" (locat. ἐν); but most naturally it belongs with

*(3) τοῦ κλήρου—"the inheritance . . . that *consists of* the kingdom of light" (epex. ἐν) or *"that is [τοῦ] *in* the realm of light" (locat. ἐν) (cf. v. 5).

In view of the contrast with "the dominion/realm of darkness" (v. 13a), art. φωτί probably means "the realm/kingdom of light" (cf. 3:1; Eph. 1:20), which is further defined in v. 13b as "the kingdom of his [God's] dearly loved Son" and therefore refers to a present reality (cf. ἔχομεν in v. 14).

VERSE 13

ὃς ἐρρύσατο ἡμᾶς

3 sg. aor. mid. indic. of ῥύομαι, rescue, deliver (someone from something, τινὰ ἔκ/ἀπό τινος). The rescue and transference (μετέστησεν, v. 13b) occurred either at the death of Christ (in a collective and proleptic sense) or at the individual believer's conversion. On either view, the aors. are constative, viewing an act or successive acts as a whole (cf. v. 7). Ἡμᾶς refers to Paul, Timothy, and the addressees as typical of all believers. The change from 2 pl. (ὑμᾶς, v. 12) to 1 pl. (ἡμᾶς, v. 13) is not uncommon in Paul (cf. 2:13-14; Rom. 6:14-15). Ὅς may be causal (cf. R 960): "for He rescued us" (Barclay; sim. JB).

ἐκ τῆς ἐξουσίας τοῦ σκότους

"From the dominion of darkness" (Goodspeed, NIV; sim. Weymouth). Ἐξ-ουσία is a key word in Pauline and biblical theology. It is derived from ἔξεστι ("it is possible") and has a wide range of meaning: (1) freedom of choice or of action, (2) arbitrary or delegated power exercised by a person, (3) the person thus empowered, a bearer of authority, and (4) the sphere or domain where that power or rule is exercised (cf. BAGD 277d-278d). Here it means "power" (2) or "domain" (4); the Eng. word "dominion" reproduces the ambiguity. Rather than simply saying "from darkness" (ἐκ τοῦ σκότους, which would be parallel to ἐν τῷ φωτί, v. 12b), Paul introduces ἐξουσία as a parallel to βασιλεία

(v. 13b) and to show that the darkness was not merely a state but an active authority (A. S. Peake, EGT 3.501).

After ἐκ τῆς ἐξουσίας the gen. τοῦ σκότους (from σκότος, -ους, τό, darkness) could be poss. ("the power possessed by darkness" [here personified]) or subj. ("the power exercised by [the prince of] darkness") or even epex. ("the power which is Darkness"), but it is probably qualitative ("the dominion that is characterized by darkness").

καὶ μετέστησεν εἰς τὴν βασιλείαν

3 sg. aor. act. indic. of μεθίστημι, transfer, remove: "and transferred us [ἡμᾶς, from v. 13a] into the kingdom." V. 13 describes two actions of God the Father (ὅς) that are sequential (first rescue, then transference) or, better, concurrent (rescue by transference). With εἰς, the vb. μεθίστημι can mean "transplant into" or "transport to" (of population resettlement; cf. BAGD 499a). If the pref. μεθ- (= μετά) has special import with εἰς, the mng. will be "brought us away into (NEB)/safe into (GNB)/over into (Barclay)." This clause introduces the last of three grounds for thanksgiving to the Father (viz. vv. 12b, 13a, 13b).

τοῦ υἱοῦ τῆς ἀγάπης αὐτοῦ

An accumulation of gens. is typical of Paul. Lit. "of the Son (poss. gen.) of the love (qualitative gen.—see below) of him" (poss. gen.). It would seem that for Paul the kingdom of Christ was an alternative designation for the kingdom of God during the period between the resurrection of Christ and the arrival of the End (cf. 1 Cor. 15:23-25; Eph. 5:5; 2 Tim. 4:1, 18; Matt. 13:41). See For Further Study 14, "The Kingdom Concept in Paul."

Some commentators take τῆς ἀγάπης as a gen. of origin or source: "begotten of (the Father's essence =) love" (Lightfoot 140, following Augustine). TCNT renders "who is the embodiment of his love" (epex. gen.). Probably, however, this gen. should be taken as qualitative ("beloved," "dearly loved"; see on v. 5), the whole phrase being equivalent to τοῦ ἀγαπητοῦ υἱοῦ αὐτοῦ (cf. Mk. 1:11) or τοῦ ἠγαπημένου υἱοῦ αὐτοῦ (cf. Eph. 1:6; thus Moule, *Idiom Book* 175 and Moule 58, "probably"; Zerwick, *Analysis* 448; TDNT 8.369 n. 246) and meaning "his beloved Son" (BAGD 6a; cf. R 496) or "the Son whom he loves" (sim. JB, NIV). In this Sem. idiom the pers. pron. αὐτοῦ, which denotes poss., properly belongs to τοῦ υἱοῦ but is actually attached to the dependent qualitative gen. (T 214; Turner, *Style* 91; R 497; cf. Z § 41).

The imagery of vv. 12-13 suggests that believers have been rescued from the gloomy domain and tyrannical rule of Satan by being transplanted as free colonists into the kingdom and peaceable sovereignty of Christ, to become citizens in the realm of light.

VERSE 14

ἐν ᾧ ἔχομεν τὴν ἀπολύτρωσιν

This clause marks the transition from the recitation of three of God's redemptive acts (vv. 12-13) to the celebration of Christ's person and work (vv. 14-20) where three successive rel. prons., ἐν ᾧ (v. 14), ὅς (v. 15), and ὅς (v. 18), and eleven instances of the pers. pron. αὐτός occur, all referring to Christ.

Although the nearest antecedent to ἐν ᾧ is αὐτοῦ (= the Father), the actual antecedent is τοῦ υἱοῦ. Ἐν is almost certainly locat., "in union with whom" (on the ἐν Χριστῷ concept see on v. 2), although Goodspeed (sim. TCNT) takes it as instr.—"by whom we have been ransomed from captivity." After the three aors. in vv. 12-13, the pres. ἔχομεν stresses the ongoing and permanent result of the Father's threefold action: "we enjoy the possession of" (cf. Moffatt). While it is improper to suggest that ἀπολύτρωσις, -εως, ἡ, always denotes "release from (ἀπό) bondage through the payment of a ransom (λύτρον)," here it does seem to mean "redemption" in the sense of release from bondage to sin, given the imagery of v. 13a and the ref. to sins in v. 14b. See For Further Study 15, "Redemption in Paul."

τὴν ἄφεσιν τῶν ἁμαρτιῶν

"Redemption" is defined here as "the forgiveness of sins," τὴν ἄφεσιν (ἄφεσις, -εως, ἡ, release, pardon, forgiveness) being acc. in epex. appos. to τὴν ἀπολύτρωσιν. Τῶν ἁμαρτιῶν is an obj. gen. (cf. Eph. 1:7), with the art. probably denoting poss., "our sins" (RV ["our redemption . . . our sins"], TCNT, Goodspeed, NEB ["our release . . . our sins"], GNB). On the ἁμαρτ- word group, see Turner, *Words* 412-413; on ἄφεσις, ibid. 371.

TRANSLATION

[9] That is why, ever since we heard this, we also have not ceased praying for you, asking that you may be filled with the knowledge of God's will by having all spiritual wisdom and discernment. [10] You will then lead a life that is worthy of the Lord and that seeks to please him in everything, bearing fruit in every kind of good deed and growing in the knowledge of God, [11] being empowered with all power through his glorious strength for endurance and patience of every kind, and joyfully [12] giving thanks to the Father who has qualified you to share the inheritance of his people in the kingdom of light. [13] He has rescued us from the dominion of darkness and transferred us into the kingdom of his dearly loved Son, [14] in whom we have redemption, the forgiveness of sins.

EXPANDED PARAPHRASE

[9] Because of this encouraging news about you, from the very day we heard it we also have never stopped praying for you. Our request to God is that he may fill you with a knowledge of what his will is by giving you every form of spiritual wisdom and discernment. [10] Once you have this you will lead a life that is worthy of the Lord Jesus and that aims to give him complete satisfaction in every respect. Your life will then be marked by perennial fruit-bearing in every kind of good deed, by continuous growth in your knowledge of God, [11] by a constant supply of strength generated by his glorious power for every form of endurance and patience, [12] and by continual and joyful thanksgiving to God the Father, the one who has entitled you to receive a share in the heritage that belongs to his people in the kingdom of light. [13] Yes, in the kingdom of light, for he has rescued us from the dominion that is characterized by darkness and has transferred us as free colonists into the kingdom of the Son whom he loves so dearly. [14] In union with this Son we have gained and now enjoy release from bondage, namely the forgiveness of our sins.

FOR FURTHER STUDY

11. Prayer in Paul (1:9-12)

Brown, C., NIDNTT 2.882-886.

Coggan, F. D., *The Prayers of the New Testament* (New York: Harper and Row, 1967) 87-167.

Mullins, T. Y., "Petition as a Literary Form," *NovT* 5 (1962) 46-54.

Schönweiss, H. and Brown, C., NIDNTT 2.873-875.

*Stanley, D. M. *Boasting in the Lord. The Phenomenon of Prayer in Saint Paul* (New York: Paulist, 1973).

Wiles, G. P., *Paul's Intercessory Prayers* (Cambridge: Cambridge University, 1974).

See also For Further Study 6, "Pauline Thanksgivings" (1:3).

12. The Will of God (1:9)

Friesen, G. with Maxson, J. R., *Decision Making and the Will of God. A Biblical Alternative to the Traditional View* (Portland: Multnomah, 1980).

McCasland, S. V., IDB 4.844-848.

Michaels, J. R., ISBE 4.1064-1067.

*Müller, D., NIDNTT 3.1015-1023.

Schrenk, G., TDNT 1.629-637; 3.44-62.

"The Will of God," a series in *ExpT* 72 (1960-61) 68-71 (C. L. Mitton); 115-117 (G. B. Caird); 142-145 (J. A. Allan); 167-169 (F. J. Taylor); 237-240 (G. Johnston).

13. The Concept of Inheritance in Paul (1:12)

Eichler, J., NIDNTT 2.295-303.

Foerster, W., TDNT 3.781-785.

Hammer, P. L., IDB 5.428-429.

Hester, J. D., *Paul's Concept of Inheritance* (Edinburgh: Oliver & Boyd, 1968).

*Lyall, F., *Slaves, Citizens, Sons: Legal Metaphors in the Epistles* (Grand Rapids: Zondervan, 1984) 101-117.

Turner, *Words* 133-134.

14. The Kingdom Concept in Paul (1:13)

*Kennedy, H. A. A., *St. Paul's Conceptions of the Last Things* (London: Hodder, 1904^2) 282-341.

Shires, H. M., *The Eschatology of Paul in the Light of Modern Scholarship* (Philadelphia: Westminster, 1966), esp. 60-63.

Vos, G., *The Pauline Eschatology* (Grand Rapids: Eerdmans, 1961 reprint of 1930 ed.) 226-260.

15. Redemption in Paul (1:14)

Hill, D., *Greek Words and Hebrew Meanings* (Cambridge: Cambridge University, 1967) 49-81.

Lyall, F., *Slaves, Citizens, Sons: Legal Metaphors in the Epistles* (Grand Rapids: Zondervan, 1984) 153-175.

Lyonnet, S. and Sabourin, L., *Sin, Redemption, and Sacrifice* (Rome: Pontifical Biblical Institute, 1970) 79-103.

*Morris, L., *The Apostolic Preaching of the Cross* (Grand Rapids: Eerdmans, 1965^3) 11-64.

————, *The Atonement: Its Meaning and Significance* (Downers Grove: IVP, 1983) 106-131.

Warfield, B. B., *Biblical Doctrines* (New York: Oxford University, 1929) 327-398.

HOMILETICAL SUGGESTIONS

Paul's Intercession for the Colossians (1:9-14)

1. Its commencement and frequency (ἀφ' ἧς ἡμέρας ἠκούσαμεν, οὐ παυόμεθα, v. 9a)
2. Its principal content (αἰτούμενοι ἵνα κτλ., v. 9b): a request for wisdom and discernment and thus knowledge of God's will
3. Its intended results (vv. 10-14): a life (περιπατῆσαι) that is:
   (a) worthy of the Lord (ἀξίως τοῦ κυρίου, v. 10a)
   (b) pleasing to the Lord (εἰς πᾶσαν ἀρεσκείαν, v. 10a)
   (c) marked by:
      (i) fruitfulness of action (. . . καρποφοροῦντες, v. 10b)
      (ii) growth in knowledge (αὐξανόμενοι κτλ., v. 10b)
      (iii) power for endurance (. . . δυναμούμενοι κτλ., v. 11)
      (iv) gratitude to God (. . . εὐχαριστοῦντες κτλ., v. 12a)
         for qualification (τῷ ἱκανώσαντι κτλ., v. 12b)
            deliverance (ἐρρύσατο κτλ., v. 13a; ἀπολύτρωσιν, v. 14)
            transference (μετέστησεν κτλ., v. 13b)

The Normal Christian Life (1:10-12a; cf. 2:6b-7)

1. Pleasing the Lord (v. 10a) by:
2. Perennial fruit-bearing (v. 10a)
3. Continuous growth (v. 10b)
4. Patience endurance (v. 11)
5. Constant thanksgiving (v. 12a)

The Father's Threefold Action (1:12b-13)

1. Granting entitlement to shared inheritance (v. 12b)
2. Carrying out a rescue from the dominion of darkness (v. 13a)
3. Effecting a transference into the kingdom of light (v. 13b; cf. v. 12b)

II. Christ's Work and Paul's Mission
(1:15–2:3)

A. THE SUPREMACY OF CHRIST
IN CREATION AND REDEMPTION (1:15-20)

15 ὅς ἐστιν εἰκὼν τοῦ θεοῦ τοῦ ἀοράτου, πρωτότοκος πάσης κτίσεως, 16 ὅτι ἐν αὐτῷ ἐκτίσθη τὰ πάντα ἐν τοῖς οὐρανοῖς καὶ ἐπὶ τῆς γῆς, τὰ ὁρατὰ καὶ τὰ ἀόρατα, εἴτε θρόνοι εἴτε κυριότητες εἴτε ἀρχαὶ εἴτε ἐξουσίαι· τὰ πάντα δι' αὐτοῦ καὶ εἰς αὐτὸν ἔκτισται, 17 καὶ αὐτός ἐστιν πρὸ πάντων καὶ τὰ πάντα ἐν αὐτῷ συνέστηκεν. 18 καὶ αὐτός ἐστιν ἡ κεφαλὴ τοῦ σώματος, τῆς ἐκκλησίας· ὅς ἐστιν ἀρχή, πρωτότοκος ἐκ τῶν νεκρῶν, ἵνα γένηται ἐν πᾶσιν αὐτὸς πρωτεύων, 19 ὅτι ἐν αὐτῷ εὐδόκησεν πᾶν τὸ πλήρωμα κατοικῆσαι 20 καὶ δι' αὐτοῦ ἀποκαταλλάξαι τὰ πάντα εἰς αὐτόν, εἰρηνοποιήσας διὰ τοῦ αἵματος τοῦ σταυροῦ αὐτοῦ, δι' αὐτοῦ εἴτε τὰ ἐπὶ τῆς γῆς εἴτε τὰ ἐν τοῖς οὐρανοῖς.

STRUCTURE

The most noteworthy feature of this section is its symmetry, achieved through the repetition of words or phrases in corresponding positions. This extensive parallelism, together with certain rhetorical devices, such as chiasmus, have prompted many scholars to suggest that vv. 15-20 form a traditional christological "hymn." But elevated diction and complex rhetorical structure do not necessarily mean that these six verses constitute a hymn, particularly when there is no recognizable metrical pattern. See Lohse 41-46; O'Brien 32-37; and For Further Study 16, "Christological Hymns in the NT." In the following structural analysis, the elaborate balancing (which is reproduced in the format of the Translation, below) will become clear. Boxes and lines are used to draw attention to three interlocked instances of chiasmus (A–B–B–A). See For Further Study 46, "Chiasmus in the NT" (Phlm. 5).

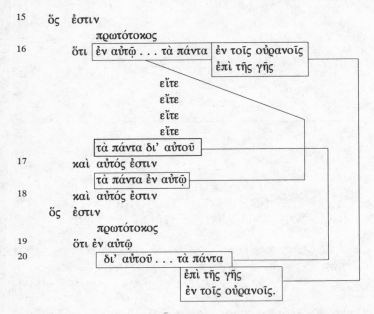

¹⁵ ὅς ἐστιν
       πρωτότοκος
¹⁶ ὅτι ἐν αὐτῷ ... τὰ πάντα   ἐν τοῖς οὐρανοῖς
                                 ἐπὶ τῆς γῆς
                  εἴτε
                  εἴτε
                  εἴτε
                  εἴτε
         τὰ πάντα δι' αὐτοῦ
¹⁷ καὶ αὐτός ἐστιν
         τὰ πάντα ἐν αὐτῷ
¹⁸ καὶ αὐτός ἐστιν
   ὅς ἐστιν
       πρωτότοκος
¹⁹ ὅτι ἐν αὐτῷ
²⁰   δι' αὐτοῦ ... τὰ πάντα
         ἐπὶ τῆς γῆς
         ἐν τοῖς οὐρανοῖς.

From this it may be seen that there are three main ways of dividing the "hymn":

(1) vv. 15-17
    vv. 18-20   πρωτότοκος and καὶ αὐτός ἐστιν occur in both sections

(2) vv. 15-18a
    vv. 18b-20   ὅς ἐστιν begins each section

(3) vv. 15-16   ὅς ἐστιν κτλ.
    vv. 17-18a   καὶ αὐτός ἐστιν occurs twice
    vv. 18b-20   ὅς ἐστιν κτλ.

We shall follow the first division, in which vv. 15-17 deal with the supremacy of Christ in creation (πρωτότοκος, "the firstborn [over all creation]"; καὶ αὐτός ἐστιν, "and he is [before everything]"), and vv. 18-20 describe his supremacy in redemption (καὶ αὐτός ἐστιν, "and he is [the head of the Body, the Church]"; πρωτότοκος, "the firstborn [from the dead]"). A similar link between creation and redemption, nature and grace, cosmology and soteriology is found in the christological passages or "hymns" in John 1:1-18 and Hebrews 1:1-4.

VERSE 15

ὅς ἐστιν εἰκὼν τοῦ θεοῦ τοῦ ἀοράτου

Ὅς (nom. sg. masc. of rel. pron. ὅς, ἥ, ὅ) refers to the "dearly loved Son" (v. 13). Ἐστιν is a timeless/atemporal present (cf. Z § 372): either Jesus, as God's Son, is eternally the outward projection of the Father, or after his incarnation Jesus remains forever God's visible expression.

Εἰκών (-όνος, ἡ, image) is nom. after the vb. εἰμί, and is anar. because a pred. noun after εἰμί often lacks the article (cf. 2 Cor. 4:4). It is definite ("the image"; "the visible representation," Weymouth) although anar. An εἰκών is a "likeness" or a "visible expression." The degree of resemblance between the archetype and the copy must be determined by the word's context but could range from a partial or superficial resemblance to a complete or essential likeness. Given 1:19; 2:9, εἰκών here signifies that Jesus is an exact, as well as a visible, representation of God. See Lightfoot 142-144; H. Kleinknecht, TDNT 2.388-390, 395-396; Turner, *Words* 225-227.

Τοῦ θεοῦ may be classified broadly as gen. of relationship (see BDF § 162; T 212; Z § 39: "general gen.") or more narrowly as gen. of poss. ("the image of God" = the image that God has), but it could also be seen as an obj. gen. (Jesus "images" God). Τοῦ θεοῦ τοῦ ἀοράτου means the same as τοῦ ἀοράτου θεοῦ, "of the invisible God" (see BDF § 270; T 185 on the position of attrib. adjs.). The adj. ἀοράτου (ἀόρατος, -ον, a two-termination adj.), which stands in contrast to εἰκών ("visible expression"), is used to describe not merely what has not been seen (= unseen) but also what cannot be seen by mortal sight (= invisible; as also in v. 16). The invisible God, who dwells in unapproachable light (1 Tim. 6:16), is visibly expressed in his Son (cf. Jn. 1:18; 12:45; 14:9).

πρωτότοκος πάσης κτίσεως

Like εἰκών, πρωτότοκος (-ον, a two-termination adj., "firstborn") is anar. but definite (see 1:15a). The "firstborn" was either the eldest child in a family or a person of preeminent rank. The use of this term to describe the Davidic king in Ps. 88:28 (LXX; = Ps. 89:27, EVV), "I will also appoint him my firstborn (πρωτότοκον), the most exalted of the kings of the earth," indicates that it can denote supremacy in rank as well as priority in time. But whether the πρωτό-element in the word denotes time, rank, or both, the significance of the -τοκος element as indicating birth or origin (from τίκτω, give birth to) has been virtually lost except in ref. to lit. birth (Lk. 2:7; cf. W. Michaelis, TDNT 6.878).

Κτίσις, -εως, ἡ, creation, creature. Πάσης κτίσεως could be distributive in sense, "every creature" (BAGD 455d, 631b) or "every created thing" (R 772, with hesitation); or collective, even though πάσης is anar., "the whole of creation" (T 199-200) or "all creation" (Lightfoot 145-146; Lohse 32, 48-49). This gen. is either obj., "supreme over all creation"; or gen. of comparison (for this use, see BDF § 185; Moule, *Idiom Book* 42; R 516; T 216), "prior to all creation," with the superlative πρωτό- ("first") having a comp. sense ("earlier [than]"; "begotten before all creation," Barclay; see T 32; Turner, *Insights* 23-24 for such a usage). It could scarcely be partitive gen. (see on 1:12), "first(born) among all created things," with πάσης κτίσεως denoting the whole of which the πρωτότοκος was the first part, since (1) v. 16a distinguishes Jesus from "all creation" when it affirms that "the whole universe" (τὰ πάντα) was created "in" him; (2) if Paul had believed that Jesus was the first of God's creatures to be formed, the adj. πρωτόκτιστος ("created first") or πρωτόπλαστος ("formed first") might have been expected instead of πρωτότοκος, and v. 16a would have continued "for all other things were created in him" (ὅτι ἐν αὐτῷ ἐκτίσθη πάντα τὰ ἄλλα). But for a defense of the tr. "archetype of all creation," see Turner, *Insights* 122-124.

VERSE 16

ὅτι ἐν αὐτῷ ἐκτίσθη τὰ πάντα ἐν τοῖς οὐρανοῖς καὶ ἐπὶ τῆς γῆς

In BGk ὅτι ranges in meaning from a weak "for" to a strong "because" (cf. T 318). Here (as a strong "for") it introduces the reason for Christ's priority over all creation: "for in him all things were created." Ἐκτίσθη (3 sg. aor. pass. indic. of κτίζω, create) refers to creation's occurrence in the past, the constative aor. pointing to creation either as a single action or as a process or series of actions viewed as a whole. The vb. is sg. with a neut. pl. subj. (τὰ πάντα), but this general rule of CGk is not always followed in BGk (BDF § 133; T 312-313; R 403-404). As opposed to πάντα, which means "all things," "everything" in a distributive sense, τὰ πάντα means "all things collectively" (Lightfoot 149). This totality is here "all things in heaven and on earth," and not exactly "the universe, namely, things in heaven and things on earth" (which would require τὰ πάντα τὰ ἐν τοῖς οὐρανοῖς καὶ τὰ ἐπὶ τῆς γῆς, as in TR; on this textual question, see Lightfoot 149-150).

The prep. phrase ἐν αὐτῷ may be instr. ("by him"), comparable in sense with δι' αὐτοῦ ("through him," v. 16d; thus BDF § 219[1]; Zerwick, *Analysis* 448; Lohse 50 and n. 129) or even causal ("because of") (T 253; but cf. later Turner, *Insights* 124), but a locat. or local sense is to be preferred. "All things in heaven and on earth" were created *in* God's beloved Son (v. 13), not in the sense that he was the preexistent or ideal archetype of creation but in the sense that creation occurred "within the sphere of" Christ. In his person resided the creative energy that produced all of creation (Vincent 897; cf. R 587-588); in the work of creation God did not act apart from Christ.

τὰ ὁρατὰ καὶ τὰ ἀόρατα

Ὁρατός, -ή, -όν, visible. For ἀόρατος see on v. 15. The neut. pl. of an adj. with the art. denotes a class (cf. BDF § 263[4]): "things visible and things invisible." It is possible that τὰ ὁρατά corresponds to ἐπὶ τῆς γῆς and τὰ ἀόρατα to ἐν τοῖς οὐρανοῖς, so that there is a chiasmus (A–B–B–A): what is on earth is visible, what is in heaven is invisible. But it is more likely that we have here two different but partially overlapping classifications of reality—one by locality (earth—heaven), the other by essence (visible—invisible; cf. Lightfoot 149).

εἴτε θρόνοι εἴτε κυριότητες εἴτε ἀρχαὶ εἴτε ἐξουσίαι

"Things invisible" are now defined (cf. NEB, "the invisible orders of . . .") in a typical but not exhaustive list of four classes of supernatural powers or spiritual beings, each class being introduced by the particle εἴτε, used here as a copulative (cf. T 333). By metonymy θρόνοι are probably angelic occupants of heavenly thrones, while κυριότητες (nom. pl. of κυριότης, -ητος, ἡ, "ruling power, dominion"), ἀρχαί, and ἐξουσίαι are supernatural potentates who exercise (respectively) "dominion," "rule," and "authority" in heavenly realms. See further Turner, *Words* 28-32, 115-116, 348-349, 448-449; For Further Study 27, "Principalities and Powers in Paul" (2:10, 15).

τὰ πάντα δι’ αὐτοῦ καὶ εἰς αὐτὸν ἔκτισται

Ἔκτισται is 3 sg. pf. pass. indic. of κτίζω, create. Note the chiasmus: ἐκτίσθη (aor.) τὰ πάντα . . . τὰ πάντα . . . ἔκτισται (pf.). In nonliterary HGk, and to some extent in the NT, the distinction between the aor. and pf. tenses tends to become blurred so that we find both aoristic pfs. and perfective aors. (see Moulton 140-145; T 68-72, 81-85), but where the same vb. (here κτίζω) is used in successive sentences with the same subj. (τὰ πάντα) and in the same voice (pass.), we should probably distinguish between the tenses rather than attribute the change to stylistic variation (cf. ἐγένετο . . . γέγονεν, Jn. 1:3). Turner proposes: ". . . were once created (ἐκτίσθη) . . . have been created (and now exist) (ἔκτισται)" (*Insights* 125; cf. Weymouth; BDF § 342[1]; R 896). The pf. here emphasizes the state resulting from the past event of creation, pointing not to continuous acts of creation (true though such an idea may be in a limited sense) but to the permanent "createdness" of creation. All things have been created, and remain in their created existence, through Christ and for him. Thus the universe (τὰ πάντα) has an ongoing relationship to Christ. Ἔκτισται is thus a prelude to συνέστηκεν (see comments on v. 17b).

Δι’ αὐτοῦ (the α of διά is elided before an initial diphthong; cf. BDF § 17) indicates the agency of Christ in creation. But since this prep. + gen. can express ultimate cause (e.g., Rom. 11:36) as well as intermediate agency, there may be no special emphasis here on Christ's mediatorial or cooperative role in creation (Z § 113; Harris 1182). It is perfectly legitimate, however, to see behind the passives ἐκτίσθη and ἔκτισται an allusion to God as Creator (thus O'Brien 45 and GNB), who acts in, through, and for Christ. Εἰς αὐτόν might mean "for him," i.e., for his benefit or glory (thus equivalent to αὐτῷ), or it might mean "to him," i.e., with him as the ultimate goal (τέλος) or, as Zerwick expresses it (in Aristotelian terminology), the "final cause" (Z §§ 109, 287). On this second view, there is now, and will be at the End, "a teleological convergence of reality on Christ" (Harris 1186; cf. Rev. 22:13).

VERSE 17

καὶ αὐτός ἐστιν πρὸ πάντων

Although some NT uses of αὐτός anticipate MGk, where αὐτός means "he, this, that" and not "himself" (cf. BDF § 277[3]; T 40), here and in v. 18a the wider context indicates that the word is clearly emphatic: "he himself," "he and no other" (cf. T 40; R 679). Among supernatural potentates Jesus has no rival for the lordship of the universe (v. 17a) and the church (v. 18a).

Αυτος εστιν may be accented in two ways: as αὐτὸς ἔστιν, "he himself exists"; or as αὐτός ἐστιν, "he himself is," where ἐστιν is a mere copula uniting subj. and pred. On this point of accentuation, see MH 203; R 233-234. Like πρωτότοκος in v. 15, πρό may denote time ("before"), status ("supreme over"), or both. Four options in translation emerge:

(1) "He himself exists before all things" (temporally; sim. R 234, 622 ["probably"], 679; Lightfoot 153-154; Moule 66-67). The pres. ἔστιν is used, rather than the impf. ἦν ("he existed," Goodspeed, JB; sim. GNB), because he continues to exist, and because, corresponding to the first pers. ἐγώ εἰμι ("I am"), αὐτὸς ἔστιν denotes Christ's absolute existence (cf. Jn. 8:58) and therefore indicates that his preexistence is not simply premundane but also eternal. Cf. Weymouth: "And HE IS before all things" (citing Exod. 3:14; Jn. 8:48).

(2) "He himself exists in supremacy over all things."

(3) "He himself is before all things" (temporally; sim. O'Brien 47). Such preexistence would imply preeminence.

(4) "He himself is supreme over all things" (sim. Lohse 32, 52; W. Michaelis, TDNT 6.879). In this case ἐστιν denotes Christ's timeless existence.

While πρό does not often denote priority of importance (BAGD 702a cites Jas. 5:12; 1 Pet. 4:8), it would seem unwise to exclude here this notion of supremacy of status, given the use of πρωτότοκος in v. 15 and of πρωτεύων in v. 18. If, then, this clause expresses the dual concept of time and status (cf. Robertson, *Pictures* 479; Harris 1177), this ambiguity may be reproduced in Eng. with "he himself is before all things" or "he is prior to all" (Moffatt) or "he exists (ἔστιν) before everything" (NEB).

Πάντων could be masc., referring to the θρόνοι κτλ., but the use of τὰ πάντα in vv. 16 (twice), 17b, and 20 suggests it is neut. ("all things," "everything"; so also Lohse 52 n. 142).

καὶ τὰ πάντα ἐν αὐτῷ συνέστηκεν

As in v. 16d, τὰ πάντα refers to "the universe" (BAGD 633b; R 773-774, "the sum of things"). As in v. 16a, ἐν αὐτῷ is locat. ("in him") rather than instr. ("by him," R 534; Weymouth has "in and through Him"). Συνέστηκεν is 3 sg. (with neut. pl. subj.) pf. act. indic. of συνίστημι, cohere; here an intrans. pf. with a pres. meaning. "In him all things hold together." What Christ has created he maintains in permanent order, stability, and productivity. He is the source of the unity (συν-, together) and cohesiveness or solidarity (συν-ίστημι, cohere) of the whole universe. But it is not impossible that συνίστημι denotes subsistence rather than coherence: "all things have their existence in him" (W. Kasch, TDNT 7.897). Commentators who regard v. 17 as transitional (see above, "Structure," [3]) and therefore as dealing with both creation and redemption argue that this vb. indicates that both the physical universe and the Church owe their coherence to Christ, and that πρὸ πάντων (v. 17a) denotes his priority over the new creation as well as the old.

VERSE 18

καὶ αὐτός ἐστιν ἡ κεφαλὴ τοῦ σώματος, τῆς ἐκκλησίας

On αὐτός, see v. 17a: "he himself," "he and no other" (T 41). The one who is the creative center and focus of the universe (v. 16) and the source of its cohesion (v. 17b) is also (καί) "the head of the Body, which is the Church." As in vv. 15a, 18b, and perhaps 17a, ἐστιν is a simple copula; it is inappropriate here to tr. "he exists (αὐτὸς ἔστιν) as the head. . . ." Κεφαλή is nom. after the vb. εἰμί, and its art. state points to a reciprocal proposition, i.e., an abs. identification: Christ, and no one else, is the head. See For Further Study 17, "Christ as Head of the Church."

Τοῦ σώματος may be classed either as an obj. gen. (the "head" is sovereign over, or the ruler of, the body) or more generally as a gen. of relation or reference. It is art. because the noun on which it depends (ἡ κεφαλή) is art. (the canon of Apollonius), but the art. could, in addition, indicate poss., "his body" (note αὐτοῦ in the parallel, v. 24b; thus Goodspeed, GNB, JB). Τῆς ἐκκλησίας is in epex. appos. to τοῦ σώματος (Z § 45): his body is the (universal) church (BAGD 241a). On the use of ἐκκλησία in Paul, see O'Brien 57-61.

ὅς ἐστιν ἀρχή

῞Ος (nom. sg. masc. of the rel. pron. ὅς, ἥ, ὅ) refers back to αὐτός (v. 18a), and has a causal sense (Robertson, *Pictures* 480; A. S. Peake, EGT 3.507): "in that he is." Jesus is the head of the church inasmuch as he is its ἀρχή ("in virtue of his primacy," Moffatt), its originating cause and the source of its life (cf. Acts 3:15; Rev. 22:13). Although ἀρχή is a def. pred. noun that follows the vb. (see "Colwell's Rule" in the Glossary), it is anar. in that it is an abstract noun used abs., without ref. to a particular situation (cf. Z § 176).

πρωτότοκος ἐκ τῶν νεκρῶν

Since πρωτότοκος ("firstborn") is asyndetic, this phrase may define more precisely the ground for Christ's headship already stated. He is head of the Church "in that he is the beginning (ἀρχή), being the first (πρωτότοκος) to rise from the dead" (cf. Acts 26:23; Moffatt). Alternatively, the phrase may state a second ground for that headship: not only is Jesus the cause of the Church's existence and the origin of its vitality (ἀρχή); he is also the pioneer and guarantor of a resurrection from death to immortality (cf. Rom. 6:9; 1 Cor. 15:20, 23). Whereas in v. 15b πρωτότοκος may refer to both time and status, here only temporal priority is signified, since the word is followed by ἐκ τῶν νεκρῶν, and not simply τῶν νεκρῶν (as in Rev. 1:5, where both time and status may be denoted). Yet this primacy in time implies superiority in rank, as v. 18c shows. ᾿Εκ is not causal—"because of [his resurrection from] the dead" (which would require ἐξ ἀναστάσεως νεκρῶν, as in Rom. 1:4)—but locat., either "from among the dead" (Weymouth, NIV) or "from death" (οἱ νεκροί standing for ὁ θάνατος, the concrete for the abstract).

ἵνα γένηται ἐν πᾶσιν αὐτὸς πρωτεύων

Γένηται is 3 sg. 2 aor. mid. subjunc. (after ἵνα) of dep. γίνομαι, be, become. Πρωτεύων is the nom. sg. masc. pres. (act.) ptc. of πρωτεύω, be first, occupy the foremost place. ῞Ινα may be telic ("in order that"; sim. Robertson, *Pictures* 480; W. Michaelis, TDNT 6.882) or ecbatic ("with the result that"; cf. Moffatt, "—that gives him pre-eminence over all"); a result is merely an achieved purpose. ῞Ινα γένηται . . . πρωτεύων is a periphrastic construction (R 375; T 89; cf. BDF § 354; Horsley 4.66) related to πρωτότοκος κτλ.: "that he might become (or be) preeminent," or "so that he came to have (or has) first place." But πρωτεύων could be an honorific title (Horsley 2.96; cf. 4.172), "the Preeminent One," being anar. because qualitative.

Γίνομαι often means no more than εἰμί, but a contrast between the ἐστιν of v. 17a and the γένηται of v. 18c is probably intended: in relation to the universe Christ is and always was supreme, but in relation to the Church he became supreme by his resurrection to immortality.

As in vv. 17a and 18a, αὐτός is emphatic: "he alone became preeminent." Πρωτεύων summarizes the principal emphasis of this christological "hymn"— the supremacy of Christ, which is sole (cf. αὐτός) and universal (cf. ἐν πᾶσιν, "in all things"). It is possible that πᾶσιν (dat. pl. of πᾶς, all, every) is masc., referring back to τῶν νεκρῶν, "among all the dead"; but as in v. 17a this use of anar. πᾶς is almost certainly neut., "in all spheres," "in every realm," the natural creation and the spiritual creation, the universe and the Church.

VERSE 19

ὅτι ἐν αὐτῷ εὐδόκησεν πᾶν τὸ πλήρωμα κατοικῆσαι

3 sg. aor. act. indic. of εὐδοκέω, be well pleased; resolve. Πλήρωμα, -ατος, τό, fullness (see the discussions of this word in Lightfoot 255-271; Moule 164-169; G. Delling, TDNT 6.298-305). Κατοικῆσαι is aor. act. inf. of κατοικέω, dwell. Ὅτι ("for," "because") introduces the ground or basis (vv. 19-20) for the universal sovereignty of Christ (v. 18c) which has been the theme of vv. 15-18b. The basic reason that Christ is Lord of creation and has become Lord of the Church is that God in all his fullness was pleased to dwell in him and to reconcile the universe through him.

If God is taken to be the implied subj. (from v. 15 or v. 13) of εὐδόκησεν (thus Lightfoot 156), then an acc. and inf. construction follows: "God resolved that all the fullness (acc.) should dwell (inf.) in him [= Christ]" (cf. G. Schrenk, TDNT 2.741 and n. 16; NEB, GNB) or "it was the good pleasure *of the Father* that in him should all the fulness dwell" (RV; sim. TCNT, Weymouth, NAB; G. Delling, TDNT 6.303). Alternatively, πᾶν τὸ πλήρωμα may be the subj. (nom.), conceived of either impersonally ("all the fullness"; BAGD 319b; Lohse 32, 56-58; cf. Moffatt) or personally ("God in all his fullness"; Moule 70, 164-169; O'Brien 51, 53; sim. Barclay). Two considerations support the latter option. First, the expressions εὐδόκησεν and ἀποκαταλλάξαι . . . εἰς αὐτόν ("to reconcile . . . to himself"; see below) suggest a pers. subj. Second, ὁ θεός need not be supplied from v. 15 as the subj., since the masc. sg. ptc. εἰρηνο-ποιήσας in v. 20 and the close parallel to 1:19 in 2:9 ("all the fullness of the Godhead" = "the Godhead in all its fulness," TCNT) show that πᾶν τὸ πλήρωμα may be cstr. as "God in all his fullness." Πᾶν τό signifies "all the (fullness)," with no part excepted (see above on v. 4).

Κατοικῆσαι is commonly taken as an ingressive aor. (for this use, see BDF § 331; R 834; T 71-72; Z § 250), denoting entrance upon a state: "God in all his fullness was pleased (or resolved) to take up residence in him" (sim. ZG 604; Barclay; O'Brien 53; G. Delling, TDNT 6.303). This residence began at the incarnation; to place it at Jesus' baptism (Mk. 1:11, note εὐδόκησα) would imply an adoptionist christology. More probably, however, this inf. is a constative or global aor. (see above on v. 7), with the time of the residence left undefined, though it would certainly include the incarnate and risen life of Christ (note the pres. tense κατοικεῖ in 2:9). Correspondingly, εὐδόκησεν is also probably a constative aor.: it was by God the Father's choice and at his good pleasure that all divine attributes and powers resided in the person of Jesus (ἐν αὐτῷ).

VERSE 20

καὶ δι' αὐτοῦ ἀποκαταλλάξαι τὰ πάντα εἰς αὐτόν

Aor. act. inf. of ἀποκαταλλάσσω, reconcile. Etymologically the vb. might be taken to mean "to effect a thorough (-κατα-) change (-αλλάσσω) back (ἀπο-)" (MH 298), but the prefix ἀπο- may emphasize completeness; i.e., no supplementary sacrifice by some supraterrestrial being is needed. This inf. is coordinate (καί) with κατοικῆσαι and is also dependent on εὐδόκησεν: "God in all his fullness was pleased to dwell . . . and to reconcile." These two infs., both constative aors., are not contemporaneous, for ἀποκαταλλάξαι is restricted to the cross-work of Christ (cf. εἰρηνοποιήσας κτλ., v. 20b), and the indwelling was a prerequisite for the reconciliation as well as continuing beyond it. Here, as in 2 Cor. 5:19a, soteriology finds its basis in ontology.

It is tempting to take δι' αὐτοῦ . . . εἰς αὐτόν in ref. to Christ, as in v. 16d. Certainly δι' αὐτοῦ (see on v. 16 for this elision) denotes the agency of the incarnate Christ in the work of reconciliation, just as v. 16d depicts the agency of the preincarnate Christ in the work of creation. But since reconciliation for Paul was always reconciliation "to God" (Rom. 5:10; 2 Cor. 5:19; Eph. 2:16), εἰς αὐτόν should be referred not to Christ (as BAGD 92d, "in his own person"; Lohse 59 n. 201) but to God (so most EVV; Moule, Idiom Book 119; F. Büchsel, TDNT 1.259; A. Oepke, TDNT 2.432; G. Schrenk, TDNT 2.741). That Paul did not write ἑαυτῷ, "to himself" (as in 2 Cor. 5:18, 19), is no objection to this view, for: (1) εἰς + acc. may stand for the dat. (T 236, 253); and (2) evidently αὐτόν could function in HGk. as a reflexive (cf. Metzger 616; Z § 211; ZG 604), although it would also be possible to print αὐτόν (= ἑαυτόν by contraction; so Moule 169-170; see also MH 180-181; WH 144-145). If, then, εἰς αὐτόν means "to himself" (viz. God), it is an instance of a "construction according to sense" (see T 311-312), for the subj. of the sentence is πᾶν τὸ πλήρωμα (neut.).

Τὰ πάντα is the dir. obj. of ἀποκαταλλάξαι and means "the universe." Here it embraces inanimate nature (cf. v. 20c; Rom. 8:19-21), the world of humankind (cf. vv. 20c, 21, 22; 2 Cor. 5:19a), and those angelic powers that were at variance with God (cf. vv. 16, 20c). Verses 21-23, especially the conditional clause in v. 23a, make it clear that while the whole universe has now been restored to its God-ordained destiny, viz. its proper relation to Christ, in an objectively real reconciliation, still the benefits of this reconciliation are not experienced by individual human beings automatically, apart from their faith.

εἰρηνοποιήσας διὰ τοῦ αἵματος τοῦ σταυροῦ αὐτοῦ

Nom. sg. masc. of aor. act. ptc. of εἰρηνοποιέω, make peace. This aor. ptc. expresses neither antecedent action nor merely contemporaneous action but rather identical, modal action: "God . . . was pleased . . . to reconcile . . . by making peace" (sim. Goodspeed, GNB, NIV). There were not two separate actions (reconciliation, making peace) but only one (reconciliation) whose mode of accomplishment is then specified ("by making peace"; cf. Burton § 139, 141), so that the reconciliation is related to the "pacification" as fact to method (cf. Burton § 121, 140). Like εἰς αὐτόν (see v. 20a above), εἰρηνοποιήσας is a "construction according to sense," the masc. form agreeing with πᾶν τὸ πλήρωμα (neut.) conceived of personally (Moule 70).

Διὰ τοῦ αἵματος is parallel to δι᾽ αὐτοῦ in v. 20a. God's reconciliation was achieved through Christ—specifically, by God's making of peace through Christ's blood. Αἷμα in this context denotes life offered up sacrificially and voluntarily in death (see A. M. Stibbs, *The Meaning of the Word "Blood" in Scripture* [London: Tyndale, 1948]; Turner, *Words* 51-54). Τοῦ σταυροῦ is gen. of reference or relation (but T 212 speaks of a gen. of "place where"): "(through his blood) shed on the cross" (BAGD 765a; Goodspeed, NIV; sim. Weymouth), "through the shedding of his blood upon the cross" (NEB). Αὐτοῦ, a gen. of poss., relates to the whole phrase τοῦ αἵματος τοῦ σταυροῦ, not simply to τοῦ σταυροῦ ("the blood of his cross," Moffatt, RSV).

δι᾽ αὐτοῦ εἴτε τὰ ἐπὶ τῆς γῆς εἴτε τὰ ἐν τοῖς οὐρανοῖς

Although omitted in some Alexandrian and Western mss., perhaps due to homoeoteleuton and haplography after τοῦ σταυροῦ αὐτοῦ, the phrase δι᾽ αὐτοῦ (see on v. 16 for this elision) is probably to be retained in the text, being read by 𝔭⁴⁶ ℵ A C syrᵖ, ʰ copᵇᵒ goth *al* and printed in square brackets in all three

UBS editions (see Metzger 621). It should be cstr. with ἀποκαταλλάξαι, not
with εἰρηνοποιήσας, and is not so much resumptive ("through him, *I say*," RV)
as an emphatic repetition from v. 20a ("through him alone," NEB), comparable
in effect to αὐτός in vv. 17a, 18a, 18c. Forms of αὐτός are used eleven times
in vv. 15-20 in ref. to Christ.

Εἴτε . . . εἴτε here introduces two all-embracing categories, in explication
of τὰ πάντα (v. 20a): "all things . . . whether things on earth or things in
heaven." In v. 16, however, the fourfold εἴτε enunciates four examples of τὰ
ἀόρατα. "On earth" and "in heaven" in vv. 16a, 20c need not imply that "earth"
and "heaven" themselves are excluded from the reconciliation, for the τὰ πάντα
that stands before these phrases in vv. 16a, 20c is used in vv. 16d and 17b in
clear ref. to the universe in its entirety.

TRANSLATION

The translation is laid out here in accordance with the discussion of the
structure of the passage (see above). No conclusions regarding "hymnic"
structure are implied.

[15] He is the image of the invisible God,
    the firstborn over all creation,
[16]   for in him all things in heaven and
             on earth were created,
    things visible and things invisible,
    whether thrones
      or   dominions
      or   principalities
      or   powers—
    all things have been created
  through him and for him.
[17]   And he himself is before everything,
    and in him all things hold together.
[18]   And he himself is the head of the Body, the Church.
  He is the beginning,
    the firstborn from the dead,
      so that in everything he alone became preeminent,
[19]   for in him God in all his fullness was pleased to dwell
[20]   and through him to reconcile all things to himself
    by making peace through his blood shed on the cross
   —through him, whether things on earth
        or   things in heaven.

EXPANDED PARAPHRASE

[15] This one who redeemed us is the exact and visible Expression of the God whom no one can see. Being the image of God, he is also the Firstborn—prior to all creation and supreme over it, [16] because it was in his person that all things in heaven and on earth were once created, things that can be seen by the human eye, and those things that cannot be seen, whether they be the angelic occupants of heavenly thrones or supernatural beings who exercise dominion or rule or authority—all these things were created, and now exist, through him and for him. [17] He—and no one else—is before everything in time and rank, and it is in his person and by his agency that all things hold together and are sustained. [18] What is more, he himself is the Head of his body, which is the Church. This is because he is its cause and the source of its life, and also because as the Firstborn he was the first person to rise from the dead to immortality, and as a result he himself became preeminent and peerless in every realm. [19] All this is true of Jesus because it was God's choice and pleasure to have all divine attributes and powers reside in Jesus [20] and to reconcile the whole universe to himself through him by making peace through the blood Jesus shed on the cross—to reconcile all things through him alone, whether they be things on earth or things in heaven.

FOR FURTHER STUDY

16. Christological Hymns in the NT (1:15-20)

Balchin, J. F., "Colossians 1:15-20: An Early Christian Hymn? The Arguments from Style," Vox Evangelica 15 (1985) 65-93.

Beasley-Murray, P., "Colossians 1:15-20: An Early Christian Hymn Celebrating the Lordship of Christ," Pauline Studies, ed. D. A. Hagner and M. J. Harris (Grand Rapids: Eerdmans, 1980) 169-183.

Martin, R. P., "An Early Christian Hymn (Col. 1:15-20)," EQ 36 (1964) 195-205.

————, Carmen Christi. Philippians ii.5-11 in Recent Interpretation and in the Setting of Early Christian Worship (Cambridge: Cambridge University, 1967; reprint Grand Rapids: Eerdmans, 1983).

————, "Aspects of Worship in the New Testament Church," Vox Evangelica 2 (1963) 6-32.

*————, ISBE 2.788-790.

Sanders, J. T., The New Testament Christological Hymns (Cambridge: Cambridge University, 1971).

17. Christ as Head of the Church (1:18)

*Barth, M., *Ephesians* (Garden City, NY: Doubleday, 1974) 1.183-199.

Sabourin, L., *The Names and Titles of Jesus,* tr. M. Carroll (New York: Macmillan, 1967) 93-98.

Schlier, H., TDNT 3.673-682.

Taylor, V., *The Names of Jesus* (London: Macmillan, 1953) 100-103.

Turner, *Words* 201.

18. Reconciliation in Paul (1:20)

Fitzmyer, J. A., "Reconciliation in Pauline Theology," *No Famine in the Land,* ed. J. W. Flanagan and A. W. Robinson (Missoula, MT: Scholars, 1975) 155-177.

Marshall, I. H., "The Meaning of 'Reconciliation,' " *Unity and Diversity in New Testament Theology,* ed. R. A. Guelich (Grand Rapids: Eerdmans, 1978) 117-132.

Martin, R. P., "Reconciliation and Forgiveness in Colossians," *Reconciliation and Hope,* ed. R. Banks (Grand Rapids: Eerdmans, 1974) 104-124.

————, *Reconciliation. A Study of Paul's Theology* (Atlanta: John Knox, 1981).

*Morris, L., *The Apostolic Preaching of the Cross* (Grand Rapids: Eerdmans, 1965[3]) 186-223.

————, *The Atonement. Its Meaning and Significance* (Downers Grove: IVP, 1983) 132-150.

O'Brien, P. T., "Col. 1:20 and the Reconciliation of all Things," *The Reformed Theological Review* 33 (1974) 45-53.

Taylor, V., *Forgiveness and Reconciliation* (London: Macmillan, 1946[2]) 70-108.

HOMILETICAL SUGGESTIONS

The Supremacy of Christ in Creation and Redemption (1:15-20)

1. Supremacy in Creation (vv. 15-17)
   As the Image of the invisible God (v. 15a)
   As the Firstborn over all creation (v. 15b)
   As the Creator of all things (v. 16a, b)
   As the Goal of all things (v. 16c)
   As the One "before" everything (v. 17a)
   As the Sustainer of all things (v. 17b)
2. Supremacy in Redemption (vv. 18-20)

As the Head of the Body, the Church (v. 18a)
As the Beginning (v. 18b)
As the Firstborn from the dead (v. 18c)
As the Possessor of all God's fullness (v. 19)
As the Agent of God's reconciliation (v. 20)

Five Titles of Christ (1:15, 18)

In relation to God:
    1. Image: the exact and visible Expression of God (v. 15a)
In relation to the first creation:
    2. Firstborn: the Supreme Lord over all creation (v. 15b)
In relation to the Church:
    3. Head: the undisputed Authority and Ruler (v. 18a)
In relation to the new creation:
    4. Beginning: the creative Pioneer and constant Source (v. 18b)
    5. Firstborn: the Pioneer of a resurrection to immortality (v. 18c)

Reconciliation (1:19-20)

1. Its Subject: "all the fullness" = God in all his fullness (v. 19; cf. 2 Cor. 5:18a, 19a)
2. Its Achievement:
    (a) "through him (Christ)" (v. 20a, c; cf. Rom. 5:11; 2 Cor. 5:18-19; Eph. 1:9-10; 2:16)
    (b) "by making peace through his blood shed on the cross" (v. 20b; cf. Rom. 5:10a; Eph. 2:15-16)
3. Its Scope: "all things . . . whether things on earth or things in heaven" (v. 20a, c; cf. Rom. 5:10; 2 Cor. 5:19a; Eph. 1:10)
4. Its Goal: "to himself (God)" (v. 20a; cf. Rom. 5:10a; 2 Cor. 5:18, 19a; Eph. 2:16)

B. RECONCILIATION AND THE COLOSSIANS (1:21-23)

21 Καὶ ὑμᾶς ποτε ὄντας ἀπηλλοτριωμένους καὶ ἐχθροὺς τῇ διανοίᾳ ἐν τοῖς ἔργοις τοῖς πονηροῖς, 22 νυνὶ δὲ ἀποκατήλλαξεν ἐν τῷ σώματι τῆς σαρκὸς αὐτοῦ διὰ τοῦ θανάτου, παραστῆσαι ὑμᾶς ἁγίους καὶ ἀμώμους καὶ ἀνεγκλήτους κατενώπιον αὐτοῦ, 23 εἴ γε ἐπιμένετε τῇ πίστει τεθεμελιωμένοι καὶ ἑδραῖοι καὶ μὴ μετακινούμενοι ἀπὸ τῆς ἐλπίδος τοῦ εὐαγγελίου οὗ ἠκούσατε, τοῦ κηρυχθέντος ἐν πάσῃ κτίσει τῇ ὑπὸ τὸν οὐρανόν, οὗ ἐγενόμην ἐγὼ Παῦλος διάκονος.

STRUCTURE

Paul now applies the general statement of cosmic reconciliation (v. 20) to the Colossians, repeating the theme of reconciliation accomplished by God through the death of Christ (vv. 21-22). Verse 23 reiterates four motifs found in vv. 4-6 of the thanksgiving: faith, hope, the hearing of the gospel, and its worldwide dissemination.

And you
    at one time estranged (v. 21a)   (previous state)
    but now he has reconciled (v. 22a)   (present condition)
      in order to present you (v. 22b)   (purpose of reconciliation)
        provided you continue (v. 23a)   (condition of presentation)
καὶ ὑμᾶς
    ποτε ὄντας ἀπηλλοτριωμένους
    νυνὶ δὲ ἀποκατήλλαξεν
      παραστῆσαι ὑμᾶς
        εἴ γε ἐπιμένετε

VERSE 21

Καὶ ὑμᾶς ποτε ὄντας ἀπηλλοτριωμένους

Ὄντας is acc. pl. masc. of the pres. ptc. of εἰμί, be. Ἀπηλλοτριωμένους is acc. pl. masc. of the pf. pass. ptc. of ἀπαλλοτριόω, alienate, estrange. These two ptcs., which agree with ὑμᾶς (the dir. obj. of ἀποκατήλλαξεν, v. 22), form a periph. pf. (cf. Eph. 2:12; R 375, 910; T 89), denoting the continuous, settled state of alienation or estrangement from God (cf. BDF § 352; Burton § 155; F. Büchsel, TDNT 1.265) that was the condition of the Colossians—and Gentiles in general—prior to (cf. ποτέ) their reconciliation. After ὄντας the pf. ptc. functions like an adj. (Burton § 420): "estranged as you once were" (Weymouth), "being alienated [from God]." NEB, GNB, NIV rightly supply "from

God." The anar. adv. ptc. ὄντας may be concessive (cf. 2:13): "although you were formerly alienated" (NASB).

Whether καὶ ὑμᾶς introduces a consequence ("and so you. . . ," "you also") or a new point ("moreover, you . . ."), vv. 21-22 indicate that reconciliation is personal as well as cosmic in its effects. Ποτέ, an enclitic particle (BAGD 695a), refers not to a single particular occasion but to the earlier period of alienation ("formerly," "at one time") and anticipates νυνὶ δέ (v. 22a).

καὶ ἐχθροὺς τῇ διανοίᾳ

Ἐχθρούς agrees with ὑμᾶς . . . ὄντας and here bears an act. (not pass., "hated") meaning, being either an adj. ("hostile") or a subst. ("enemies"). Τῇ διανοίᾳ (from διάνοια, -ας, ἡ, mind, attitude) is a locat. dat. ("in") or a dat. of ref. or respect ("with ref./respect to") and may be a distributive sg. ("in your minds," NIV; for distributive sg., see BDF § 140; R 409; T 23-25). Tr. the whole phrase either "enemies in your minds" (the art. denoting poss.) or "hostile in attitude" (thus BAGD 187b; Goodspeed). Καί could be ascensive (see Col. 3:4): "estranged . . . and even hostile" (Weymouth).

ἐν τοῖς ἔργοις τοῖς πονηροῖς

Ἐν is probably causal ("because of [your evil deeds]"; sim. GNB, NIV; Harris 1175, 1192): evil action promoted a hostile attitude. But the prep. could be locat. ("in the midst of," Barclay; "as expressed in"; cf. G. Harder, TDNT 6.557 n. 73) or circumstantial ("and engaged in [doing wrong]," Goodspeed). The adj. πονηροῖς is in the alternative attributive position where both subst. and adj. are emphatic (R 776-777; but cf. BDF § 270), with the phrase meaning "(your) evil deeds/wicked works" (the art. with ἔργοις perhaps denoting poss.) or "wickedness" (TCNT)/"evil-doing" (Moffatt) (where the concrete represents the abstract).

VERSE 22

νυνὶ δὲ ἀποκατήλλαξεν

3 sg. aor. act. indic. of ἀποκαταλλάσσω, reconcile. As in v. 20 and elsewhere in Paul, the subj. of this vb. is God (Lohse 64 n. 17; NEB), not Christ (as Moffatt, NAB). Also as in v. 20, the aor. is constative. Νυνί, an intensive form of νῦν with the same mng. (BDF § 64[2]; BAGD 546b), is contrasted with ποτέ (v. 21a) and refers to the present order, not simply the present time (Lightfoot 159; G. Stählin, TDNT 4.1116-1118). Δέ opposes an implied concession: "although you were once . . . yet now. . . ."

Although the rdg. ἀποκατήλλαξεν (UBS[3] with a "D" rating) has early and geographically diversified textual support, some scholars (e.g., Metzger 622; and esp. Lightfoot 159, 246, 249-250) prefer ἀποκατηλλάγητε (2 pl. aor. pass. indic.). The latter is supported by B Hilary Ephraem and (in effect) by 𝔭[46] and 33 and was preferred in UBS[1, 2] with a "D" rating because it more easily accounts for the rise of the other four rdgs. (see UBS textual apparatus). On the other hand, it may be an awkward (given ὑμᾶς in v. 21a) scribal attempt to have Paul address the Colossians more directly (with the second person; cf. Lohse 64 n. 16).

Associated with this textual problem is the question of punctuation in vv. 20-22. There are two main options (cf. Moule 72):

(1) a period at the end of v. 21, with that verse understood as the continuation of what precedes, ἀποκατηλλάγητε read in v. 22a, and ὑμᾶς in v. 22b understood reflexively (". . . to reconcile all things [v. 20] . . . [v. 21], including you . . . [v. 22]. But now you have been reconciled . . . in order to present yourselves . . ."); or

(2) a period at the end of v. 20, with either
*(a) ἀποκατήλλαξεν (so UBS[3]), or
(b) ἀποκατηλλάγητε in v. 22a (so UBS[1, 2]), with this vb. regarded either as anacoluthic after ὑμᾶς (so B. M. Metzger in Metzger 622), or as part of a parenthesis (νυνὶ . . . θανάτου, v. 22a; so WH) so that παραστῆσαι (v. 22b) is dependent on εὐδόκησεν (v. 19) and itself governs ὑμᾶς ποτε κτλ. (v. 21; Lightfoot 159-160).

ἐν τῷ σώματι τῆς σαρκὸς αὐτοῦ διὰ τοῦ θανάτου

Τῆς σαρκός (lit. "of flesh") is a Sem. or qualitative gen. (R 496; T 213; MH 440) equivalent in mng. to the adj. σάρκινος ("fleshy"). Here it has a neutral sense ("physical") and not a pejorative sense ("dominated by the flesh") as in 2:11, although σάρξ here includes the ideas of physical limitation (BAGD 744a), suffering, and mortality. Tr. "his physical/earthly human body." The qualification τῆς σαρκός is added to ἐν τῷ σώματι to distinguish the physical body from the spiritual Body of Christ (v. 18; cf. Eph. 2:14, 16), or to oppose a docetic christology.

Although JB construes αὐτοῦ with θανάτου and divides the whole phrase into two parts ("by his death and in that mortal body"), it is more probable that:

(1) αὐτοῦ belongs to the whole preceding expression, "his physical body," with the art. before θανάτου denoting poss., and that

(2) a single idea is being expressed, either "by (instr. ἐν) his physical body through (his) death" (cf. NIV), or "through Christ's death in (locat. ἐν) his physical body" (cf. NEB). In either case διά expresses means (Moule, *Idiom*

Book 56; BAGD 180a). Reconciliation was effected not by Christ's assumption of an earthly body but by his death in a physical body (cf. Rom. 5:10a).

παραστῆσαι ὑμᾶς

Aor. inf. act. of παρίστημι, present. God, the implied subj. of ἀποκατήλλαξεν, is also the subj. of παραστῆσαι, with ὑμᾶς (acc. pl.) its dir. obj. Given the condition that follows in v. 23a, this constative inf. should be seen as telic, not consec. (so also Zerwick, *Analysis* 448; Robertson, *Pictures* 482): God's "presentation" of the Colossians and all believers is a purpose to be accomplished in the future, not a result already achieved. Here the vb. may have legal overtones (H. Währisch, NIDNTT 3.924-925; Lohse 65; O'Brien 68-69) or a sacrificial setting (Lightfoot 161; Moule 73; but see B. Reicke, TDNT 5.841 for a different proposal). Citing Eph. 5:27; Col. 1:22, 28; 2 Tim. 2:15, BAGD (627d-628a) suggests that in these passages "present" is almost equivalent to "make" or "render."

ἁγίους καὶ ἀμώμους καὶ ἀνεγκλήτους

It is possible that the second and third adjs. qualifying ὑμᾶς (ἀμώμους, from ἄμωμος, -ον, without blemish; ἀνεγκλήτους, from ἀνέγκλητος, -ον, blameless) may define the first (ἁγίους): "holy, that is (καί), without blemish or blame" (cf. NIV). But the repeated καί suggests, rather, three distinct descriptions (as in v. 23a), one positive ("holy") and two negative with the negating α-privative ("free from blemish and beyond accusation").

κατενώπιον αὐτοῦ

Κατενώπιον is an "improper" prep. (see MH 293, 328-332; R 553-554, 636-648) meaning "in the presence of, before." Αὐτοῦ refers to God, not Christ (although αὐτοῦ in v. 22a refers to Christ; cf. the two referents of αὐτός in v. 20a; F. Büchsel, TDNT 1.259). Accordingly κατενώπιον αὐτοῦ means "before himself" (NEB; for this refl. use of the pers. pron., see R 680-681; T 41; Z §§ 208, 211) or "in his (own) presence/sight"; BAGD 421c paraphrases the expression, "in the sight of God on his heavenly throne" (cf. 1 Thess. 3:13). Like justification, reconciliation anticipates the positive verdict of God regarding believers at the Great Assize on the day of Christ (cf. 1 Cor. 1:8). But, adducing the parallel in Eph. 1:4, Lightfoot (160-161) prefers to see a ref. to God's present approval in this phrase.

VERSE 23

εἴ γε ἐπιμένετε τῇ πίστει

2 pl. pres. act. indic. of ἐπιμένω, continue, remain. Εἴ γε ("if indeed," "provided that," "if only"; encl. γέ emphasizes εἰ, BDF § 439; R 1148; T 331) expresses an actual condition: the future divine "presentation" (but not the reconciliation) is in fact conditional on future human perseverance. Yet, since εἰ is followed by the pres. indic. *and* Paul is confident about the Colossian Christians' present spiritual condition (2:5b), this condition is neither a hypothesis nor simply a hope but a condition that Paul is confident or assumes will be fulfilled: "if you continue—and I am confident/I am assuming that you will" (sim. Thrall 87-88).

Ἐπιμένετε expresses active persistence, i.e., perseverance, rather than mere passive continuance. Τῇ πίστει is locat. and should be construed with what precedes, although the two adjs. that follow also relate to πίστις (cf. Barclay, "if only you remain grounded and established in the faith"), which may here refer to "the Faith" (Acts 6:7; Jude 3, 20), to the apostolic gospel (thus O'Brien 69), or to personal faith. Tr.: "if indeed you adhere/remain true to the Faith"; or "provided that you persist in faith/continue having faith." See For Further Study 19, "Christian Perseverance."

τεθεμελιωμένοι καὶ ἑδραῖοι

Nom. pl. masc. (agreeing with the subj. of ἐπιμένετε) of the pf. pass. ptc. of θεμελιόω, lay a foundation, establish. Ἑδραῖος, -αία, -αῖον means (etym.) "not easily changing one's abode" (ἕδρα, abode; Zerwick, *Analysis* 448), and thus fig. "firm, steadfast." If the architectural symbolism behind the adj. ptc. τεθεμελιωμένοι was preserved in general usage, the sense is "with your foundation established and your structure immovable (ἑδραῖοι)." But both terms are more probably related to the πίστις Paul has just mentioned. Tr.: "if at least you continue firm and steadfast in the exercise of faith" (Goodspeed). Paraphrase: "if indeed you continue exercising faith—faith in which you were once (implied in the pf. tense) firmly founded and now should be steadfast" (ἑδραῖοι resuming the thought of perseverance found in ἐπιμένετε).

καὶ μὴ μετακινούμενοι

Nom. pl. masc. (agreeing with the subj. of ἐπιμένετε) of the pres. mid./pass. ptc. of μετακινέω, shift, (re)move. This ptc. defines the two preceding terms negatively (μή, the usual negating particle with ptcs. in HGk.; BDF §§426, 430; R 1136-1139; T 284-285) and may be mid., "not (constantly, pres. ptc.) shifting," "without ever shifting" (Weymouth), "never abandoning" (TCNT); or pass., "not being moved," "never to be dislodged" (NEB).

ἀπὸ τῆς ἐλπίδος τοῦ εὐαγγελίου οὗ ἠκούσατε

2 pl. aor. act. indic. of ἀκούω, hear. Gen. τοῦ εὐαγγελίου could be poss. ("from the hope that belongs to/is attached to the gospel"), epex. ("the hope which is the gospel"), or partitive ("the hope which forms part of/is contained within the gospel"), but is rather to be viewed as subj. ("the hope that is held out in/kindled by [BAGD 318a]/based on [BAGD 253b] the gospel"; sim. TCNT, Weymouth, NEB, GNB; J. Schneider, TDNT 3.720). The case of the rel. pron. οὗ (gen. sg. neut.) is an instance either of the attraction of the rel. into the case of its antecedent (assuming an original ὅ, acc. of thing heard and understood) or of the gen. of the thing heard (with or without understanding; on the acc. and gen. with ἀκούω, see BDF § 173[1, 2]; R 506-507, 717; T 161, 233-234; Turner, *Insights* 87-90; Z § 69).

τοῦ κηρυχθέντος

Gen. sg. neut. (agreeing with τοῦ εὐαγγελίου) of the aor. pass. ptc. of κηρύσσω, proclaim. This art. ptc., which here describes (rather than identifies) the gospel (cf. Burton §§ 295, 426), is equivalent to a rel. clause (cf. BDF § 412; R 764; T 152): "which has been proclaimed."

ἐν πάσῃ κτίσει

Κτίσις, -εως, ἡ, creation, creature. This prep. phrase may be tr. in two basic ways:

(1) "in the whole of creation" (Moule 73-74; cf. RV, ASV, NEB), where ἐν 'has the distributive sense of "throughout"; πάσῃ κτίσει is equivalent to πάσῃ τῇ κτίσει (cf. v. 6 and Mk. 16:15; thus T 200; ZG 605; cf. Z §§188, 190) and κτίσις = κόσμος (cf. v. 6), the inhabited world; or

*(2) "to every creature" (Moffatt; BAGD 455d; 631b; Lohse 66-67; sim. R 772), "to all mankind," where ἐν = εἰς (cf. T 249, 257; unless we translate "in [the hearing of] every creature"); anar. πᾶς (sg.) has its customary distributive sense of "every" (cf. Z § 188); and κτίσις virtually means "human being" (cf. W. Foerster, TDNT 3.1028-1029).

τῇ ὑπὸ τὸν οὐρανόν

In this art. prep. phrase τῇ agrees with κτίσει and functions as a rel. pron. introducing a restrictive rel. clause: "that is found under heaven/under the sky/beneath the arch of heaven" = "on earth" (BAGD 594a; 843c). JB renders ἐν πάσῃ . . . οὐρανόν, "to the whole human race"; GNB, "to everybody in the world." Like v. 6 ("all over the world"), this statement is hyperbolic (sim. Horsley 4.79), highlighting the proclamation of the good news not to every person on earth without exception but to every type of person in every place (cf. v. 23). But for a different view, see O'Brien 71, 72.

οὗ ἐγενόμην ἐγὼ Παῦλος διάκονος

The rel. pron. οὗ (gen. sg.) refers back to τοῦ εὐαγγελίου (neut., v. 23a) rather than αὐτοῦ (masc., second occurrence in v. 22, referring to God). 1 sg. 2 aor. mid. indic. of dep. γίνομαι, become, be; in ref. to Paul's Damascus commissioning (cf. Acts 9:15; 22:14-15; 26:16-18). Ἐγώ is probably emphatic (cf. 2 Cor. 10:1; cf. BDF § 277[1]; R 677, 693; T 37-40; Z § 198). Tr.: "I, Paul, have become its (viz. the gospel's) servant."

TRANSLATION

[21] Although you were at one time estranged from God and enemies in your minds because of your evil deeds, you also [22] he has now reconciled through Christ's death in his physical body. He did this in order to present you holy and without blemish or reproach in his sight—[23] provided that you persist in faith, established, steadfast, and not shifting from the hope generated by the gospel which you heard. This gospel has been proclaimed to every creature under heaven, and I, Paul, have become its servant.

EXPANDED PARAPHRASE

[21] This universal reconciliation includes you Colossians, although you were at one time in a state of alienation from God and were his inveterate enemies in thought and attitude because of your evil actions. [22] But as things now stand, God has reconciled you to himself by means of Christ's death in his physical body. God's purpose in all this was to present you in his own presence at the End as people who will then be without any sin, without blemish, and beyond accusation. [23] But this will occur only if you continue to exercise faith, the faith in which you were once firmly founded and now should be steadfast, refusing to shift from the hope that is held out to you in the good news which you heard. This good news has been proclaimed to every person beneath heaven's orb. And I, Paul, have been entrusted with the task of communicating the good news.

FOR FURTHER STUDY

19. Christian Perseverance (1:23)

Berkouwer, G. C., *Faith and Perseverance* (Grand Rapids: Eerdmans, 1958).

Brown, S., *Apostasy and Perseverance in the Theology of Luke* (Rome: Pontifical Biblical Institute, 1969).

*Marshall, I. H., *Kept by the Power of God: A Study of Perseverance and Falling Away* (London: Epworth, 1969).

Pieper, F., *Christian Dogmatics. Vol. III* (Saint Louis: Concordia, 1953) 89-100.

*Strong, A. H., *Systematic Theology* (Philadelphia: Judson, 1907) 881-886.

HOMILETICAL SUGGESTIONS

Reconciliation and the Colossians (1:21-23)

1. Their previous state: alienated and enemies (v. 21)
2. Their present condition: reconciled through Christ (v. 22a)
3. Their future destiny: presented blameless before God (v. 22b)
4. Their present duty: persisting in faith and maintaining hope (v. 23)

The Christian—Where From and Where To? (1:21-23)

1. By nature we were at enmity with God (v. 21).
2. By grace we have been reconciled to God (v. 22a).
3. By grace and perseverance we shall be presented irreproachable before God (vv. 22b-23a).

C. PAUL'S STEWARDSHIP OF GOD'S MYSTERY (1:24-29)

24 Νῦν χαίρω ἐν τοῖς παθήμασιν ὑπὲρ ὑμῶν, καὶ ἀνταναπληρῶ τὰ ὑστερήματα τῶν θλίψεων τοῦ Χριστοῦ ἐν τῇ σαρκί μου ὑπὲρ τοῦ σώματος αὐτοῦ, ὅ ἐστιν ἡ ἐκκλησία, 25 ἧς ἐγενόμην ἐγὼ διάκονος κατὰ τὴν οἰκονομίαν τοῦ θεοῦ τὴν δοθεῖσάν μοι εἰς ὑμᾶς πληρῶσαι τὸν λόγον τοῦ θεοῦ, 26 τὸ μυστήριον τὸ ἀποκεκρυμμένον ἀπὸ τῶν αἰώνων καὶ ἀπὸ τῶν γενεῶν—νῦν δὲ ἐφανερώθη τοῖς ἁγίοις αὐτοῦ, 27 οἷς ἠθέλησεν ὁ θεὸς γνωρίσαι τί τὸ πλοῦτος τῆς δόξης τοῦ μυστηρίου τούτου ἐν τοῖς ἔθνεσιν, ὅ ἐστιν Χριστὸς ἐν ὑμῖν, ἡ ἐλπὶς τῆς δόξης· 28 ὃν ἡμεῖς καταγγέλλομεν νουθετοῦντες πάντα ἄνθρωπον καὶ διδάσκοντες πάντα ἄνθρωπον ἐν πάσῃ σοφίᾳ, ἵνα παραστήσωμεν πάντα ἄνθρωπον τέλειον ἐν Χριστῷ· 29 εἰς ὃ καὶ κοπιῶ ἀγωνιζόμενος κατὰ τὴν ἐνέργειαν αὐτοῦ τὴν ἐνεργουμένην ἐν ἐμοὶ ἐν δυνάμει.

STRUCTURE

The link between this paragraph and the previous one is provided by the repeated clause ". . . whose servant I (Paul) have become":

23b . . . τοῦ εὐαγγελίου. . .   οὗ ἐγενόμην ἐγὼ Παῦλος   διάκονος
24b-25a . . . ἡ   ἐκκλησία,   ἧς ἐγενόμην ἐγὼ   .   διάκονος

As a servant of the gospel (v. 23b) Paul suffers for the sake of the Colossians and the whole Church of Christ (v. 24). As a servant of the Church (vv. 24b, 25a) Paul discharges his stewardship of God's mystery (vv. 25b-27a) by toiling at the task of proclaiming Christ (vv. 28-29), whose indwelling of believers is the essence of the mystery (v. 27b).

Contained within this paragraph is a remarkable series of identifications:

v. 24a, b	Paul's παθήματα	=	Christ's θλίψεις (implied by the parallelism between v. 24a and 24b—viz. 1 sg. pres. indic. act. vb. + ἐν phrase + ὑπέρ phrase)
v. 24c	Christ's body	=	the Church (ὅ ἐστιν)
vv. 25b, 26a	God's message	=	the mystery (τὸ μυστήριον being in epex. appos.)
v. 27b	the mystery	=	Christ in you (ὅ ἐστιν)
	Christ in you	=	your hope of glory (ἡ ἐλπίς being in epex. appos.)

VERSE 24

Νῦν χαίρω

After a succession of first pers. pls. in vv. 3-14, Paul uses sgs. in vv. 24-25, 29 (but pls. in v. 28), following ἐγενόμην ἐγώ (v. 23). Νῦν is not transitional ("now then"), but temporal, referring either to Paul's present imprisonment and suffering ("right now"; cf. 4:3), or, more generally, to the present era and his role as a servant of the gospel (v. 23; "now" = "as things now stand"; cf. BAGD 545d).

ἐν τοῖς παθήμασιν ὑπὲρ ὑμῶν

Ἐν is less likely to be causal ("because of") than locat., here denoting not the reason for his joy ("I rejoice in/over") but its circumstances ("I rejoice in the midst of," BAGD 873d; "amid," Weymouth), as though Paul had written χαίρω πάσχων. That the sufferings (παθήμασιν, dat. pl. of πάθημα, -ατος, τό, suffering) are Paul's, not Christ's, is shown by (1) the two 1 sg. vbs. followed by ἐν τῇ σαρκί μου, (2) the phrase ὑπὲρ ὑμῶν (not ἡμῶν), (3) the parallel in 2 Cor. 1:5-7, and (4) the fact that τοῖς after χαίρω probably denotes poss.: "my sufferings" (ℵ³ 81 syrʰ actually add μου). Παθήμασιν may be a generalizing (or categorical) pl. (cf. T 26-27; Z § 7): "the suffering I endure" (NAB), "what was suffered" (NIV). Ὑπὲρ ὑμῶν, "for your sake/benefit," refers to the Colossians and other Christians in the Lycus Valley (cf. 4:16).

καὶ ἀνταναπληρῶ τὰ ὑστερήματα τῶν θλίψεων τοῦ Χριστοῦ

1 sg. pres. act. indic. of ἀνταναπληρόω, fill up. Καί introduces an explanation of the preceding statement: "in fact," almost "in that." Τὰ ὑστερήματα (acc. pl. of ὑστέρημα, -ατος, τό, lack, deficiency) is a generalizing pl. (cf. T 26-27; Z § 7): "what is lacking," "whatever lack may still exist" (BAGD 73a), "what still remains" (GNB). It is a measurable deficiency, which implies a predetermined quota or fullness (πλήρωμα; cf. ἀντανα-πληρῶ).

Τῶν θλίψεων may be partitive gen. ("from the afflictions" [JB mg.], denoting the whole of which τὰ ὑστερήματα is a part) or a gen. of respect/ref./relation ("in regard to [Christ's] afflictions," NIV).

Ὁ Χριστός may here denote an individual (either Jesus Christ or the Messiah), or it may have a collective reference (the people of the Messiah, the messianic community; cf. 1 Cor. 12:12). If the gen. τοῦ Χριστοῦ is poss., the sense will be "the afflictions to be endured by Christ" (cf. F. Hauck, TDNT 3.806; JB) or "the afflictions destined for Messiah's people"; if subj., "the afflictions imposed by Christ"; if qualitative, "Christian afflictions" or "messianic afflictions/woes"; if denoting ref. or relation, "the afflictions that result from union with Christ" (cf. G. Delling, TDNT 6.307 n. 3) or "afflictions endured for Christ's sake" or "afflictions like those of Christ."

The pref. ἀντι- in ἀντ-ανα-πληρῶ could signify substitution (the fullness replaces the deficiency; or Paul suffers vicariously) or benefit (ἀντι- resuming the ὑπέρ ["on behalf of"] that precedes and anticipating the ὑπέρ that follows [cf. Moule 78-79; *Idiom Book* 71]), but in compounds ἀντί (basically "opposite") generally denotes (1) reciprocal action (MH 296-297) or *(2) correspondence: here, "in my turn" (cf. R 574; Robertson, *Pictures* 484) or "on my part" (RV). On this latter view, this pref. implies a distinction between the persons suffering (Lightfoot 163, 164) and may indicate (a) that Paul for his part was now suffering as Christ himself had earlier suffered, although in a different way and for a different purpose, or (b) that either the supply corresponded to the deficiency, although not necessarily in extent, or Paul's sufferings corresponded to Christ's afflictions. Given 2:9-15, Paul is certainly not suggesting that Christ's atoning sacrifice was in any way deficient or in need of supplementation. Nor need we suppose that Paul believed that he himself was exhausting the deficiency (*pace* H. Schlier, TDNT 3.143): NASB has "I do my share . . . in filling up . . ." (sim. GNB, JB).

From this bewildering variety of options, two major interpretations may be isolated:

(1) Paul regarded his sufferings as a servant of the gospel as his part of what still remained of the sufferings due to all who are united with Christ, the suffering Son of Man (cf. Acts 14:22; Rom. 8:17-18; 1 Thess. 3:3). Any suffering endured by the servant of Christ in the service of Christ and for the benefit of his Church is part of "the afflictions of Christ" (cf. Acts 9:4-5, 16; 2 Cor. 1:5).

*(2) Paul viewed his apostolic suffering as his own distinctive contribution toward reducing the "deficiency" in the divinely appointed quota of sufferings to be patiently endured by the messianic community of the last days prior to the end of the Age. On this view the expression αἱ θλίψεις τοῦ Χριστοῦ may be the Christian equivalent of the Jewish apocalyptic notion of "the birthpangs of the Messiah," "the messianic woes" that were to precede the end of the Age (cf. Matt. 24:6-8; Mk. 13:7-8; Lohse 69-71; Moule 76-78; O'Brien 78-80).

ἐν τῇ σαρκί μου

To be cstr. with ἀνταναπληρῶ, not with τὰ ὑπερήματα κτλ. (as Moffatt). Ἐν may be locat. ("in") or instr. ("by means of") and σάρξ may mean "(physical) body" (= τὸ σῶμα τῆς σαρκός, v. 22a; cf. 2 Cor. 4:10; Gal. 6:17), "flesh," "person," or, by metonymy, "(by means of my) physical sufferings" (GNB). Since τῇ alone could denote possession, μου is probably emphatic. Tr.: "in my own person" (TCNT, Weymouth, Goodspeed).

ὑπὲρ τοῦ σώματος αὐτοῦ

This phrase generalizes the earlier particular ὑπὲρ ὑμῶν (W. Michaelis, TDNT 5.933): Paul's sufferings benefited (ὑπέρ) not only the Colossians but also the whole Body of Christ.

ὅ ἐστιν ἡ ἐκκλησία

Ὅ (nom. sg. neut. of the rel. pron. ὅς, ἥ, ὅ) is nom. because it is the subj. of the rel. clause, although its antecedent is gen. (σώματος, neut. sg.). Ὅ ἐστιν is regularly used in explanations ("that is") even when the antecedent is not neut. (BAGD 584c, d). Pred. nouns are normally anar. (BDF § 273; T 183). Because the pred. ἐκκλησία (here the universal Church, BAGD 241a) is art., the proposition is reciprocating, with the subj. and the pred. denoting the same entity (cf. R 767-769): the Body of Christ is exclusively the Church, and the Church is exclusively the Body of Christ. See For Further Study 21, "The Church as the Body of Christ."

VERSE 25

ἧς ἐγενόμην ἐγὼ διάκονος

1 sg. 2 aor. mid. indic. of dep. γίνομαι, become, be. The rel. pron. ἧς (gen. sg. fem., antecedent ἐκκλησία) may have causal overtones (as also οἷς in v. 27; cf. R 724-725): ". . . for the sake of his Body, the Church, inasmuch as I have become its servant."

κατὰ τὴν οἰκονομίαν τοῦ θεοῦ τὴν δοθεῖσάν μοι

Κατά may indicate the standard ("according to," RV; BAGD 559d), the means ("by," NIV; "through," NAB; Zerwick, *Analysis* 449), or the cause ("as a result of," "by virtue of," NEB; cf. TCNT). Οἰκονομία, -ας, ἡ, denotes basically the office or function of a steward (O. Michel, TDNT 5.151-153; O'Brien 81-82). Here EVV render it variously: "stewardship" (NASB), "commission" (NIV, NAB), "task" (NEB), "office" (RSV).

While some take τοῦ θεοῦ as qualitative gen. ("divine office," RSV; BAGD 559d; G. Friedrich, TDNT 3.717 n. 17; O. Michel, TDNT 5.152; Lohse 68, 72 and n. 36; cf. Moffatt), it seems preferable in light of τὴν δοθεῖσάν μοι, which immediately follows, to take it as subj. (or gen. of author/origin)—"the commission from God given to me" (cf. NASB) = "the commission God gave me" (NAB, NIV; cf. NEB). Δοθεῖσαν is acc. sg. fem. (agreeing with τὴν

οἰκονομίαν) of the aor. pass. ptc. of δίδωμι, give, followed by dat. (here the
encl. μοι). This art. ptc., which here is restrictive (rather than explanatory) in
function, identifying rather than merely describing (cf. Burton §§ 295, 426),
is equivalent to a rel. clause (cf. BDF § 412; R 764; T 152): "which was given
to me."

εἰς ὑμᾶς

It is possible to construe this with what follows ("to present *to you* the word
of God in its fullness," NIV) where the phrase denotes the persons addressed
and is equivalent to ὑμῖν (A. Oepke, TDNT 2.425), but the parallel in Eph. 3:2,
the juxtaposition of the two pronouns (μοι εἰς ὑμᾶς), and the position of the
phrase suggest it should be taken with what precedes: "that God gave me with
regard to you" (εἰς of ref.) or "assigned to me by God for your benefit" (NEB;
cf. Weymouth, TCNT, NASB; εἰς = dat. of advantage, cf. BAGD 229d).

πληρῶσαι τὸν λόγον τοῦ θεοῦ

Aor. act. inf. of πληρόω, bring to completion (BAGD 671b). This inf. could be
final (thus Zerwick, *Analysis* 449; "the commission given to me that I might
fully proclaim . . ."), but is more probably epex., defining the content of τὴν
οἰκονομίαν κτλ. ("the commission. . . , namely, to declare fully . . ."; "That
office is to make the word of God fully known," Barclay). "The word of God"
is the message of the gospel (v. 5; cf. BAGD 478b), the message about Christ,
which comes from God (τοῦ θεοῦ, subj. gen.) and which Paul must "declare
. . . in all its fulness" (TCNT), or, possibly, God's work of evangelization (τοῦ
θεοῦ, poss. gen.) that Paul must complete (ZG 605).

VERSE 26

τὸ μυστήριον

Τὸ μυστήριον is in epex. appos. (R 398-400; T 206) to τὸν λόγον, and therefore
is acc., not nom. (although neut. forms are the same for these two cases).
Because Eng. "mystery" is ambiguous, μυστήριον is sometimes rendered
"secret" (Goodspeed, NEB, GNB), "open secret" (Moffatt), "Truth" (TCNT),
"hidden truth(s)," or "secret plan of salvation." In Pauline usage, it denotes in
general a divine truth, unknowable by humankind apart from revelation and
once hidden but now disclosed in the gospel era as embodied in the person of
Christ. More specifically it refers to God's secret plan of salvation involving
the admission of the Gentiles into the freshly constituted people of God and
into the benefits of the new covenant on equal terms with the Jews (Eph. 3:4-6).
See For Further Study 22, " 'Mystery' (μυστήριον) in Paul."

τὸ ἀποκεκρυμμένον

Acc. sg. neut. (agreeing with τὸ μυστήριον) of the perf. pass. ptc. of ἀποκρύπτω, hide away. This art. attrib. ptc., equivalent to a rel. clause (cf. BDF § 412; R 764, 1106-1108; T 152), is restrictive rather than explanatory in import (cf. Burton §§ 295, 426), identifying which "mystery" is being referred to, viz. "the mystery that has been kept secret."

ἀπὸ τῶν αἰώνων καὶ ἀπὸ τῶν γενεῶν

With νῦν δέ following, ἀπό (+ gen.) is more probably temp. in both instances (lit. "from/since the ages and generations" = "from ages and generations past," NAB; "for [= during] ages and generations," RSV, NIV; Lohse 68, 74) than local ("from [the people of] former ages and generations"). It is therefore highly unlikely that αἰῶνες are principalities and powers (cf. 1 Cor. 2:8) or personified Aeons (BAGD 28b; see *per contra* H. Sasse, TDNT 1.207) or angels (RSV mg.). The repeated ἀπὸ τῶν before γενεῶν is probably due to Sem. influence, but it is possible to take the first ἀπό temp. and the second locally—"through all past ages and from all mankind" (GNB; cf. Eph. 3:5). ZG (605; cf. Z § 184) sees the repetition as distinguishing eternity (αἰῶνες, the measureless periods of eternity—Zerwick, *Analysis* 449) from the beginnings of human history.

νῦν δὲ ἐφανερώθη

3 sg. aor. pass. indic. of φανερόω, reveal, make known; (pass.) become known, be disclosed (followed by the dat. τοῖς ἁγίοις). This cstr. is an anacoluthon (marked by a dash in UBS[3] and some EVV) because the subj. of this vb. is τὸ μυστήριον, which is in the acc. case, in appos. to τὸν λόγον. On this transition from ptc. (ἀποκεκρυμμένον) to finite vb. (ἐφανερώθη), see BDF § 468(3); MH 429; R 440. The aor. is constative, referring to a series of disclosures conceived of unitarily, and after νῦν may be translated (as in v. 22a) by an Eng. perf. or pres. ("has been/is now disclosed").

τοῖς ἁγίοις αὐτοῦ

Αὐτοῦ refers to God, not Christ (note ὁ θεός in the parallel, v. 27a). Τοῖς ἁγίοις, "God's people" (NEB), may be "holy apostles and [NT] prophets" (Eph. 3:5); or Gentiles (τὰ ἔθνη, v. 27b); or, as is probable, all believers (cf. 1:2; 3:12), as recipients of the word of God (v. 25b; cf. Eph. 3:9). That is, through the proclamation and acceptance of the message of the gospel, God's mystery is divulged to believers in general.

VERSE 27

οἷς ἠθέλησεν ὁ θεός

Dat. pl. masc. of the rel. pron. (the antecedent is τοῖς ἁγίοις). 3 sg. aor. act. indic. of θέλω, wish. For the aug. ἠ- instead of ἐ- and the relation of θέλω to the CGk vb. ἐθέλω, see BDF §§ 66(3), 101 (under θέλειν); MH 188; R 205-206. This aor. could be timeless ("God's plan is," GNB; "it is His will," Moffatt) but is probably constative, here denoting either God's settled purpose prior to and during the disclosure (ἐφανερώθη; "it was God's purpose," JB) or his decision prior to the disclosure ("God had chosen"; "God willed," NASB).

γνωρίσαι

Aor. act. inf. of γνωρίζω, make known. This is a complementary inf. after ἠθέλησεν (cf. BDF § 392[1]; R 1077-1078) and refers to the same action as that denoted by ἐφανερώθη; that is, the making known of the glorious riches of the mystery (v. 27a) is identical with the revelation of the mystery (v. 26b). As with ἧς in v. 25a, οἷς may have causal overtones (cf. R 724-725): "for God chose to divulge to them [his people]. . . ."

τί τὸ πλοῦτος τῆς δόξης

Τί (nom. sg. neut. of τίς, τί, interr. pron. who? what?) introduces an indir. question (viz. τί [ἐστιν τὸ πλοῦτος] . . . ἔθνεσιν; BAGD 163c) that is the obj. of γνωρίσαι. Used with a noun denoting quality or quantity (here τὸ πλοῦτος, wealth, riches; sometimes masc. in the NT, BDF § 51[2]; MH 127; R 262), τί may mean "what sort of" (= ποῖον; BAGD 819b) or "how great," "how vast" (Weymouth).

Τὸ πλοῦτος is pred. after τί, with ἐστιν understood, and is therefore nom. Gen. τῆς δόξης may be:

*(1) Sem.: "the glorious riches" (NIV); "the glorious wealth" (Moffatt), or
 (2) poss.: lit. "belonging to the glory,"
     (a) where τὸ πλοῦτος is descriptive of the δόξα, "(all) the rich glory" (JB) or
     (b) where δόξα means "glorious revelation," "the richness of the glorious manifestation" (cf. Lightfoot 162, 167).

τοῦ μυστηρίου τούτου

Τούτου (gen. sg. neut. of οὗτος, αὕτη, τοῦτο, this) is a demonstrative adj. used in the pred. position (R 700-701) and agreeing with μυστηρίου, and alludes to τὸ μυστήριον in v. 26. Τοῦ μυστηρίου (gen.) may be

*(1) poss.: "the glorious riches that characterize this mystery"; "the glorious wealth which this secret holds" (Moffatt); "this rich and glorious secret" (GNB),

 (2) subj.: "the glory beyond price which this mystery brings" (NAB), or

 (3) obj.: "the glorious revelation of this mystery" (Lightfoot 162).

ἐν τοῖς ἔθνεσιν

The position of this prep. phrase makes it awkward to construe it with γνωρίσαι (as in NIV, "to make known among the Gentiles," where ἐν = "among"; cf. BAGD 258d). Rather it modifies τί τὸ πλοῦτος κτλ.: "how great are the glorious riches of this mystery [displayed] among the Gentiles" (sim. NEB; Lightfoot 167; TCNT, ". . . when proclaimed among the Gentiles"). It was in the Gentile mission that the riches and splendor of God's plan of salvation were evident. But it is not impossible that ἐν = εἰς (cf. T 257), so that ἐν τοῖς ἔθνεσιν could mean "to pagans" (JB) or "for all peoples" (GNB), "for the Gentile world" (Weymouth).

ὅ ἐστιν Χριστός

Ὅ (nom. sg. neut. of rel. pron.) is nom. because it is the subj. of the rel. clause, although its antecedent is gen. (μυστηρίου, neut. sg.). Sometimes ὅ ἐστιν is a formulaic phrase unrelated to gender, "that is to say" (BDF § 132[2]; BAGD 584c, d). Χριστός, like ἐκκλησία in v. 24c, is a nom. pred. after the vb. εἶναι. In general the use of the article with proper names is impossible to regularize (cf. BDF § 260; T 165-166), but in Paul's letters Χριστός is commonly anar. (R 760, 795), and in stylized formulae such as "Christ in you" nouns are regularly anar. (cf. BDF § 252).

ἐν ὑμῖν

This means either "in your midst," "among you" (Lohse 68, 76 and nn. 65-66; TCNT, Moffatt, NEB mg., JB), or "(with)in you," "in your hearts" (most EVV have "in you" = "within you"). In the light of Rom. 8:10; 2 Cor. 13:5; Gal. 2:20; Eph. 3:17, "in you" is to be preferred, although ὑμῖν refers to the Colossians not exclusively but as representatives of both the Gentiles (the principal emphasis in the context; cf. G. Bornkamm, TDNT 4.820; Lightfoot 167) and all believers. The μυστήριον is both personal (Χριστός) and experiential (ἐν ὑμῖν).

ἡ ἐλπὶς τῆς δόξης

Ἐλπίς refers to an assured hope, not a vague possibility or even merely an expectation. The art. ἡ denotes poss. ("your hope," JB, NAB; cf. TCNT), and δόξης as a dependent gen. is art. according to the canon of Apollonius. Δόξης is an obj. gen.: "your hope of [sharing in the] glory [of God, Rom. 5:2; of Christ, Rom. 8:17; Col. 3:4]." But since Christ himself is described as the believer's ἐλπίς (1 Tim. 1:1; cf. BAGD 253b, c), it is not impossible that this gen. is qualitative, "your glorious hope" (Barclay). The whole phrase is in epex. appos. to Χριστὸς ἐν ὑμῖν: the indwelling of the exalted Christ in individual believers is their assurance of coming glory, "the promise of glorification" (Goodspeed). Cf. Eph. 1:13-14, where the indwelling Spirit is called the pledge of inheritance.

VERSE 28

ὃν ἡμεῖς καταγγέλλομεν νουθετοῦντες πάντα ἄνθρωπον καὶ διδάσκοντες πάντα ἄνθρωπον

1 pl. pres. act. indic. of καταγγέλλω, proclaim, declare. Nom. pl. masc. (agreeing with ἡμεῖς) of the pres. act. ptc. of νουθετέω, admonish, warn. Nom. pl. masc. (agreeing with ἡμεῖς) of the pres. act. ptc. of διδάσκω, teach.

Ὅν (acc. sg. masc. of the rel. pron. ὅς, ἥ, ὅ) is acc. because within the rel. clause it is the obj., although its antecedent is nom. (Χριστός, masc. sg.). On this asyndetic rel. pron. (as also in v. 29a), see R 724. The pl. ἡμεῖς, after the succession of sgs. in vv. 24-25, refers generally to the apostles and evangelists or specifically to Paul and his coworkers such as Epaphras (1:7-8; 4:12-13).

The two pres. ptcs. express less probably the means of the proclamation (as Lohse 77; O'Brien 87, 88) than its accompanying circumstances: "while/as we admonish and teach" (sim. NAB). For the adv. ptc. denoting circumstance or manner, see BDF §§ 417-418; Burton § 444; R 1127-1128; T 153-157). Admonition and teaching are two natural and necessary concomitants of the proclamation of the mystery of Christ; but necessary concomitants are also essential ingredients. Νουθετοῦντες may relate to unbelievers and διδάσκοντες to believers ("*warning* to repent, *instructing* in the faith," Lightfoot 168, citing Acts 20:21), or both ptcs. to believers (warning against sin and error, imparting mature teaching; cf. 3:16, διδάσκοντες καὶ νουθετοῦντες ἑαυτούς).

Πάντα ἄνθρωπον occurs three times in this verse (cf. v. 23c) and emphasizes the individual members of the class (viz. ἄνθρωπος, "person"; BAGD 631b): "every person," "everyone" (Goodspeed), "everyone without distinction" (NEB; cf. 1 Thess. 2:11). On anar. πᾶς see on v. 9. Through this emphasis on the universal applicability of the gospel Paul counteracts any intellectual elitism or exclusiveness: there is no special gospel or teaching for a spiritual or intellectual elite.

ἐν πάσῃ σοφίᾳ

"With all wisdom" (NIV), "with all possible wisdom" (Weymouth; ἐν denoting attendant circumstances or mode/manner; cf. T 252) or "by means of wisdom of every sort" (instrumental ἐν, so Zerwick, *Analysis* 449; cf. T 252-253 for this usage). On anar. πᾶς, see on v. 9. It is unlikely that the phrase defines the content of the teaching ("we . . . teach everyone all our wisdom," Goodspeed; "in every aspect of wisdom"), since the obj. of διδάσκειν is always acc. and never expressed by ἐν + dat.

ἵνα παραστήσωμεν πάντα ἄνθρωπον τέλειον ἐν Χριστῷ

1 pl. aor. act. subjunc. of παρίστημι, present (on the mng. of this vb., see on v. 22). In conjunction with the adj. τέλειος, -α, -ον (perfect, mature), παρίστημι may mean "make . . . complete" (BAGD 628a) or "render . . . mature," but the eschatological and forensic sense of παρίστημι seems more apposite. The goal (telic ἵνα) of the apostolic proclamation of Christ, which was attended by admonition and teaching, was to present before God at the Last Judgment (or in the present age—so Lohse 78 n. 80) every person to whom the proclamation was made, τέλειος ἐν Χριστῷ. In Pauline usage τέλειος does not describe a person initiated into mystic rites (as BAGD 809b, c ["probably"]) but rather a person mature in faith (cf. v. 23a) and in the knowledge of God's will (cf. v. 9c), someone who has attained mature adulthood (ἀνὴρ τέλειος) and is no longer misled by false doctrine (Eph. 4:13-14; cf. Heb. 5:14). See For Further Study 23, "Christian Perfection." Here ἐν Χριστῷ means either "(as a mature individual) in union with Christ" (GNB; cf. TCNT) or "(as a mature member) of Christ's body" (NEB), the individual and corporate senses (respectively) of this phrase, rather than "(made perfect) through Christ" (Weymouth).

VERSE 29

εἰς ὃ καὶ κοπιῶ ἀγωνιζόμενος

Κοπιῶ is 1 sg. pres. act. indic. of κοπιάω, work with effort, toil. Ἀγωνιζόμενος is nom. sg. masc. of the pres. mid. ptc. of dep. ἀγωνίζομαι, strive, contend. Ὅ (acc. [after εἰς] sg. neut. of the rel. pron. ὅς, ἥ, ὅ) refers back to a total concept (cf. BAGD 584d; R 714), either the bringing of every individual into God's presence as a mature Christian, or, more comprehensively, the whole process of proclamation—admonition—teaching—presentation. Καί emphasizes specificity ("to achieve this *very* goal"; cf. BAGD 443c) or may give greater independence to the rel. clause (BAGD 393d; cf. Z § 463). With the sg. κοπιῶ we pass from the general task of preachers (note the five pls. in

v. 28) to Paul's own devotion as an individual pastor. Ἀγωνιζόμενος expresses circumstances attendant (see v. 28) on Paul's toiling ("I am toiling
strenuously," NEB; "I labor, striving," BAGD 15b), although this ptc. may
possibly define the finite vb. ("I toil, in that I strive"; cf. 1 Tim. 4:10, εἰς
τοῦτο γὰρ κοπιῶμεν καὶ ἀγωνιζόμεθα). See For Further Study 24, "Athletic
Imagery in Paul."

κατὰ τὴν ἐνέργειαν αὐτοῦ τὴν ἐνεργουμένην ἐν ἐμοὶ ἐν δυνάμει

Ἐνεργουμένην is acc. sg. fem. (agreeing with τὴν ἐνέργειαν, from ἐνέργεια,
-ας, ἡ, working, operation) of the pres. mid./pass. ptc. of ἐνεργέω, be at work,
operate; probably mid. (BAGD 265c: "operates," "is at work," cf. NEB) but
could be pass. ("is being effected"; see O'Brien 91 and refs. there). It is a
restrictive art. ptc., equivalent to a rel. clause ("that operates"; see the similar
ptcs. in vv. 5, 25, 26 and refs. there). Κατά here denotes not simply correspondence ("in accordance with") or proportion ("in proportion to") but either cause
("because of") or, better, means ("using"; "in reliance upon," Weymouth), so
that the whole κατά phrase may be tr. "impelled by that energy of his" (NAB,
αὐτοῦ, poss. gen.) or "with the energy which he supplies" (where αὐτοῦ refers
to Christ, the nearest explicit referent, and is subj. gen.).

Ἐν ἐμοί means "within me," that is, "in my life." After a "proper"
preposition such as ἐν the accented forms of the oblique cases of sg. ἐγώ are
generally used (i.e., here, ἐμοί rather than μοι; BDF § 279; cf. BAGD 217c).
Ἐν δυνάμει may express attendant circumstances ("[along] with power") or
more probably is adv. ("powerfully," BAGD 207d, 261a). For these two uses
of ἐν, see T 252.

TRANSLATION

²⁴ I rejoice now in the midst of my sufferings for your sake, and for my part I
am filling up in my own person what is still lacking with regard to the
afflictions of Christ, for the sake of his Body, which is the Church. ²⁵ I have
become a servant of the Church by virtue of the commission God gave me
with regard to you, to declare fully the word of God— ²⁶ the mystery kept
secret for ages and generations past but now disclosed to God's people. ²⁷ For
God chose to divulge to his people how great are the glorious riches of this
mystery displayed among the Gentiles, which is Christ within you, your hope
of glory. ²⁸ It is this Christ that we proclaim as we admonish and teach everyone
with all wisdom, so that we may present everyone mature in Christ. ²⁹ To
achieve this I toil and strive with the energy that Christ powerfully generates
within me.

EXPANDED PARAPHRASE

[24] Now, when I recognize the privilege of my apostolic vocation, I rejoice even in the midst of all that I am suffering for your sake. In fact, through this personal suffering of mine I am making my distinctive contribution toward filling up whatever remains to be endured of "the afflictions of Christ." All this is for the sake of his body, the universal Church, [25] whose servant I have become as a result of the commission entrusted to me by God with regard to you, the task of fully proclaiming to you Gentiles the message of God. [26] This message is none other than the sacred secret of God's plan of salvation that was hidden during all the past ages and generations but has now been disclosed to the new and holy people of God. [27] For in his eternal counsel God had chosen to divulge this mystery to his people in all its glory and richness displayed in the Gentile mission. What is this mystery or sacred secret? Christ indwelling you Gentiles (and all believers), which is your assurance of a share in his glory. [28] And this is the Christ we proclaim when we warn every unbeliever and teach every believer with all possible wisdom, our aim being to present every believer mature and perfect as a member of Christ's body who is in personal union with Christ. [29] In my eager desire to achieve all this, I toil and earnestly strive, energized by the power of the indwelling Christ that is so mightily at work in my life.

FOR FURTHER STUDY

20. Christian Suffering (1:24)

*Ahern, B. M., "The Fellowship of His Sufferings (Phil 3,10). A Study of St. Paul's Doctrine on Christian Suffering," *CBQ* 22 (1960) 1-32.

Bowker, J., *Problems of Suffering in Religions of the World* (Cambridge: Cambridge University, 1970).

Lewis, C. S., *The Problem of Pain* (London: Bles, 1940; New York: Macmillan, 1962).

Proudfoot, C. M., "Imitation or Realistic Participation? A Study of Paul's Concept of 'Suffering with Christ,'" *Interpretation* 17 (1963) 140-160.

Robinson, H. W., *Suffering Human and Divine* (London: SCM, 1940).

Schweitzer, A., *The Mysticism of Paul the Apostle,* tr. W. Montgomery (London: Black, 1931) 141-159.

Sutcliffe, E. F., *Providence and Suffering in the Old and New Testaments* (London: Nelson, 1953).

21. The Church as the Body of Christ (1:24)

Best, E., *One Body in Christ* (London: SPCK, 1955).

Cerfaux, L., *The Church in the Theology of St. Paul* (New York: Herder, 1959) 262-286.

*Gundry, R. H., *Sōma in Biblical Theology* (Cambridge: Cambridge University, 1976) 223-244.

Jewett, R., *Paul's Anthropological Terms* (Leiden: Brill, 1971) 200-230.

Käsemann, E., *Perspectives on Paul* (Philadelphia: Fortress, 1971) 102-121.

Minear, P. S., *Images of the Church in the New Testament* (Philadelphia: Westminster, 1960) 173-220.

Robinson, J. A. T., *The Body* (London: SCM, 1952).

Schweizer, E., *The Church as the Body of Christ* (Richmond: John Knox, 1964).

————, TDNT 7.1067-1081.

22. "Mystery" (μυστήριον) in Paul (1:26-27)

Barker, G. W., ISBE 3.451-455.

Barth, M., *Ephesians* (Garden City, NY: Doubleday, 1974) 1.123-127.

Bornkamm, G., TDNT 4.819-824.

Brown, R. E., "The Semitic Background of the New Testament *Mysterion*," *Biblica* 39 (1958) 426-448; 40 (1959) 70-87 (reprinted as *The Semitic Background of the Term "Mystery" in the New Testament* [Philadelphia: Fortress, 1968]).

Caragounis, C. C., *The Ephesian Mysterion* (Lund: Gleerup, 1977).

Coppens, J., " 'Mystery' in the Theology of Saint Paul and its Parallels at Qumran," J. Murphy-O'Connor, ed., *Paul and Qumran* (Chicago: Priory, 1968) 132-158.

Liefeld, W. L., ZPEB 4.327-330.

Robinson, J. A., *St. Paul's Epistle to the Ephesians* (London: Macmillan, 1928²) 234-240.

*Turner, *Words* 281-285.

23. Christian Perfection (1:28)

Delling, G., TDNT 8.73-77.

Dieter, M. E., et al., *Five Views on Sanctification* (Grand Rapids: Zondervan, 1987).

Du Plessis, P. J., *ΤΕΛΕΙΟΣ: The Idea of Perfection in the New Testament* (Kampen: Kok, 1959).

Flew, R. N., *The Idea of Perfection in Christian Theology* (Oxford: Oxford University, 1934; New York: Humanities, 1968).

LaRondelle, H. K., *Perfection and Perfectionism. A Dogmatic-Ethical Study of Biblical Perfection and Phenomenal Perfection* (Kampen: Kok, 1971).

Lindström, H., *Wesley and Sanctification* (London: SCM, 1946).

Peterson, D. G., *Hebrews and Perfection* (Cambridge: Cambridge University, 1982).

*Turner, *Words* 324-329.

24. Athletic Imagery in Paul (1:29)

Gardiner, E. N., *Athletics of the Ancient World* (Oxford: Clarendon, 1930).

————, *Greek Athletic Sports and Festivals* (London: Macmillan, 1910).

Howson, J. S., *The Metaphors of Paul* (London: Strahan, 1868; Boston: American Tract Society, 1872) 125-176.

Pfitzner, V. C., *Paul and the Agon Motif: Traditional Athletic Imagery in the Pauline Literature* (Leiden: Brill, 1967).

*Ringwald, A., et al., NIDNTT 1.644-652.

Stauffer, E., TDNT 1.134-140, 637-639.

HOMILETICAL SUGGESTIONS

Paul's Stewardship of God's Mystery (1:24-29)

1. Paul's sufferings for the sake of the Church (v. 24)
2. Paul's stewardship as servant of the Church (v. 25)
3. God's mystery, once hidden but now revealed (vv. 26-27)
4. Paul's proclamation of the mystery of the indwelling Christ (v. 28)
5. Paul's toil, empowered by Christ (v. 29)

Proclaiming Christ (1:28), or Declaring the Whole Counsel of God (Acts 20:27)

1. Its nature: we must fully declare God's message (v. 25b)
   we must warn unbelievers (νουθετοῦντες, v. 28a)
   we must teach believers (διδάσκοντες, v. 28a)
2. Its scope: we must exclude no one (πάντα ἄνθρωπον, three times in v. 28)
3. Its purpose: we aim to bring everyone to Christian maturity (v. 28b)

D. PAUL'S SPIRITUAL STRUGGLE (2:1-3)

1 Θέλω γὰρ ὑμᾶς εἰδέναι ἡλίκον ἀγῶνα ἔχω ὑπὲρ ὑμῶν καὶ τῶν ἐν Λαοδικείᾳ καὶ ὅσοι οὐχ ἑόρακαν τὸ πρόσωπόν μου ἐν σαρκί, 2 ἵνα παρακληθῶσιν αἱ καρδίαι αὐτῶν, συμβιβασθέντες ἐν ἀγάπῃ καὶ εἰς πᾶν πλοῦτος τῆς πληροφορίας τῆς συνέσεως, εἰς ἐπίγνωσιν τοῦ μυστηρίου τοῦ θεοῦ, Χριστοῦ, 3 ἐν ᾧ εἰσιν πάντες οἱ θησαυροὶ τῆς σοφίας καὶ γνώσεως ἀπόκρυφοι.

STRUCTURE

In one sentence Paul informs his readers of the fourfold purpose of his spiritual struggle for them:

Θέλω γὰρ ὑμᾶς εἰδέναι		Paul's desire
ἡλίκον ἀγῶνα ἔχω		Paul's struggle
ὑπὲρ ὑμῶν	καὶ	
τῶν ἐν Λαοδικείᾳ καὶ		beneficiaries of the struggle
ὅσοι		
ἵνα παρακληθῶσιν		
συμβιβασθέντες . . .	καὶ	fourfold purpose
εἰς πᾶν πλοῦτος		of the struggle
εἰς ἐπίγνωσιν		

VERSE 1

θέλω γὰρ ὑμᾶς εἰδέναι

Γάρ introduces an illustration ("for," "indeed") of the struggle mentioned in 1:29 (note ἀγωνιζόμενος . . . ἀγῶνα, 1:29; 2:1). Εἰδέναι is the pf. act. inf. of οἶδα, a pf.-pres. with a pres. mng., "know" (BAGD 555d; MH 220-221; R 881; T 82). This is a complementary inf. after θέλω (BDF § 392[1]; R 1077-1078). If (as here) the subj. of the inf. is not the same as the subj. of the governing vb. (θέλω), it is expressed by the acc. (here ὑμᾶς).

ἡλίκον ἀγῶνα ἔχω

Ἡλίκον is acc. sg. masc. from ἡλίκος, -η, -ον, how great. This interr. adj. (sometimes called an interr. pron., e.g., T 50) here introduces an indir. question after οἶδα (BAGD 556b; R 733). It agrees with ἀγῶνα (acc. sg. from ἀγών, -ῶνος, ὁ, contest, struggle, concern; see Turner, *Words* 81-82), which is acc. as the obj. of ἔχω. Lit.: "how great a struggle I have" (BAGD 345c); thus "how hard I am struggling" (NAB), "how strenuously I am striving," "in how severe a struggle I am engaged" (Weymouth). Although ἀγών may refer in general to

Paul's unremitting toil for the furtherance of the gospel (cf. Phil. 1:12, 30), including his intense pastoral concern (cf. 2 Cor. 11:28) and his perpetual struggle against his opponents (e.g., 1 Cor. 15:32; 16:9), here, as in 4:12, the primary ref. is to the spiritual warfare of wrestling in prayer. See For Further Study 11, "Prayer in Paul" (1:9-12).

ὑπὲρ ὑμῶν καὶ τῶν ἐν Λαοδικείᾳ

Ὑπὲρ ὑμῶν could mean "with respect to you," "[I am struggling] over you," but should instead be rendered "for your sake" or "on your behalf" (NASB). Τῶν is gen. (pl. masc. of the def. art.) after ὑπέρ: οἱ ἐν Λαοδικείᾳ means "those who are at/in Laodicea," here "Christ's People at Laodicea" (TCNT). For the art. with prep. phrases, see BDF § 266; R 766; T 14-15, 221.

καὶ ὅσοι οὐχ ἑόρακαν

3 pl. pf. act. indic. of ὁράω, see. TR has ἑωράκασιν, the more usual form (but cf. ἑώρακαν in Lk. 9:36). The 3 pl. pf. ending -ασι(ν) sometimes yielded to the influence of the 3 pl. first aor. ending -αν, being the only difference between pf. and first aor. endings in the indic. act. (see BDF § 83[1]; Moulton 52; MH 193; R 336-337). The neg. particle is οὐχ before rough breathings.

Ὅσοι is nom. pl. masc. of ὅσος, -η, -ον, as great, as much, (pl.) as many; correlative with πόσος, how great; how much, (pl.) how many, or with τοσοῦτος, so great, so much, (pl.) so many (BAGD 586b, c). Before this correlative, which is nom. as the subj. of the vb. οὐχ ἑόρακαν, a form such as πόσων or τούτων or τοσούτων (all gen. after ὑπέρ) should be supplied as antecedent: "and for as many as have not seen" (RV), "and for all who." Ὅσοι introduces the general class of persons to which the Colossians and Laodiceans belong—"all the others who" (cf. Lightfoot 28 n. 4, 170; ZG 605). (Note: the single prep. ὑπέρ; αὐτῶν [v. 2] clearly refers to all three groups; v. 4 reverts to the second pers. [ὑμᾶς] of v. 1a, ὑμᾶς . . . ὑμῶν.) Paul is thinking of other Christians in the Lycus Valley, such as those at Hierapolis (4:13), who, like the Colossians and Laodiceans, had not met him personally.

τὸ πρόσωπόν μου ἐν σαρκί

"To see someone's face" is a circumlocution for "to see someone" (BAGD 578a; cf. 721a). With τὸ πρόσωπον the prep. phrase ἐν σαρκί means "face-to-face" (BAGD 743c; JB) or "in person"/"personally" (NASB). Since to "see" (ἑόρακαν) was not simply to "look at," it is also appropriate to render the whole clause "all who have not met me personally" (NIV; O'Brien 73) or "all who do not know me personally" (Goodspeed; Lohse 68, cf. 80 n. 95; sim. Weymouth, GNB). Paul is emphasizing that his struggle was for Christians personally unknown to him yet spiritually dear to him.

VERSE 2

ἵνα παρακληθῶσιν αἱ καρδίαι αὐτῶν

3 pl. aor. pass. subjunc. of παρακαλέω, comfort, encourage (but in defense of the meaning "strengthen" here, see O'Brien 92-93). Ἵνα introduces the first of four stated purposes of Paul's ἀγών (see above on Structure); but it is not impossible that ἵνα expresses a wish (volitive ἵνα) with θέλω understood (cf. T 103, 138; thus Moffatt, NEB, NAB). In place of the expected second pers. ὑμῶν (cf. vv. 1a, 4), we find third pers. αὐτῶν, doubtless under the influence of the two nearest antecedents (viz. τῷ ἐν Λ. καὶ ὅσοι).

συμβιβασθέντες ἐν ἀγάπῃ

Nom. pl. masc. of the aor. pass. ptc. of συμβιβάζω, knit together, unite (as in 2:19; Eph. 4:16); but some opt for the meaning "instruct" (as in Acts 9:22; 19:33; 1 Cor. 2:16; so Vulg.; O'Brien 73, 93; Turner, *Words* 233-234; cf. Moffatt). This vb. is the causal form of βαίνω, go; thus "make go together (σύν)," "cause to join."

Συμβιβασθέντες is an anacoluthon, since it would be fem. [-θεῖσαι] if agreeing with καρδίαι, or gen. if agreeing with αὐτῶν (TR actually has συμβιβασθέντων). Numerous explanations have been given:

(1) It agrees with an unexpressed αὐτοί, the pers. equivalent of αἱ καρδίαι αὐτῶν (cf. RV).

*(2) It is a nominative *ad sensum* ("in accordance with the sense"; T 230; Moule 86) or a "hanging nominative" (*nominativus pendens;* Moule, *Idiom Book* 105; cf. 31).

(3) It is an impv. ptc. where there is an ellipse of ἔστε (2 pl. impv. of εἰμί, be), a form never found in the LXX or NT, where γίνεσθε or ἔσεσθε replaces it (cf. Moulton 180; MH 203). Tr.: "they must be knit together."

(4) It is an abs. ptc. with an opt. sense (Lightfoot 222, but cf. his paraphrase on p. 170; see the remarks of Moulton 182-183). Tr.: "May they be united."

As an aor. ptc. following a finite vb., συμβιβασθέντες could be modal, stating the means by which the encouragement would occur: "by being knit together." But if it is temp., it describes action antecedent to the main vb. ("having been knit together," NASB) or possibly contemporaneous ("as they are knit together," RSV; cf. RV, TCNT). In either case, under the influence of the ἵνα clause, it becomes another purpose of Paul's ἀγών, and, if it denotes action antecedent to παρακληθῶσιν, a prior purpose. Tr.: "that they may be welded together in love and their hearts encouraged."

In the phrase ἐν ἀγάπῃ, the prep. is either instr. ("united by love,"

Goodspeed; cf. Z § 449; TCNT) or local ("united in love," NAB, NIV; cf. Eph. 4:16).

καὶ εἰς πᾶν πλοῦτος

Εἰς introduces a third purpose of Paul's ἀγών (see above on Structure) or, alternatively, the purpose (so NIV; O'Brien 73) or result (so GNB) of the encouragement and union (v. 2a). There is no need to construe εἰς with συμ-βιβασθέντες alone (as Z § 449: "love is the cause of the union and greater knowledge is its effect") or to regard it as expressing direction after an impli-cation of motion in συμβιβασθέντες (Lightfoot 171).

Generally, with an anar. noun πᾶς means "every (kind of)" (see 1:10), but here, in conjunction with the abstract noun πλοῦτος (neut.; wealth, riches; see on 1:27), it clearly means "all the wealth" (Moffatt, NASB), "the full wealth" (NEB, GNB), or possibly "the full blessedness" (TCNT) or "all the benefit" (Goodspeed). On this exceptional use of πᾶς, see R 772 ("with the abstract word 'every' and 'all' amount practically to the same thing"); T 199-200; Z § 190.

τῆς πληροφορίας τῆς συνέσεως

Πληροφορία, -ας, ἡ, full assurance, certainty, conviction; or possibly, fullness (cf. BAGD 670c). The gen. is probably epex. ("the full wealth [consisting] of conviction," Moule 86; "all the rich fullness"), but it could be subj. ("all the wealth that comes from the full assurance [of understanding]," NASB; sim. Lightfoot 170) or descriptive of the σύνεσις ("the full riches of complete understanding," NIV).

On the other hand, τῆς συνέσεως (gen. sg. of σύνεσις, ἡ, understanding, insight) is probably subj. ("conviction which is the result of insight," T 211; "conviction that is brought by understanding"; sim. Moffatt, NEB, GNB; BAGD 670c; Moule 86) rather than merely poss. ("the full assurance attached to understanding").

εἰς ἐπίγνωσιν τοῦ μυστηρίου τοῦ θεοῦ

Unlike the third purpose of Paul's ἀγών (viz. εἰς πᾶν πλοῦτος κτλ.), this fourth and final stated aim (telic εἰς) is not introduced by καί, which suggests that Paul is here redefining his aim or stating it comprehensively. But the εἰς could be ecbatic ("resulting in," NASB; sim. GNB) or even temp. ("until," JB). On ἐπίγνωσις, see on 1:9 and note γνῶσις in 2:3. Since Paul's readers already had a knowledge of God's mystery (1:27), the pref. ἐπι- may signify "full" (Wey-mouth), "deeper," "perfect" (TCNT), or "true" (NASB) knowledge (cf. JB: "until you really know").

Τοῦ μυστηρίου is obj. gen. and τοῦ θεοῦ poss.: "deeper knowledge of

God's mystery." These two art. nouns well illustrate the "canon of Apollonius" (see 1:5) and the principal exception to that rule (cf. Moule, *Idiom Book* 114-115; T 180): (a) being a governed noun, θεοῦ is art., like its governing noun, μυστηρίου; (b) although its governing noun ἐπίγνωσιν is anar., μυστηρίου is art.

Χριστοῦ

There are no fewer than fifteen textual variants at the end of this verse. All three UBS edd. prefer τοῦ θεοῦ, Χριστοῦ with a "B" rating ("there is some degree of doubt"), a rdg. that is supported by two proto-Alexandrian texts (𝔭⁴⁶ B) and two Western Fathers (Hilary, Pelagius) and that best accounts for the other variants, which all arose as attempts to resolve the syntactical ambiguity of the juxtaposed genitives, τοῦ θεοῦ Χριστοῦ, through omission, explanation, or amplification. See the discussion in Metzger 622; B. M. Metzger, *The Text of the New Testament* (New York: Oxford University, 1968²) 236-238; WH 125-126; Lightfoot 171, 246, 250-251; Lohse 81-82.

Even with this preferred rdg. grammatical ambiguities remain:

*(1) Gen. Χριστοῦ may be in epex. appos. to τοῦ μυστηρίου: "God's mystery, which is Christ" (thus most grammarians, commentators, and EVV). This understanding is supported by 1:27 and is reflected in a textual variant that has strong Western support, . . . τοῦ θεοῦ ὅ ἐστιν Χριστός. Χριστοῦ is anar. although the subst. in appos. is usually art. (T 206).

(2) Χριστοῦ might also be in epex. appos. to τοῦ θεοῦ: "the mystery of God, even/who is Christ." Such a bold explicit equation of ὁ θεός with Χριστός (not of Χριστός with ὁ θεός) is, however, without parallel in the NT.

(3) Or Χριστοῦ could be poss., denoting relationship: "the mystery of Christ's God," "that open secret of God, the Father of Christ" (Moffatt). Although Eph. 1:17 affords a Pauline parallel to the idea of "the God of Christ," it would seem inappropriate for Paul to emphasize the subordination of Christ when the false teaching he was opposing called into question or undermined the sovereignty of Christ.

VERSE 3

ἐν ᾧ

While the antecedent of ᾧ (dat. sg. masc. or neut. of the rel. pron. ὅς, ἥ, ὅ) could be μυστηρίου (neut.; "the mystery . . . in which"; sim. Goodspeed, JB), it is more likely to be the nearer antecedent, Χριστοῦ (masc.; so most EVV). But there is ultimately no difference in meaning since Christ is the mystery of God (1:27; 2:2). This rel. clause explains the equation τὸ μυστήριον τοῦ θεοῦ

= Χριστός (v. 2d) or justifies the pursuit of a deeper knowledge of Christ (v. 2d). As such it may have causal overtones: "for in Christ. . . ."

πάντες οἱ θησαυροὶ τῆς σοφίας καὶ γνώσεως

Θησαυροί, from θησαυρός, -οῦ, ὁ, something stored up, treasure; treasure chest. In the pred. position with an art. noun πᾶς means "all (without exception)" (see on 1:4): "All the treasures of wisdom and knowledge (without exception)." The art. with θησαυροί probably denotes poss., "God's treasures" (NEB).

As a dependent gen. σοφίας is, like θησαυροί, art. (the canon of Apollonius—see on 2:2), while γνώσεως (gen. of γνῶσις, ἡ, knowledge) is anar. because of the intimate relationship between "wisdom" and "knowledge" (cf. Rom. 11:33; cf. Z § 184). These two gens. stand in the broadest possible relation to θησαυροί—"all the treasures that are involved in having wisdom and knowledge" (gens. of ref. or relation).

εἰσιν . . . ἀπόκρυφοι

Nom. pl. masc. (agreeing with θησαυροί) of ἀπόκρυφος, -ον (two-termination adj.), hidden. If εἰσιν (3 pl. pres. of εἰμί, be) . . . ἀπόκρυφοι are cstr. together, the sense is "all the treasures . . . are stored up/deposited" or "lie hidden" in Christ (sim. BAGD 361d; TCNT, Moffatt, NEB); if they are separated in sense (cf. 3:1), then tr. "all the treasures . . . reside in him in a hidden manner," so that εἰσιν affirms the existence of the θησαυροί in him and ἀπόκρυφοι is a "secondary predicate" (Lightfoot 173) expressing the manner of their existence (cf. Lohse 82 n. 115). In the former case Paul is rebutting the view that true spiritual knowledge resides elsewhere than in Christ. In the latter case he is expressing the paradox that the treasures of wisdom and knowledge, although localized in and revealed through Christ, remain hidden in him, as though they beckoned the investigator or surpassed all human effort to exhaust them. It is improbable that ἀπόκρυφοι is an attrib. adj. ("in whom there resides all the hidden treasures. . . ," sim. GNB), for that would require πάντες οἱ θησαυροὶ . . . οἱ ἀπόκρυφοι or πάντες οἱ ἀπόκρυφοι θησαυροί.

TRANSLATION

[1]For I want you to know how strenuously I am striving for you, for those at Laodicea and all who have not seen me personally, [2] that they may be welded together in love and their hearts may be encouraged, also that they may gain the full wealth of conviction that is brought by understanding and come to a deeper knowledge of God's mystery, which is Christ. [3] For in him all God's treasures of wisdom and knowledge are stored up.

EXPANDED PARAPHRASE

[1] Indeed, I want you to be fully aware of my ongoing and intense wrestling in prayer for the spiritual welfare of you and the Laodicean believers and all others in the Lycus Valley who have yet to meet me in person. [2] The aim of this spiritual wrestling of mine is multiple: that they all may be welded together and established in mutual love and that their hearts and yours may be encouraged and strengthened; that they may gain assured conviction in its full richness, a conviction that comes from spiritual insight and an understanding mind, and may have an enriched appreciation and knowledge of God's mystery, which is nothing other than Christ himself. [3] For it is in Christ—and Christ alone—that the full treasury of God's wisdom and knowledge is stored up.

HOMILETICAL SUGGESTIONS

Paul's Spiritual Struggle (2:1-3)

1. Its nature (ἡλίκον ἀγῶνα ἔχω, v. 1a)
2. Its beneficiaries (ὑπὲρ κτλ., v. 1b)
3. Its objectives (v. 2):
    (a) encouragement of heart (ἵνα παρακληθῶσιν κτλ., v. 2a)
    (b) unity in love (συμβιβασθέντες ἐν ἀγάπῃ, v. 2b)
    (c) full assurance through understanding (εἰς πᾶν πλοῦτος κτλ., v. 2c)
    (d) more profound penetration of God's mystery (εἰς ἐπίγνωσιν κτλ., v. 2d)
4. The justification of this fourth, comprehensive objective (3.d.): Christ is the Reservoir of God's wisdom and knowledge (ἐν ᾧ κτλ., v. 3)

Wrestling in Prayer (2:1-2)

1. What are its *characteristics* (v. 1)?
    (a) It should be intense (ἡλίκον)
    (b) It should be ongoing (ἔχω)
    (c) It should be for others, even those personally unknown
2. What are its *aims* (v. 2)?
    (a) hearts that are encouraged (v. 2a)
    (b) persons who are united in love (v. 2b)
    (c) intellectual and spiritual understanding that generates conviction (v. 2c)
    (d) deeper knowledge of Christ (v. 2d)

III. Error and Its Remedy (2:4–3:4)

A. WARNING AGAINST SPECIOUS PHILOSOPHY (2:4-8)

4 Τοῦτο λέγω ἵνα μηδεὶς ὑμᾶς παραλογίζηται ἐν πιθανολογίᾳ. 5 εἰ γὰρ καὶ τῇ σαρκὶ ἄπειμι, ἀλλὰ τῷ πνεύματι σὺν ὑμῖν εἰμι, χαίρων καὶ βλέπων ὑμῶν τὴν τάξιν καὶ τὸ στερέωμα τῆς εἰς Χριστὸν πίστεως ὑμῶν.
6 Ὡς οὖν παρελάβετε τὸν Χριστὸν Ἰησοῦν τὸν κύριον, ἐν αὐτῷ περιπατεῖτε, 7 ἐρριζωμένοι καὶ ἐποικοδομούμενοι ἐν αὐτῷ καὶ βεβαιούμενοι τῇ πίστει καθὼς ἐδιδάχθητε, περισσεύοντες ἐν εὐχαριστίᾳ. 8 βλέπετε μή τις ὑμᾶς ἔσται ὁ συλαγω-γῶν διὰ τῆς φιλοσοφίας καὶ κενῆς ἀπάτης κατὰ τὴν παράδοσιν τῶν ἀνθρώπων, κατὰ τὰ στοιχεῖα τοῦ κόσμου καὶ οὐ κατὰ Χριστόν·

STRUCTURE

In this paragraph Paul warns the Colossians of two dangers confronting them: (a) that of being deluded by beguiling sophistry (v. 4), and (b) that of being carried off as booty by empty, delusive philosophy (v. 8).

(a)	Τοῦτο λέγω ἵνα μηδεὶς	the danger of
	ὑμᾶς παραλογίζηται	being deceived
	ἐν πιθανολογίᾳ	by persuasive argument
	ἐν αὐτῷ περιπατεῖτε	the protection available:
	ἐρριζωμένοι	living in Christ, and
	ἐποικοδομούμενοι	four characteristics
	βεβαιούμενοι	of this life
	περισσεύοντες	
(b)	βλέπετε μή τις	the danger of
	ὑμᾶς . . . ὁ συλαγωγῶν	being kidnapped
	διὰ τῆς φιλοσοφίας καὶ	by meaningless,
	κενῆς ἀπάτης	deceptive philosophy

85

κατά   ⎫   the origin and content
κατά   ⎬   of this philosophy
οὐ κατὰ Χριστόν ⎭

VERSE 4

Τοῦτο λέγω ἵνα μηδεὶς ὑμᾶς παραλογίζηται

Μηδείς is nom. sg. masc. of the subst. and adj. μηδείς, μηδεμία, μηδέν, nobody, no. Ἵνα μηδείς, "in order that no one," "to prevent anyone" (TCNT) is equivalent to μή τις, "lest anyone" (v. 8). Παραλογίζηται is 3 sg. pres. mid. subjunc. (after ἵνα) of dep. παραλογίζομαι, deceive/delude by false reckoning or reasoning (see MM 487; see MH 319 on παρα-, "aside").

It is possible that ἵνα is impv. and τοῦτο prospective: "What I mean is this: let no one deceive you" (sim. Goodspeed, NEB mg., GNB; Moule 88; *Idiom Book* 145). On impv. ἵνα see BDF § 388; Moule, *Idiom Book* 144-145; T 94-95, 102; Z § 415; for prospective τοῦτο, cf. 1 Cor. 1:12; Gal. 3:17. More probably, however, ἵνα is telic and τοῦτο retrospective (as in Jn. 5:34): "I am telling you this so that no one may delude you" (sim. most EVV and commentators). Λέγω refers to the present written communication (BAGD 469d) and the antecedent of τοῦτο is either vv. 1-3 in general, or v. 3 in particular (viz. the all-sufficiency and finality of Christ as God's disclosed mystery).

ἐν πιθανολογίᾳ

Ἐν is instr.—either "by (means of)" or "with" (= "using"). Πιθανολογία (-ας, ἡ), from πιθανός ("persuasive") and λόγος ("word, argument, speech"), was used in CGk in a positive sense of (the use of) probable argument rather than conclusive proof (ἀπόδειξις; cf. 1 Cor. 2:4). Here it is used in a pejorative sense and variously rendered "beguiling speech" (RSV; Lohse 68), "plausible sophistry" (Weymouth), "specious arguments" (Goodspeed, NEB, JB, NAB—taking the noun as a generic sg. [cf. BAGD 657b]), or "persuasiveness of speech" (RV).

VERSE 5

εἰ γὰρ καί

This verse affords evidence (γάρ, "for") of Paul's concern for his readers' spiritual welfare (1:29; 2:1) or supplies the reason why they are not really candidates for deception (v. 4). Εἰ . . . καί (here "although," "even if," not "if indeed") introduces a concessive clause whose apodosis begins with ἀλλά, "yet," "certainly," "at least" (cf. BDF § 448[5]).

τῇ σαρκὶ ἄπειμι, ἀλλὰ τῷ πνεύματι σὺν ὑμῖν εἰμι

1 sg. pres. act. indic. of ἄπειμι, be absent, be away. Some tr. (Weymouth, Goodspeed, NIV) supply "from you" (ἀφ' ὑμῶν) to balance "with you" (σὺν ὑμῖν). The τῇ σαρκί—τῷ πνεύματι antithesis is not moral but physical: "in body" (= τῷ σώματι, 1 Cor. 5:3)—"in spirit" (RSV). The articles are either generic (denoting a category) or poss. Whether we classify these words as datives of manner (thus ZG 606) or respect (Zerwick, *Analysis* 449; cf. Z § 53), the meaning is the same: "physically"—"spiritually" (so also Moule, *Idiom Book* 46; cf. T 239). To render τῇ πνεύματι by "in the Spirit" (as Lohse 68, 83) destroys the parallelism with τῇ σαρκί. On Paul's "spiritual" presence, see O'Brien 98.

χαίρων καὶ βλέπων

Nom. sg. masc. (agreeing with the sg. subj. of εἰμι) of the pres. act. ptc. of χαίρω, rejoice, and βλέπω, see. Both ptcs. describe circumstances that accompany Paul's spiritual presence with and among the Colossians (σὺν ὑμῖν εἰμι). It could be that two separate thoughts are being expressed—"I rejoice with you (or, about you; or, at being with you) and in addition see . . ."—but it is better to find here a case of hendiadys, "rejoicing to see" (BDF § 471[5]; RSV; Lohse 68, 84; sim. BAGD 392a, 873d and most EVV) or "viewing with joy" (BDF § 471[5]).

ὑμῶν τὴν τάξιν καὶ τὸ στερέωμα

Here Paul may be employing two military metaphors, perhaps suggested by the circumstances of his imprisonment. On this view, τάξις (-εως, ἡ) depicts the "orderly array" (Lightfoot 173, 174; NEB) of military formation, while στερέωμα (-ατος, τό) refers to the "solid front" (Lightfoot 174; Moffatt) of a closed phalanx or bulwark. But the words were also used in a general sense, τάξις meaning "orderliness" or "good order" (RSV, NAB), and στερέωμα "solidity" (Goodspeed), "stability" (NASB), or "resolute firmness" (GNB).

A poss. pron. commonly follows an art. noun (cf. τῆς . . . πίστεως ὑμῶν, v. 5d) but may precede it (ὑμῶν τὴν τάξιν, v. 5c; cf. T 189). Here (v. 5c) the poss. pron. may be placed first to highlight Paul's interest in his readers and their spiritual attainment. It is quite possible that this ὑμῶν qualifies both τὴν τάξιν and τὸ στερέωμα and that the phrase τῆς εἰς Χριστὸν πίστεως ὑμῶν also should be construed with both of these nouns (see G. Bertram, TDNT 7.614 for this latter point). But, probably because of the repeated ὑμῶν and the difficulty of the concept of ἡ τάξις . . . τῆς . . . πίστεως, most EVV and commentators restrict the first ὑμῶν to τὴν τάξιν and take the phrase τῆς . . . πίστεως ὑμῶν only with τὸ στερέωμα.

τῆς εἰς Χριστὸν πίστεως ὑμῶν

Εἰς Χριστόν defines the obj. of "your faith," being equivalent to an obj. gen. (cf. BAGD 663a, b). Τῆς . . . πίστεως (art. in accordance with the canon of Apollonius) is probably a poss. gen.: "the firmness of (= attaching to/charac- terizing) your faith in Christ" (NAB; sim. Moffatt, Goodspeed, NASB) or "(I . . . delight to see) how firm your faith in Christ is" (NIV). "Your firm faith" fails to reflect the subst. τὸ στερέωμα, which is more emphatic than an adj. Alternatively, τῆς . . . πίστεως may be a subj. gen., esp. if στερέωμα is a military metaphor: "the firm front which your faith in Christ presents" (NEB; sim. Weymouth); "the unbroken front resulting from your faith in Christ" (TCNT).

VERSE 6

ὡς οὖν παρελάβετε

2 pl. second aor. act. indic. of παραλαμβάνω, receive (as a tradition); accept. Here the vb. denotes not simply passive receipt of Christian tradition (as NEB, "Jesus was delivered to you") but active acceptance of the person who was the essence of that tradition (cf. BAGD 619d; GNB). With a finite vb. ὡς is rarely causal ("since"; BAGD 898b; cf. BDF § 453[2]); here it is a comp. conj. ("as," "just as") used without its correlative οὕτως ("so"; cf. BAGD 897b, c). Οὖν, "so then," grounds the impv., "continue to walk in him" (v. 6b), in the Colos- sians' demonstrated faith in Christ (v. 5b).

τὸν Χριστὸν Ἰησοῦν τὸν κύριον

There are six different ways to tr. this unique phrase (but cf. Eph. 3:11), depending on whether Χριστός functions as a proper name or as a title.

(1) As a proper name:
    (a) "Christ Jesus as Lord" (GNB, NIV; O'Brien 101, 105)
    (b) "Christ Jesus the Lord" (RV, RSV, NASB, NAB; Lohse 92, 93)
(2) As a title:
    (a) "Jesus . . . as Christ and Lord" (NEB; cf. Moule 89-90)
    (b) "Jesus, the Christ, as your Lord" (TCNT)
    (c) "the Christ, Jesus, as your Lord" (Goodspeed)
  *(d) "the Christ, even Jesus the Lord" (Lightfoot 173, 174; sim. Wey- mouth, Moffatt ["the messiah, . . ."], JB; Robertson, *Pictures* 489; Vincent 905)

That Χριστός is art. and stands first suggests that it is titular (cf. Moule 89; T 167), "the Messiah," "the Christ"; that κύριος is art. even without the poss. pron. ἡμῶν (see Eph. 3:11) suggests that it is not pred., "as (your) Lord" (as the anar. κύριος is in the expression Ἰησοῦν Χριστὸν κύριον in 2 Cor. 4:5). These two considerations favor 2 (d)—either "the Christ, even Jesus the Lord," or "the Messiah, Jesus the Lord." The whole expression appears to be a combination of two early christological confessions, ὁ Χριστὸς Ἰησοῦς, "Jesus is the Messiah" (Acts 18:5, 28; cf. 2:36; 9:22; 17:3), and κύριος Ἰησοῦς, "Jesus is Lord" (Rom. 10:9; 1 Cor. 12:3; cf. Phil. 2:11), with the one common element and proper name being anar. (Ἰησοῦν) and the two titular elements being art. and (here) not pred. (τὸν Χριστὸν . . . τὸν κύριον).

ἐν αὐτῷ περιπατεῖτε

2 pl. pres. act. impv. (here not indic.) of περιπατέω, go about; live, walk, conduct oneself. In the indic.-impv. dialectic of this verse (παρελάβετε—περιπατεῖτε; cf. 3:1-2), the pres. after the aor. should be rendered "continue to live" (NIV) or "go on walking" (T 75). Given the pervasive influence of Paul's ἐν Χριστῷ formula, ἐν here is less probably instr. ("by him" = "by his power") than locat., either "in union with him" (TCNT, NEB, GNB), "as incorporated in him" (Moule 90), or indicating Christ as the sphere circumscribing the entire life of the believer.

VERSE 7

ἐρριζωμένοι καὶ ἐποικοδομούμενοι ἐν αὐτῷ

Nom. pl. masc. (agreeing with the pl. subj. of παρελάβετε) of the pf. pass. ptc. of ῥιζόω, cause to take root; (pass.) be firmly rooted/established. Vbs. in ῥ- usually reduplicate by ἐρρ- (MH 193). Nom. pl. masc. of the pres. pass. ptc. of ἐποικοδομέω, build on/up (possibly mid., as Weymouth: "continually building yourselves up").

These are the first two of four ptcs. (the other two being βεβαιούμενοι and περισσεύοντες), all syntactically related to the preceding impv. περιπατεῖτε (v. 6b). Some EVV (viz. NEB, GNB, JB) cstr. all of these ptcs. as virtual impvs. because of their relation to περιπατεῖτε, but it is preferable to regard them as adv. ptcs. of attendant circumstance (see BDF § 418[5]; Burton §§ 449-450; R 1125-1128; T 154 for this category), describing not the exclusive means by which the περιπατεῖν takes place, but four typical characteristics of the Christian's conduct (cf. the same phenomenon after the same vb. in 1:10-12). The first three ptcs. are pass., implying that divine action is essential in Christian growth.

Whether or not the transition from ἐρριζωμένοι to ἐποικοδομούμενοι represents a change of metaphor from agricultural to architectural (note the similar combination of metaphors in 1 Cor. 3:9 and Eph. 3:17 and the fact that ῥιζόω was also used of buildings), the alteration of tense from pf. to pres. is significant. A previous rooting is implied and the present rootage is stressed in the pf. ptc. ἐρριζωμένοι, whereas the ongoing process of edification is emphasized by the pres. ptc. ἐποικοδομούμενοι. Tr.: "now rooted and being built up in him."

Because the prep. phrase ἐν αὐτῷ belongs to both ptcs. (see TCNT, NEB, GNB, NAB), it should probably be rendered simply "in him [viz. Jesus the Lord, v. 6a]," a central notion in 2:6-15. But it is perfectly admissible to tr. it differently with each ptc., "you must be rooted in him and built on him" (JB; cf. GNB; BAGD 305c, "upon him"; and 1 Cor. 3:11), where ἐν αὐτῷ = ἐπ᾽ αὐτῷ (cf. Eph. 2:20) or ἐπ᾽ αὐτόν (cf. 1 Cor. 3:12). The ἐπ(ι)- in ἐποικοδομούμενοι could mean "(built) up," as in Jude 20, or could point to the successive layers of the building built one upon (ἐπί) another (Lightfoot 175).

καὶ βεβαιούμενοι

Nom. pl. masc. (agreeing with the pl. subj. of παρελάβετε) of the pres. pass. ptc. of βεβαιόω, confirm, establish, strengthen. Since this is the third of four adv. ptcs. of attendant circumstance (see previous note), the καί is conj., not epex. (as if it introduced a redefinition of the two preceding ptcs.). Tr.: "(and) becoming (more and more) established," "growing ever stronger" (NAB).

τῇ πίστει

As in 1:23, it is unclear whether πίστις here bears (a) a subj. sense (faith as the act of believing), or (b) an obj. sense (the faith as the obj. or content of belief), although the ref. to teaching that immediately follows favors the latter. The dat. τῇ πίστει may be:

(1) instr.:
   (a) "by your faith [in Christ, cf. v. 5b]" (Lightfoot 173, 175: "faith is, as it were, the cement of the building"; NEB mg.; cf. TCNT; the art. here denotes poss.) or
   (b) "held firm by the faith (you have been taught)" (JB),
(2) dat. of ref. or relation: "growing stronger with respect to faith/the faith," or
(3) locat.:
   (a) "in faith" (BAGD 138c; Goodspeed, NAB) or "in your faith" (RV, NASB, GNB)
   *(b) "in the faith" (ZG 606; Moffatt, RSV, NIV; Lohse 92, 94; O'Brien 101, 108).

καθὼς ἐδιδάχθητε

2 pl. aor. pass. indic. of διδάσκω, teach, alluding to the instruction given by Epaphras and others (cf. 1:7; 2:6a). Καθώς (= κατά + ὡς) is a conj. introducing a comparison, "just as." This clause may qualify only βεβαιούμενοι κτλ. (thus Weymouth, Moffatt, NEB, JB) but more probably it relates to all three preceding ptcs. (thus, apparently, TCNT, Goodspeed, NASB, GNB, NAB).

περισσεύοντες

Nom. pl. masc. (agreeing with the pl. subj. of ἐδιδάχθητε) of the pres. act. ptc. of περισσεύω, abound, overflow (or possibly, excel—thus BAGD 651a). Being asyndetic (with no preceding καί), this ptc. could be related to βεβαιούμενοι κτλ. only, but it is better to attribute the "absence" of καί to stylistic variation and regard the ptc. as the fourth and last adv. ptc. of attendant circumstance related to περιπατεῖτε (see v. 7a).

ἐν εὐχαριστίᾳ

Εὐχαριστία, -ας, ἡ, can denote the attitude of thankfulness ("gratitude") or the actual rendering of thanks ("thanksgiving"; BAGD 328c) in informal or formal prayers or hymns. Ἐν εὐχαριστίᾳ defines the sphere in which (locat. ἐν) the overflow was evident ("abounding in thanksgiving," RSV) or the element that formed the content of the overflow (instr. ἐν; "overflowing with gratitude," NASB, NAB; cf. Moffatt, NEB, NIV; BAGD 328c).

Representatives of the Alexandrian, Western, and Byzantine text families read ἐν αὐτῇ ἐν εὐχαριστίᾳ, where ἐν αὐτῇ = ἐν πίστει ("overflowing with faith and thanksgiving," TCNT; this rdg. is also reflected in Goodspeed and preferred by Lightfoot 173, 175). But this rdg. is doubtless secondary, having arisen by assimilation to 4:2, while the predominantly Western rdg. ἐν αὐτῷ ἐν εὐχαριστίᾳ ("abounding in Christ with thanksgiving") arose subsequently under the influence of the two preceding instances of ἐν αὐτῷ in this sentence (vv. 6b, 7a). See Metzger 622.

VERSE 8

βλέπετε μή τις ὑμᾶς ἔσται

2 pl. pres. act. impv. of βλέπω, see, see to it, take care. 3 sg. fut. indic. of εἰμί, be. When βλέπω is followed by a clause that defines the act or condition to be avoided, it is usually followed by μή (or μήποτε or μήπως) and the aor. subj. (e.g., Matt. 24:4), but here, exceptionally (cf. Heb. 3:12), it is followed by the fut. indic. (ἔσται; cf. BAGD 143d, 517b; R 995). This tends to make the danger more imminent and the warning more urgent (cf. Moulton 178; although

Moulton himself prefers to see μή as introducing a cautious assertion: "Take heed! perhaps there will be someone who. . . ," 192-193; cf. R 1169). Μή τις, "lest anyone," "that no one" (τις, nom. sg. masc. [subj. of ἔσται] of the encl. indef. pron. τις, τι, anyone, anything; someone, something).

ὁ συλαγωγῶν

Nom. sg. masc. (agreeing with τις) of the pres. act. ptc. of συλαγωγέω, a NT *hapax legomenon* meaning "carry off (ἄγω) as booty (σύλημα)," although other meanings are possible, viz. "kidnap," "exploit," "take captive," "make a prey of." This art. ptc. restricts the sense of τις (cf. Burton § 424) and is equivalent to a rel. clause, ὃς συλαγωγήσει (BAGD 551b, c; BDF § 412[4]; Moulton 228; R 764). Lit.: "Take care lest there will be anyone who carries you off as spoil." Although τις is indef., Paul probably has a specific individual in mind, the foremost advocate or a vocal proponent of the erroneous philosophy, who could at any time carry the Colossians away from the truth into error and consequent slavery. The dramatic juxtaposition, τις ὑμᾶς (where the normal word-order would have been μή τις ἔσται ὑμᾶς κτλ.: Moule, *Idiom Book* 168), highlights their real peril. The pres. tense of the ptc. is timeless and could refer either to a single act or to repeated action.

διὰ τῆς φιλοσοφίας καὶ κενῆς ἀπάτης

Two nouns in the gen. after διά express the means by which the capture of the Colossians would take place: φιλοσοφία, -ας, ἡ, philosophy; ἀπάτη, -ας, ἡ, deception, deceit(fulness). Lit.: "through philosophy and empty deceit" (κενῆς, gen. sg. fem. of κενός, -ή, -όν, empty, vain; agreeing with ἀπάτης). The single prep. and art. qualifying both nouns suggest that one conceptual entity, not two, is being named (cf. R 737) and therefore that καί is epex. "through a philosophy which is empty deceit," "through hollow and deceptive philosophy" (NIV). By the term φιλοσοφία, thus qualified, Paul means neither philosophy in general nor classical Gk. philosophy specifically but so-called philosophy (cf. O. Michel, TDNT 9.185-187; Lightfoot 176-177), what is falsely termed philosophy (cf. 1 Tim. 6:20), "philosophy" that has the mere "appearance of wisdom" (cf. 2:23), almost "philosophizing" or "intellectualism." It is possible that the art. τῆς is poss., referring to τις (thus RV, TCNT, Weymouth) and that both nouns are generic sgs.: "by means of such a person's speculations, which are meaningless delusions."

κατὰ τὴν παράδοσιν τῶν ἀνθρώπων

This phrase qualifies φιλοσοφίας κτλ., not ὁ συλαγωγῶν. Κατά sets forth the basis ("based on," NEB; "which depends on," NIV) or *source ("derived from," "which comes from," GNB) of the "philosophy," viz. "the tradition of humans" (παράδοσις, -εως, ἡ, a handing down/over; what is handed down, i.e., tradition). The gen. τῶν ἀνθρώπων, which is art. in accordance with the canon of Apollonius, is less probably obj. ("directed to humans," "for the observance of humankind") than subj. ("emanating from humans," "man-made"; "handed down by humans," GNB) or *adj. ("human," TCNT, Goodspeed, NIV).

κατὰ τὰ στοιχεῖα τοῦ κόσμου καὶ οὐ κατὰ Χριστόν

A στοιχεῖον (neut.) is a constituent element of a series (of a στοῖχος, row, line, series); κατὰ στοιχεῖον, for example, means "in the order of the letters (of the alphabet)," "alphabetically." Four principal meanings have been given to τὰ στοιχεῖα τοῦ κόσμου (see For Further Study 25, "Τὰ στοιχεῖα τοῦ κόσμου" for bibliographical references):

(1) "the (material) elements of which the universe is composed" (cf. 2 Pet. 3:10, 12; sim. NEB mg.; E. Schweizer);
(2) "the elemental forces operating in the world" (A. J. Bandstra);
(3) "the elementary teaching(s) of the world" (sim. RV, TCNT, Weymouth, NEB mg., NASB, JB, NIV; Lightfoot 178; E. de W. Burton; Moule 90-92), where τοῦ κόσμου may mean:
  (a) (teaching) about the universe,
  (b) (teaching) restricted to this world,
  (c) (teaching) regarding materialistic matters, or
  (d) (teaching) possessed by humankind; or
*(4) "the elemental spirits of the world" (sim. Moffatt, NEB, GNB; Lohse 96-99; O'Brien 102, 110, 129-132; Cannon 220-223; Turner 88-91), where τοῦ κόσμου may mean:
  *(a) (spirits) belonging to this world/universe,
  (b) (spirits) that operate in the world, or
  (c) (spirits) that control the world.

Except in 3(d) and 4(a), which cstr. it as poss. gen., τοῦ κόσμου is elsewhere cstr. as gen. of relation or ref., that broadest category of the gen. whose meaning is determined by the context. In 4(a-c) the "elemental spirits" are usually identified with the "rulers" (ἄρχοντες) of 1 Cor. 2:6, 8, the "world rulers" (κοσμοκράτορες) of Eph. 6:12, and the "powers and authorities" (ἀρχαὶ καὶ ἐξουσίαι) of 2:15 (cf. 2:10), whose demonic aim is to enslave the human race (cf. 2:20-22; Gal. 4:3, 9).

Some EVV, esp. those preferring view 3 above, take κατά in an identical sense in each of its three occurrences in v. 8b: RV, "after"; Weymouth, "following"; NASB, "according to"; NIV, "which depends on"; GNB, "which comes from" (preferring view 4 above). But it is preferable, esp. if view 4 is adopted, to take the first κατά as denoting the origin or source of the "philosophy" ("human tradition," as opposed to divine revelation), the second κατά as describing its content or substance (τὰ στοιχεῖα κτλ.), and the third as introducing the negation of the two preceding clauses (the essential weakness of this "philosophy" was that Christ was neither its source nor its substance; sim. Lightfoot 177-179; Lohse 96). Tr.: "derived from human tradition and centered on the elemental spirits of the universe, but not based on Christ" (sim. NEB, "based on . . . and centred on . . . and not on Christ"). Alternatively, the third κατά phrase (οὐ κατὰ Χριστόν) may relate solely to the second (thus TCNT, "following . . . and dealing with . . . , and not with Christ"). On καὶ οὐ, see R 1164. See above, For Further Study 8, "The Colossian Heresy" (1:5).

TRANSLATION

[4] I am telling you this so that no one may delude you by persuasive argument. [5] For though I am physically absent, yet I am spiritually present with you and delighted to see your orderliness and the stability of your faith in Christ. [6] So just as you received the Messiah, Jesus the Lord, continue to walk in him, [7] now rooted and being built up in him, becoming established in the faith, as you have been taught, and overflowing with gratitude. [8] Take care that no one carries you off as spoil by an empty, deceptive philosophy derived from human tradition and centered on the elemental spirits of the universe, but not based on Christ.

EXPANDED PARAPHRASE

[4] My aim in telling you all this is that none of the false teachers talk you into error and delude you by the use of persuasive language or plausible argument. [5] For even if I may be absent from you in body, I am certainly present with you in spirit, and I am delighted to see how orderly your Christian life is and how solid and stable your faith in Christ. [6] You personally embraced the Christian tradition that recognizes the Messiah to be Jesus the Lord. So then, continue living in him, [7] for at the time of your conversion you were first rooted in him and remain so but now you need to be progressively built up on him and established in the faith, in keeping with the instruction that you have received from Epaphras and others. Also see to it that you always overflow with gratitude. [8] Maintain a constant watch lest anyone take you captive through a seductive type of "philosophy" that is hollow and deceptive and that comes from mere human tradition and whose focus is on the elemental spirits of the universe and not on the one source of divine revelation and depository of divine truth—Christ himself.

FOR FURTHER STUDY

25. Τὰ στοιχεῖα τοῦ κόσμου (2:8, 20)

Bandstra, A. J., *The Law and the Elements of the World* (Kampen: Kok/Grand Rapids: Eerdmans, 1964).

Burton, E. de W., *A Critical and Exegetical Commentary on the Epistle to the Galatians* (Edinburgh: T. & T. Clark, 1921) 510-518.

Cannon 220-223.

Delling, G., TDNT 7.670-687.

Esser, H.-H., NIDNTT 2.451-453.

Lohse 96-99.

*O'Brien 129-132.

Reicke, B., "The Law and this World according to Paul. Some Thoughts concerning Gal. 4:1-11," *JBL* 70 (1951) 259-276.

Schweizer, E., "Christianity of the Circumcised and Judaism of the Uncircumcised. The Background of Matthew and Colossians," *Jews, Greeks and Christians. Religious Cultures in Late Antiquity,* ed. R. G. Hamerton-Kelly and R. Scroggs (Leiden: Brill, 1976) 245-260.

―――, "Slaves of the Elements and Worshipers of Angels: Gal. 4:3, 9 and Col. 2:8, 18, 20," *JBL* 107 (1988) 455-468.

Turner, *Words* 88-91.

HOMILETICAL SUGGESTIONS

Warning against Specious Philosophy (2:4-8)

1. The danger of being talked into error (παραλογίζεσθαι) by specious argument (ἐν πιθανολογίᾳ; vv. 4-7)
   (a) evidence of Paul's concern for the Colossians' welfare: his joy in their orderliness and stability (v. 5)
   (b) protection against this danger:
      (i) recalling Christian tradition (ὡς . . . παρελάβετε, v. 6a)
      (ii) life in union with Christ (ἐν αὐτῷ περιπατεῖτε, v. 6b), marked by:
         (α) rootage in Christ (v. 7a)
         (β) building on Christ (v. 7a)
         (γ) stability in the faith (v. 7b)
         (δ) overflow of thanksgiving (v. 7c)
2. The danger of being carried off as spoil (συλαγωγεῖν) by hollow deceptive philosophy (διὰ τῆς φιλοσοφίας καὶ κενῆς ἀπάτης; v. 8)

(a) origin (κατά) of this philosophy: human tradition
(b) content (κατά) of this philosophy: the elemental spirits of the universe
(c) protection against this danger: Christ, who is neither the source nor
the substance (οὐ κατά) of this philosophy

The Indicative–Imperative Dialectic (παρελάβετε— περιπατεῖτε, 2:6)

1. As you received (παρελάβετε) the Messiah, Jesus the Lord,
2. [So then] live your lives (περιπατεῖτε) in union with him.

The Normal Christian Life (2:6b-7; cf. 1:10-12a)

1. Living in union with Christ (ἐν αὐτῷ περιπατεῖτε, v. 6b)
2. Firm rootage in Christ (ἐρριζωμένοι . . . ἐν αὐτῷ, v. 7a)
3. Continuous building on Christ (ἐποικοδομούμενοι ἐν αὐτῷ, v. 7a)
4. Being increasingly established in the faith (βεβαιούμενοι τῇ πίστει, v. 7b)
5. Constant gratitude to God (περισσεύοντες ἐν εὐχαριστίᾳ, v. 7c)

B. CHRIST, THE REMEDY AGAINST ERROR (2:9-15)

9 ὅτι ἐν αὐτῷ κατοικεῖ πᾶν τὸ πλήρωμα τῆς θεότητος σωματικῶς, 10 καὶ ἐστὲ ἐν
αὐτῷ πεπληρωμένοι, ὅς ἐστιν ἡ κεφαλὴ πάσης ἀρχῆς καὶ ἐξουσίας, 11 ἐν ᾧ καὶ
περιετμήθητε περιτομῇ ἀχειροποιήτῳ ἐν τῇ ἀπεκδύσει τοῦ σώματος τῆς σαρκός,
ἐν τῇ περιτομῇ τοῦ Χριστοῦ, 12 συνταφέντες αὐτῷ ἐν τῷ βαπτισμῷ, ἐν ᾧ καὶ
συνηγέρθητε διὰ τῆς πίστεως τῆς ἐνεργείας τοῦ θεοῦ τοῦ ἐγείραντος αὐτὸν ἐκ
νεκρῶν· 13 καὶ ὑμᾶς νεκροὺς ὄντας ἐν τοῖς παραπτώμασιν καὶ τῇ ἀκροβυστίᾳ τῆς
σαρκὸς ὑμῶν, συνεζωοποίησεν ὑμᾶς σὺν αὐτῷ, χαρισάμενος ἡμῖν πάντα τὰ παραπτώματα, 14 ἐξαλείψας τὸ καθ᾽ ἡμῶν χειρόγραφον τοῖς δόγμασιν ὃ ἦν ὑπεναντίον
ἡμῖν, καὶ αὐτὸ ἦρκεν ἐκ τοῦ μέσου προσηλώσας αὐτὸ τῷ σταυρῷ· 15 ἀπεκδυσάμενος τὰς ἀρχὰς καὶ τὰς ἐξουσίας ἐδειγμάτισεν ἐν παρρησίᾳ, θριαμβεύσας
αὐτοὺς ἐν αὐτῷ.

STRUCTURE

```
9 ὅτι              ἐν      αὐτῷ ... πᾶν τὸ  πλήρωμα
10   καὶ ἐστὲ      ἐν      αὐτῷ              πεπληρωμένοι
                          ὅς ἐστιν κτλ.
11                ἐν      ᾧ καὶ περιετμήθητε περιτομῇ ἀχειροποιήτῳ
                                    ἐν τῇ ἀπεκδύσει κτλ.
                                    ἐν τῇ περιτομῇ κτλ.
12 συνταφέντες            αὐτῷ ἐν τῷ βαπτισμῷ
                              ἐν ᾧ καὶ
   συνηγέρθητε
13 συνεζωοποίησεν ... σὺν αὐτῷ, χαρισάμενος
14                             ἐξαλείψας ... καὶ ... ἦρκεν ...
                                                      προσηλώσας
15                             ἀπεκδυσάμενος ...   ἐδειγμάτισεν ...
                                                      θριαμβεύσας
              ἐν       αὐτῷ
```

From this it is apparent that the paragraph falls into three sections:

(1) Two reasons that Christ is the remedy against error and the standard of
    truth (vv. 9-10; cf. κατὰ Χριστόν, v. 8c):
    (a) his deity (v. 9) and
    (b) Christian completeness in him (v. 10).
(2) The means by which believers have appropriated this completeness (vv.
    11-13b):
    (a) heart-circumcision, characteristic of Christ's followers (v. 11),

(b) burial with Christ in baptism (v. 12a), and

(c) resurrection with Christ in baptism (vv. 12b-13b).

(3) God's action through Christ (vv. 13c-15):

(a) forgiveness of trespasses (v. 13c),

(b) cancellation of indebtedness (v. 14), and

(c) disarming of opposition (v. 15).

Three further points are noteworthy.

(1) Two themes are prominent—"in Christ" (vv. 9, 10, 11, 15) and "with Christ" (vv. 12, 13).

(2) There are two interesting changes of person in v. 13—in the subj., from second person (vv. 10-12) to third person, and in pers. prons., from second person (vv. 13a, b) to first person (v. 13c).

(3) The parallelism between the verbal forms in vv. 14-15 is pronounced—temporal aor. ptc., finite vb., modal aor. ptc.

VERSE 9

ὅτι ἐν αὐτῷ κατοικεῖ

3 sg. pres. act. indic. of κατοικέω, dwell, live. Here ὅτι is causal, introducing two reasons (vv. 9, 10a) that Christ is the antidote to the error of the false teachers and the norm for the assessment of truth (cf. κατὰ Χριστόν, v. 8c); ὅτι is not recitative here, introducing a christological or baptismal hymn. Since this verse speaks of Christ, not the believer, ἐν αὐτῷ does not have its customary sense of "in union with him" or "incorporate in him"; rather, here it means "in his person." Κατοικεῖ is a timeless pres., "permanently dwells," "continues to live" (see notes on ἐστιν [1:15] and κατοικῆσαι [1:19]). Distinguishing κατοικεῖν (permanent residence) from παροικεῖν (temporary residence), Lightfoot proposes the tr. "has its fixed abode" (157, 179).

πᾶν τὸ πλήρωμα τῆς θεότητος

With an art. sg. noun πᾶς means "all (the)," "the whole" (BAGD 631d) so that πᾶν τὸ πλήρωμα means "all the fullness" or "the entire fullness," no element of the fullness being excepted (cf. Z § 188). Unlike 1:19, this expression is here qualified by the gen. τῆς θεότητος ("of the Godhead," "of deity"), which may be epex. (see JB [study ed.], note e) or poss., and defines precisely what dwells in the person of Christ in its total plenitude. If there is a valid distinction between the two words, θεότης (-ητος, ἡ) refers to the divine essence, "deity" (deitas), the being of God (θεός), while θειότης (-ητος, ἡ, used in Rom. 1:20) refers to the divine qualities, "divinity" (divinitas), the quality of being divine (θεῖος). If τῆς θεότητος = τοῦ θεοῦ (abstract for concrete; cf. BAGD 358c), it would be proper to render the whole phrase "God in all his fullness" (cf. notes on 1:19), but there is no need to depart from the abstract, "the entire Fulness of deity" (Moffatt), "the complete being of the Godhead" (NEB), or "the Godhead in all its fulness" (TCNT).

Since πᾶν is pleonastic with πλήρωμα and ἐν αὐτῷ is emphatic by position, the whole statement is probably polemical: it is in Christ, and Christ alone, that the sum total of the fullness of the Godhead, no part or aspect excepted, permanently resides in bodily form. See For Further Study 26, "The Deity of Christ."

σωματικῶς

This adv. has been rendered in four main ways, here listed in descending order of probability:

*(1) "In bodily form" (NASB, NAB, NIV; O'Brien 102, 113), "embodied" (Weymouth, Goodspeed, NEB), "bodily" (RV, RSV; BAGD 800b; Lohse 92, 100 and nn. 46, 47), or "incarnate" (TCNT).

(2) "In one person" (cf. Eph. 2:16, ἐν ἑνὶ σώματι), where the emphasis is on the singularity of the embodiment: the fullness of Deity is not dispersed throughout a series of spiritual intermediaries but is completely localized in one person. For σωματικῶς meaning "in person" in the papyri, see Horsley 3.86.

(3) "In reality," "actually" (cf. 2:17, "the reality [σῶμα] is found in Christ," Goodspeed; cf. BAGD 800b, "in reality, not symbolically").

(4) "Corporately" (NEB mg.), i.e., as manifested through the Body of Christ, the Church (cf. 1:24).

See further the discussions in Moule 92-94; O'Brien 112-113.

Σωματικῶς describes the permanent (cf. κατοικεῖ) *post-incarnational state* of Christ, viz. "having bodily form," and does not point directly to the act of incarnation, as Lightfoot suggests ("'corporeally,' i.e. 'assuming a bodily form, becoming incarnate,'" cf. Jn. 1:14) (180). The separation of κατοικεῖ from σωματικῶς suggests that two distinct affirmations are being made (cf. Vincent 906): that the total plenitude of the Godhead dwells in Christ eternally and that this fullness now permanently resides in the incarnate Christ in bodily form. It is true that before the incarnation the πλήρωμα did not reside in Christ σωματικῶς; it is not true that before the incarnation the πλήρωμα did not reside in him at all. Thus Paul implies both the eternal deity and the permanent humanity of Christ. Moreover, κατοικεῖ . . . σωματικῶς implies that both before and after his resurrection Christ "possessed" a σῶμα (cf. 1:22; 1 Cor. 15:44; Phil. 3:21).

VERSE 10

καὶ ἐστὲ ἐν αὐτῷ πεπληρωμένοι

Ἐστέ is 2 pl. pres. indic. of εἰμί, be. Πεπληρωμένοι is nom. pl. masc. (agreeing with the subj. of ἐστέ) of the pf. pass. ptc. of πληρόω, fill, bring to completion, fulfill. Some find here two predicates: "you are in him, having been made complete" (sim. Vincent 906; Lightfoot 180). But most regard ἐστὲ . . . πεπληρωμένοι as a periph. pf. (pres. of εἰμί + pf. ptc.; so Robertson, *Pictures* 491; T 89) and ἐν αὐτῷ ("in union with him," Goodspeed, GNB) as the sole predicate: "and in him you have been brought to completion" (NEB), where "God" is the implied agent.

Although πληρόω is sometimes followed by ἐν + dat. of that which fills (Eph. 5:18), ἐν αὐτῷ does not here mean "with him," nor should "with it [i.e., all the fullness of deity]" be supplied (as in Goodspeed, TCNT; cf. NAB, "yours is a share of this fullness"). But the verbal link with v. 9 is clear: "you have been made full (πεπληρωμένοι) in him, in whom all the fullness (πλήρωμα) of deity resides." It is not impossible that ἐν is instr.—"you are filled absolutely by Him as the Giver" (G. Delling, TDNT 6.292).

What constitutes the "completeness" that believers have in Christ? It could be full acceptance before God, "fullness of life" (RSV; sim. Moffatt, GNB; cf. Jn. 10:10), corporate completeness or complementarity as the Body of Christ, individual integrity, or the satisfaction of every spiritual need.

ὅς ἐστιν ἡ κεφαλὴ πάσης ἀρχῆς καὶ ἐξουσίας

Nom. sg. masc. of the rel. pron. ὅς, ἥ, ὅ, agreeing with its antecedent αὐτῷ in number and gender, but as subj. of ἐστιν its case is nom. (cf. R 712). Κεφαλή is a nom. complement after the vb. εἰμί, and its art. shows this is a reversible proposition (cf. 1:18, 24). For anar. πᾶς, see on 1:9. The two gens. are obj. Tr.: "who is the head over every power and authority"—this, by reason of creation (1:15b-16) and conquest (2:15), perhaps stated against the view that certain angels or spiritual powers shared Christ's mediatorial role. That these angelic or cosmic rulers and potentates were closely associated is shown by the single πάσης (cf. the repeated art. in 2:15a). If ἀρχῆς and ἐξουσίας are generic sgs., we could tr.: "all rulers and powers." See For Further Study 27, "Principalities and Powers in Paul."

VERSE 11

ἐν ᾧ καὶ

Dat. (after ἐν) sg. masc. of the rel. pron. ὅς, ἥ, ὅ, referring to Christ (like ἐν αὐτῷ in vv. 9a, 10a and ὅς in v. 10b): "in union with Christ" (GNB), "by your union with him" (TCNT), or "through your relation to him" (Goodspeed). Καί signifies "in addition to your completeness in him (v. 10a)."

περιετμήθητε περιτομῇ ἀχειροποιήτῳ

2 pl. aor. pass. indic. of περιτέμνω, cut (off) around, circumcise (see Horsley 3.81; Turner, *Words* 71-72). The -ι of περί is retained before the aug. ε. This constative aor. points (in this case) to a single action in the past, viz. circumcision at the time of conversion or baptism (cf. v. 12). As with the passives in v. 12, God is the implied agent. The anar. cognate noun περιτομή is a dat. of means: "you were circumcised with a circumcision" (RSV). Ἀχειροποιήτῳ is dat. sg. fem. (agreeing with περιτομῇ) of ἀχειροποίητος, -ον, a two-termination adj. meaning "not made by (human) hand," i.e., "spiritual" (see Turner, *Words* 363). This περιτομὴ ἀχειροποίητος is to be equated with the περιτομὴ τοῦ Χριστοῦ of v. 11c (BAGD 653a).

ἐν τῇ ἀπεκδύσει

Ἀπεκδύσει is dat. (after ἐν) sg. of ἀπέκδυσις, -εως, ἡ, the act of taking off clothes (nouns in -σις are nouns of action, MH 373). In the double pref., -εκ- means "off from" and ἀπ(ο)- is either intensive or perfective ("completely," NAB; cf. JB, "the complete stripping"; Moulton 111-112; MH 297-298, 310; Lightfoot 187). If τῇ denotes poss., it refers either to the Colossian believers (note περιετμήθητε) or to Christ (note ἐν ᾧ), either "your" or "his (stripping off)." Ἐν may be:

(1) instr., "by putting off" (RSV, Lohse 92; also JB; ZG 606),
*(2) temp., "when you threw off" (Weymouth, TCNT), or
(3) epex., "consisting of the removal," "in the removal" (NASB; cf. NIV).

τοῦ σώματος τῆς σαρκός

Τοῦ σώματος is an obj. gen. after ἀπεκδύσει, indicating what is stripped off. Τῆς σαρκός could be an epex. gen. after τοῦ σώματος ("the whole body *which consists* of the flesh"; so Lightfoot 182, who paraphrases "the body with all its corrupt and carnal affections"), but is more probably a "Hebrew" or adj. gen. where the gen. of an abstract noun is used in place of an adj. of quality (MH 440), either "his physical body" (in ref. to Christ; Moule 96), or "your fleshly body" (in ref. to believers; BAGD 83c; sim. ZG 606; JB), "your sinful nature" (Weymouth), "this sinful self" (GNB). In one case σάρξ is an ethically neutral term ("physical"; "earthly," TCNT), in the other, a pejorative moral term ("fleshly," "sinful"; cf. 2:18).

ἐν τῇ περιτομῇ τοῦ Χριστοῦ

As in the previous phrase, ἐν may be:

(1) instr., "by the circumcision of Christ" (NASB) or "with Christ's circum-
    cision" (NAB; sim. Moffatt, GNB, NIV),
(2) temp., "when you . . . received the circumcision of the Christ" (TCNT),
    or
*(3) epex., "in true Christian circumcision" (Weymouth; sim. NEB mg., JB;
    cf. NEB, "this is Christ's way of circumcision").

The gen. τοῦ Χριστοῦ may be construed in any one of three ways:

(1) obj., "the circumcision performed on Christ/experienced by Christ,"
    alluding not to his circumcision on the eighth day (Lk. 2:21) but to his
    death when he stripped off his physical body (Moule 96; O'Brien 117;
    NEB mg.),
(2) subj., "a circumcision effected by Christ" (Goodspeed; sim. GNB, NIV;
    Vincent 907), alluding to the "circumcision of the heart," although
    Goodspeed interprets it to be the removal of the "material nature"; or to
    "the circumcision willed by Christ" (cf. Zerwick, *Analysis* 450), or
*(3) poss., "Christ's circumcision" (NAB; sim. NEB, JB; cf. Turner, *Words*
    365) or *adj., "Christian circumcision" (Weymouth), or the so-called
    "mystical genitive" where τοῦ Χριστοῦ = ἐν Χριστῷ, "the circumcision
    undergone (by those) in Christ" (cf. Z §§ 38-39; ZG 606).

From these various options regarding ἐν and τοῦ Χριστοῦ three main possibilities emerge. "Also in him you were circumcised with a circumcision not performed by human hands, . . .":

(1) ". . . a circumcision (epex. ἐν) performed by Christ (subj. gen.), in the
    stripping off (epex. or temp. ἐν) of the sinful nature" (sim. Goodspeed,
    GNB, NIV). The major difficulty here is that the circumcision is simul-
    taneously in or through Christ (ἐν ᾧ) and by Christ (τοῦ Χριστοῦ, subj.
    gen.).
(2) ". . . when (temp. ἐν) Christ stripped off his physical body in (epex. ἐν)
    his own (obj. gen.) circumcision" (sim. Moule 94-96; O'Brien 116-117).
    Neither of the parallels alleged to support this understanding is conclu-
    sive: in 1:22 the reference to Christ's physical body is made clear by

αὐτοῦ; it is unlikely that Christ is the unexpressed subj. of the cognate
vb. (ἀπεκδυσάμενος) in 2:15 (see discussion below).
*(3) ". . . when (temp. ἐν) you stripped off your fleshly nature in (epex. ἐν)
Christ's (poss. gen.) circumcision," i.e., in a Christian circumcision of
the heart (sim. Weymouth and, in part, JB). Ἀπεκδυσάμενοι τὸν παλαιὸν
ἄνθρωπον in 3:9 (cf. 3:5) is a significant parallel.

On the third of these views, which is to be preferred, v. 11 presents
spiritual circumcision, not baptism, as the Christian counterpart to physical
circumcision. A contrast is implied between circumcision as an external, physical act performed by human hands on a portion of the flesh eight days after
birth and circumcision as an inward, spiritual act carried out by divine agency
on the whole fleshly nature at the time of regeneration. Although the OT knew
of such a "circumcision of the heart" (Deut. 10:16, 30:6; Jer. 4:4; Ezek. 44:7),
Paul speaks of this divestiture of the old man as distinctively "Christ's circumcision," a circumcision that characterizes the followers of Christ.

VERSE 12

συνταφέντες αὐτῷ

Nom. pl. masc. (agreeing with the pl. subj. of περιετμήθητε, v. 11) of the second
aor. pass. ptc. of συνθάπτω, bury together with; pass. be buried with (+ dat.
αὐτῷ). In relation to the finite vb. περιετμήθητε, this aor. ptc. here does not
express antecedent action (first burial, then circumcision), but either contemporaneous action (circumcision and burial occurring simultaneously at baptism) or subsequent action (first spiritual circumcision [? = death with Christ;
cf. v. 20], then burial with Christ; cf. Rom. 6:3-8). The pref. of a compound
vb. (such as συν-θάπτω) is sometimes repeated as a separate prep. (as in v. 13,
συνεζωοποίησεν ὑμᾶς-σὺν αὐτῷ, the only such use of σύν in the NT); sometimes
a different prep. is used; and sometimes, as here, there is no repetition of the
pref. (cf. Moule, *Idiom Book* 90-91; R 559-562).

ἐν τῷ βαπτισμῷ

There are two NT words for "baptism": βαπτισμός, -ου, ὁ, the act or process
of dipping, washing, or immersion; and βάπτισμα, -ατος, τό, the rite or ordinance of baptism. On the basis of external evidence alone, neither of the
alternative rdgs. (βαπτισμῷ, βαπτίσματι, both dat. [sg.] after ἐν) is more likely
than the other, but βαπτισμῷ is to be preferred (UBS gives it a "C" rating in
all edd.) as the more difficult rdg. because (a) here it bears the unusual sense
of "rite of baptism"; and (b) in the early church it was the less common term

for Christian baptism. See Metzger 623; Lightfoot 182. On the βαπτ- word group, see Turner, *Words* 37-41.

'Εν is locat. ("in [the rite of] baptism"; Barclay has "in the act of baptism") or temp. ("at your baptism"; "when you were baptised," GNB, JB). The art. τῇ may indicate that the well-known Christian rite is spoken of or may be poss. ("in your baptism," Weymouth, Moffatt). See For Further Study 28, "Christian Baptism."

ἐν ᾧ καί

There are two possible antecedents of ᾧ (dat. sg. masc. or neut. of the rel. pron. ὅς, ἥ, ὅ):

(1) αὐτῷ = Christ (thus W. Grundmann, TDNT 7.792 and n. 122; Lohse 92, 99, 104 n. 73; O'Brien 102, 119) or

*(2) βαπτισμῷ or the alternative rdg. βαπτίσματι (so RV, TCNT, Weymouth, Moffatt, Goodspeed, RSV, NEB, NASB, GNB, JB, Barclay, NAB; Lightfoot 183; Robertson, *Pictures* 492; A. Oepke, TDNT 1.545).

Although *prima facie* v. 11a affords an exact parallel to (1) (where ἐν ᾧ καί can refer only to Christ), several considerations count against this view:

(a) The true parallel to ἐν ᾧ . . . συνηγέρθητε is the immediately preceding συνταφέντες . . . ἐν τῷ βαπτισμῷ;

(b) it is more natural to regard the καί as linking συνηγέρθητε with συνταφέντες than with the more remote περιετμήθητε;

(c) the concept of resurrection with Christ in baptism is expressed in Rom. 6:4, 8-11, 13; and

(d) it is awkward to envisage spiritual resurrection as being both *with* Christ and *in* Christ (Eph. 2:6 is not a precise parallel because of different word-order).

'Εν could be instr. (thus JB, "by baptism"; Moffatt, "thereby") but more probably is locat. ("in which" or "in baptism"; thus most EVV).

συνηγέρθητε

2 pl. aor. pass. indic. of συνεγείρω, cause to rise up with; pass. be raised/rise up with. Tr.: "you were raised along with (συν-) him (= Christ)," "you shared his resurrection." God is the implied agent; cf. vv. 12b, 13b. The ref. is to a past, spiritual resurrection to "newness of life" (Rom. 6:4), not a future, somatic resurrection to immortality, although the former both precedes and guarantees the latter. For Paul the resurrection of believers is a two-stage event—a resurrection with Christ in baptism (cf. Eph. 2:5-6), and a resurrection to become like Christ at the End (Rom. 8:29; Phil. 3:20-21). See For Further Study 29, "Resurrection with Christ."

διὰ τῆς πίστεως τῆς ἐνεργείας τοῦ θεοῦ

"Through your belief," διά + gen. expressing means (or even cause, "because you believed," NAB; see BAGD 180b for this latter use of διά) and the art. denoting poss. (as NEB, JB, NIV). Πίστις has a subj. (or act.) sense, "trust," "confidence" (BAGD 663a). Τῆς ἐνεργείας (gen. sg. of ἐνέργεια, -ας, ἡ, working, action, operation) is obj. gen., for in Paul the gen. after πίστις normally expresses the obj. of faith unless it refers to the person who believes. Τοῦ θεοῦ will then be a subj. gen.—"through your faith in the effective power exercised by God." Both gens. are art. on the basis of the canon of Apollonius. Conceivably, however, these two gens. could be (respectively) subj. and poss.—"through the faith produced (in you) by the activity of God" (cf. Weymouth).

τοῦ ἐγείραντος αὐτὸν ἐκ νεκρῶν

Gen. sg. masc. (agreeing with τοῦ θεοῦ) of the aor. act. ptc. of ἐγείρω, arouse, raise. This art. ptc., which here describes (rather than identifies) God (cf. Burton §§ 295, 426), is equivalent to a rel. clause (cf. BDF § 412; R 764; T 152): "who raised him [Christ, vv. 11c, 12a] from the dead." Ἐκ νεκρῶν means "from the realm of (ἐκ) the dead (οἱ νεκροί)," "from among the dead" (Weymouth); or, if νεκροί stands for θάνατος (concrete for abstract), "from death" (GNB) (cf. 1:18). The expression is anar., being a common, stereotyped prep. phrase (cf. BDF § 255; T 180).

VERSE 13

καὶ ὑμᾶς νεκροὺς ὄντας

Since v. 13 is a restatement of v. 12b, καὶ ὑμᾶς should be rendered not "you also," but "and you" or "Yes, you . . ." (Goodspeed). Ὑμᾶς is "you Gentiles," while ἡμῖν (v. 13c) is "all of us, Jews and Gentiles" (cf. Lightfoot 175-176). Lit. "and you, being dead" (RV).

Ὄντας is acc. pl. masc. (agreeing with ὑμᾶς, the obj. of συνεζωοποίησεν) of the pres. ptc. of εἰμί, be. It is an anar. adv. ptc. that is temp. ("when you were dead," NASB, NIV; NAB, "even when . . .") or concessive ("although you were dead," NEB; cf. Moffatt and 1:21) in mng. "You who were dead" (Goodspeed; cf. TCNT) would have been expressed with ὑμᾶς τοὺς ὄντας νεκρούς. Because of its relation to the finite vb. συνεζωοποίησεν, which is aor., this ptc. refers to past time. Although in v. 12 νεκροί refers to those physically dead, here it is used of persons spiritually dead (cf. Rom. 7:9) rather than of those liable to physical or eternal death.

ἐν τοῖς παραπτώμασιν καὶ τῇ ἀκροβυστίᾳ τῆς σαρκὸς ὑμῶν

Παραπτώμασιν is dat. pl. of παράπτωμα, -ατος, τό, trespass, transgression, sin (see Turner, *Words* 414-415). Ἀκροβυστίᾳ is dat. sg. of ἀκροβυστία, -ας, ἡ, (the state of) uncircumcision; the Gentiles. Σάρξ may refer to "the material that covers the bones of a human . . . body" (BAGD 743b), "flesh," or to the body (cf. Rom. 8:13), or to the sinful nature (cf. 2:11). "The uncircumcision of your flesh" will therefore mean either "your uncircumcised flesh" (BAGD 33d; cf. Moffatt), "your physical uncircumcision" (cf. Goodspeed), or "your uncircumcised nature" (TCNT), "the uncircumcision of your sinful nature" (NIV). Given the probable distinction between σάρξ and τὸ σῶμα τῆς σαρκός ("fleshly nature," 2:11), the former option is to be preferred; that is, the physical uncircumcision of the Gentiles was a symbol of their alienation from God (cf. Eph. 2:11-12) and unregenerate state.

When, as here, two nouns are coordinated but differ in gender and number, the repetition of the article is customary (R 789). On the other hand, the single ἐν illustrates the close connection between sin and paganism; the Gentiles were pagan sinners (cf. 1 Pet. 4:3-4). This ἐν may be:

(1) instr., "through" (RV),
(2) locat., "in" (BAGD 534d; R 658; Weymouth, Moffatt, NASB, NIV; Lohse 92, 107 and n. 90), or
*(3) causal, "because of" (TCNT, NEB, GNB, JB; Lightfoot 184; O'Brien 122)

Tr.: "and when you were dead because of your trespasses and your uncircumcised flesh. . . ."

συνεζωοποίησεν ὑμᾶς σὺν αὐτῷ

3 sg. aor. act. indic. of συζωοποιέω, make alive together with (someone). Before the aug. ε- the ν that was assimilated before ζ reappears. The parallel in Eph. 2:4-5 shows that "God" is the unexpressed subj. of the vb. and that σὺν αὐτῷ means not "with Himself [Christ]" (Weymouth) but "together with him [Christ]." Σύν does not mean "at the same time as," or even "in the same way as," but rather "along with" in the sense of "in the wake of." It is not that the spiritual resurrection of believers occurred at the time of the bodily resurrection of Christ or simply that his resurrection formed the pattern for theirs. Rather, the resurrection of Christians from spiritual deadness to new life is grounded in, and a consequence of, Christ's own rising from the realm of the dead to immortal life. See For Further Study 29, "Resurrection with Christ."

This second ὑμᾶς in v. 13 is resumptive, being repeated for clarity (R 1205) after the lengthy qualification of the first ὑμᾶς. Supported by א* A

C K 1739 syr^{p, h} cop^{sa, bo} *al* and given a "C" rating in the three UBS edd., it
is omitted in some MSS, doubtless to avoid apparent redundancy and the
awkward juxtaposition of ὑμᾶς and ἡμῖν, and is replaced in other MSS (notably
p⁴⁶ B 33) by ἡμᾶς in assimilation to the ἡμῖν that follows. See Metzger 623.

χαρισάμενος ἡμῖν πάντα τὰ παραπτώματα

Nom. sg. masc. (agreeing with the unexpressed subj. of συνεζωοποίησεν) of
the aor. mid. ptc. of dep. χαρίζομαι, bestow freely; forgive (+ dat. of person
forgiven [here ἡμῖν] and acc. of thing forgiven [πάντα τὰ παραπτώματα, acc. pl.
of παράπτωμα, -ατος, τό, trespass, transgression, sin]). Grammatically, this
bestowal of divine forgiveness is contemporaneous with the divine vivification
("though logically antecedent," Robertson, *Pictures* 494) or antecedent to it
(as RSV, "having forgiven us all our trespasses").

After the repeated ὑμᾶς in v. 13a and b, ἡμῖν adverts to "Jews and Gentiles
alike" (Lightfoot 176; cf. 184). After ἡμῖν, the art. τά is clearly poss. On πᾶς
with an art. pl. noun, see on 1:4. Tr.: "all our sins, none excluded."

VERSE 14

ἐξαλείψας τὸ καθ' ἡμῶν χειρόγραφον τοῖς δόγμασιν ὃ ἦν ὑπεναντίον ἡμῖν

Nom. sg. masc. (agreeing with the unexpressed subj. of συνεζωοποίησεν) of
the aor. act. ptc. of ἐξαλείφω, wipe out; obliterate, remove, destroy. The pref.
ἐξ- has perfective force (cf. MH 308-309), "cancelled out" (NASB) or
"completely obliterated." The ptc. probably denotes action simultaneous with
χαρισάμενος, which it explains (Robertson, *Pictures* 494), but it could specify
a new, subsequent action—"Further, he cancelled . . ." (note the καί before
ἦρκεν, v. 14b).

A χειρόγραφον (-ου, τό) was a handwritten document (cf. MH 271) or
note of any description, and in particular a signed certificate of debt in which
the signature legalized the debt (cf. Phlm. 18-19), a promissory note signed by
the debtor (cf. E. Lohse, TDNT 9.435). Suggested identifications of this IOU
or bond are numerous, the most probable being the Mosaic law itself (cf. Eph.
2:15), regarded as a bill of debt; or a writ of accusation regarding the Mosaic
law; or the Jewish obligation to keep the Mosaic law and the Gentile obligation
to keep the moral law, the one debt being acknowledged by contract (Deut.
27:9-26), the other by conscience (Rom. 2:14-16). See further O'Brien 124-
125.

The position of καθ' ἡμῶν shows that it qualifies τὸ χειρόγραφον: "the
bond that stood against us" (BAGD 201c, 880d; cf. 405d, Goodspeed), a sense

that Vincent (908) paraphrases as "which stood to our debit, binding us legally."
It is also possible that this prep. phrase (κατά + gen.) means "that testified
against us" or "which was made out against us" (Lohse 92).

If καθ' ἡμῶν highlights the brute fact of indebtedness, the rel. clause ὅ
ἥν ὑπεναντίον ἡμῖν emphasizes the direct and active opposition of the signed
statement of indebtedness: "which was directly hostile to us" (TCNT). Not
only was the χειρόγραφον an accusation of guilt; it also constituted a threat of
penalty because of human inability to discharge the debt. Ὅ is nom. sg. neut.
(agreeing with χειρόγραφον in number and gender, but being the subj. of ἥν it
is nom.) of the rel. pron. Ὑπεναντίον is nom. sg. neut. (agreeing with ὅ) of
ὑπεναντίος, -α, -ον, opposed, hostile (+ dat.; here ἡμῖν).

Τοῖς δόγμασιν (dat. pl. δόγμα, -ατος, τό, decree, ordinance) probably
refers to the demands of the Mosaic law (thus G. Kittel, TDNT 2.231). This
expression has been construed in several ways:

(1) with ἐξαλείψας: the law was abrogated
     (a) "by means of (instr. dat.) the precepts" of the gospel (cf. Lightfoot
          186 on the Greek Fathers), or
     (b) "through (instr. dat.) [Christ's keeping of] the decrees" of the law;
(2) with καθ' ἡμῶν:
     (a) "the bond that was against us by (instr. dat.) its ordinances" (RV
          mg.; sim. Zerwick, *Analysis* 450; NAB), or
     (b) the writing that witnesses against mankind "in virtue of (causal dat.)
          the ordinances" (J. Schneider, TDNT 7.577);
(3) with ὅ ἥν ὑπεναντίον ἡμῖν: the certificate of indebtedness "which was
     against us because of (causal dat.) the decrees" (T 242; sim. Lohse 92,
     109-110, who suggests [109] that τοῖς δόγμασιν is placed first to empha-
     size the legal basis for the certificate's testimony against mankind);
(4) with both καθ' ἡμῶν and ὅ ἥν κτλ.: "the IOU which, because of (causal
     dat.) the regulations, was against us and stood opposed to us" (O'Brien
     102, 125; cf. RSV); or
*(5) with χειρόγραφον, understanding τοῖς δόγμασιν as:
     (a) dat. after the vb. "subscribe to" implied in χειρόγραφον: "our sub-
          scription to the ordinances" (the view of J. A. T. Robinson, cited by
          Moule 98; *Idiom Book* 45 n. 2; cf. T 219). This could be classified
          as a dat. of ref. or respect,
     (b) locat. dat. after an implied γεγραμμένον: "the bond written in ordi-
          nances" (RV),
     (c) epex. dat.: "the bond that consisted of ordinances" (TCNT; so also
          NASB; G. Kittel, TDNT 2.231; Lightfoot 185; cf. Moffatt; Moule,
          Idiom Book 45; ἐν δόγμασιν in Eph. 2:15), or

*(d) associative dat. or dat. of accompanying circumstances (cf. BDF
        § 198; T 240-241): "the written code, with its regulations" (NIV),
        "the bond, ordinances and all" (sim. Weymouth, GNB; cf. BAGD
        201c; Goodspeed).

καὶ αὐτὸ ἦρκεν

3 sg. pf. act. indic. of αἴρω, lift up, take away. With ἦρκεν there is a change
from ptcs. to a finite vb. and from aors. to a pf. This pf. tense points to present
freedom from indebtedness after the complete abrogation (ἐξαλείψας) of the
bond. Αὐτό (acc. sg. neut. of αὐτός, -ή, -ό, he, she, it) refers back to τὸ . . .
χειρόγραφον.

ἐκ τοῦ μέσου

Whether or not ἐκ (τοῦ) μέσου αἴρειν (found also in 1 Cor. 5:2) is a "phraseo-
logical Latinism" equivalent to *de medio tollere* ("do away with, abolish"), as
BDF § 5(3b) asserts (against this see Lohse 110 n. 121), ἐκ τοῦ μέσου is certainly a "prepositional circumlocution" (R 648) meaning "from our midst,"
"aside," and reinforcing the sense of ἦρκεν. Lit. tr.: "and he has taken it away
from our midst" = "he has set it aside" (NEB), "he has taken it out of our way"
(TCNT; cf. RV), "he has done away with it completely" (cf. GNB), "he has
removed it from sight" (cf. Lightfoot 176, 187).
       God is clearly the subj. of συνεζωοποίησεν (v. 13) (see Lightfoot 183).
But, arguing that ἀπεκδυσάμενος (v. 15) can mean only "having divested himself" and must therefore refer to Christ, some commentators find a change of
subj. from God to Christ either at ἐξαλείψας (an option preferred by Moule
100-101), at ἦρκεν (Lightfoot 183, 187), or at ἀπεκδυσάμενος (GNB). Most
EVV, however, retain God as the subj. throughout vv. 13-15, and this seems
preferable.

προσηλώσας αὐτὸ τῷ σταυρῷ

Nom. sg. masc. (agreeing with the unexpressed subj. of ἦρκεν) of the aor. act.
ptc. of προσηλόω, nail (fast) τί (acc.) τινι (dat.), something (here αὐτό =
χειρόγραφον) to something (here τῷ σταυρῷ). This adv. ptc. may be simply
temp. ("having nailed it to the cross," NASB), but given that this is an aor. ptc.
following a finite aor. vb., it is more probably modal, specifying (in a paradox;
cf. ἑαυτὸν ἐκένωσεν . . . λαβών, Phil. 2:7) the means by which the removal of
the certificate of debt took place (cf. Burton §§ 139-141): "he has set it aside
by nailing it to the cross" (sim. TCNT, GNB, JB; J. Schneider, TDNT 7.577;
cf. Goodspeed). What is envisaged is not the actual destruction of the bond
(*pace* Lightfoot 176, 187), but the cancellation of its validity by the death of
Christ.

VERSE 15

ἀπεκδυσάμενος τὰς ἀρχὰς καὶ τὰς ἐξουσίας

Nom. sg. masc. (agreeing with the unexpressed sg. subj. of ἦρκεν) of the aor. mid. ptc. of ἀπεκδύομαι. This vb. is found only twice in the NT, here and in 3:9 (ἀπεκδυσάμενοι). In each case it is mid. with the obj. in the acc. Here it is an adv. ptc. denoting action antecedent to the finite vb. ἐδειγμάτισεν ("he displayed in public"). If it is mid. proper, it means "he divested/stripped himself" (see the defense of this meaning in Lightfoot 187-189) of the powers and authorities that encircled him like a garment. If the mid. is here used with an act. mng. (so BDF § 316[1]; R 805; Z § 235; A. Oepke, TDNT 2.319; T 55, but see Turner's later *Insights* 133-134), the sense will be "he disarmed" the powers and authorities or "he stripped" them of their armor or their power. Yet even here the mid. sense is not really lost, for the action is performed for the subject's own interest. We concur with MH 310 that ἀπεκδύομαι connotes the complete (ἀπ[ο]-) stripping of oneself or another person, in one's own interest. The other ambiguity in this clause is whether God or Christ is the subj.

The following options of translation emerge:

*(1) With God the subj. and ἀπεκδ. act. in mng.: "He [God] disarmed the principalities and powers" (RSV; sim. BAGD 83c; A. Oepke, TDNT 2.319; Goodspeed, NASB, NAB, NIV; NEB mg., "despoiled"; Lohse 92, 111-112, "stripped"; O'Brien 102, 126-127, "stripped . . . of their authority and dignity").

(2) With Christ the subj. and ἀπεκδ. act. in mng.: "Christ stripped the spiritual rulers and authorities of their power" (GNB mg.).

(3) With God the subj. and ἀπεκδ. mid. in mng.: "He [God] discarded the cosmic powers and authorities like a garment" (but it is unclear in this NEB rendering, as also in RV and TCNT, whether or not a change of subj. from God [v. 13] to Christ is intended).

(4) With Christ the subj. and ἀπεκδ. mid. in mng.: "He [Christ] divested himself of the rulers and authorities" (sim. Weymouth, GNB; Lightfoot 176, 187-189; Moule 99-102).

All of these renderings assume that τὰς ἀρχὰς καὶ τὰς ἐξουσίας is the obj. of ἀπεκδυσάμενος. But the NEB mg. (following the Latin Fathers—see Lightfoot 188) takes this phrase as the obj. of ἐδειγμάτισεν ("he . . . made a spectacle of the cosmic powers and authorities") and supplies "his physical body" (τὸ σῶμα τῆς σαρκὸς αὐτοῦ, cf. 1:22) as the obj. of ἀπεκδυσάμενος: "he [Christ] stripped himself of his physical body" (sim. RV mg.). While v. 11 is a possible parallel, nothing in the immediate context suggests this daring metaphor.

The repetition of the art. with ἐξουσίας suggests that two sets of entities (not one) are envisaged. Since on any view ἀπεκδυσάμενος implies conflict and conquest, "the powers and authorities" will be hostile forces, whether cosmic, angelic, or demonic. See on v. 10 and For Further Study 27, "Principalities and Powers."

ἐδειγμάτισεν ἐν παρρησίᾳ

3 sg. aor. act. indic. of δειγματίζω, make an example (δεῖγμα) of, make a public spectacle of; expose (see H. Schlier, TDNT 2.31). The implied obj. is τὰς ἀρχὰς κτλ. Since this vb. already denotes a public display, the prep. phrase ἐν παρρησίᾳ, with ἐν expressing manner (R 589) or attendant circumstance, will here mean "boldly" (Weymouth, NEB mg.; Lightfoot 189-190; Moule 100) rather than "in public," "openly."

θριαμβεύσας αὐτούς

Nom. sg. masc. (agreeing with the unexpressed subj. of ἐδειγμάτισεν) of the aor. act. ptc. of θριαμβεύω. This vb. was originally intr. in mng., "celebrate a triumph," but is trans. in the NT (found only here and in 2 Cor. 2:14), "lead in (a) triumphal procession" or "exhibit in a public procession," with acc. of the persons led in procession (here αὐτούς) or of the spoils of war on display in the procession (cf. BAGD 363d; BDF § 148[1]; MH 400). Like προσηλώσας in v. 14, this ptc. is an aor. ptc. of identical action (see Burton §§ 139-141), here specifying the means by which the public display occurred: "he boldly displayed them in public by leading them in triumphal procession" (sim. GNB). If the ptc. is temp. (". . . when he led them . . ."; sim. TCNT, Weymouth), the sense is not materially altered, for the temp. and modal categories of the adv. ptc. are closely related (cf. T 154-157, who has a single "modal-temporal" category).

After the two fem. nouns ἀρχάς and ἐξουσίας, one would expect αὐτάς (acc. pl. fem. of αὐτός, -ή, -ό), not αὐτούς (acc. pl. masc.). This is a case of "construction according to sense" (constructio ad sensum; T 40), showing that the powers and authorities are not abstract entities but personal beings (cf. BDF § 134[3]).

ἐν αὐτῷ

In this phrase, which concludes this paragraph as it began it (v. 9a), ἐν could be locat. ("in," "on") or instr. ("by," "through"), and the antecedent of αὐτῷ could be τῷ σταυρῷ in v. 14 or αὐτῷ in v. 13, i.e., the cross or Christ. It is highly improbable that τὸ χειρόγραφον is the antecedent (unless it is understood as "this cancelled bond") or that ἐν αὐτῷ = ἐν αὑτῷ (rough breathing), "by himself" (cf. Vulg., in semetipso). Thus we find in the EVV, on the one hand, "in him"

(RSV, NIV mg.; Lohse 92, 99, 112-113, 113 n. 145; O'Brien 128; cf. 102), "in the person of Christ" (NAB), "through him" (BAGD 363d; Goodspeed, NASB); and on the other, "in it" (RV, RSV mg.; cf. Moffatt), "on the cross" (TCNT; Moule 102; cf. NEB, GNB; Lightfoot 176, 190), "by the cross" (NIV; cf. ZG 607; Weymouth). If Christ is taken to be the subj. in v. 15, then ἐν αὐτῷ will refer to the cross. As Lightfoot (190) puts it, "the convict's gibbet is the victor's car."

TRANSLATION

[9] For in him there dwells the whole fullness of deity in bodily form. [10] And you have your completeness in him, who is the head over every power and authority. [11] Also in him you were circumcised with a circumcision not performed by human hands, when you stripped off your fleshly nature in Christ's circumcision. [12] You were buried with him in baptism, and in baptism you were raised with him through your faith in the action of God who raised him from the dead. [13] And when you were dead because of your trespasses and your uncircumcised flesh, God brought you to life together with Christ. He forgave us all our trespasses, [14] cancelled the bond, along with its decrees, that stood against us and threatened us, and has set it aside by nailing it to the cross. [15] And after disarming the powers and authorities, he boldly displayed them in public by leading them in triumphal procession through Christ.

EXPANDED PARAPHRASE

[9] For it is in Christ, and Christ alone, that all the fullness of God's being now has its permanent abode in bodily form. [10] And therefore it is in him who is completely God that you have come to completeness, the satisfaction of every spiritual need—in Christ, who is the sovereign head over every cosmic power and authority, whether conceivable or real. [11] Furthermore, it is also in Christ that you were circumcised, but this circumcision was no external rite performed by human hands on actual flesh. Rather, it involved the stripping off of your fleshly nature in a heart-circumcision characteristic of the followers of Christ. [12] This heart-circumcision took place at the time of your baptism, when you were identified with Christ not only in burial but also in resurrection, for you were spiritually raised with him through your faith in the powerful activity of God, the God who demonstrated that power by raising Jesus from the dead. [13] Indeed! For when you were spiritually dead because of your trespasses and because you were rank pagans without knowledge of the true God, God raised you to spiritual life in union with Christ whom he raised. And not only so: At

that time he also forgave us all our trespasses; [14] he completely cancelled the certificate of indebtedness—broken decrees and all—that stood as a testimony against us and was an ominous threat to us; in fact he has removed it altogether from sight by nailing it to the cross; [15] what is more, after he had rendered the powers and authorities helpless, he boldly exposed them to public display when, through Christ's death, he led them in his triumphal procession as his enemy captives.

FOR FURTHER STUDY

26. The Deity of Christ (2:9)

Berkouwer, G. C., *The Person of Christ*, tr. J. Vriend (Grand Rapids: Eerdmans, 1954).

Brunner, E., *The Mediator*, tr. Olive Wyon (Philadelphia: Westminster, 1934).

Cullmann, O., *The Christology of the New Testament*, tr. S. C. Guthrie and C. A. M. Hall (Philadelphia: Westminster, 1963[2]).

Grillmeier, A., *Christ in Christian Tradition*, vol. 1, tr. J. Bowden (Atlanta: John Knox, 1975[2]).

Longenecker, R. N., *The Christology of Early Jewish Christianity* (London: SCM, 1970; reprint Grand Rapids: Baker, 1981).

Mackintosh, H. R., *The Doctrine of the Person of Jesus Christ* (Edinburgh: Clark, 1914[3]).

Morris, L., *The Lord From Heaven* (Grand Rapids: Eerdmans, 1958).

Nash, H. S., "θειότης—θεότης (Romans 1:20; Col. 2:9)," *JBL* 18 (1899) 1-34.

Pannenberg, W., *Jesus—God and Man*, tr. L. L. Wilkins and D. A. Priebe (Philadelphia: Westminster, 1968).

Rawlinson, A. E. J., *The New Testament Doctrine of the Christ* (New York: Longmans, 1929).

Rowdon, H. H., ed., *Christ the Lord. Studies in Christology presented to Donald Guthrie* (Downers Grove: IVP, 1982).

Taylor, V., *The Person of Christ in New Testament Teaching* (London: Macmillan, 1958).

Warfield, B. B., *The Lord of Glory* (New York: American Tract Society, 1907).

*Wells, D. F., *The Person of Christ* (Westchester, IL: Crossway, 1984).

27. Principalities and Powers in Paul (2:10, 15)

Berkhof, H., *Christ and the Powers*, tr. J. H. Yoder (Scottdale, PA: Herald, 1977).

Caird, G. B., *Principalities and Powers: A Study in Pauline Theology* (Oxford: Clarendon, 1956).

Carr, W., *Angels and Principalities: The Background, Meaning and Development of the Pauline Phrase* "hai archai kai hai . . . exousiai" (Cambridge: Cambridge University, 1981).

Cullmann, O., *The State in the New Testament* (London: SCM, 1957) 95-114.

Heuvel, A. van den, *These Rebellious Powers* (London: SCM, 1966).

Lee, J. Y., "Interpreting the Demonic Powers in Pauline Thought," *NovT* 12 (1970) 54-69.

Macgregor, G. H. C., "Principalities and Powers: The Cosmic Background of Paul's Thought," *NTS* 1 (1954-55) 17-28.

Morrison, C. D., *The Powers That Be: Earthly Rulers and Demonic Powers in Romans 13:1-7* (London: SCM, 1960).

*O'Brien, P. T., "Principalities and Powers and their Relationship to Structures," *Reformed Theological Review* 40 (1981) 1-10.

Schlier, H., *Principalities and Powers in the New Testament* (New York: Herder, 1961).

Wink, W., *Unmasking the Powers: The Invisible Powers that Determine Human Existence* (Philadelphia: Fortress, 1986).

28. Christian Baptism (2:12)

Aland, K., *Did the Early Church Baptize Infants?* tr. G. R. Beasley-Murray (Philadelphia: Westminster, 1963).

Beasley-Murray, G. R., *Baptism in the New Testament* (Grand Rapids: Eerdmans, 1962).

*Bridge, D. and Phypers, D., *The Water That Divides: The Baptism Debate* (Downers Grove, IL: IVP, 1977).

Dixon, N., *Troubled Waters* (London: Epworth, 1979).

Flemington, W. F., *The New Testament Doctrine of Baptism* (London: SPCK, 1957).

Howard, J. K., *New Testament Baptism* (London: Pickering and Inglis, 1970).

Jeremias, J., *Infant Baptism in the First Four Centuries,* tr. D. Cairns (Philadelphia: Westminster, 1960).

Jewett, P. K., *Infant Baptism and the Covenant of Grace* (Grand Rapids: Eerdmans, 1978).

Marcel, P. C., *The Biblical Doctrine of Infant Baptism,* tr. P. E. Hughes (London: Clarke, 1953).

Moody, D., *Baptism: Foundation for Christian Unity* (Philadelphia: Westminster, 1967).

Murray, J., *Christian Baptism* (Grand Rapids: Baker, 1952).

Schnackenburg, R., *Baptism in the Thought of St. Paul*, tr. G. R. Beasley-Murray (New York: Herder, 1964).

White, R. E. O., *The Biblical Doctrine of Initiation* (London: Hodder, 1960).

29. Resurrection with Christ (2:12-13)

Faw, C. E., "Death and Resurrection in Paul's Letters," *The Journal of Bible and Religion* 27 (1959) 291-298.

Glasson, T. F., "Dying and Rising with Christ," *The London Quarterly and Holborn Review* 186 (1961) 286-291.

Grundmann, W., TDNT 7.781-797.

*Harris, M. J., *Raised Immortal. Resurrection and Immortality in the New Testament* (Grand Rapids: Eerdmans, 1985) 101-108.

Ridderbos, H., *Paul: An Outline of His Theology*, tr. J. R. de Witt (Grand Rapids: Eerdmans, 1975) 206-214.

Tannehill, R. C., *Dying and Rising with Christ* (Berlin: Töpelmann, 1967).

Wilson, W. E., "The Development of Paul's Doctrine of Dying and Rising Again with Christ," *ExpT* 42 (1930-31) 562-565.

HOMILETICAL SUGGESTIONS

Christ, the Remedy against Error (2:9-15)

1. Why is Christ the remedy against error and the standard of truth (cf. κατὰ Χριστόν, v. 8c)? (vv. 9-10)
    (a) Because the fullness of deity resides in him (v. 9) and
    (b) because Christians have completeness in him, the universal Head (v. 10).
2. How were Christians brought to his completeness? (vv. 11-13b)
    (a) By circumcision of the heart, as followers of Christ (v. 11),
    (b) by being buried with Christ (v. 12a), and
    (c) by being raised with Christ when spiritually dead (vv. 12b-13b).
3. What did God achieve through Christ's death? (vv. 13c-15)
    (a) The forgiveness of trespasses (v. 13c),
    (b) the cancellation of indebtedness (v. 14), and
    (c) the disarming of opposition (v. 15).

Christian Circumcision (2:11)

1. It involves the heart, not the body (ἀχειροποιήτῳ).
2. It involves the excision of the whole fleshly nature, not a mere portion of the flesh (ἐν τῇ ἀπεκδύσει τοῦ σώματος τῆς σαρκός).
3. It is spiritual surgery performed on Christ's followers at the time of their regeneration (ἐν τῇ περιτομῇ τοῦ Χριστοῦ).

Resurrection with Christ (2:12-13; cf. Rom. 6:1-11; Eph. 2:1-10)

1. It occurs in baptism (. . . βαπτισμῷ, ἐν ᾧ καί, v. 12a).
2. It comes about through faith in God (v. 12b).
3. It brings the spiritually dead to life (v. 13a).
4. It involves identification with Christ in his resurrection (σὺν αὐτῷ, v. 13b; cf. v. 12b).

The Sinner's IOU to God (2:14)

1. Its existence:
   (a) It is a signed statement of indebtedness, a promissory note (χειρό-γραφον);
   (b) it refers to broken laws (τοῖς δόγμασιν);
   (c) it stands as a silent testimony against us (καθ᾽ ἡμῶν); and
   (d) it is a witness hostile to us (ὃ ἦν ὑπεναντίον ἡμῖν).
2. Its destruction:
   (a) It is completely cancelled (ἐξαλείψας), and
   (b) totally removed (αὐτὸ ἦρκεν ἐκ τοῦ μέσου), by being
   (c) nailed to Christ's cross (προσηλώσας αὐτὸ τῷ σταυρῷ).

C. WARNING AGAINST MYSTICAL LEGALISM (2:16-19)

16 Μὴ οὖν τις ὑμᾶς κρινέτω ἐν βρώσει καὶ ἐν πόσει ἢ ἐν μέρει ἑορτῆς ἢ νεομηνίας ἢ σαββάτων, 17 ἅ ἐστιν σκιὰ τῶν μελλόντων, τὸ δὲ σῶμα τοῦ Χριστοῦ. 18 μηδεὶς ὑμᾶς καταβραβευέτω θέλων ἐν ταπεινοφροσύνῃ καὶ θρησκείᾳ τῶν ἀγγέλων, ἃ ἑόρακεν ἐμβατεύων, εἰκῇ φυσιούμενος ὑπὸ τοῦ νοὸς τῆς σαρκὸς αὐτοῦ, 19 καὶ οὐ κρατῶν τὴν κεφαλήν, ἐξ οὗ πᾶν τὸ σῶμα διὰ τῶν ἁφῶν καὶ συνδέσμων ἐπιχορηγούμενον καὶ συμβιβαζόμενον αὔξει τὴν αὔξησιν τοῦ θεοῦ.

STRUCTURE

Paul alerts his readers to a further pair of dangers (cf. ἵνα μηδείς, v. 4; μή τις, v. 8), thus specifying in more detail the nature of the "philosophy" of v. 8.

A. μὴ . . . τις	the danger of
ὑμᾶς κρινέτω (v. 16)	illegitimate accusation
ἐν βρώσει	⎧ regarding
καὶ ἐν πόσει	⎨ religious
ἢ ἐν μέρει κτλ.	⎩ observances
B. μηδεὶς	the danger of
ὑμᾶς καταβραβευέτω (v. 18)	unjustifiable disqualification,
θέλων	and its means.
ἐμβατεύων	⎧ Paul's description
φυσιούμενος	⎨ and criticism of
οὐ κρατῶν τὴν κεφαλήν	⎩ the false teachers.
ἐξ	source of growth,
διά	channels of nourishment
	and means of unification
	of the Body

VERSE 16

Μὴ οὖν τις ὑμᾶς κρινέτω

3 sg. pres. act. impv. of κρίνω, judge. In general μή + pres. impv. either demands the termination of some action already begun ("stop . . . !"), or, as here, depicts action that must always be avoided (cf. BDF §§ 335, 336[3]; Burton § 165; Moule, *Idiom Book* 135; Moulton 122-126; R 853-854, 890, 947; T 74-78). It issues general directions (that are less dramatic than those expressed by μή + aor. subjunc.) about a course of conduct to be avoided. Being parallel to καταβραβευέτω ("disqualify," "rob of a prize," "condemn," v. 18), κρινέτω clearly has a pejorative sense: not "adjudicate," but "pass an unfavorable

judgment upon" (BAGD 452 b, c), "sit in judgment" (Weymouth), "take (you) to task" (TCNT, Moffatt, NEB; Lightfoot 191), "pass judgment on" (RSV, NAB; Lohse 114; O'Brien 135). In the light of (cf. οὖν, "therefore") God's triumph in Christ over all spiritual powers that would enslave human beings (vv. 8, 15), the Colossians should resolutely resist any effort that certain propagandists (cf. μὴ . . . τις [. . . κρινέτω], "Do not . . . allow any one," TCNT; sim. Weymouth, NEB) might make to restrict their freedom by legalistic regulations.

ἐν βρώσει καὶ ἐν πόσει

Βρῶσις, -εως, ἡ, eating; food. Πόσις, -εως, ἡ, drinking; drink. Nouns with the suf. -σις generally denote "names of action" *(nomina actionis),* verbal abstracts (MH 373)—thus "eating," "drinking" (TCNT, Weymouth, Moffatt; Lohse 114-115). But, by metonymy, βρῶσις can be equivalent to βρῶμα," food," and πόσις to πόμα, "drink" (thus RSV, NASB; O'Brien 135), so that one could tr. "what you eat or drink" (Goodspeed, NEB, GNB, NAB, NIV).

’Εν is locat./referential ("in the matter of," "regarding"; sim. most EVV) or conceivably instr./causal ("by," NIV; "on the basis of"). Prep. phrases are often anar. (cf. 2:1, 12). The repeated ἐν shows that dietary regulations concerning food and drink are being viewed separately.

ἢ ἐν μέρει ἑορτῆς ἢ νεομηνίας ἢ σαββάτων

Tr.: "or with regard to" (BAGD 280b, 506b), where ἐν μέρει (+ gen.) is a stylistic variation of the previous simple ἐν, used to avoid a succession of five datives. The first ἤ ("or") introduces a third category (after βρῶσις and πόσις; note the threefold ἐν) that consists of three alternatives separated by the second and third uses of ἤ.

’Εορτή, -ῆς, ἡ, festival, feast. Νεομηνία, -ας, ἡ, new moon; first of the month. Remarkably, σάββατον, -ου, τό in either the sg. or the pl. can mean either "sabbath" or "week" (see BAGD 739 a, b, c; BDF § 141[3]; T 27). Tr. "or concerning [the observance of, NEB] a festival, a new moon, or a sabbath day." But it is also possible that the first two nouns are generic sgs. and therefore may be tr. as pls. ("or in connexion with observance of festivals or new moons or sabbaths," Moffatt; sim. JB), or that Paul is referring to "the matter of annual or monthly or weekly festivals" (TCNT; cf. Goodspeed, NAB; and note the reverse order in Gal. 4:10). The three nouns are anar. after ἐν μέρει, in accordance with the canon of Apollonius.

VERSE 17

ἅ ἐστιν σκιὰ τῶν μελλόντων

The antecedent of ἅ (nom. pl. neut. of the rel. pron.) is either σαββάτων (R 712), or regulations in the three categories cited (viz. food, drink, and calendar), or the material objects implied or referred to by βρῶσις and πόσις, or the Law (S. Schulz, TDNT 7.398) as implied by the reference to three types of religious festival. Alternatively ἅ may be very general: "all such things" (GNB), as typifying the old order. As a neut. pl. subject ἅ is followed by a sg. vb. (see 1:16).

Movable ν is found even before initial consonants (here, ἐστιν σκία) (cf. BDF § 20). Σκιά, -ᾶς, ἡ, shadow, a faint outline of an object rather than the object itself. It is nom. after ἐστιν and sg. in spite of the pl. subject ἅ (cf. Gal. 5:19): "these things are a shadow." On the "shadow–reality" antithesis, see S. Schulz, TDNT 7.398; Lohse 116-117; O'Brien 139-140. "The conception of the shadow as thrown before the substance . . . implies both the *unsubstantiality* and the *supersession* of the Mosaic ritual" (Lightfoot 193).

Gen. pl. neut. (here not masc.) of the pres. act. ptc. of μέλλω, be about to. Τὰ μέλλοντα are "the things to come," where the ptc. is used abs. as an adj. that means "future," "to come" (BAGD 501c). Because the reality (the σῶμα) to which the shadow corresponds has arrived, it is appropriate to tr. "the things that were to come" (NIV; O'Brien 135; sim. Weymouth, Goodspeed), "what was to come" (NEB). "What is to come" (TCNT, NASB; cf. Moffatt) is ambiguous, since it could refer to the second Advent and subsequent events. This gen. is either obj. ("these things foreshadow what was to come") or poss./subj. ("these things are a shadow cast by future events"); "a shadow of what was to come" reproduces this ambiguity.

τὸ δὲ σῶμα τοῦ Χριστοῦ

In dramatic contrast (adversative δέ) with the insubstantial "shadow" (σκιά) is the substantial "reality" (the σῶμα): "the reality, however, belongs to Christ." Although σῶμα could also refer to the Body of Christ, the Church (cf. 1:24), or to the resurrection body of the exalted Christ, a double or triple meaning or referent for σῶμα seems improbable, given (a) the absence, on this view, of an explicit pred. and (b) the explicit contrast with σκιά (but see JB mg.; Moule 103; and NAB, "the reality is the body of Christ").

Although the NT epistles usually omit the art. with Χριστός when it is a proper noun (cf. BDF § 260[1]; R 760), art. Χριστός here is a personal name ("Christ," possibly standing for the Christian "economy" [Vincent 910] or era) rather than a title ("the Messiah"; cf. BAGD 887b). As poss. gen. τοῦ Χριστοῦ may mean, with ἐστιν understood, "belongs to Christ" (Weymouth, Moffatt, RSV, NASB; ZG 607; Moule 103), "is found in Christ" (Goodspeed, NIV), or even "is Christ" (GNB, JB).

Food regulations and calendrical observances, and all such legal prescriptions that belonged to the transitory old Age, were merely pale adumbrations of a coming permanent reality now realized in the person and gospel of Christ. The implication is that the shadows not only are now superfluous but actually disappear with the appearance of the "substance."

VERSE 18

μηδεὶς ὑμᾶς καταβραβευέτω

Nom. sg. masc. of the subst. and adj. μηδείς, μηδεμία, μηδέν, nobody; no. 3 sg. pres. act. impv. καταβραβεύω. This vb. has three possible mngs.:

*(1) "disqualify" (F. O. Francis in *Conflict* 166, 197), "declare disqualified" (Moule 104), used of the negative decision of an "umpire" (βραβεύς);

(2) "rob of a (rightful) prize (βραβεῖον)" (sim. RV, Weymouth, NASB, NAB; Lightfoot 190, 193; Zerwick, *Analysis* 451, "arbitrarily declare someone unworthy of the prize of heaven"); the prize would be the benefits of salvation or eternal life (cf. 2 Tim. 4:8); TCNT, however, has "defraud you of the reality" (cf. σῶμα); and

(3) "condemn" (= κατακρίνω; GNB; Lohse 114, 117; O'Brien 135, 141).

The intr. vb. βραβεύω ("act as an umpire") becomes trans. with the pref. κατά- ("against"; thus "give a decision against," "decide against") and therefore may take an acc. (ὑμᾶς; cf. MH 316). Tr.: "Let no one disqualify you."

θέλων ἐν ταπεινοφροσύνῃ καὶ θρησκείᾳ τῶν ἀγγέλων

Nom. sg. masc. (agreeing with μηδείς) of the pres. act. ptc. of θέλω. This ptc. may be cstr.:

(1) in an adv. sense with καταβραβευέτω: "willfully" (cf. 2 Pet. 3:5), "of his own mere will" (RV mg.), "intentionally" (BDF § 148[2]); cf. Moffatt, "Let no one lay down rules for you as he pleases (θέλων), with regard to (ἐν) . . .";

(2) in an adv. or adj. sense with ἐν ταπεινοφροσύνῃ: lit. "willingly by humility" = "by a voluntary humility" (RV; Robertson, *Pictures* 496);

(3) as a ptc. of attendant circumstance, with τοῦτο ποιεῖν understood: "desirous of effecting it [the disqualification] by . . .";

(4) in a modal sense, θέλων ἐν being a Septuagintalism (cf. 2 Sam. 15:26; 1 Kgs. 10:9; Ps. 111:1, LXX) meaning "delighting in" (BAGD 355c;

G. Schrenk, TDNT 3.45 n. 13; Lightfoot 193; Moule 104; *Idiom Book* 183; O'Brien 135, 142): "by delighting in" (NASB); or
*(5) in a modal sense, with θέλω meaning "order, require": "by insisting on" (ZG 607; NAB; cf. RSV, GNB).

In 3:12 ταπεινοφροσύνη, -ης, ἡ (lowliness of mind, humility) is clearly a positive virtue, but here as in 2:23 it has negative overtones—either "false humility" (GNB, NIV), "so-called 'humility'" (TCNT), "flaunted humility," or "self-abasement" (RSV, NASB), "self-mortification" (NEB; cf. W. Grundmann, TDNT 8.22-23). But some regard it as a technical term for "fasting" (Moffatt; F. O. Francis, *Conflict* 167-171, 181) or "readiness to serve" (Lohse 114, 117-118, 126).

The nonrepetition of the prep. ἐν (contrast v. 16) before θρησκεία (-ας, ἡ, [cultic] worship) points to the close conceptual link between this self-humiliation and angel-worship. It may even be a case of hendiadys, false humility expressed in angel-worship: "by insisting on servility in the worship of angels" (NAB). Τῶν ἀγγέλων could possibly be subj. gen. ("the worship [of God] by angels"; "angelic worship," F. O. Francis, *Conflict* 176-183; O'Brien 135, 142-143) but more probably it is obj. ("worship paid to angels," R 500; sim. BAGD 7d; "angel-worship," TCNT, NEB). On "The Cult of Angels at Colossae," see A. L. Williams, *Journal of Theological Studies* 10 (1909) 413-438. What Paul is countering here is not Christian humility but that parade of misguided, false humility or self-humiliation that imagines that God is so holy that he is accessible only through angelic mediation (cf. Lightfoot 101, 115-116).

ἃ ἑόρακεν ἐμβατεύων

῝Α is acc. (as dir. obj. of ἑόρακεν) pl. neut. of the rel. pron. Ἑόρακεν is 3 sg. pf. act. indic. of ὁράω, see. Lit.: "the things that (= what) (such a person) has seen" = "his visions" (Moffatt; cf. Weymouth, Goodspeed, NASB) or "his own experience" (NAB), or even "his visionary (= mystical) experiences."

Nom. sg. masc. of the pres. act. ptc. of ἐμβατεύω. This is the first of three temp. adv. ptcs. (ἐμβατεύων . . . φυσιούμενος . . . οὐ κρατῶν) agreeing with the subject of καταβραβευέτω. These three ptcs. depict the circumstances attendant on the attempted disqualification ("while . . ."). The mng. of ἐμβατεύων is far from clear (see BAGD 254b; MM 205-206; Lohse 119-120; Moule 104-106; F. O. Francis, *Conflict* 171-176, 197-207). Alternatives include:

(1) "taking his stand on" (Weymouth, RSV, NASB; sim. RV mg., NAB), virtually "parading" (cf. Lightfoot 190) or "presuming on" (Moffatt);
(2) "going into detail about" (cf. BAGD 254b; NIV, JB); and
(3) "entering into" (cf. NEB: "people who . . . try to enter into [= conative

pres.] some vision of their own"); following F. O. Francis (*Conflict* 166, 171-176, 197-207), O'Brien takes the ptc. as circumstantial: "the angelic worship [of God], which he has seen upon entering" (135; cf. 144-145).

On all three views (but not O'Brien's) the rel. clause ἃ ἑόρακεν is the obj. of ἐμβατεύων. On views (1) and (3) the background could be certain rites in the mystery religions, either when the initiate actually "entered into" the inner sanctuary that he had first seen in a vision, or when a visitor, seeking an oracular response from a god, "set foot on" or "took his stand on" the sacred area (see further W. M. Ramsay, *The Teaching of Paul in Terms of the Present Day* [New York: Hodder and Stoughton, 1914²] 283-305; H. Preisker, TDNT 2.535-536). On this basis, some propose that ἐμβατεύων has the more general sense of "at his initiation" (A. Fridrichsen, cited in Lohse 120 n. 50) or "during the mystery rites" (Lohse 114, 118-121).

The secondary addition of the negs. οὐκ (F G) or μή (C Ψ vg syr^p *al*) to ἃ probably arose when some scribes either failed to make sense of ἐμβατεύων or wanted to intensify the polemical thrust of the context (the false teachers relied on or paraded the experience of others—what they had not seen, visions they had not in fact had; cf. Metzger 623; Lightfoot 195, 252).

Because of the difficulties of this phrase, several scholars have proposed conjectural emendations (see Lightfoot 195 and the views summarized by F. F. Bruce in *The Epistles to the Colossians, to Philemon, and to the Ephesians* [Grand Rapids: Eerdmans, 1984] 120-121 with n. 130). Many of these conjectures are ingenious, but the more plausible the emendation, the more difficult it is to account for the rise of the reading ἃ ἑόρακεν ἐμβατεύων, which has the support of early representatives of the Alexandrian (p⁴⁶ ℵ* A B) and Western (D*) textual families, and which may with justification be rendered "taking his stand on his visions."

εἰκῇ φυσιούμενος ὑπὸ τοῦ νοὸς τῆς σαρκὸς αὐτοῦ

Nom. sg. masc. (agreeing with the subject of καταβραβευέτω) of the pres. pass. ptc. of φυσιόω, puff up, inflate. Εἰκῇ (adv., "without cause," BAGD 222a; "in a futile manner") should be cstr. with φυσιούμενος rather than with the preceding ἐμβατεύων since it usually stands before the word it qualifies (F. Büchsel, TDNT 2.380), although some scholars have (unnecessarily) cstr. both ptcs. together: "vainly conceited over what he beheld at his initiation" (A. Fridrichsen, cited in BDF § 154; on this view ἃ is probably acc. of respect). Tr.: "inflated without cause" (NASB), "idly puffed up" (Weymouth), "inflated with futile notions." JB takes φυσιούμενος as a refl. mid., "inflating themselves to a false importance."

Ὑπό (+ gen.) denotes agency ("by"). Νοός is gen. sg. of νοῦς, ὁ, mind, intellect, outlook (on the decl. of this noun, see BDF § 52; MH 127, 142). Τῆς σαρκός is probably a Sem. or qualitative gen. (see 1:5, 22), "fleshly," "unspiritual," "materialistic," "dominated by the senses" (ZG 608), but could be subj., "[the attitude] produced by the flesh." The third gen. (αὐτοῦ) is clearly poss. and modifies τοῦ νοὸς τῆς σαρκός, "his sensuous mind" (RSV; cf. 1:22).

Three colorful renderings of this clause may be mentioned:

• NEB: "bursting with the futile conceit of worldly minds"
• BAGD 544d: "groundlessly conceited . . . by his mind, fixed on purely physical things"
• TCNT: "(Such a man . . .) without reason is rendered conceited by his merely human intellect."

VERSE 19

καὶ οὐ κρατῶν τὴν κεφαλήν

Nom. sg. masc. (agreeing with the subject of καταβραβευέτω) of the pres. act. ptc. of κρατέω, hold fast to (and therefore: remain closely united to, BAGD 448d). In NT Gk. οὐ normally negates the indic. and μή the other moods, incl. the inf. and the ptc. (BDF §§ 426, 430; R 1136-1139; T 284-285; Z § 440). But οὐ is used with a ptc. (as here): (1) when a positive clause is followed by a neg. (R 1164) in a strong contrast (BAGD 590b) and the neg. is "clear-cut and decisive" (R 1137-1138) or (2) when οὐ is closely attached to a particular word with which it often merges to form a single concept (Z § 440 n. 2): "not adhering firmly to," denoting either loss of hold ("he has lost connection with the Head," NIV; sim. Goodspeed, TCNT; Lightfoot 190) or outright repudiation ("relinquishing," "rejecting," Zerwick, *Analysis* 451; Z § 440 n. 2). Τὴν κεφαλήν refers to Christ, who is "the Head" of the Body, his Church (cf. 1:18, 24).

ἐξ οὗ πᾶν τὸ σῶμα

Οὗ is gen. (after ἐκ; ἐξ before rough breathing) sg. masc. of the rel. pron. Its gender is assimilated to that of the antecedent (viz. Christ the Head) in place of the grammatical gender (viz. ἐξ ἧς, referring to κεφαλή, fem.; cf. Eph. 4:15-16 and BAGD 584a; R 713). If ἐξ οὗ is cstr. exclusively with αὔξει, it will denote the source (ἐκ) of the growth ("from whom," "from this source," NAB). But if this prep. phrase is related also to the two ptcs. (ἐπιχορηγούμενον, συμβιβαζόμενον), it will define the source of nourishment and unity as well as of growth ("in dependence on whom," "to whom it is due that," TCNT). Πᾶν τὸ σῶμα means "all the body, no part excepted," "the Body, in all its parts" (Weymouth), and thus "the whole body" (GNB, NIV; cf. 1:19; 2:9 and BAGD 631d).

διὰ τῶν ἀφῶν καὶ συνδέσμων ἐπιχορηγούμενον καὶ συμβιβαζόμενον

Gen. pl. of ἀφή, -ῆς, ἡ, (point of) contact, juncture; joint, ligament. Gen. pl. of σύνδεσμος, -ου, ὁ, bond; connecting bond in the body, sinew, ligament, tendon. On the use and relation of these two terms, see Lightfoot 196-198.

Nom. sg. neut. (agreeing with τὸ σῶμα) of the pres. pass. ptc. of ἐπιχορη-γέω, supply, equip. As a description of the Body's relation to the Head, this ptc. will mean "supplied with nourishment," "nourished" (Weymouth, RSV, GNB), or, more generally, "supported" (NIV; BAGD 305b; Lohse 114, 122 n. 62). Nom. sg. neut. (also agreeing with τὸ σῶμα) of pres. pass. ptc. συμβιβάζω, hold together, unite.

Διά (+ gen.) belongs with both nouns (note single prep. and art.), and probably with both ptcs. (and not simply with ἐπιχ., as Moffatt, NEB): "nourished and fitted together by its (τῶν denoting poss.) joints and sinews." If Christ is the source (ἐκ) of the body's growth, nourishment, and unity, the joints and ligaments together form the channels (διά) of supply and the means (διά) of unification. But it is not impossible that the mng. is "nourished through its joints and compacted by its ligaments." On any view, we should not expect to find physiological precision here.

αὔξει τὴν αὔξησιν τοῦ θεοῦ

3 sg. pres. act. indic. of αὔξω. Of the two pres. tense forms of this vb., αὐξάνω is both trans. ("cause to grow") and intrans. ("grow," 1:6, 10), while αὔξω is only intrans. (BAGD 121d; BDF § 101 s.v. [p. 50]). The cognate acc. τὴν αὔξησιν (αὔξησις, -εως, ἡ, growth, increase), here an acc. of "inner content" (R 478), serves only to introduce the qualifying gen. τοῦ θεοῦ (BDF § 153[1]), which may be:

*(1) subj. (or gen. of author): growth "that is stimulated/generated by God," increase "which God gives" (Zerwick, *Analysis* 451),
 (2) gen. of source: growth "which is from God" (NASB; sim. RSV, NAB; Lohse 114, 122 n. 64),
 (3) qualitative: grows with "divine" growth (BAGD 122a; sim. TCNT, Wey-mouth, Moffatt; O'Brien 148, but cf. 135), or
 (4) gen. of ref./relation: grows "according to God's design" (NEB; sim. GNB; Moule 107).

Since all three verbal forms in v. 19b are pres. tense Paul is affirming that the Body's receipt of vitality and the preservation of its integrity are ongoing processes related to its overall growth (αὔξησιν), which is simul-taneously dependent on Christ (ἐξ οὗ) and stimulated by God (τοῦ θεοῦ). See For Further Study 30, "Christian Growth."

TRANSLATION

[16] Let no one therefore sit in judgment on you regarding food and drink, or concerning a festival, a new moon, or a sabbath day. [17] These things are a shadow of what was to come; the reality, however, belongs to Christ. [18] Let no one disqualify you by insisting on self-humiliation and angel-worship, taking his stand on his visions and inflated with futile notions by his sensuous mind. [19] He does not hold firmly to the Head, in dependence on whom the whole Body, nourished and fitted together by its joints and sinews, grows with a growth stimulated by God.

EXPANDED PARAPHRASE

[16] In the light of all this, do not allow anyone to take you to task about what you eat and what you drink, or in the matter of observing yearly religious festivals or monthly new moons or weekly sabbaths. [17] These things are merely a shadow cast by a reality to come; now that reality has in fact arrived, and it is none other than the gospel of Christ. [18] Do not allow anyone who indulges and delights in self-abasement and the cultic worship of angels to declare you disqualified and thus rob you of your prize of the benefits of salvation. Such a person presumes to parade his visionary experiences, and his fleshly thought and outlook have filled him with futile ideas and conceit. [19] Moreover, he fails to adhere to Christ, the Head, although it is in dependence on him alone that the whole Body experiences growth that is stimulated by God, as it is nourished and fitted together into one by means of its joints and ligaments.

FOR FURTHER STUDY

30. Christian Growth (2:19)

Günther, W., NIDNTT 2.128-130

Jones, E. S., *Growing Spiritually* (Nashville: Abingdon, 1953).

*Montague, G. T., *Growth in Christ. A Study in Saint Paul's Theology of Progress* (Kirkwood, MO: Maryhurst, 1961).

Ramsay, W. M., *The Teaching of Paul in Terms of the Present Day* (New York: Hodder and Stoughton, 1914[2]) 100-103, 126-129.

Thomas, W. H. G., *Let Us Go On: The Secret of Christian Progress in the Epistle to the Hebrews* (Grand Rapids: Zondervan, 1944[3]).

HOMILETICAL SUGGESTIONS

Warning against Mystical Legalism (2:16-19)

1. The danger of succumbing to groundless accusations regarding:
    (a) diet (food and drink)
    (b) religious festivals
    (c) calendrical observances
    (d) sabbatarianism (v. 16),
all of which are shadows in comparison with the reality of Christ (v. 17).

2. The danger of succumbing to unjustifiable disqualification by another's insistence on:
    (a) self-humiliation and
    (b) angel-worship,
while he himself
    (a) parades his visions,
    (b) is filled with futile notions (v. 18), and
    (c) fails to adhere to Christ, the source of the Church's growth (v. 19).

D. CONSEQUENCES OF DEATH WITH CHRIST (2:20-23)

20 Εἰ ἀπεθάνετε σὺν Χριστῷ ἀπὸ τῶν στοιχείων τοῦ κόσμου, τί ὡς ζῶντες ἐν κόσμῳ δογματίζεσθε, 21 Μὴ ἅψῃ μηδὲ γεύσῃ μηδὲ θίγῃς, 22 ἅ ἐστιν πάντα εἰς φθορὰν τῇ ἀποχρήσει, κατὰ τὰ ἐντάλματα καὶ διδασκαλίας τῶν ἀνθρώπων; 23 ἅτινά ἐστιν λόγον μὲν ἔχοντα σοφίας ἐν ἐθελοθρησκίᾳ καὶ ταπεινοφροσύνῃ καὶ ἀφειδίᾳ σώματος, οὐκ ἐν τιμῇ τινι πρὸς πλησμονὴν τῆς σαρκός.

STRUCTURE

20 Εἰ ἀπεθάνετε σὺν Χριστῷ		The fact of death with Christ
		Consequent freedom from:
ἀπὸ τῶν στοιχείων κτλ.		(a) elemental spirits
ὡς ζῶντες ἐν κόσμῳ		(b) old world-order
τί . . . δογματίζεσθε		(c) regulations such as
21	Μὴ ἅψῃ	do not handle this
	μηδὲ γεύσῃ	do not taste that
	μηδὲ θίγῃς	do not touch this
22	ἅ ἐστιν πάντα	—all of them things
		destined to perish
κατὰ τὰ ἐντάλματα κτλ.		(d) compliance with human
		traditions
23	ἅτινά ἐστιν κτλ.	(e) enforced asceticism

VERSE 20

Εἰ ἀπεθάνετε σὺν Χριστῷ ἀπὸ τῶν στοιχείων τοῦ κόσμου

2 pl. second aor. act. indic. of ἀποθνήσκω, die. Because εἰ here introduces an accepted fact, not an open condition, it bears the sense "if, as is true," "since" (cf. BAGD 219c; BDF § 372[1]; Burton § 244). This death "with Christ" refers not to believers' self-denial "in union with Christ" but to their baptismal identification with Christ in his crucifixion: when he died, they died along with him (Rom. 6:3, 5, 8). See For Further Study 29, "Resurrection with Christ" (2:12-13).

ʼΑπό repeats the pref. in ἀπεθάνετε (R 559) and points not simply to the separation effected by death (Zerwick, *Analysis* 451) but also to the freedom that follows severance: "from the control of" (sim. Moule 107; O'Brien 135). In effect, ἀπό is brachylogy for "[and thus were freed] from" (sim. BAGD 86d; Goodspeed, GNB; NEB "[Did you not die with Christ and] pass beyond reach of. . . ?"). On τὰ στοιχεῖα τοῦ κόσμου, see notes on 2:8 and For Further Study

25, "Τὰ στοιχεῖα τοῦ κόσμου" (2:8, 20). Just as death dissolves a slave's bondage to his master, so death with Christ severs the Christian's bondage to "the elemental spirits of the universe."

τί ὡς ζῶντες ἐν κόσμῳ δογματίζεσθε

Nom. pl. masc. (agreeing with the subject of δογματίζεσθε) of the pres. act. ptc. of ζάω, live. Ὡς makes it clear that ζῶντες is concessive ("as though," RV, TCNT, Goodspeed, GNB, NIV; sim. NASB, Barclay). BDF (§ 425[3]) suggests that in general ὡς + ptc. conveys subjective motivation—"with the assertion that," "on the pretext that," "with the thought that" (this latter mng. would be suitable here). Or this construction may state an alleged reason which may or may not be the real reason (cf. R 966).

Ἐν κόσμῳ is def. although anar. ("in the world"; cf. ἐν σαρκί, 2:1; ἐκ νεκρῶν, 2:12; cf. R 791-792). Lit.: "as though you were living in the world" = "as though your life were still that of the world" (TCNT) or "as though you belonged to this world" (GNB; sim. Moffatt, Goodspeed, RSV; taking ζάω ἐν as meaning "belong to") or "as if you still lived in a worldly way" (O'Brien 135, taking ἐν κόσμῳ in the sense of κατὰ σάρκα, "in a worldly manner"). Paul is not denying his readers' earthly existence, only the worldly orientation of their lives.

Τί is an interr. adv. meaning "why?" (BAGD 819d) or possibly "how?" 2 pl. pres. indic. mid./pass. of δογματίζω, ordain, decree; (mid./pass.) submit to decrees (δόγματα). Δογματίζεσθε may be a reflexive/direct middle ("Why do you subject yourselves to ordinances?" R 807 ["probably"]) or a permissive use of the pass. ("Why do you let yourselves be dictated to?" ZG 608; sim. Zerwick, *Analysis* 451; BDF § 314, although § 317 shows that the mid. as well as the pass. may be permissive). On either view the sense is "Why do you submit to rules?" (sim. BAGD 201d; T 57, where δογματίζομαι is classified as intrans. act. in mng.). Paul is not merely warning of potential danger ("Why submit. . . ?") but castigating actual surrender ("Why do you submit. . . ?", or, to bring out the possible significance of the pres., "Why do you continue to submit yourselves?" Barclay).

VERSE 21

Μὴ ἅψῃ μηδὲ γεύσῃ μηδὲ θίγῃς

Ἅψῃ is 2 sg. aor. mid. subjunc. of ἅπτω, kindle; (mid.) touch, lay hold of. Γεύσῃ is 2 sg. aor. mid. subjunc. of dep. γεύομαι, taste. Θίγῃς is 2 sg. second aor. act. subjunc. of θιγγάνω, touch. In general, whereas μή + pres. impv. prohibits continued or habitual action (Moule, *Idiom Book* 135), the pres. being iter. (= frequentative), μή + aor. subjunc. expresses categorical prohibition of specific conduct, usually to prevent an action from beginning, the aor. being constative (= summary, complexive; cf. BDF §§ 335, 337[3]; Burton §§ 162-164; Moule, *Idiom Book* 135-136; Moulton 122-126; R 855-856; T 74-78). The neg. disjunctive particle μηδέ ("and . . . not," "nor") twice introduces a further negation (cf. BAGD 517d).

Although ἅπτομαι and θιγγάνω may both mean "touch," the former vb. here probably envisages more lasting contact than the superficial and temporary touch suggested by the latter vb.: "Do not handle! Do not taste! Do not even touch!" Because no objects are expressed, these regulations are probably not purely dietary. See further BAGD 102d-103a; O'Brien 149-150. Paul may be citing actual prohibitions to which the Colossians were submitting, or he may be ironically caricaturing typical regulations. Some EVV supply indefinite objects: " 'Hands off this!' 'Taste not that!' 'Touch not this!' " (Moffatt; sim. NEB, GNB); the JB paraphrases thus, " 'It is forbidden to pick up this, it is forbidden to taste that, it is forbidden to touch something else.' "

VERSE 22

ἅ ἐστιν πάντα

῞Α is nom. pl. neut. of the rel. pron. ὅς, ἥ, ὅ, followed here by the sg. vb. ἐστίν (see BDF § 133; T 312-313; R 403-404). On the antecedent of ἅ, see below under κατὰ κτλ. Movable ν is found even before initial consonants (here, ἐστιν πάντα; cf. BDF § 20). Πάντα agrees with ἅ (viz. nom. pl. neut.).

εἰς φθορὰν τῇ ἀποχρήσει

After εἶναι the prep. εἰς can mean "to serve as," "meant for," or (as here) "destined for" (cf. BAGD 225a; BDF § 145[1]). Lit.: "which things are all destined for destruction" (φθορά, -ᾶς, ἡ, ruin, destruction), i.e., they are, by divine appointment (cf. A. Oepke, TDNT 2.428), "destined to perish" (NASB, NIV; Lohse 114, 124 n. 81; Moule 108; O'Brien 135). Τῇ ἀποχρήσει (dat. sg. of ἀπόχρησις, -εως, ἡ, consumption by use, using up) is locat. ("in their use," NAB; "in being used"), temp. ("as they are used," RSV; "in the course of using them up," Moule 108), or instr. ("by being used," Moffatt; "with use," NIV). The pref. ἀπο- may be perfective ("by being used *up*"), as in the cognate vb. ἀποχράομαι, use up (MH 299).

κατὰ τὰ ἐντάλματα καὶ διδασκαλίας τῶν ἀνθρώπων;

This κατά phrase may relate specifically to the regulations cited (or comparable prohibitions; "These rules are determined by. . . ," Moffatt; sim. NAB) or, better, may be loosely attached to the whole sentence ("in compliance with"; "That is to follow. . . ," NEB; "You are following. . . ," TCNT; sim. RV, Weymouth, Goodspeed, NASB).

Ἔνταλμα, -ατος, τό, precept, injunction. Διδασκαλία, -ας, ἡ, act of teaching; teaching (= what is taught). If ἐντάλματα are specific directives, διδασκαλίαι are general instructions; thus "injunctions and teaching" (generalizing pl.), NEB; "precepts and doctrines," NAB. The intimate connection between the two terms is shown by the single prep. and the single art. (even though the genders of the two nouns differ—see BDF § 276[1]; T 181). As in 2:8, τῶν ἀνθρώπων is probably subj. ("handed down by humans"; "man-made," GNB) or adj. ("human," Moffatt, NIV; "merely human," NEB, NAB). Barclay paraphrases thus: "humanly taught and humanly imposed."

The antecedent of ἅ is ambiguous. If it is the regulations (δόγματα) implied in the vb. δογματίζεσθε or the three prohibitions just cited, the sense will be "Such/these rules (ἅ) all (πάντα) relate to things [viz. material objects] destined to be destroyed through being used" (sim. GNB, JB, NAB). But if the antecedent is the material objects that are considered impure to touch and that are implied in the prohibitions, the meaning is " 'Do not handle this!' 'Do not taste that!' 'Do not touch this!' These things (ἅ) are all (πάντα) destined to perish with use" (sim. TCNT, Moffatt, Goodspeed, NEB). The word-order of ἅ ἐστιν πάντα (not ἅ πάντα ἐστιν) supports this latter alternative, which has the effect of making v. 22a (ἅ . . . ἀποχρήσει) parenthetical (as in RV, Weymouth, NASB).

In the long, complex question that Paul poses in vv. 20-22, he is making two basic points. Since death with Christ brought emancipation from bondage to the elemental spirits, submission to the codified taboos that they promote amounts to a surrender of that liberty (εἰ . . . τί . . . ; "Since . . . why. . . ?") and a denial of the headship of Christ (v. 19). Secondly, it is incongruous for the citizens of another, heavenly world to submit to petty regulations concerning perishable items in this world, out of conformity to merely human precepts and tenets.

VERSE 23

ἅτινά ἐστιν λόγον μὲν ἔχοντα σοφίας

Ἅτινα is nom. pl. neut. of ὅστις, ἥτις, ὅ τι, who(ever); such a one who. Whether this compound indef. rel. pron. is indistinguishable from the simple def. rel. ἅ (and so is lit. "which things" = "these rules," Weymouth; cf. BDF § 293; Moule 123-124; Moulton 91-92; R 67, 726-728; T 47-48; Z §§ 215-220) or has a qualitative sense (either "things of this sort" = "such rules," GNB; or "these regulations, being what they are"), its antecedent is not ἐντάλματα καὶ διδασ-καλίας but the prohibitions in v. 21 and similar injunctions, although the δόγματα of v. 21 are included within the ἐντάλματα of v. 22.

A neut. pl. subject is followed (as in v. 22) by the sg. vb. ἐστίν, which may be complemented in any one of three ways:

(1) ἅτινά ἐστιν . . . οὐκ ἐν τιμῇ τινι κτλ., "these regulations are . . . not of any value . . ."

(2) ἅτινά ἐστιν . . . πρὸς πλησμονὴν κτλ., lit. "such regulations are . . . result-ing in (πρός) gratification . . ." = "such regulations actually lead . . . to the gratification of the flesh" (O'Brien 135, 151-152, 154-155)

*(3) ἅτινά ἐστιν . . . ἔχοντα, "such rules have. . . ," where ἐστιν . . . ἔχοντα (nom. pl. neut. [agreeing with ἅτινα] of the pres. act. ptc. of ἔχω, have) is a periph. pres. (BDF § 353[4]; R 375, 881; Robertson, *Pictures* 499; T 88; ZG 608-609).

The distance of οὐκ κτλ. or πρὸς κτλ. from ἐστίν counts against (1) and (2).

Λόγον here means "appearance" or "reputation": such rules "have the appearance of wisdom" (BAGD 477c; sim. Weymouth, RSV, NASB, NIV), "appear wise"; or "have the reputation of being wise" (BAGD 503a; sim. Lohse 114, 126 n. 96), "get the name of 'wisdom' " (Moffatt).

Μέν ("indeed," "to be sure") points to the contrast between λόγον . . . σοφίας and οὐκ ἐν τιμῇ τινι κτλ. (R 1152), between the ostensible wisdom of the ascetic regulations and their lack of actual value. Alternatively, the contrast could be supplied from the context: BAGD 503a suggests ὄντα δὲ ἄλογα, "but are foolish." Although the absence of the normal correlative of μέν, viz. an adversative δέ, produces a technical anacoluthon (cf. BDF § 447[2]), most EVV appropriately supply "but" before οὐκ κτλ.

ἐν ἐθελοθρησκίᾳ καὶ ταπεινοφροσύνῃ καὶ ἀφειδίᾳ σώματος

The compound subst. ἐθελοθρησκία, -ας, ἡ, means either "self-imposed wor-ship" (Weymouth, NIV), "self-ordained piety" (G. Delling, TDNT 6.134; cf. Turner, *Words* 493, *"free worship* or *uncontrolled worship"* (on the analogy of ἐθελοδουλεία, "voluntary slavery," in which the first element of the com-pound "governs" the second; see BDF § 118[2]); or "would-be worship" (on the analogy of ἐθελοσοφία, "would-be wisdom"; MH 290; F. O. Francis in *Conflict* 181-182). The worship envisaged is worship of God, not of angels (cf. GNB, "their forced worship of angels"). On ταπεινοφροσύνη, "flaunted humil-ity," see 2:18.

Ἀφειδία, -ας, ἡ, lit. "unsparingness" (the negating ἀ- privative + φεί-δομαι, spare); "severe treatment" (BAGD 124d; NASB, JB), with σώματος an obj. gen. (Zerwick, *Analysis* 452), "severity to the body" (RSV, NEB), "harsh treatment of the body" (TCNT, NIV). But ἀφειδίᾳ σώματος may be a periphrasis for "asceticism" (ZG 609; cf. BAGD 124d), "ascetic severity" (Weymouth; sim. Lohse 126), or even "ascetic discipline" (Goodspeed). NAB seems to cstr. the ἐθελο- ("self-imposed," "voluntary," "affected") of ἐθελοθρησκίᾳ with the two succeeding nouns as well: "their affected piety, humility, and bodily austerity."

Ἐν may be instr. ("through," "with"), locat. ("in"; "in the spheres of," O'Brien 135, 153, 156; "in promoting," RSV), or *causal ("by reason of," "as a consequence of"). The single prep. indicates the close association of "self-imposed devotion, affected humility, and bodily severity" in creating "the appearance of wisdom."

Unlike UBS[1, 2], UBS[3] places the καί before ἀφειδίᾳ in square brackets (with a "D" rating), indicating its "dubious textual validity." Without the καί (as in 𝔭[46] B 1739 al), ἀφειδίᾳ is probably in epex. appos. to ταπεινοφροσύνῃ ("self-mortification, that is, severe treatment of the body") or possibly is an instr. dat. after λόγον ἔχοντα σοφίας (". . . have an appearance of wisdom in [ἐν]. . . , by their harsh treatment of the body"). Although Lightfoot (204, 252-253) defends the omission of καί as original, this omission probably arose accidentally, καί being found in geographically diversified witnesses (see Metzger 624; Lohse 125 n. 88 for various conjectural emendations of the verse).

οὐκ ἐν τιμῇ τινι

This phrase is neither a parenthesis nor a gloss on ἀφειδίᾳ σώματος but is the contrast answering to the earlier μέν clause. "Such rules indeed (μέν) appear wise . . . but they lack any value. . . ," popular impression being pitted against actual value (τιμή). With an implied ἐστίν (from v. 23a), ἐν ("are . . . with," ἐν of attendant circumstance or accompaniment, T 252) = ἔχει ("have"); thus "they have no real value" (GNB) or "they are of no value" (RSV; BAGD 817c; sim. TCNT). Τινι is dat. sg. fem. (agreeing with τιμῇ) of the encl. indef. pron. or adj. τις, τι (gen. τινός), someone, anyone; some, any. When used with a subst. τις may mean "a kind of" (R 742; BAGD 820c), but when negated "any (at all)."

πρὸς πλησμονὴν τῆς σαρκός

Πλησμονή, -ῆς, ἡ, satiety; satisfaction; gratification. If σάρξ is given a neutral, nonmoral sense (= σῶμα), the phrase could mean "the satisfaction of natural desire," "the gratification of physical needs" (τῆς σαρκός, obj. gen.; the dominant view among the Fathers—G. Delling, TDNT 6.133). But the pejorative sense of τῆς σαρκός in the related v. 18 ("his sensuous mind") suggests that here too, where σαρκός seems to be distinguished from the preceding σώματος (of the physical frame), the term has its usual Pauline meaning of "the sinful nature," the self in opposition to God. Accordingly, πλησμονή will also be negative in connotation—"satiation," "indulgence." Πλησμονὴν τῆς σαρκός will then mean:

(1) "the gratification of the flesh" (τῆς σαρκός, obj. gen.), "the indulgence of our earthly nature" (TCNT; sim. BAGD 673a); or

(2) "fleshly gratification" (adj. gen.), "sensual indulgence" (NIV; Moule 108), "sensuality" (NEB).

If this phrase is independent, πρός denotes result: "Such precepts . . . have no (true) validity and simply serve to satisfy (pious) self-seeking" (G. Delling, TDNT 6.134). "These rules . . . are of no value, they simply pamper the flesh!" (Moffatt). On the other hand, if this phrase is construed with οὐκ ἐν τιμῇ τινι, which immediately precedes, πρός will bear its developed sense of "against" (RV, TCNT, NASB; ZG 609 "prob[ably]"; R 626, citing Acts 6:1; 2 Cor. 5:12, to which may be added 1 Cor. 6:1 and Col. 3:13). "Such rules . . . have no real value against (i.e., "in combating," Weymouth, NEB; Moule 108; "in restraining," NIV; sim. RSV, GNB; Lightfoot 204) sensual indulgence." To construe πρὸς κτλ. with ἅτινά ἐστιν (as B. Reicke, TDNT 6.725; O'Brien 135, 151-152, 154-155) creates a long parenthesis that is made awkward by the phrase οὐκ ἐν τιμῇ τινι.

See For Further Study 31, "Christian Asceticism." For other interpretations of 2:23, see Lightfoot 205-206; Lohse 124-127; Moule 108-110; O'Brien 154-155.

TRANSLATION

[20] You died with Christ and were thus freed from the elemental spirits of the universe. Why, then, as though your life were worldly, do you submit to regulations such as [21] "Do not handle this!" "Do not taste that!" "Do not touch this!" [22] —things that are all destined to perish with use—in compliance with man-made injunctions and teachings? [23] Such rules indeed appear wise by reason of their self-imposed worship, flaunted humility, and severe treatment of the body, but they lack any value in combating fleshly gratification.

EXPANDED PARAPHRASE

[20] When you died with Christ you were freed from the control of the elemental spirits of the universe. Why, then, do you live as if you still belonged to the world and were not citizens of heaven? And why do you allow yourselves to be subjected to pointless regulations such as [21] "Do not handle this thing here!"

"Do not taste that food there!" "Do not even touch that item!"? [22] Purely material things, such as food and drink, are all destined to pass out of existence as they are used! In any case, why should you be bound by merely human precepts and instructions? [23] What is more, although these regulations at first glance might appear to be wise and beneficial with their self-imposed devotion, their affected humility, and their ascetic ill-treatment of the body, they are in fact without any value at all in the very area of their apparent value, namely, in curbing sensual indulgence.

FOR FURTHER STUDY

31. Christian Asceticism (2:23)

Austgen, R. J., *Natural Motivation in the Pauline Epistles* (Notre Dame: University Press, 1966) 91-108.

Campenhausen, H. von, "Early Christian Asceticism," in his *Tradition and Life in the Church: Essays and Lectures in Church History,* tr. A. V. Littledale (Philadelphia: Fortress, 1968).

Chadwick, O., ed., *Western Asceticism* (Philadelphia: Westminster, 1958).

Hardman, O., *The Ideals of Asceticism* (London: SPCK, 1924).

Harrison, E. F., ISBE 1.313-314.

Kirk, K. E., *The Vision of God. The Christian Doctrine of the Summum Bonum* (New York: Longmans, 1932[2]).

Law, W., *A Serious Call to a Devout and Holy Life* (New York: Dutton, 1955 reprint).

*Ziesler, J. A., *Christian Asceticism* (London: SPCK, 1973/Grand Rapids: Eerdmans, 1974).

HOMILETICAL SUGGESTIONS

Consequences of Death with Christ (2:20-23)

Freedom from (ἀπό):
1. control by the elemental spirits of the universe (v. 20a)
2. the old world-order (v. 20b)
3. restrictive regulations (v. 20b)
   —that prohibit touching or eating certain things (v. 21), all of which are destined to perish when used (v. 22a)
4. bondage to merely human precepts and doctrines (v. 22b)
5. enforced ascetic disciplines (v. 23)

—that involve self-imposed devotion, flaunted humility, and harsh treatment of the body (v. 23b),

—that, in popular estimation, appear advantageous (v. 23a),

—and that, in reality, are totally ineffective in restraining self-gratification (v. 23c)

E. CONSEQUENCES OF RESURRECTION WITH CHRIST
(3:1-4)

1 Εἰ οὖν συνηγέρθητε τῷ Χριστῷ, τὰ ἄνω ζητεῖτε, οὗ ὁ Χριστός ἐστιν ἐν δεξιᾷ τοῦ θεοῦ καθήμενος· 2 τὰ ἄνω φρονεῖτε, μὴ τὰ ἐπὶ τῆς γῆς· 3 ἀπεθάνετε γάρ, καὶ ἡ ζωὴ ὑμῶν κέκρυπται σὺν τῷ Χριστῷ ἐν τῷ θεῷ. 4 ὅταν ὁ Χριστὸς φανερωθῇ, ἡ ζωὴ ὑμῶν, τότε καὶ ὑμεῖς σὺν αὐτῷ φανερωθήσεσθε ἐν δόξῃ.

STRUCTURE

1 Εἰ . . . συνηγέρθητε	τῷ	Χριστῷ,		τὰ ἄνω ζητεῖτε,
	οὗ ὁ	Χριστός ἐστιν		
2				τὰ ἄνω φρονεῖτε
3 ἀπεθάνετε γὰρ [σὺν		Χριστῷ, 2:20a]		
ἡ ζωὴ ὑμῶν . . . σὺν	τῷ	Χριστῷ		ἐν τῷ θεῷ
4	ὁ	Χριστὸς . . . ἡ ζωὴ ὑμῶν		
	σὺν	αὐτῷ φανερωθήσεσθε		ἐν δόξῃ

Five features of this paragraph deserve special mention:

(1) Εἰ . . . συνηγέρθητε τῷ Χριστῷ (v. 1a) parallels εἰ ἀπεθάνετε σὺν Χριστῷ (2:20a). One protasis introduces the consequences of death with Christ (2:20-23), the other the consequences of resurrection with Christ (3:1-4).

(2) There are two pres. impvs. (ζητεῖτε, v. 1; φρονεῖτε, v. 2), each with an identical object (τὰ ἄνω) and each with a twofold ground that is either stated (εἰ κτλ. in v. 1a; ἀπεθάνετε γάρ in v. 3a, respectively) or implied (οὗ κτλ. in v. 1b; καὶ κτλ. in vv. 3b-4, respectively).

(3) Christ is a central theme of the paragraph (there are five explicit references to him in the four verses), and prominent throughout is the concept of believers' identification with Christ (σὺν τῷ Χριστῷ . . . , σὺν αὐτῷ) in death (v. 3a), resurrection (v. 1a), life (vv. 3b, 4a), and glory (v. 4b). Note also that the next paragraph (vv. 5-11) ends with an emphasis on the centrality of Christ and actually concludes with the word Χριστός (v. 11).

(4) There is a striking instance of chiasmus (A-B-B-A) in vv. 3b-4a: ἡ ζωὴ ὑμῶν . . . Χριστῷ . . . Χριστὸς . . . ἡ ζωὴ ὑμῶν.

(5) The paragraph contains both spatial imagery (τὰ ἄνω, vv. 1, 2; τὰ ἐπὶ τῆς γῆς, v. 2) and temporal categories (past—συνηγέρθητε, v. 1; ἀπεθάνετε, v. 3; present—οὗ ὁ Χριστός ἐστιν, v. 1; κέκρυπται [stressing present consequences], v. 3; ἡ ζωὴ ὑμῶν, vv. 3, 4; future—ὅταν . . . φανερωθῇ . . . φανερωθήσεσθε, v. 4).

VERSE 1

Εἰ οὖν συνηγέρθητε τῷ Χριστῷ

2 pl. aor. pass. indic. of συνεγείρω, cause to rise up with; pass. be raised/rise up with. As in 2:20, εἰ introduces an assumed fact, "if, as is true," "since" (cf. BAGD 219c; BDF § 372[1]; Burton § 244). Οὖν looks back either to 2:20 (death with Christ implies resurrection with him; "since, therefore," TCNT; logical/inferential οὖν) or, better, to 2:12-13 (to references to being raised with Christ; "since, then," NIV; resumptive οὖν). Συνηγέρθητε is a constative aor., here denoting a single action in the past, viz. resurrection to new life in baptism (cf. Rom. 6:4). Τῷ Χριστῷ is dat. after a σύν- compound. The prefixed σύν of a compound vb. is generally not repeated with an accompanying word, 2:13 being the one NT exception (see 2:12). The presence of the article with Χριστῷ is probably not significant (see note on 2:17; cf. W. Grundmann, TDNT 9.540-541; but TCNT has "the Christ").

τὰ ἄνω ζητεῖτε

2 pl. pres. act. impv. of ζητέω, seek. "Aim at" (Moffatt; ZG 609), "keep seeking" (NASB), "aspire to" (NEB). With the neut. art., advs. such as ἄνω ("above," "upward"), esp. those denoting time and place, may become substs. (cf. BAGD 552a; BDF § 266[1]; R 547; T 14): lit. "the things above," thus "the realm above" (NEB), "the heavenly world"; τὰ ἄνω = τὰ ἐν τοῖς οὐρανοῖς (cf. F. Büchsel, TDNT 1.376).

οὗ ὁ Χριστός ἐστιν ἐν δεξιᾷ τοῦ θεοῦ καθήμενος

Οὗ, really gen. sg. masc./neut. of the rel. pron. ὅς, ἥ, ὅ, had become an adv. of place, "where," denoting either circumstances or (as here, after τὰ ἄνω) locality (cf. BAGD 589d). It is possible that the clause introduced by οὗ states the ground for the previous impv.: "for it is there that . . ." (TCNT).

Καθήμενος, nom. sg. masc. (agreeing with ὁ Χριστός) of pres. mid. ptc. κάθημαι, sit. With ἐστιν this could form a periph. pres., "is seated" (thus TCNT, Barclay, NAB, NIV; T 88; Turner *Style* 89), but, given the word-order, it is preferable to tr. "where Christ is, seated . . ." (thus RV, Weymouth, Moffatt, Goodspeed, RSV, NEB, NASB, JB; Robertson, *Pictures* 500 [but cf. R 881]; Lightfoot 207; Lohse 132, 133 n. 7; O'Brien 157, 161-162). Paul is making two distinct affirmations—Christ is resident in "the realm above"; and he is enthroned there at God's right hand. In this case the ptc. καθήμενος is adj. Just as in v. 1a the resurrection of Christ is presupposed, so here in v. 1b his ascension into heaven is assumed.

Ἐν δεξιᾷ is an abbreviation of ἐν τῇ δεξιᾷ χειρί, "at the right hand," "at the right-hand side" (GNB; cf. BAGD 174d, 389b). Δεξιός, -ά, -όν, right (as opposed to left). The expression is anar., being a common, stereotyped prep. phrase (cf. BDF § 255; T 180). Τοῦ θεοῦ is poss. gen. "God's right hand" is the place of unrivalled prestige and unparalleled authority; consequently, although believers now "sit with Christ in the heavenly places" (Eph. 2:6), they do not "sit at God's right hand in the heavenly places," as Christ does (Eph. 1:20). See For Further Study 32, "The Ascension and Session of Christ."

VERSE 2

τὰ ἄνω φρονεῖτε

2 pl. pres. act. impv. of φρονέω, think, be intent on (+ acc.). Tr.: "give your minds to" (ZG 609), "constantly fix your thoughts on." If ζητεῖτε (3:1) focuses on the practical pursuit of heavenly or spiritual goals, φρονεῖτε emphasizes the inner attitude necessary in that pursuit. " 'You must not only *seek* heaven; you must also *think* heaven' " (Lightfoot 207).

μὴ τὰ ἐπὶ τῆς γῆς

With the neut. art., prep. phrases such as ἐπὶ τῆς γῆς ("on the earth") may become substs. (cf. BAGD 551d, 552a; BDF § 266[2]; R 766; T 14-16): lit. "the things on the earth," "earthly matters." Μή is regularly used to negate substs. (R 1172). As in v. 5, γῆ denotes earth in contrast to heaven (BAGD 157d), so that the Pauline antithesis τὰ ἄνω—τὰ ἐπὶ τῆς γῆς (= τὰ κάτω, "the realm below") is spatial, "heavenly things" symbolizing "spiritual matters" or "things of the Spirit" (Rom. 8:5b) and "earthly things" betokening "unspiritual matters" or "things of the flesh" (Rom. 8:5a). Paul is not detracting from the importance of the material world and earthly concerns but rather is rejecting an earth-bound mind-set. The remedy for submission to mundane regulations (cf. 2:20-22) is concentration of desire and thought on heavenly obligations.

VERSE 3

ἀπεθάνετε γάρ

2 pl. second aor. act. indic. of ἀποθνήσκω, die. Because this same verbal form occurs in 2:20, γάρ may be resumptive: "I repeat, you died" (NEB). But more probably γάρ ("for") introduces the grounds of the twofold injunction of v. 2: believers are to fix their thoughts on the realm above because their resurrection lives are hidden with Christ in heaven; they are not to focus their attention on earthly things because in baptism they died with Christ (2:20) to worldly pursuits.

καὶ ἡ ζωὴ ὑμῶν κέκρυπται

3 sg. pf. indic. pass. of κρύπτω, hide (in a safe place, BAGD 454d). If aor.
ἀπεθάνετε points to the past act of dying with Christ in baptism (cf. Rom. 6:2-8),
pf. κέκρυπται alludes to the permanent outcome of rising with Christ in baptism:
the true life of believers "now lies hidden" (TCNT, Goodspeed) or "remains
concealed" (Robertson, *Pictures* 500) until the final revelation (v. 4). Security
as well as concealment is implied.

Καί here expresses a result, "and so," "consequently" (cf. Z § 455[b]);
in Christian baptism, life inevitably follows death. Whereas in v. 4 ἡ ζωὴ ὑμῶν
("your life") is identified *as* Christ, here ἡ ζωὴ ὑμῶν is described as "now hidden
with Christ" and refers either to believers' new, spiritual life or to their individual resurrection lives. On either view, ζωή in v. 3 is a distributive sg. (cf.
BDF § 140; R 409; T 23-25).

σὺν τῷ Χριστῷ ἐν τῷ θεῷ

Σὺν Χριστῷ does not simply mean "along with [the life of] Christ." Rather,
σύν shows that the resurrection lives of believers are intimately connected—in
symbiosis (cf. ζωὴ . . . σύν)—with the risen, heavenly life of Christ. Also it is
implied that in a spiritual, real sense believers are already living "in the
company of Christ" in the heavenly realm (cf. Eph. 2:6), all this being hidden
from human gaze. On the σὺν Χριστῷ formula, see O'Brien 169-171; Harris
1207. The phrase ἐν τῷ θεῷ is to be construed either with *κέκρυπται ("hidden
. . . in the sphere of God," locat. ἐν) or with σὺν τῷ Χριστῷ ("with Christ, who
[also] has his being in the life of God," locat. ἐν; cf. Jn. 1:18; 17:21). On dying
and rising with Christ, see above For Further Study 29, "Resurrection with
Christ" (2:12-13).

VERSE 4

ὅταν ὁ Χριστὸς φανερωθῇ

3 sg. aor. pass. subjunc. of φανερόω, reveal; (pass.) be revealed; reveal oneself,
become visible, appear. Ὅταν (= ὅτε + ἄν, "when," "whenever") + aor. subjunc.
regularly specifies a fut. action whose accomplishment precedes the action of
the principal vb. (R 972; T 112). When this cstr. is followed (as here) by τότε
("then") in the main clause, this sequence is further emphasized: "*when* (this
or that has occurred), *then* (something else will happen)" (cf. BAGD 588a,
824a). "When Christ appears . . ." refers to his second Advent. What remains
indefinite is not the fact but the time of his appearance. It is remarkable that
although the NT epistles usually omit the art. with Χριστός when it is a proper

name (cf. BDF § 260[1]; R 760), 3:1-4 contains four uses of art. Χριστός in ref. to Christ.

ἡ ζωὴ ὑμῶν

Most EVV and many commentators (Lightfoot 208; Lohse 132, 134; Moule 112; O'Brien 157, 167) prefer the rdg. ἡ ζωὴ ἡμῶν (represented by B Dᶜ syrᵖ· ʰ copˢᵃ *al*), usually on the ground that ἡμῶν would be more likely to be altered to ὑμῶν in conformity with ἡ ζωὴ ὑμῶν, which precedes in v. 3, and ὑμεῖς, which follows in v. 4b, than the reverse alteration. But in favor of the originality of ἡ ζωὴ ὑμῶν (given a "C" rating in all three UBS edd. and preferred by JB, NIV), the following points may be made:

(1) Ὑμῶν is supported by stronger external evidence, of both the Alexandrian (𝔭⁴⁶ ℵ Ψ 33 1739 *al*) and the Western (D* it vg *al*) text-types (cf. Metzger 624);

(2) The change from ὑμῶν to ἡμῶν may have been occasioned by the universalizing instinct of a scribe who did not want it to appear that Christ was "the life" solely of the Colossian Christians. He could not introduce this change in v. 3 (at ἡ ζωὴ ὑμῶν) because an identity of referent was needed in the death-life sequence of thought ("you died and your life is hidden . . ."). Verse 4 presented no such obstacle, although the transition from "our life" to "you shall appear" is awkward.

The phrase ἡ ζωὴ ὑμῶν is in epex. appos. to ὁ Χριστός, and ζωή is nom. in agreement with Χριστός. Generally appos. nouns are in the same case (which may be any case) but there is a gen. of appos. where the two substs. are in different cases (cf. BDF §§ 268, 271; R 398-400; T 206). Ζωή has the art. because a noun followed by a dependent pers. pron. (here ὑμῶν) is normally art. (although an appos. noun is in any case often art.). Tr.: "when Christ, who is your life, appears, . . ." (NIV), or "when Christ is revealed—and he is your life—you too . . ." (JB). The life of Christians *is* Christ, as well as being "hidden *with* Christ" (v. 3). It "is" Christ, not in the sense that Christ's risen life in heaven can be equated with believers' spiritual life on earth or that the Church is the resurrection body of Christ, but in the sense that Christ is the source, center, and goal of the individual and corporate lives of believers (cf. 1 Cor. 8:6; Gal. 2:20; Phil. 1:21; Col. 1:16).

τότε καὶ ὑμεῖς

Τότε answers to ὅταν: "when. . . , then" (see above on ὅταν). Καὶ ὑμεῖς, "you too," "you also." The six main NT uses of καί are: coordinative/conjunctive ("and"), adjunctive ("also"), ascensive ("even"), adversative ("but," "[and] yet"), emphatic ("indeed," "in fact"), and epex. ("that is," "namely"; see further

BDF § 442; R 426, 1179-1183; T 334-336; Z §§ 450-465). Here adjunctive
καί reinforces the effect of the repeated vb. φανερόω.

σὺν αὐτῷ φανερωθήσεσθε ἐν δόξῃ

2 pl. fut. pass. indic. of φανερόω, reveal; (pass.) be revealed; reveal oneself,
become visible, appear. This appearance of believers could be similar to the
appearance of Christ (v. 4a) in being a single, future event, subsequent to his
appearance (ὅταν . . . τότε suggesting a definite sequence of events). Alternatively, this future tense may be linear rather than punctiliar, pointing to a future
manifested state to be inaugurated by Christ's appearance. Certainly it may be
said that futurist eschatology is not absent from Colossians (see also 1:5, 12-13,
18, 22-23, 27-28; 3:6, 10, 24-25).

'Εν might denote accompanying circumstances ("attended by glory"), or
it could be instr. ("[clothed] with glory," Zerwick, *Analysis* 452) or *locat. ("in
glory" = "glorified" or "in glorified bodies"; cf. 1 Cor. 15:43; Phil. 3:21). It is
not certain whether what is referred to is God's glory (cf. Rom. 5:2), Christ's
glory ("and share his glory," GNB, taking ἐν as equivalent to ecbatic εἰς; cf.
2 Thess. 2:14), or that of believers ("in all your glory," JB; cf. 2 Tim. 2:10),
but the context favors the second alternative. Σὺν αὐτῷ means *"along with
him" at his appearance (cf. Rom. 8:17), or "in his train" since he lives in heaven
in a "body of glory" (Phil. 3:20-21) as the paradigm for believers' resurrection
transformation (1 Cor. 15:20, 23, 49).

For heightened solemnity and dramatic effect, perhaps to highlight the
certainty and wonder of this dual revelation or appearance after the dual
"hiddenness" of v. 3, v. 4 is asyndetic. On asyndeton, see BDF § 462[2];
R 443; T 340-341.

TRANSLATION

[1] If, then, you were raised with Christ, seek the realm above where Christ is,
seated at God's right hand. [2] Fix your thoughts on the realm above, not on
earthly things. [3] For you died, and so your life is now hidden with Christ in
God. [4] When Christ, who is your life, appears, then you too will appear with
him in glory.

EXPANDED PARAPHRASE

[1] In your baptism, then, you came to share in Christ's resurrection. In light of
this, always seek whatever belongs to that heavenly realm above, where the
risen Christ now reigns, seated at God's right hand in the place of unrivaled
honor and authority. [2] Focus your attention and your thoughts exclusively and

constantly on the heavenly realm above, not on the earthly realm below. [3] This is appropriate and necessary, for in baptism you died with Christ to sin and the world and now your new, spiritual life, enjoyed in union with Christ, is concealed in the safekeeping of God in heaven. [4] Although your life is now hidden, when this Christ, who is your very Life, appears at his second Advent and his glory is manifested, then you too will fully share in his appearance and in the open display of his glory.

FOR FURTHER STUDY

32. The Ascension and Session of Christ (3:1)

Davies, J. G., *He Ascended into Heaven* (London: Lutterworth, 1958).

Donne, B. K., *Christ Ascended* (Exeter: Paternoster, 1983).

Harris, M. J., *Raised Immortal: Resurrection and Immortality in the New Testament* (London: Marshall, 1983/Grand Rapids: Eerdmans, 1985) 76-94.

Hay, D. M., *Glory at the Right Hand: Psalm 110 in Early Christianity* (Nashville: Abingdon, 1973).

Loader, W. R. G., "Christ at the Right Hand—Ps. cx.1 in the New Testament," *NTS* 24 (1977-78) 199-217.

Milligan, W., *The Ascension and Heavenly Priesthood of our Lord* (Edinburgh: T. & T. Clark, 1891).

Swete, H. B., *The Ascended Christ: A Study in the Earliest Christian Teaching* (London: Macmillan, 1922).

*Toon, P., *The Ascension of our Lord* (Nashville: Nelson, 1984).

HOMILETICAL SUGGESTIONS

Consequences of Resurrection with Christ (3:1-4)

1. Pursuit of (ζητεῖτε) the realm above (τὰ ἄνω, v. 1a), because of:
   (a) resurrection with Christ (εἰ . . . συνηγέρθητε τῷ Χριστῷ, v. 1a)
   (b) the session of Christ (οὗ ὁ Χριστός ἐστιν . . . καθήμενος, v. 1b)
2. Preoccupation with (φρονεῖτε) the realm above (τὰ ἄνω, v. 2a), because of:
   (a) death with Christ (ἀπεθάνετε γάρ, v. 3a),
   (b) identification with Christ (σὺν τῷ Χριστῷ . . . σὺν αὐτῷ) in life (vv. 3b, 4a) and glory (v. 4b)

"With Christ" (3:1-4)

    1. In death to sin, self, and the world (v. 3a; cf. 2:20; Rom. 6:6, 11)

    2. In spiritual resurrection to newness of life (v. 1a; cf. 2:12-13; Rom. 6:4; Eph. 2:5-6)

    3. In new, spiritual life, aliveness to God (vv. 3b, 4a; cf. Rom. 6:11, 13)

    4. In resurrection glory (v. 4b; cf. Rom. 8:17-18; 2 Thess. 1:10)

    See For Further Study 29, "Resurrection with Christ" (2:12-13).

IV. Exhortation to Holiness (3:5–4:6)

A. "PUTTING OFF" VICES (3:5-11)

5 Νεκρώσατε οὖν τὰ μέλη τὰ ἐπὶ τῆς γῆς, πορνείαν, ἀκαθαρσίαν, πάθος, ἐπιθυμίαν κακήν, καὶ τὴν πλεονεξίαν ἥτις ἐστὶν εἰδωλολατρία, 6 δι' ἃ ἔρχεται ἡ ὀργὴ τοῦ θεοῦ· 7 ἐν οἷς καὶ ὑμεῖς περιεπατήσατέ ποτε ὅτε ἐζῆτε ἐν τούτοις. 8 νυνὶ δὲ ἀπόθεσθε καὶ ὑμεῖς τὰ πάντα, ὀργήν, θυμόν, κακίαν, βλασφημίαν, αἰσχρολογίαν ἐκ τοῦ στόματος ὑμῶν· 9 μὴ ψεύδεσθε εἰς ἀλλήλους, ἀπεκδυσάμενοι τὸν παλαιὸν ἄνθρωπον σὺν ταῖς πράξεσιν αὐτοῦ, 10 καὶ ἐνδυσάμενοι τὸν νέον τὸν ἀνακαινούμενον εἰς ἐπίγνωσιν κατ' εἰκόνα τοῦ κτίσαντος αὐτόν, 11 ὅπου οὐκ ἔνι Ἕλλην καὶ Ἰουδαῖος, περιτομὴ καὶ ἀκροβυστία, βάρβαρος, Σκύθης, δοῦλος, ἐλεύθερος, ἀλλὰ τὰ πάντα καὶ ἐν πᾶσιν Χριστός.

STRUCTURE

5	Νεκρώσατε . . . τὰ μέλη		*First imperative*
	πορνείαν,	ἀκαθαρσίαν	{ five vices
	πάθος,	ἐπιθυμίαν κακήν	{ to be
	πλεονεξίαν		{ extirpated
6	δι' ἃ ἔρχεται ἡ ὀργὴ τοῦ θεοῦ		{ two grounds
7	ἐν οἷς . . . περιεπατήσατε . . . ἐν τούτοις		{ for this action
8	ἀπόθεσθε . . . τὰ πάντα		*Second imperative*
	ὀργήν,	θυμόν	{ five vices
	κακίαν,	βλασφημίαν	{ to be
	αἰσχρολογίαν		{ repudiated
9	μὴ ψεύδεσθε εἰς ἀλλήλους		*Third imperative*
	ἀπεκδυσάμενοι	τὸν παλαιὸν	ἄνθρωπον	{ two grounds
10	ἐνδυσάμενοι	τὸν νέον	[ἄνθρωπον]	{ for this action

144

11   ὅπου οὐκ ἔνι   Ἕ. καὶ Ἰ.   ⎧ abolition
                                π. καὶ ἀκ.   ⎪ of
                                   β., Σ.   ⎨ distinctions
                                δ. καὶ ἐλ.   ⎩
            ἀλλὰ   τὰ πάντα καὶ   ⎧ centrality
                                ἐν πᾶσιν Χριστός ⎩ of Christ

The structure revolves around three impvs., νεκρώσατε (v. 5), ἀπόθεσθε
(v. 8), and μὴ ψεύδεσθε (v. 9). Of these, the first two are aor. and the third pres.,
but all three are negative in connotation, being the opposite of the two positive
pres. impvs. in vv. 1-2 (τὰ ἄνω ζητεῖτε . . . τὰ ἄνω φρονεῖτε). Both νεκρώσατε and
ἀπόθεσθε have dir. objs. (τὰ μέλη and τὰ πάντα, respectively) that are both defined
by lists of five vices in grammatical appos. to the dir. objs. (cf. the five virtues
listed in v. 12). Both νεκρώσατε and μὴ ψεύδεσθε are followed by a statement of
two grounds for the injunction, explicit grounds in the case of μὴ ψεύδεσθε (viz.
the causal ptcs. ἀπεκδυσάμενοι [v. 9] and ἐνδυσάμενοι [v. 10], "because you have
put off . . . and put on . . ."), and implicit grounds in the case of νεκρώσατε (viz.
God's impending wrath [v. 6], a past repudiation of sin [v. 7]).

VERSE 5

Νεκρώσατε οὖν

2 pl. aor. act. impv. of νεκρόω, put to death. Οὖν looks back to vv. 1-4, in
particular to v. 3a, and possibly also to 2:20a: "you died (ἀπεθάνετε), rose with
Christ, and will be glorified with him; therefore put to death. . . ." A similar
movement from a doctrinal indicative to an ethical imperative is found in vv.
8-10: "put off . . . do not lie . . . since you have stripped off . . ." (cf. Rom.
6:1-14). See For Further Study 33, "Doctrinal Indicative—Ethical Imperative."

τὰ μέλη τὰ ἐπὶ τῆς γῆς

Occasionally τὰ μέλη has been construed as an art. nom. used as a voc., and τὰ
ἐπὶ τῆς γῆς as the obj. of νεκρώσατε: "Members [of the Body of Christ], put to
death what is earthly in you" (sim. Turner, *Insights* 104-105). Although possible
grammatically, this interpretation would be convincing only if Paul had added
τοῦ σώματος (cf. 1 Cor. 12:12, 22) or τοῦ Χριστοῦ (cf. 1 Cor. 6:15; 12:27) to τὰ
μέλη, or had written ὑμεῖς οὖν τὰ μέλη νεκρώσατε κτλ. ("You, therefore, as
members [of the Body], must put to death . . ."). Rather, τὰ μέλη is acc. as the
obj. of νεκρώσατε, with τὰ ἐπὶ τῆς γῆς as an adj. phrase describing τὰ μέλη: lit.
"the members, the on-the-earth [members]," "the members that are on the earth."

To clarify the meaning of this puzzling phrase, several points must be made:

(1) Μέλη are bodily limbs (eye, hand, foot, etc.).
(2) The first τά is poss., "your limbs" (some mss. add ὑμῶν).
(3) Τὰ ἐπὶ τῆς γῆς does not mean "the things on the earth" as in v. 2b, for here in v. 5 τά repeats the art. of μέλη before the prep. phrase ἐπὶ τῆς γῆς, which functions as an adj. in the alternative attrib. position (as in, e.g., ὁ ἄνθρωπος ὁ ἀγαθός; cf. BDF § 270; R 776-777; T 185).
(4) In an instance of catachresis, Paul says "Put to death your *limbs* . . ." rather than simply "put off immorality . . ." (cf. v. 8), not because here "*limbs*" *mean* "deeds," as in Iranian thought (so Lohse 137), but because bodily members can become "instruments of wickedness" (Rom. 6:13; cf. Matt. 5:29-30; 18:8-9). Paul is not advocating ascetic suppression or rejection of bodily desires and functions; he is rather calling for termination of the immoral and self-centered use of physical limbs or organs. Not "those parts of your nature that are earthly" (sim. BAGD 501d), "what is earthly in you" (RSV; BAGD 535c); but, "your limbs as used for earthly purposes" (sim. Moule 115).

πορνείαν, ἀκαθαρσίαν, πάθος, ἐπιθυμίαν κακήν

Lightfoot (209) begins a new construction here, regarding these accs. (along with τὴν πλεονεξίαν) as "prospective accusatives" governed by a vb. such as ἀπόθεσθε ("put off") in v. 8. He contends that, as it stands, the sentence is dislocated. But it is perfectly adequate to regard these accs. as in appos. to τὰ μέλη (so also Lohse 136; O'Brien 174, 177), agreeing in case (acc.) as is required for appos., but not in number. Yet the appos. is bold, for Paul is thereby juxtaposing instruments (μέλη) and the actions performed by them. In such lists of vices or virtues, asyndeton is natural (cf. BDF § 460[2]).

Πορνεία, -ας, ἡ, "immorality," denotes every type of improper sexual intercourse, including sexual activity outside marriage (both adultery and fornication). When associated with πορνεία, ἀκαθαρσία, -ας, ἡ ("impurity," Moffatt, JB, NIV; "uncleanness," TCNT, NAB; "indecency," NEB, GNB), regularly refers to sexual sins. In this context πάθος, -ους, τό, signifies sensual craving, sexual passion (BAGD 603a), "lust" (NEB, NIV), and ἐπιθυμία κακή, "debased passion," "foul desires" (generic sg.) of a sexual character.

καὶ τὴν πλεονεξίαν

Καί, "and especially" (Lightfoot 210). Πλεονεξία -ας, ἡ, is "a craving to have more" (πλέον ἔχειν), grasping, self-seeking acquisitiveness, "ruthless greed" (NEB). This noun, unlike those that precede, is art., for any one of the following reasons: (1) only πλεονεξία is defined as "idolatry"; (2) the following rel. clause has the effect of making πλ. def. (BDF § 258[1]; R 758); (3) specific instances of covetousness may be in view (cf. Z §§ 176-178: with abstract nouns the art. may indicate "concrete application"); (4) the art. is anaphoric, pointing to "that πλ. known to all" (ZG 609) which must be avoided at all costs.

ἥτις ἐστὶν εἰδωλολατρία

Ἥτις is nom. sg. fem. of the indef. rel. pron. ὅστις, ἥτις, ὅ τι (= ὅς + encl. τις; see MH 179), who(ever); such a one who. It is fem. sg. in agreement with its antecedent πλεονεξία, but nom. as the subj. of ἐστίν. Tr.: "and especially ruthless greed, which is idolatry" (εἰδωλολατρία, -ας, ἡ, nom. after εἰμί; see Turner, *Words* 229). Ἥτις may be equivalent here to the simple rel. pron. ἥ, or it may mean "which, by its very nature" (emphasizing a characteristic quality), or it may have a causal sense, "inasmuch as" (Zerwick, *Analysis* 452; cf. Z § 215; sim. Lightfoot 210, "for"; Vincent 913, "seeing it stands in the category of"). See further BAGD 587a, b. See For Further Study 34, "Catalogs of Virtues and Vices."

VERSE 6

δι' ἃ ἔρχεται

3 sg. pres. mid. indic. of dep. ἔρχομαι, come. Ἃ is acc. (after διά, "on account of," "because of," with α elided before a rough breathing) pl. neut. of the rel. pron. ὅς, ἥ, ὅ, the antecedent being either the sins listed in v. 5 ("on account of these very sins," Weymouth; "because of these," NEB, NIV) or, less probably, those sins along with comparable sins ("because of such things," GNB). Ἔρχεται is a gnomic pres., enunciating a principle of universal and permanent validity, "(always) comes," or a futuristic pres., depicting the certainty of future divine action, "will (certainly) come," "is coming." Either way, the word-order (vb.—subject) points to the impendence of wrath.

ἡ ὀργὴ τοῦ θεοῦ

Τοῦ θεοῦ may be merely a poss. gen. ("the wrath God has") but more probably is subj. ("the wrath God [has and] exhibits"). It seems far more likely, considering that God is the personal sustainer as well as author of the moral law and that sinners are his "enemies" (Rom. 5:10; cf. Col. 1:21), that ὀργή is an *affectus* ("feeling," "emotion"), God's eternal opposition to sin and sinners, than an *effectus* ("action," "activity"), an impersonal principle of retribution or law of cause and effect in a moral universe. The latter view tends to evacuate the personal gen. of any signficance. Nor is there need, if ὀργή is opposition felt or displayed, to render ἡ ὀργὴ τοῦ θεοῦ by "God's dreadful judgment" (NEB, reflecting Moule 117, "disaster from God," "God's terrible judgments"). See For Further Study 35, "The Wrath of God."

Widely diversified and early mss. add after θεοῦ the phrase ἐπὶ τοὺς υἱοὺς τῆς ἀπειθείας (enclosed in square brackets in all three UBS edd. and given a "D" rating; cf. Metzger 624-625). Tr.: (lit.) "on (ἐπί + acc.) the children of disobedience" (ἀπείθεια, -ας, ἡ), "on disobedient people," "upon those who do not obey him" (GNB). Υἱοί + gen. = "those characterized by," "those given over to" (cf. BDF § 162[6]; MH 441; T 208; Z §§ 42-43). But the rdg. is probably a secondary addition to the text that arose from the parallel in Eph. 5:6 (lit. "for because of these things [διὰ ταῦτα γάρ] the wrath of God comes upon the children of disobedience"), which provided, in the phrase τοὺς υἱοὺς τῆς ἀπειθείας, a natural antecedent for the rel. ἐν οἷς (v. 7a), construing it as masc. ("among whom"). With Lightfoot (211, 244-245), Lohse (139 n. 30), and O'Brien (173, 186), we prefer the shorter text, represented by 𝔓⁴⁶ B (?D*) copˢᵃ ethʳᵒ and several Fathers, which omits the phrase.

VERSE 7

ἐν οἷς καὶ ὑμεῖς περιεπατήσατέ ποτε

2 pl. aor. act. indic. of περιπατέω, walk; conduct one's life, live (see Turner, Words 41-42). The -ι of περί is retained before the aug. ε (cf. 2:11). As in 1:10, this aor. is constative (see on 1:7), here encompassing the previous (cf. the encl. ποτέ, once, formerly) sinful lives of Paul's readers in a single glance. Οἷς is dat. (after ἐν) pl. masc./neut. of the rel. pron. ὅς, ἥ, ὅ. If τοὺς υἱοὺς τῆς ἀπειθείας is read in v. 6b, οἷς could be masc., "among whom," "in the company of such people" (locat. ἐν); but to live among unbelievers was no sin (cf. 1 Cor. 5:10). Rather, οἷς is neut., having the same antecedent as ἅ in v. 6a, viz. the sins enumerated in v. 5; thus "in which," "in these sins" (sim. Lightfoot 211; Lohse 136, 140 n. 31). Καὶ ὑμεῖς, "you also," i.e., along with other godless Gentiles. Tr.: "You also once practiced these sins," "such was your own former behavior."

ὅτε ἐζῆτε ἐν τούτοις

2 pl. impf. act. indic. of ζάω, live. Τούτοις is dat. (after ἐν) pl. masc./neut. of the demonstrative pron. or adj. οὗτος, αὕτη, τοῦτο, this. As with οἷς (v. 7a), unless "children of disobedience" is read in v. 6b, τούτοις is neut. and refers to the vices listed in v. 5, "in these very sins" (locat. ἐν), which is stronger than ἐν αὐτοῖς, "in them," would be. However, in tr., to avoid repeating "(in) these

sins" (ἐν οἷς . . . ἐν τούτοις), we might render the second phrase "(in) that way,"
although it might also mean "under their power," referring to the sins (Weymouth; sim. GNB). The temp. conj. ὅτε looks back to ποτέ, ". . . formerly, when
you spent your life that way."

If there is a distinction between περιπατεῖν ἐν and ζῆν ἐν, both of which
could be tr. "live in," the former refers to actual conduct (e.g., Eph. 2:10), and
the latter to general life-style. Note also: (1) the juxtaposition of a constative
aor. and a durative impf. ("Your own former conduct was marked by these
same sins when you used to live that way"); (2) the chiasmus (A-B-B-A), ἐν
οἷς . . . περιεπατήσατε . . . ἐζῆτε ἐν τούτοις.

VERSE 8

νυνὶ δὲ ἀπόθεσθε καὶ ὑμεῖς τὰ πάντα

2 pl. second aor. mid. impv. of ἀποτίθημι, put off, lay aside; (mid.) rid oneself
of. This drastic repudiation would doubtless involve many isolated acts, but
Paul thinks of the repeated action as a unit (hence the aor.), as he did with
νεκρώσατε in v. 5. Νυνὶ δέ, "but now" (cf. 1:22), complements the ποτὲ ὅτε of
v. 7. Καί may emphasize ὑμεῖς, "you yourselves, in spite of your past, must in
fact lay aside . . ."; or it may be adjunctive, "in addition to putting to death the
vices mentioned, rid yourselves of these further sins."

Τὰ πάντα is the obj. of ἀπόθεσθε and could be retrospective ("all these
sins" in v. 5b, "all this," BAGD 633b), prospective ("all of the following sins"
of v. 8b), or undefined ("the sum total of sin, including . . ."). Certainly, (1) the
stress is on the totality, with no exceptions envisaged (this is the effect of the
art.), in anticipation of v. 9, "the old nature/humanity" *in toto;* (2) the vices
listed in v. 8b must be included. The ποτὲ . . . νυνὶ δέ antithesis in vv. 7 and 8
serves to unite the two catalogs of vices, for ἐν οἷς looks back to the list in
v. 5b and τὰ πάντα looks forward to the list in v. 8b (O'Brien 174, 186).

ὀργήν, θυμόν, κακίαν, βλασφημίαν, αἰσχρολογίαν ἐκ τοῦ στόματος ὑμῶν

As in v. 5, a pl. obj. (τὰ πάντα) is followed by five sg. nouns in appos. If ὀργή
("wrath") and θυμός (-οῦ, ὁ, "rage") are to be distinguished (see Lightfoot 212),
the former denotes chronic anger, the latter a passionate outburst of anger.
Κακία, -ας, ἡ, malicious spite. Βλασφημία (-ας, ἡ) is abusive or scurrilous
language directed against God ("blasphemy") or a human being ("slander," the
mng. here; see further Turner, *Words* 46-48). Αἰσχρολογία, -ας, ἡ, foul language, obscene speech.

In the phrase ἐκ τοῦ στόματος ὑμῶν, "from your mouth," "from your lips"
("mouth" standing for "lips," by synecdoche), ὑμῶν is a poss. gen. and accounts

for the art. with στόματος (see on 3:4), while στόματος is a distributive sg. (cf. BDF § 140; R 409; T 23-25). The phrase may be cstr. with:

(1) ἀπόθεσθε: "Get rid of these out of your mouth— . . ." (sim. Moule 117-118, tentatively),
(2) both βλασφημίαν and αἰσχρολογίαν: "abusive and filthy language from your mouths"; "No insults or obscene talk must ever come from your lips" (GNB), or
*(3) αἰσχρολογίαν alone: "foul talk from your mouth" (RSV), "foul-mouthed language."

Against (1) is: (i) the distance of the prep. phrase from the vb. and (ii) the need, on this view, for the first three terms to bear a restricted mng. (viz. a *verbalized* expression of anger, rage, and spite).

VERSE 9

μὴ ψεύδεσθε εἰς ἀλλήλους

2 pl. pres. mid. impv. of dep. ψεύδομαι, speak falsely, lie. Because μή + pres. impv. prohibits either the continuation of action ("cease to") or a course of action that must always be avoided ("keep from"; see on 2:16), this clause may mean:

(1) "Stop lying to one another" (NEB, NAB); "Tell no more untruths" (ZG 609); or
(2) "Do not lie to one another" (RSV, NASB, GNB, Barclay; sim. RV, Moffatt, NIV); "Never lie to one another" (TCNT; sim. JB); "Do not indulge in the habit of lying to one another."

Most EVV rightly take εἰς as indicating direction, "to one another," but conceivably it could express opposition (= hostile direction), "against one another" (cf. BAGD 229b), "at one another's expense."

ἀπεκδυσάμενοι

Nom. pl. masc. (agreeing with the pl. subject of ψεύδεσθε) of the aor. mid. ptc. of ἀπεκδύομαι, strip off completely (see on 2:15). Lightfoot (208, 212-213), Lohse (136, 141), and TCNT construe this ptc. and the ptc. ἐνδυσάμενοι in v. 10 as impv. in sense, "put off . . . put on . . . ," and therefore as comparable to ἀπόθεσθε ("put off") in v. 8 and ἐνδύσασθε ("put on") in v. 12. Since these two ptcs. are syntactically related to the impv. ψεύδεσθε, this is a possible construction, but there are compelling reasons for taking both ptcs. as causal adv. ptcs., specifying the twofold ground for the injunction μὴ ψεύδεσθε, "Do

not lie to one another, for you have stripped off . . . and have put on . . ." (sim.
RV, Weymouth, RSV, NASB, GNB, NIV; R 1128; Robertson, *Pictures* 502;
ZG 609; O'Brien 173, 189; C. Maurer, TDNT 6.644 n. 5):

(1) Throughout vv. 1-15 the basis for exhortation is repeatedly the central
facts of salvation (vv. 1, 2-3, 5, 7-8, 12, 13, 15).

(2) Ἐνδυσάμενοι ("you have put on," v. 10) provides the natural basis for
ἐνδύσασθε οὖν (*"therefore* put on," v. 12a); cf. "you died . . . therefore
put to death" (vv. 3, 5).

(3) If the ptcs. derived their impv. force from ψεύδεσθε, we would expect
this impv. also to be aor. (viz. μὴ ψεύσησθε).

(4) After the prohibition "do not lie," some adversative would be natural
before a further imperative: "but rather (μᾶλλον δέ or ἀλλά) put off. . . ."

(5) An impv. ἐνδυσάμενοι κτλ. ("put on . . .") ill accords with a section that
focuses on vices, not virtues (contrast v. 12).

(6) In the parallel passage (Eph. 4:22-25), the command to "put away false-
hood" (v. 25) is based (διό, "therefore") on a prior "putting off" (v. 22)
and "putting on" (v. 24).

τὸν παλαιὸν ἄνθρωπον

Paul's contrast between ὁ παλαιὸς ἄνθρωπος (v. 9) and ὁ νέος [ἄνθρωπος]
(v. 10) is not only a contrast between "the old self" and "the new self"
(Weymouth, NASB, GNB, Barclay; sim. Goodspeed, NIV), "the old nature"
and "the new nature" (Moffatt, RSV, NEB), but also between the Humanity in
Adam and the new Humanity in Christ. Ἄνθρωπος has both individual and
collective overtones: this individual "man" or "Man(kind)" as a whole is "old"
(παλαιός, -ά, -όν) in the sense of belonging to the "earlier, unregenerate" state
(BAGD 605d). See For Further Study 36, "The 'Old Person/Humanity' and
the 'New Person/Humanity.'"

σὺν ταῖς πράξεσιν αὐτοῦ

Dat. pl. (after σύν) of πρᾶξις, -εως, ἡ (course of) action; evil deed; (pl.) behavior.
The term generally has negative ethical connotations; thus "(the òld self) with
its evil practices" (NASB), including the vices mentioned in vv. 5 and 8. Αὐτοῦ
refers to ὁ παλαιὸς ἄνθρωπος and may be poss. ("that characterized it") or subj.
("that expressed it").

VERSE 10

καὶ ἐνδυσάμενοι τὸν νέον

Nom. pl. masc. (agreeing with the pl. subj. of ψεύδεσθε) of the aor. mid. ptc.

of ἐνδύω, clothe; (mid.) clothe oneself in, put on oneself. The ptc. is adv. with a causal sense (see on v. 9). Ἄνθρωπον is to be supplied from v. 9 with the adj. νέον. No consistent distinction can be drawn between the NT adjs. νέος (-α, -ον) and καινός (-ή, -όν), "new," esp. since the two roots are juxtaposed here (νέον . . . ἀνακαινούμενον), as also in the parallel passage, Eph. 4:23-24 (ἀνανεοῦσθαι . . . καινόν; see further BAGD 394a-c, 536a-b; J. Behm, TDNT 3.447-454; 4.896-901). Because ἐνδύομαι has Χριστόν as its obj. in Rom. 13:14 and Gal. 3:27, it is tempting to identify the "new person/humanity" as Christ himself. But this view destroys the "old person/humanity—new person/humanity" parallel (Christians do not "put off" Adam) and ignores the fact that the "new person" is being "renewed" and that this renewal promotes conformity to Christ as the image of God (see below).

τὸν ἀνακαινούμενον

Acc. sg. masc. (agreeing with τὸν νέον [ἄνθρωπον]) of the pres. pass. ptc. of ἀνακαινόω, renew (see Turner, *Words* 399-401). This is an explanatory art. ptc. (cf. Burton §§ 295, 426), equivalent to a rel. clause (cf. BDF § 412; R 764, 1106-1108; T 152): "which is being constantly renewed" (NEB), with God or the Spirit (cf. Tit. 3:5) as the implied agent. Paradoxically, the "new person/humanity" is continuously (pres. tense) being made new "again" (ἀνα-; cf. MH 295), in progressive conformity to the divine image (2 Cor. 3:18; 4:16; see below).

εἰς ἐπίγνωσιν

Ἐπίγνωσις here may merely be equivalent to γνῶσις (see on 1:9 and on 1:6 [ἐπέγνωτε]), but if it forms a goal or outcome of the constant remolding, it means "ever-increasing knowledge" (Zerwick, *Analysis* 452), "true knowledge" (NASB, JB), or "full knowledge" (BAGD 55c; Weymouth, GNB; sim. Barclay; cf. 1 Cor. 13:12). The unexpressed obj. of the ἐπίγνωσις is God (cf. 1:10; thus Moffatt, Goodspeed, NEB, GNB), or God's will (cf. 1:9), or even Christ (cf. 2:2; Eph. 1:17; 4:13).

Εἰς may be understood as:

(1) expressing direction: "towards true knowledge" (JB; sim. Weymouth, NASB),

(2) equivalent to a locat. ἐν: "in the sphere of knowledge," "in knowledge" (thus BAGD 291c; 455d; TCNT, RSV, NAB, NIV; Lohse 136, 142; O'Brien 173, 191, 192) or "in knowledge" = "with respect to [εἰς] knowledge,"

(3) telic: "for full knowledge" (BAGD 55c; sim. RV, Moffatt, Goodspeed, GNB),

(4) consec.: "leading to knowledge" (ZG 609; sim. NEB), or

*(5) temp.: "until it reaches fulness of knowledge" (Barclay; cf. Eph. 4:13).

κατ' εἰκόνα τοῦ κτίσαντος αὐτόν

Κατά (the final α is elided before an initial diphthong; cf. BDF § 17; MH 61-62; R 206-208) here means "in conformity with," "after the pattern of" (+ acc.). On εἰκών, -όνος, ἡ, "image," see on 1:15. Κτίσαντος is gen. sg. masc. of the aor. act. ptc. of κτίζω, create. With the art. (τοῦ) this ptc. is subst., ὁ κτίσας (cf. Matt. 19:4) being "he who created," "the Creator."

Although the tr. of this clause, which should be cstr. with τὸν ἀνακαινούμενον, is straightforward (viz. "after the image of its creator"), three identifications need to be made:

(1) Εἰκόνα probably refers to Christ, who is the image of God (1:15; 2 Cor. 4:4), rather than to God himself (cf. Gen. 1:26), for Paul is discussing the renewal of the "new person/humanity," not the re-creation of the first person, and in his thought Christ is the paradigm for believers' transformation (Rom. 8:29; 1 Cor. 15:49; 2 Cor. 3:18).

(2) Τοῦ κτίσαντος refers to God, not Christ, for in the Pauline corpus the expressed or implied subj. of κτίζω is always God. For this gen., see on τοῦ θεοῦ in 1:15. The aor. is constative, speaking of some indefinite time or times in the past.

(3) Αὐτόν refers to "the new person" or the new Humanity, not mankind in itself or Christ as the new Man, for (i) the only explicit antecedent to αὐτόν is τὸν νέον [ἄνθρωπον]; (ii) "the old person/humanity" can neither be equated with the first person nor be considered a divine creation; and (iii) in no sense would Paul say that God "created" Christ (cf. 1:16-17).

If these identifications are correct, Paul is affirming that God created "the new person/humanity" and is now renewing it after the pattern of Christ, who is God's image. The Creator's aim in this re-creation is not exactly the restoration in the creature of the pristine divine image, now tarnished by sin, but rather the construction of a new image, that of Christ. This ongoing process continues until a full knowledge of God is acquired and Christians finally bear "the image of the heavenly man" (1 Cor. 15:49; cf. Rom. 8:29) as the result of a resurrection transformation.

VERSE 11

ὅπου οὐκ ἔνι

Ὅπου is a particle indicating place, "where," which here refers back either to *the new Humanity itself or to the refashioning of "the new person/humanity" or to the image of the re-creation. Ἔνι is the original and strengthened form of ἐν, with ἐστίν understood, and thus stands for ἔνεστιν, "is in," "is present" (BDF § 98; MH 306; R 313; Robertson, *Pictures* 503). In the NT it is always found with the neg. οὐκ: "there is not," "there does not exist," "there cannot be." Both fact and possibility are negated.

Ἕλλην καὶ Ἰουδαῖος, περιτομὴ καὶ ἀκροβυστία

Ἕλλην, -νος, ὁ, a Greek; a Gentile. When the term is used with Ἰουδαῖος (-ου, ὁ, Jew), the whole human race is signified (H. Windisch, TDNT 1.552; 2.515-516; cf. Rom. 1:16). In a threefold grouping, Ἕλληνες are "non-Jews of Greek origin and culture" (H. Windisch, TDNT 1.553) and βάρβαροι are non-Greeks in origin or culture (H. Windisch, TDNT 1.551-552). The sgs. are generic and so may be rendered "Gentiles and Jews" (GNB). Dissimilar entities may be associated by καί (R 1188).

"Circumcision" (περιτομή) and "uncircumcision" (ἀκροβυστία, -ας, ἡ, foreskin) are abstracts for concrete (BAGD 33d, 653a), and correspond to the previous pair of words, forming a chiasmus A-B-B-A (BDF § 477[2]; Turner, *Style* 97): "the circumcised" (= Jews) and "the uncircumcised" (= Gentiles; cf. Rom. 3:29-30). See Turner, *Words* 71-72.

βάρβαρος, Σκύθης, δοῦλος, ἐλεύθερος

While the fourth pair are opposites ("slave, freeman" [ἐλεύθερος, -ου, ὁ]), the third pair are not, for the Scythian (Σκύθης, -ου, ὁ, an inhabitant of what is now southern Russia) was a notorious example of the "barbarian" (βάρβαρος, -ου, ὁ), the non-Greek who could not speak Greek. See further Lightfoot 214-217.

Paul's point in v. 11a is that in the new Humanity, just as old practices were abandoned (v. 9b), so too traditional distinctions are obliterated, whether they be racial, ceremonial, cultural, or social.

ἀλλὰ τὰ πάντα καὶ ἐν πᾶσιν Χριστός

Ἀλλά, "on the contrary," "rather," looks back to the listed distinctions, all now eradicated. Although Χριστός is anarthrous and πάντα art., "Christ" is the subj. and "everything" is the pred., with ἐστίν understood. "Christ is all" does not mean he is the sum total (τὰ πάντα) of all that exists (= pantheism) but that he is "absolutely everything," all that matters. Ἐν πᾶσιν could be neut. (Christ is "present in everything" [cf. 1:17b], "active in all circumstances") but is far more likely to be masc.—either "in all people" (not a Pauline sentiment) or *"in all of you" who belong to the new Humanity and are being progressively renewed (cf. 1:27).

Καί shows that two distinct ideas are being expressed, as in Eph. 4:6 (διὰ πάντων καὶ ἐν πᾶσιν), not one, as in 1 Cor. 15:28 and Eph. 1:23 (τὰ πάντα ἐν πᾶσιν): not, "Christ is all in all" (Barclay), or "Christ is everything in all of you" (NAB), but "Christ is all and in all" (RV, RSV, NASB; Lohse 136, 145; O'Brien 173, 193). Christ amounts to everything and indwells all—without distinction—who belong to his new people.

TRANSLATION

[5] Therefore put to death your limbs as used for earthly purposes—immorality, impurity, lust, evil craving, and especially ruthless greed, which is idolatry. [6] These sins incur God's wrath. [7] You also once practiced these sins when you used to live that way. [8] But now you are in fact to put all these off—anger, rage, spite, slander, foul-mouthed language. [9] Do not lie to one another, for you have stripped off the old nature with its practices [10] and have put on the new nature which is being renewed after the image of its Creator until it reaches full knowledge of him. [11] Here no distinction exists between Greek and Jew, circumcision and uncircumcision, barbarian, Scythian, slave and freeman, but Christ is everything and in all.

EXPANDED PARAPHRASE

[5] So then, give evidence of your death to the world: regard your bodily limbs as completely dead with respect to their former earthly actions—immorality and impurity of any and every type, sensual craving and debased passion, and especially covetousness, which makes the desire to get and to have into a god. [6] Never forget that it is these very sins that bring God's wrath. [7] There was a time when you yourselves also indulged in these sins, when your life was given over to such action. [8] But as things now stand, you must put off all sins of any kind, including chronic anger, sudden rage, malicious spite, slanderous talk, and foul-mouthed language. [9] Do not lie to one another in either word or deed; remember that you have stripped off forever the old Adamic nature, the old Humanity, together with the actions that expressed it, [10] and have put on the new nature you have in Christ, the new Humanity, which is being renewed day by day in conformity with Christ, who is the image of the God who created this new nature, until it finally attains full knowledge of God and his will. [11] In this new Humanity, the Church, all personal distinctions are eradicated—between Greek and Jew, the circumcised and the uncircumcised, barbarian, Scythian, the slave and the freeman. On the contrary, Christ himself amounts to everything and he is in all of you.

FOR FURTHER STUDY

33. Doctrinal Indicative—Ethical Imperative (3:5, 8-10)

*Dennison, W. D., "Indicative and Imperative: The Basic Structure of Pauline Ethics," *Calvin Theological Journal* 14 (1979) 55-78.

Furnish, V. P., *Theology and Ethics in Paul* (Nashville: Abingdon, 1968), esp. 224-227.

Ridderbos, H., *Paul. An Outline of His Theology,* tr. J. R. de Witt (Grand Rapids: Eerdmans, 1975) 253-258, 270-271.

Schnackenburg, R., *The Moral Teaching of the New Testament,* tr. J. Holland-Smith and W. J. O'Hara (New York: Seabury, 1965) 268-277.

Tannehill, R. C., *Dying and Rising with Christ* (Berlin: Töpelmann, 1967).

34. Catalogs of Virtues and Vices (3:5-8, 12-14)

Cannon 51-94.

Carrington, P., *The Primitive Christian Catechism: A Study in the Epistles* (Cambridge: Cambridge University, 1940).

Daube, D., *The New Testament and Rabbinic Judaism* (New York: Arno, 1973, reprint of 1956 edition) 90-140.

Easton, B. S., "New Testament Ethical Lists," *JBL* 51 (1932) 1-12.

Horst, P. W. vån der, "Observations on a Pauline Expression," *NTS* 19 (1973-74) 181-187.

Hunter, A. M., *Paul and His Predecessors* (London: SCM, 1961[2]) 52-57, 128-131.

McEleney, N. J., "The Vice Lists of the Pastoral Epistles," *CBQ* 36 (1974) 203-219.

Schweizer, E., "Traditional Ethical Patterns in the Pauline and post-Pauline Letters and their Development (Lists of Vices and House-tables)," in *Text and Interpretation,* ed. E. Best and R. McL. Wilson (Cambridge: Cambridge University, 1979) 195-209.

*Seitz, O. J. F., IDB 3.137-139.

Selwyn, E. G., *The First Epistle of St. Peter* (Grand Rapids: Baker, 1981, reprint of 1947[2]) 363-466.

35. The Wrath of God (3:6)

Berkouwer, G. C., *Sin,* tr. P. C. Holtrop (Grand Rapids: Eerdmans, 1971) 354-423.

Dahlberg, B. T., IDB 4.903-908.

Erlandsson, S., "The Wrath of YHWH," *Tyndale Bulletin* 23 (1972) 111-116.

Hahn, H. C., NIDNTT 1.107-113.

Hanson, A. T., *The Wrath of the Lamb* (London: SPCK, 1957).

Macgregor, G. H. C., "The Concept of the Wrath of God in the New Testament," *NTS* 7 (1960-61) 101-109.

Morris, L., *The Apostolic Preaching of the Cross* (Grand Rapids: Eerdmans, 1965³) 147-154, 179-184, 208-213.

*———, *The Cross in the New Testament* (Grand Rapids: Eerdmans, 1965) 189-192.

O'Brien 184-185.

Stählin, G., TDNT 5.419-447.

Tasker, R. V. G., *The Biblical Doctrine of the Wrath of God* (London: Tyndale, 1957²).

Travis, S. H., *Christ and the Judgement of God* (London: Marshall Pickering, 1986).

White, W., Jr., ZPEB 5.990-995.

36. The "Old Person/Humanity" and the "New Person/Humanity" (3:9-10)

Barth, M., *Ephesians 4–6* (Garden City, NY: Doubleday, 1974), 536-545.

Behm, J., TDNT 3.449-453.

*Harrisville, R. A., "The Concept of Newness in the New Testament," *JBL* 74 (1955) 69-79.

Jeremias, J., TDNT 1.365-366.

Robinson, J. A. T., *The Body. A Study in Pauline Theology* (Chicago: Regnery, 1952).

Scroggs, R., *The Last Adam. A Study in Pauline Anthropology* (Philadelphia: Fortress, 1966).

Shedd, R. P., *Man in Community* (Grand Rapids: Eerdmans, 1964), esp. 155-156.

Tannehill, R. C., *Dying and Rising with Christ* (Berlin: Töpelmann, 1967).

HOMILETICAL SUGGESTIONS

"Putting off" Vices (3:5-11)

1. Put to death (νεκρώσατε) your bodily limbs as used for earthly purposes (v. 5a):
> immorality—impurity
> lust—evil craving, and
> ruthless greed, which is idolatry (v. 5b)
> because: (a) you have died (with Christ, 2:20) to the world and its sin

(ἀπεθάνετε . . . νεκρώσατε οὖν, vv. 3, 5)
(b) such sins incur God's wrath (δι' ἅ, v. 6)
(c) such conduct belongs to your past (ποτέ, v. 7)
2. Put off (ἀπόθεσθε) all the following vices (v. 8a):
anger—rage
spite—slander
foul language from your mouth
3. Put an end to lying (μὴ ψεύδεσθε) to one another (v. 9a) because:
(a) you have put off the old Humanity, your Adamic nature, along with
its characteristic conduct (v. 9b)
(b) you have put on the new Humanity, your new nature in Christ, which
is being constantly renewed (v. 10b) and in which all traditional barriers
are abolished and Christ is central (v. 11).

The Two Humanities or Natures (3:9b-11)

1. The Old:
(a) its customary practices (v. 9b; listed in vv. 5b, 8b)
(b) it has been stripped off like a garment needing to be discarded
(ἀπεκδυσάμενοι, v. 9)
2. The New:
(a) its constant renewal (v. 10b)
(b) it has been put on like a garment suitable for every occasion
(ἐνδυσάμενοι, v. 10a)

Christian Renewal (3:10)

1. It began at the point of regeneration (ἐνδυσάμενοι).
2. It continues in the process of sanctification (τὸν ἀνακαινούμενον).
3. It is modeled on Christ, the perfect Image of the God (1:15) who created
the new Humanity (κατ' εἰκόνα τοῦ κτίσαντος αὐτόν).
4. It will issue in a perfect knowledge of God (εἰς ἐπίγνωσιν; cf. 1 Cor.
13:12b).

B. "PUTTING ON" VIRTUES (3:12-17)

12 Ἐνδύσασθε οὖν ὡς ἐκλεκτοὶ τοῦ θεοῦ, ἅγιοι καὶ ἠγαπημένοι, σπλάγχνα οἰκ-τιρμοῦ, χρηστότητα, ταπεινοφροσύνην, πραΰτητα, μακροθυμίαν, 13 ἀνεχόμενοι ἀλλήλων καὶ χαριζόμενοι ἑαυτοῖς ἐάν τις πρός τινα ἔχῃ μομφήν· καθὼς καὶ ὁ κύριος ἐχαρίσατο ὑμῖν οὕτως καὶ ὑμεῖς· 14 ἐπὶ πᾶσιν δὲ τούτοις τὴν ἀγάπην, ὅ ἐστιν σύνδεσμος τῆς τελειότητος. 15 καὶ ἡ εἰρήνη τοῦ Χριστοῦ βραβευέτω ἐν ταῖς καρδίαις ὑμῶν, εἰς ἣν καὶ ἐκλήθητε ἐν ἑνὶ σώματι· καὶ εὐχάριστοι γίνεσθε. 16 ὁ λόγος τοῦ Χριστοῦ ἐνοικείτω ἐν ὑμῖν πλουσίως, ἐν πάσῃ σοφίᾳ διδάσκοντες καὶ νουθετοῦντες ἑαυτοὺς ψαλμοῖς, ὕμνοις, ᾠδαῖς πνευματικαῖς ἐν τῇ χάριτι ᾄδοντες ἐν ταῖς καρδίαις ὑμῶν τῷ θεῷ· 17 καὶ πᾶν ὅ τι ἐὰν ποιῆτε ἐν λόγῳ ἢ ἐν ἔργῳ, πάντα ἐν ὀνόματι κυρίου Ἰησοῦ, εὐχαριστοῦντες τῷ θεῷ πατρὶ δι᾽ αὐτοῦ.

STRUCTURE

```
12 Ἐνδύσασθε οὖν
                σπλάγχνα      οἰκτιρμοῦ
                χρηστότητα,   ταπεινοφροσύνην
                πραΰτητα,     μακροθυμίαν
13 ἀνεχόμενοι   ἀλλήλους καὶ
   χαριζόμενοι  ἑαυτοῖς
                καθὼς καὶ ὁ κύριος ἐχαρίσατο ὑμῖν
                οὕτως καὶ ὑμεῖς·
14 [ἐνδύσασθε]
                τὴν ἀγάπην
                ὅ ἐστιν σύνδεσμος τῆς τελειότητος.
15         καὶ ἡ εἰρήνη τοῦ Χριστοῦ  βραβευέτω      ἐν ταῖς καρδίαις ὑμῶν
      εἰς ἣν καὶ                     ἐκλήθητε
           καὶ                       εὐχάριστοι γίνεσθε.
16         ὁ λόγος τοῦ Χριστοῦ ἐνοικείτω     ἐν ὑμῖν
           ἐν πάσῃ σοφίᾳ διδάσκοντες καὶ
                         νουθετοῦντες   ἑαυτοὺς
           ἐν τῇ χάριτι  ᾄδοντες        ἐν ταῖς καρδίαις ὑμῶν
17         καὶ πᾶν ὅ τι  ἐὰν ποιῆτε  ἐν λόγῳ ἢ
                                     ἐν ἔργῳ

   [ποιεῖτε]  πάντα              ἐν ὀνόματι        κυρίου Ἰησοῦ,
                                 εὐχαριστοῦντες . . . δι᾽  αὐτοῦ.
```

(1) Verses 12-17 correspond to vv. 5-11 in issuing specific ethical directives and in being positive exhortation ("putting on" virtues) after negative

injunction ("putting off" vices). Each section (viz. vv. 5-11, 12-17) is linked with what precedes by οὖν ("therefore") and begins with an aor. impv. (νεκρώσατε, v. 5; ἐνδύσασθε, v. 12), which is followed by a tabulation of five items (vices and virtues, respectively).

(2) The two pres. ptcs. in v. 13 (ἀνεχόμενοι, χαριζόμενοι) derive their impv. force from ἐνδύσασθε (v. 12), an impv. on which they are grammatically dependent. Ἐνδύσασθε is to be supplied in v. 14 with the direct obj. τὴν ἀγάπην.

(3) Verses 15-17 form a distinct unit, with two third person pres. impvs. (βραβευέτω, ἐνοικείτω) that relate to "the peace of Christ" (v. 15) and "the word of Christ" (v. 16) respectively, and two second person pres. impvs. (γίνεσθε, v. 15; [ποιεῖτε], v. 17).

(4) The three pres. ptcs. in v. 16 (διδάσκοντες, νουθετοῦντες, ᾄδοντες) are dependent on ἐνοικείτω and are probably modal ("*by* teaching and admonishing, . . . and *by* singing"). The pres. ptc. εὐχαριστοῦντες in v. 17 is dependent on an implied ποιεῖτε and is circumstantial ("all the while giving thanks").

VERSE 12

Ἐνδύσασθε οὖν ὡς ἐκλεκτοὶ τοῦ θεοῦ

2 pl. aor. mid. impv. of ἐνδύω, clothe; (mid.) clothe oneself in, put on oneself. Either "put on" (RV, RSV, NEB, NASB) or "clothe yourselves with" (TCNT, GNB, NAB, NIV). Οὖν ("therefore") alludes to 3:10: "since you have put on the new person, which is being progressively renewed, effect that renewal by putting on the virtues that are characteristic of this new nature." A further reason for the injunction "put on" is introduced by causal ὡς: "inasmuch as (ὡς; Zerwick, *Analysis* 452) you are God's chosen people" (sim. NAB). But BAGD (898a) sees this ὡς as introducing an actual, characteristic quality. Either way, Paul is enjoining the Colossians to wear those moral garments that are appropriate to their calling and status.

Ἐκλεκτοί is nom. pl. masc. (agreeing with the subj. implied in ἐνδύσασθε) of ἐκλεκτός, -ή, -όν, chosen (see Turner, *Words* 127-129). As is customary in Gk., the masc. gender is used when both males and females are included (cf. BDF § 135[2]; R 412; T 22). Being qualitative in emphasis, this adj. is anar., "as chosen ones." On the relation between κλητοί ("called") and ἐκλεκτοί see Lightfoot 218. Also see For Further Study 37, "Predestination and Election." Τοῦ θεοῦ is either poss. ("as God's elect," RV; "as God's chosen people," NIV), or subj. after the verbal idea (ἐκλέγομαι, choose) implied in ἐκλεκτοί ("as persons chosen by God," Goodspeed).

ἅγιοι καὶ ἠγαπημένοι

Nom. pl. masc. (agreeing with the pl. subj. of ἐνδύσασθε) of the perf. pass. ptc. of ἀγαπάω, love. God is the implied agent; thus, "loved by God" (cf. BAGD 5a), "his beloved" (NEB), or "those on whom God has set his love" (a paraphrase that brings out the sense of the pf. tense and that distinguishes this verbal adj. from ἀγαπητοὶ θεοῦ [e.g., Rom. 1:7], "God's beloved"). On God's electing love, see E. Stauffer, TDNT 1.49-52. These two adjs. are not voc. but attrib. of ἐκλεκτοί: "God's chosen people, who are holy and loved by him."

σπλάγχνα οἰκτιρμοῦ

Σπλάγχνον, -ου, τό, always pl. in the NT; entrails, inward parts; heart (as the seat of the emotions); affection (see Turner, *Words* 78-80). Like the four abstract nouns that follow this phrase, σπλάγχνα is acc. after ἐνδύσασθε, and anar. as an abstract noun expressing a quality without particular ref. to specific, concrete expressions of that quality (cf. BDF § 258; T 176-177; and esp. Z §§ 176-179; but see Moule, *Idiom Book* 111-112; R 758, 794).

Οἰκτιρμός, -οῦ, ὁ, pity, mercy, compassion. In the other four NT uses of this word, it is pl. The gen. is qualitative, lit. "a heart of (= characterized by) compassion" (RV, NASB), thus "a compassionate heart" or "heartfelt compassion" (BAGD 561d), or, if it is a case of hendiadys, "compassion" (BAGD 264b), "tenderheartedness" (Weymouth).

χρηστότητα, ταπεινοφροσύνην, πραΰτητα, μακροθυμίαν

See note above for the case and the anar. state of these abstracts. Χρηστότης, -ητος, ἡ, kindness, kindliness, goodness, generosity. Ταπεινοφροσύνη, -ης, ἡ, humility, lowliness of mind (but see 1:18, 23 for a pejorative use of this word, "flaunted humility"; see further Turner, *Words* 216-218). Πραΰτης, -ητος, ἡ, courtesy, gentleness, meekness. On the diacritical mark over υ, called diaeresis (which prevents -αυ- from being regarded as a diphthong and shows that each vowel has its own sound), see BDF § 15; MH 50; R 204-205. Μακροθυμία, -ας, ἡ, patience, patient endurance, long-suffering, forbearance. See above For Further Study 34, "Catalogs of Virtues and Vices" (3:5-8, 12-14).

VERSE 13

ἀνεχόμενοι ἀλλήλων καὶ χαριζόμενοι ἑαυτοῖς

Nom. pl. masc. (agreeing with the pl. subj. of ἐνδύσασθε, v. 12) of the pres. mid. ptc. of ἀνέχω, (mid.) put up with, bear with (+ gen. of person, acc. of thing). ᾽Αλλήλων, gen. of the reciprocal pron. ἀλλήλους (acc.), ἀλλήλοις (dat.), "one another," is by nature always pl. and never nom. This gen. after ἀνέχομαι may be explained as specifying the cause of emotion (BDF § 176[1]; T 234), although Robertson (*Pictures* 504; cf. R 692) speaks of an "ablative" (= ablatival gen.; "holding yourselves back *from* one another").

Nom. pl. masc. of the pres. mid. ptc. of dep. χαρίζομαι, give freely, graciously confer; forgive (+ dat. of person forgiven [here ἑαυτοῖς] and acc. of thing forgiven [as in 2:13]). The refl. pron. ἑαυτοῖς (dat. pl. of ἑαυτοῦ, -ῆς, -οῦ) stands for the reciprocal pron. ἀλλήλοις (BDF § 287; Moule, *Idiom Book* 120; R 690; T 43-44), probably for stylistic variety (as in Eph. 4:32). There is therefore no difference in meaning here between ἀλλήλων and ἑαυτοῖς, both meaning "one another" (or "each other"), although Lightfoot (219) alleges that the reciprocal ἑαυτῶν emphasizes corporate unity. In the appropriate case, ἑαυτοῦ may be used of all three persons (apart from first person sg.; "I myself" is αὐτὸς ἐγώ, e.g., Rom. 7:25; see BAGD 211d, 212a-c): thus "ourselves; yourself, yourselves; himself, herself, itself, themselves."

These two pres. ptcs., grammatically dependent on the impv. ἐνδύσασθε (v. 12a), are unlikely to be modal in force ("put on . . . by forbearing . . . and forgiving") since the graces listed in v. 12b are wider than mutual toleration and forgiveness. Rather, they may express attendant circumstances ("put on. . . , forbearing one another and forgiving each other," RSV; sim. RV, TCNT, Weymouth, NASB; see 2:7 for this usage), or, alternatively, they may be cstr. as impvs. on the basis of their syntactical relation to ἐνδύσασθε ("Bear with one another; forgive each other," JB; sim. Moffatt, Goodspeed, NEB, GNB, NAB, NIV; R 1418; Lohse 136, 147; O'Brien 195, 201). Moreover, these ptcs. may describe specific instances of μακροθυμία—or even of all the Christian graces mentioned (cf. Moffatt).

ἐάν τις πρός τινα ἔχῃ μομφήν

3 sg. pres. act. subjunc. of ἔχω, have. Ἐάν (= εἰ + ἄν) followed by the pres. subjunc. in the protasis of a cond. sentence expresses a fut. cond. that is general or iter. (the so-called "third class" cond.; cf. the Glossary and BDF §§ 371[4], 373[1]; Moule, *Idiom Book* 148-149; R 1004-1007, 1016-1020; T 114; Z §§ 320-322, 325, 327). That grounds for complaint will arise among members of a congregation is here regarded as at least a distinct possibility, if not a probability. "If, as may well happen, anyone (τις, nom. sg. masc. of the encl. indef. pron.) has a grievance against (πρός; see BAGD 710c) someone else (τινα, acc. sg. masc. of the encl. indef. pron., anyone, someone). . . ." Μομφή, -ῆς, ἡ, means "cause for complaint," "ground for blame," "grievance," not "quarrel" or "wrangle."

καθὼς καὶ ὁ κύριος ἐχαρίσατο ὑμῖν οὕτως καὶ ὑμεῖς

3 sg. aor. mid. indic. of dep. χαρίζομαι, give freely; forgive (+ dat. of person forgiven [ὑμῖν]). Καί appears in both elements of the comparison (καθὼς . . . οὕτως, "just as . . . so"), emphasizing both the correlation and the contrast (cf. Lightfoot 133 on 1:6). With ὑμεῖς, καί is adjunctive and χαρίζεσθε (2 pl. pres. mid. impv.) is to be understood: "so you also must forgive" (RSV). Complementing this principle, "forgive because forgiven," is the teaching of Jesus in Matt. 6:12, 14-15; 18:23-35, "forgive in order to be forgiven." See For Further Study 38, "Forgiveness."

The reading κύριος (cf. Matt. 18:27) is supported by strong Alexandrian (𝔭⁴⁶ A B) and Western (D* F G itᵈ, ᵍ vg al) witnesses and is to be preferred over the variant Χριστός (read by a wide variety of mss. and reflected in Moffatt). Although the latter reading probably identifies correctly "the Lord" (Moule 123), it removes the ambiguity from κύριος (viz. God or Christ) and is therefore probably secondary as a less difficult rdg., as also are the other two variants, θεός (ℵ*) and the conflated rdg. θεὸς ἐν Χριστῷ (33 arm), which have been harmonized with Eph. 4:32 (cf. Metzger 625; Lightfoot 220).

VERSE 14

ἐπὶ πᾶσιν δὲ τούτοις τὴν ἀγάπην

Πᾶσιν is dat. (after ἐπί) pl. neut. of πᾶς, πᾶσα, πᾶν, all, every. Τούτοις is dat. pl. neut. (agreeing with πᾶσιν) of the demonstrative pron. and adj. οὗτος, αὕτη, τοῦτο, this. Tr.: "all these things" (= virtues or qualities or articles of clothing). Ἐπί may have any one of three meanings:

*(1) "in addition to" (BDF § 235[3]; R 605; Z § 128; Lohse 136; Moule 123; O'Brien 195, 203; sim. BAGD 287b; NASB, GNB),
 (2) "over" (= "on top of" [Zerwick, *Analysis* 453], developing the clothing imagery; TCNT, JB, NAB, NIV; sim. Weymouth), or
 (3) "above (all)" (Moffatt; ZG 610; cf. NEB, "to crown all").

"Above all these things" (RV; sim. RSV) could be (3) or (2).

With τὴν ἀγάπην, we should probably supply ἐνδύσασθε, "put on," from v. 12 (thus most EVV; O'Brien 195, 203; Robertson, *Pictures* 504), although more general vbs. could be supplied, such as "add" (on the basis of ἐπί = "in addition to"; GNB; G. Delling, TDNT 8.79 and n. 7) or "there must be" (NEB, perhaps reflecting an impv. ἔχοντες; sim. Moffatt). The art. with ἀγάπην suggests that concrete expressions of love, love dramatized, is in mind (cf.

Z § 176). On the ἀγαπ- word group, see Turner, *Words* 261-268; For Further
Study 39, "Love."

ὅ ἐστιν

Nom. sg. neut. of the rel. pron. ὅς, ἥ, ὅ. Some suggest that this expression is
formulaic and explanatory, "which is," "that is to say," the vernacular equivalent of the literary τοῦτ᾽ ἔστιν (or τουτέστιν). The neut. rel. is used without
ref. to the gender of either the antecedent (ἀγάπην, fem.), the word explained,
or the pred. subst. (σύνδεσμος, masc., although ℵ* D* read ὅς [cf. Lightfoot
247]), the word that explains (cf. BDF § 132[2]; BAGD 584d; Robertson,
Pictures 504; R 411, but cf. R 713). Alternatively, the antecedent of ὅ may be
the general concept of "the putting on of love" or of "love-put-on," i.e., love
in action (cf. R 713). Accordingly, this expression should not be classified as
a solecism (as it is by T 317; Turner, *Style* 86).

σύνδεσμος τῆς τελειότητος

Σύνδεσμος, -ου, ὁ, that which fastens or binds together; thus link, bond, joint,
ligament (see 2:19). As a philosophical term, it denotes that which overcomes
duality or plurality by producing unity (cf. G. Fitzer, TDNT 7.856-859). There
is no evidence that it denotes a belt or "girdle" (TCNT; so also Robertson,
Pictures 504, and Zerwick, *Analysis* 453) that holds clothes together. Being
pred., this noun is anar., although def. "Which is the bond" may be rendered
"which binds together" (sim. Goodspeed, RSV, NEB, NAB, NIV). What love
or dramatized love "binds together" may be: *(a) the virtues, viewed as garments (thus Goodspeed, JB, NAB, NIV; and, apparently, RSV, NEB, GNB),
or (b) fellow-believers (G. Delling, TDNT 8.79; Lohse 149; O'Brien 204).
    The gen. τῆς τελειότητος (τελειότης, -ητος, ἡ, perfection, completeness)
is not likely to be poss. ("the bond belonging to perfection") or subj. ("the bond
produced by perfection"). This leaves three options:

(1) epexegetic/appositional: "the bond that consists of perfection" (sim.
    Robertson, *Pictures* 504);
(2) qualitative/descriptive: "the bond characterized by perfection," "the per-
    fect bond" (Barclay; NASB, "the perfect bond of unity"; sim. Wey-
    mouth), "the bond of perfection" (sim. RV), or, if τελειότης is taken to
    mean "perfect unity" (some Western witnesses [D* F G it] actually read
    ἑνότητος, from ἑνότης, -ητος, ἡ, unity), "the bond of perfect unity"
    (BAGD 785c) or ". . . which binds all things together in perfect unity"
    (GNB; sim. RSV, NIV); or
*(3) objective: "the bond that produces perfection" (BDF § 163, citing A. Fri-

drichsen; sim. T 212; Lohse 136, 148-149; O'Brien 195, 203-204, 213), or "the bond that perfects."

What love or love-in-action "perfects" or "completes" may be: *(a) the virtues (thus Goodspeed, JB, NAB; cf. Zerwick, *Analysis* 453, "without love the virtues, as it were, melt away"); (b) "the whole" (NEB; sim. TCNT); or (c) the Christian community (Lohse 149).

VERSE 15

καὶ ἡ εἰρήνη τοῦ Χριστοῦ βραβευέτω

3 sg. pres. act. impv. of βραβεύω. Originally this word depicted the task of the umpire (the βραβεύς or βραβευτής) of "directing" the athletic games and "deciding" the winners of the contest (E. Stauffer, TDNT 1.637-638). Then it came to have more general applications—to arbitrate, give a verdict, preside, rule, control, or hold sway.

It is improbable that τοῦ Χριστοῦ should be classified as a "mystical" gen. (see T 212 for this category): "the peace belonging to those who are in the Body of Christ" or "the peace you have through your union with Christ." Rather, this gen. is subj.: either "the peace that Christ gives" (GNB; sim. TCNT, Weymouth; cf. R 499) or "the peace brought by Christ" (BAGD 227d). Cf. Jn. 14:27; 2 Thess. 3:16.

ἐν ταῖς καρδίαις ὑμῶν

Not "among you" (= ἐν ὑμῖν [v. 16] or ἐν μέσῳ ὑμῶν), but "(with)in your hearts" (locat. ἐν). Here καρδία may signify the mind or the thinking process (thus GNB, "in the decisions you make") or, by synecdoche, the whole person. Tr.: "let the peace that Christ gives act as arbitrator in your hearts." That is, "in making your decisions, in choosing between alternatives, in settling conflicts of will, a concern to preserve the inward and communal peace that Christ gave and gives should be your controlling principle" (cf. Eph. 4:3).

εἰς ἣν καὶ ἐκλήθητε

2 pl. aor. indic. pass. of καλέω, call. God is the implied agent. Ἥν, acc. (after εἰς) sg. fem. (agreeing with the antecedent, ἡ εἰρήνη) of the rel. pron. ὅς, ἥ, ὅ. After the vb. καλεῖν, εἰς defines the goal or purpose, "to experience," "to share in." Καί either strengthens the rel. ("to enjoy *this very* peace") or is emphatic ("for you were, *indeed,* called to share in this peace"). The rel. may be causal (cf. R 960), "since . . . you have been called to that peace" (NAB; sim. Goodspeed, Barclay, NIV).

ἐν ἑνὶ σώματι

Dat. sg. neut. (agreeing with σώματι) of the cardinal numeral εἷς, μία, ἕν, one. Ἐν may express here:

(1) cause: "(called to this peace) *in that* you belong to a single body,"
(2) instrumentality: "through your incorporation into the one Body of Christ,"
(3) purpose: "so that you might be united in one body" (Barclay) or result: "so that you form one body" (ἓν = telic or ecbatic εἰς), or
*(4) attendant circumstances: "as members of one Body" (TCNT; sim. Weymouth, Moffatt, NEB, JB, NAB, NIV; Lightfoot 221; cf. T 264).

The use of ἓν σῶμα in Rom. 12:5 and Eph. 4:4 (cf. 1 Cor. 12:12) suggests that the "one body" here is not a single local congregation but the one universal Body of Christ (cf. 1:18, 24). See above For Further Study 21, "The Church as the Body of Christ" (1:24).

καὶ εὐχάριστοι γίνεσθε

2 pl. pres. mid. impv. of dep. γίνομαι, be, become. Like ἔσεσθε (2 pl. fut. of εἰμί), γίνεσθε takes the place of ἔστε (2 pl. impv. of εἰμί), which does not occur in the LXX or NT (MH 203). Εὐχάριστος, -ον, thankful (both feeling grateful and expressing gratitude); a two-termination adj. Although found only here in the Gk. Bible, this adj. was commonly used in inscriptions of those who were "grateful" to their benefactors (MM 268). Tr.: "always be thankful" (JB), "and be filled with gratitude" (NEB), "and show yourselves thankful" (TCNT; sim. ZG 610), "make it your habit to be thankful."

VERSE 16

ὁ λόγος τοῦ Χριστοῦ

This phrase may mean "the word spoken by Christ" (τοῦ Χριστοῦ, subj. gen.; cf. GNB, "Christ's message"), "the Christian message" (BAGD 478b; adj. gen.), or *"the teaching concerning Christ" (Weymouth; sim. O'Brien 206-207, 213; obj. gen.). The rendering "the message of Christ" (Goodspeed, NEB, JB; sim. TCNT) could be subj. or obj. gen.—or both—and thus reflects the ambiguity of the Gk. Some mss. read θεοῦ (A C* 33) or κυρίου (א* I), the more usual qualifiers of ὁ λόγος in Paul, but Χριστοῦ has strong and wide external support (𝔓⁴⁶ B D G Ψ 1739 Byz Lect it vg syrʰ copˢᵃ al) and is the more difficult reading (cf. Metzger 625).

ἐνοικείτω ἐν ὑμῖν πλουσίως

3 sg. pres. act. impv. of ἐνοικέω, live in, dwell in. The concept is dynamic, not static: "the message of Christ" is not merely to be present as a resident but is to be operative as a powerful force. Ἐν ὑμῖν (note the repetition of the pref. ἐν- from the compound vb.; cf. R 559-560) is ambiguous, for it could mean "within you" (NASB), "in your hearts" (Weymouth, Lightfoot 222; sim. TCNT), or, in a corporate sense, "among you" (NEB; G. Delling, TDNT 8.498 n. 63; Lohse 136, 150), "in your midst" (Moffatt). The adv. πλουσίως may be cstr. with ἐνοικείτω ("richly," RV, RSV, NASB, Barclay, NIV; O'Brien 195, 207; "abundantly," Lohse 136, 150 ["in rich abundance"]) or with ὁ λόγος τοῦ Χριστοῦ ("in all its richness," NEB, GNB, JB; sim. TCNT, Moffatt, NAB; "as a rich treasure," Weymouth).

ἐν πάσῃ σοφίᾳ

"With all (possible) wisdom," "with the utmost wisdom" (NEB), ἐν denoting attendant circumstances or mode/manner. Construing the phrase closely with ὁ λόγος and πλουσίως, Moffatt renders it "with all its wealth of wisdom" (sim. Goodspeed).

In the latter part of v. 16 there are three decisions to be made with regard to punctuation:

(1) Take ἐν πάσῃ σοφίᾳ
    (a) with ἐνοικείτω (or ὁ λόγος; RV, Goodspeed, Moffatt; WH 1.449) or
 *(b) with διδάσκοντες καὶ νουθετοῦντες ἑαυτούς (most EVV; UBS; Lohse 136, 151; O'Brien 195, 208).

Two observations support (b): ἐνοικείτω is already qualified by πλουσίως; if ἐν πάσῃ σοφίᾳ has the sense "in a tactful manner," it accords better with "teaching" than "indwelling."

(2) Construe ψαλμοῖς . . . πνευματικαῖς
    (a) with διδάσκοντες καὶ νουθετοῦντες ἑαυτούς (RV, Weymouth, Moffatt, Goodspeed; WH 1.449; Lightfoot 222; O'Brien 195, 207 and esp. 208-209) or
 *(b) with ᾄδοντες (most EVV; Lohse 136, 151).

In favor of (b): three different words for "song" seem more suitable with "singing" than with "teaching" (1 Cor. 14:26 and Eph. 5:19 notwithstanding); the dats. ψαλμοῖς κτλ. may be instr. ("with/using") rather than indicative of content (normally expressed by the acc. after ᾄδω). The one difficulty with (b) is that the ptc. ᾄδοντες then bears the weight of three qualifying statements.

(3) Take ἐν τῇ χάριτι
    (a) with διδάσκοντες κτλ. (Goodspeed; WH 1.449; Lightfoot 223) or
  *(b) with ᾄδοντες κτλ. (most EVV; Lohse 136; Moule 126; O'Brien 195, 208, 210).

On view (b), ἐν τῇ χάριτι ᾄδοντες is then parallel to ἐν πάσῃ σοφίᾳ διδάσκοντες κτλ.

From these punctuation alternatives two main options in translation emerge:

(1) Representing 1(a), 2(a), and 3(a) and reflecting the punctuation in WH 1.449:
"Let the message of Christ live in your hearts in all its wealth of wisdom. Teach it to one another and train one another in it with thankfulness, with psalms, hymns, and sacred songs, and sing to God with all your hearts" (Goodspeed).
*(2) Representing 1(b), 2(b), and 3(b):
"Let the word of Christ dwell in you richly as you teach and admonish one another with all wisdom, and as you sing psalms, hymns and spiritual songs with gratitude in your hearts to God" (NIV).

διδάσκοντες καὶ νουθετοῦντες ἑαυτούς

Nom. pl. masc. of the pres. act. ptcs. of διδάσκω, teach, and νουθετέω, admonish, warn. These two ptcs. may be:

(1) adverbial, expressing
    (a) circumstances attendant on ἐνοικείτω, "as you teach and admonish" (RSV [pre-1971 printings], NIV; O'Brien 195; sim. RV, NASB),
  *(b) the means by which the message of Christ is operative, "by teaching and admonishing" (it is implied that the content of the teaching and the means of the admonition is "the message of Christ"; on this view these are pres. ptcs. of identical action, where the finite vb. ἐνοικείτω is related to the ptcs. as fact to method; cf. Burton §§ 120-121), or
    (c) the outcome or evidence of the indwelling word, "so that you teach and admonish"; or
(2) imperatival, being dependent on the impv. ἐνοικείτω: "teach and admonish" (TCNT, Weymouth; sim. Moffatt, Goodspeed, NEB, GNB, JB, Barclay, NAB; BDF § 468[2]; Moulton 181; Robertson, *Pictures* 505; T 303 and Turner, *Insights* 166 [ἔστε is to be supplied]; ZG 610, "probably" [cf. Z § 373]; Lightfoot 221, 222; Lohse 136, 150 n. 141).

On either view, the cstr. is an anacoluthon, since ὁ λόγος is the subj. but the two nom. pl. ptcs. (and ᾄδοντες—see below) refer to persons indicated by ὑμῖν

(Gk. dislikes a succession of ptcs. in the dat.). The noms. may be explained as "hanging nominatives" (Moule, *Idiom Book* 105; cf. 31) or noms. *ad sensum* ("in accordance with the sense"; see T 230). Cf. 2:2.

As in v. 13, the refl. pron. expresses reciprocal action (T 43). That is, ἑαυτούς ("yourselves" = ὑμᾶς αὐτούς) has the sense of ἀλλήλους ("one another").

ψαλμοῖς, ὕμνοις, ᾠδαῖς πνευματικαῖς

These dats. are either instr. ("by means of," O'Brien 195, 208; "with"), locat. ("in," NAB), or dats. of accompanying circumstance ("with," "making use of"). The distinction between these three categories is imprecise; most EVV have the ambiguous prep. "with." But a distinction ought to be drawn between ᾄδω + acc. ("sing a song," as in Rev. 5:9; 14:3; 15:3) and ᾄδω + dat. (as here; but RSV, GNB, JB, NIV have "sing psalms . . .").

Ψαλμός, -οῦ, ὁ, psalm. Ὕμνος, -ου, ὁ, hymn. Ὠδή, -ῆς, ἡ, song. It is impossible to differentiate these words with any precision, for all may denote a song of praise to God (see H. Schlier, TDNT 1.164-165; Lightfoot 222-223). However, ψαλμοῖς may refer to OT psalms or songs, ὕμνοις to NT hymns about Christ or Christian canticles, and ᾠδαῖς to spontaneous hymnody; in this case Paul might be listing three types of Christian hymnody—songs from Scripture, songs about Christ, and songs from the Spirit. Also, since ψάλλω originally meant "pluck a stringed instrument," ψαλμός could allude to musical accompaniment (cf. Moffatt, "with the music of psalms"; Turner, *Words* 353).

The adj. πνευματικαῖς, although fem. in agreement with the nearest noun, ᾠδαῖς (cf. R 655; T 311), could qualify all three terms ("by means of Spirit-inspired psalms, hymns and songs," O'Brien 195, 210; sim. Lohse 136, 151 and n. 151). But whether πνευματικός here means "prompted by the Spirit" (Lohse 136, 151 n. 151; sim. Zerwick, *Analysis* 453; G. Delling, TDNT 8.498), "spiritual" (= "of the spiritual life," Moffatt; "arising from or reflecting the [Christian's] spirit"), or "sacred" (TCNT, Goodspeed, GNB), the adj. seems more appropriately used of spontaneous "songs" than more formal "psalms" or "hymns" already in existence. Moreover, since ᾠδή is the widest term, denoting any type of song, and ψαλμός always and ὕμνος usually bear a religious sense, a restriction of the meaning of ᾠδή is apposite (A. S. Peake, EGT 3.541). Tr.: "spiritual songs" (RV, RSV, NEB, NASB, NIV).

ἐν τῇ χάριτι ᾄδοντες ἐν ταῖς καρδίαις ὑμῶν τῷ θεῷ

Nom. pl. masc. of the pres. act. ptc. of ᾄδω, sing. Like the two earlier pres. ptcs. in this sentence, ᾄδοντες is dependent on ἐνοικείτω and may be adv. (*circumstantial, "as you sing," RSV, NIV; sim. RV, TCNT, NASB; or consec., "so that . . . you sing") or impv. (Weymouth, Moffatt, Goodspeed, NEB, GNB, JB, NAB; T 303 and Turner, *Insights* 166; Lightfoot 222; Lohse 136).

Whereas א* A C omit the art. with χάριτι (the rdg. adopted by WH and UBS[1, 2]), important Alexandrian (𝔭[46] א[2] B Ψ 1739 Clement-Alex) and Western witnesses (D* F G) include it, and this is the preferable rdg. (so also UBS[3], in square brackets; Lightfoot 223; Lohse 151-152; Moule 126). The art. with χάριτι may be anaphoric, pointing back to εὐχάριστοι ("thankful," v. 15) or to the thanksgiving known to be God's due.

The first ἐν in this clause may be:

*(1) circumstantial: "with [God's] grace (in your hearts)" (RV); "with grati-
     tude" (JB, Barclay, NIV); "gratefully" (NAB; Moule 125-126); "with
     thankfulness" (Goodspeed, RSV; sim. GNB); "thankfully" (NEB;
     O'Brien 195, 210), or
 (2) local: "since you stand in grace" (Lohse 136, 151-152).

But, on the basis of Ps. 137:5 (LXX), Turner suggests that ᾄδειν ἐν (ἐν = Heb. *b*[e]) is a Hebraism for "sing of" (= about); thus "sing of grace in your hearts" (*Style* 93).

Ἐν ταῖς καρδίαις ὑμῶν means "in your hearts" (locat. ἐν, as in v. 15), or "with [all] your heart(s)" (circumstantial ἐν) = "fervently," "with enthusiasm." The indir. obj. τῷ θεῷ can be cstr.:

 (1) with ἐν τῇ χάριτι: singing "with thankfulness in your hearts to God"
     (RSV; sim. NIV; apparently RV, NASB); or
 (2) with ᾄδοντες:
     (a) singing "to God in your hearts" (but Paul is unlikely to be thinking
         of inward, nonvocal praise or even of the inner spirit of praise),
     (b) singing "to God with thanksgiving in your hearts" (GNB; sim. JB;
         cf. Moffatt, "praise God with thankful hearts"), or
    *(c) singing "to God gratefully with all your heart" (sim. O'Brien 195).

In the place of θεῷ some authorities read κυρίῳ (K Ψ* Byz Lect goth *al*) but this is undoubtedly secondary, being assimilated to Eph. 5:19 (Metzger 625). See For Further Study 40, "Worship in the NT."

VERSE 17

καὶ πᾶν ὅ τι ἐὰν ποιῆτε

2 pl. pres. act. subjunc. (in an indef. rel. clause) of ποιέω, do. Πᾶν is a nom. abs. or "hanging nom." (*nominativus pendens;* cf. Matt. 10:32; Lk. 12:10; Jn. 17:2; thus Robertson, *Pictures* 506; Lightfoot 224; cf. BDF § 466[3]; R 436-

437) that is resumed by πάντα (acc.). Ὅ τι, acc. sg. neut. of the compound indef. rel. pron. ὅστις, ἥτις, ὅ τι, who(ever), what(ever). The combination πᾶν ὅ or (as here) πᾶν ὅ τι means "whatever" (BAGD 632a), while ἐάν (a variant of ἄν after rels., BAGD 211d; BDF § 107) serves to heighten the indefiniteness of ὅ τι (BAGD 586d). Tr.: "and whatever you are doing" ("whatever you do" is ambiguous in Eng.).

ἐν λόγῳ ἢ ἐν ἔργῳ

"Whether in word (= speech) or in deed (= action)." Since this phrase explicates πᾶν ὅ τι ἐάν, the ἐν is epex. (or "descriptive"—thus Moule, *Idiom Book* 79, who tr. "whether it is a matter of words or actions"; cf. T 265).

πάντα ἐν ὀνόματι κυρίου Ἰησοῦ

From the earlier vb. ποιῆτε one must supply the impv. ποιεῖτε (2 pl. pres. act. impv. of ποιέω; cf. Moulton 181, 183). The cstr. is πᾶν (nom. sg. abs.) ὅ τι (acc. sg.) ἐὰν ποιῆτε . . . πάντα (acc. pl.) [ποιεῖτε]: "whatever you are doing, . . . do all things. . . ."

"In the name of" could mean "as representatives of" (locat. ἐν, "under the name of") or "while calling on the name of," i.e., in prayer (circumstantial ἐν; cf. BAGD 572d). This universal exhortation of v. 17a (cf. 1 Cor. 10:31) sums up the more specific preceding injunctions (vv. 12-16). Not only Christian worship (v. 16) but the Christian's entire life should be conducted in Christ's name.

εὐχαριστοῦντες τῷ θεῷ πατρὶ δι' αὐτοῦ

Nom. pl. masc. (agreeing with the pl. subj. of ποιῆτε or of the supplied ποιεῖτε) of the pres. act. ptc. of εὐχαριστέω, give thanks. This could be an independent impv. ptc. ("Give thanks to God the Father through him," NAB; sim. TCNT, Goodspeed; Lohse 136), but more probably it is a circumstantial ptc., related to the implied impv. ποιεῖτε ("as you give thanks," GNB; sim. most EVV). The expression of thanks to God should be the concomitant of all Christian behavior. See above For Further Study 6, "Pauline Thanksgivings" (1:3).

Early and diversified witnesses (𝔭⁴⁶ᵛⁱᵈ ℵ A B C 1739 syrᵖ copˢᵃ, ᵇᵒ goth eth Ambrose) support this unusual rdg., τῷ θεῷ πατρί, which scribes altered by inserting καί before πατρί under the influence of passages such as 1 Cor. 15:24; Eph. 5:20; Phil. 4:20. See note at 1:3 and cf. Metzger 626; Lightfoot 224, 248. Δι' αὐτοῦ (see on 1:16 for this elision) points to the role of Christ as intermediary (cf. Eph. 2:18; 1 Tim. 2:5) and advocate (Rom. 8:34) rather than as high priest.

TRANSLATION

[12] Therefore, as God's chosen people, who are holy and loved by him, put on heartfelt compassion, kindness, humility, gentleness, and patience. [13] You are to bear with one another, and if anyone has a grievance against someone else, you are to forgive one another. Just as the Lord forgave you, so you also must forgive. [14] And in addition to all these garments, put on love, which is the bond that perfects them all. [15] And let the peace that Christ gives rule in your hearts, for you were actually called to experience this peace as members of one Body. Also be thankful. [16] Let the message of Christ dwell in you richly by your teaching and admonishing one another in all wisdom, as you sing to God gratefully with all your heart, using psalms, hymns, and spiritual songs. [17] And whatever you are doing, whether in word or in deed, do everything in the name of the Lord Jesus, giving thanks to God the Father through him.

EXPANDED PARAPHRASE

[12] So then, since you are God's chosen people, his Elect, dedicated to his service and the objects of his special love, clothe yourselves appropriately— with tenderhearted compassion, kindness, humility, gentleness of spirit, and patient endurance. [13] You must patiently bear with one another and readily forgive one another if anyone has a complaint against his neighbor. The Lord readily forgave you; so you, for your part, ought to follow his example and readily forgive. [14] And in addition to all these garments just mentioned, clothe yourselves with the robe of love, for when this final, outer garment is put on, it binds together and perfects all the other virtues. [15] And let the preservation of the peace that Christ gives be the determinative factor in your decision-making, for in reality your Christian calling as fellow members of the one Body of Christ is to share in that peace. And always remember to be grateful. [16] Let the message of Christ be operative in your hearts and in your midst and enrich you with all its wealth through your teaching and admonishing one another with all possible wisdom, as you sing to God with thanksgiving and with your whole heart—not simply with your lips—using psalms, hymns, and spiritual songs. [17] To sum up: whatever you are doing, whether it be speech or action, do everything in the name of the Lord Jesus, at the same time giving thanks to God the Father on the basis of the mediatorial work of Christ.

FOR FURTHER STUDY

37. Predestination and Election (3:12)

Berkouwer, G. C., *Divine Election,* tr. H. Bekker (Grand Rapids: Eerdmans, 1960).

Boettner, L., *The Reformed Doctrine of Predestination* (Grand Rapids: Eerdmans, 1954).

Bromiley, G. W., ISBE 3.945-951.

Coenen, L., NIDNTT 1.533-543.

Davidson, F., *Pauline Predestination* (London: Tyndale, 1946).

Jacobs, P. and Krienke, H., NIDNTT 1.695-696.

Jocz, J., *A Theology of Election: Israel and the Church* (New York: Macmillan, 1958).

Mendenhall, G. E., IDB 2.76-82.

Murray, J., ZPEB 2.270-274.

Reid, W. S., ISBE 2.56-57.

Ridderbos, H., *Paul. An Outline of his Theology* (Grand Rapids: Eerdmans, 1975) 341-354.

*Rowley, H. H., *The Biblical Doctrine of Election* (London: Lutterworth, 1950).

Schmidt, K. L., TDNT 3.487-496.

Schrenk, G., TDNT 4.172-192.

Stendahl, K., "The Called and the Chosen: An Essay on Election," in *The Root of the Vine,* ed. A. Fridrichsen (London: Dacre, 1953) 63-80.

Strong, A. H., *Systematic Theology* (Old Tappan, NJ: Revell, reprint of 1907 ed.) 779-790.

Warfield, B. B., *Biblical and Theological Studies,* ed. S. G. Craig (Philadelphia: Presbyterian and Reformed, 1952) 270-333.

———, *Biblical Doctrine* (New York: Oxford University, 1929) 3-67.

38. Forgiveness (3:13)

Bultmann, R., TDNT 1.509-512.

*Mackintosh, H. R., *The Christian Experience of Forgiveness* (London: Nisbet, 1927).

Martin, R. P., "Reconciliation and Forgiveness in the Letter to the Colossians," in *Reconciliation and Hope,* ed. R. Banks (Grand Rapids: Eerdmans, 1974) 104-124.

Monsma, P. H., ZPEB 2.596-600.

Morris, L., *The Cross in the New Testament* (Grand Rapids: Eerdmans, 1965).

Morro, W. C., and Harrison, R. K., ISBE 2.340-344.

Quanbeck, W. A., IDB 2.314-319.

Redlich, E. B., *The Forgiveness of Sins* (Edinburgh: T. & T. Clark, 1937).

Taylor, V., *Forgiveness and Reconciliation* (New York: St. Martin's, 1946[2]) 1-28.

Telfer, W., *The Forgiveness of Sins* (London: SCM, 1959).

Vorländer, H., NIDNTT 1.697-703.

39. Love (3:14)

Burnaby, J., *Amor Dei* (London: Hodder, 1938).

Furnish, V. P., *The Love Command in the New Testament* (Nashville: Abingdon, 1972)

Günther, W., Link, H. G., and Brown, C., NIDNTT 2.538-551.

*Harrelson, W., "The Idea of Agape in the New Testament," *Journal of Religion* 31 (1951) 169-182.

Johnston, G., IDB 3.168-178.

Lewis, C. S., *The Four Loves* (New York: Harcourt, 1960).

Moffatt, J., *Love in the New Testament* (London: Hodder & Stoughton, 1929).

Montefiore, H. W., " 'Thou Shalt Love the Neighbour as Thyself,' " *NovT* 5 (1962) 157-170.

Morris, L., *Testaments of Love. A Study of Love in the Bible* (Grand Rapids: Eerdmans, 1981).

Nygren, A., *Agape and Eros.* Part I: *A Study of the Christian Idea of Love.* Part II: *The History of the Christian Idea of Love,* tr. P. S. Watson (Philadelphia: Westminster, 1953).

Piper, J., *'Love Your Enemies.' Jesus' Love Command in the Synoptic Gospels and the Early Christian Paraenesis* (New York: Cambridge University, 1979).

Spicq, C., *Agape in the New Testament,* 3 vols., tr. Marie A. McNamara and Mary H. Richter (St. Louis: B. Herder, 1963-66).

Stählin, G., TDNT 9.113-171.

Stauffer, E., TDNT 1.35-55.

Turner, G. A., ISBE 3.173-176.

Warfield, B. B., "The Terminology of Love in the New Testament," *Princeton Theological Review* 16 (1918) 1-45, 153-203.

40. Worship in the NT (3:16)

Bromiley, G. W., ZPEB 5.969-975, 984-990.

Cranfield, C. E. B., "Divine and Human Action: the Biblical Concept of Worship," *Interpretation* 22 (1958) 387-398.

Cullmann, O., *Early Christian Worship*, tr. A. S. Todd and J. B. Torrance (London: SCM, 1953).

Delling, G., *Worship in the New Testament*, tr. P. Scott (Philadelphia: Westminster, 1962).

Greeven, H., TDNT 6.758-766.

Hahn, F., *The Worship of the Early Church*, tr. D. E. Green, ed. J. Reumann (Philadelphia: Fortress, 1973).

Hess, K., NIDNTT 3.544-553.

Martin, R. P., *Worship in the Early Church* (Grand Rapids: Eerdmans, 1975).

———, ISBE 5.1124-1133.

*Moule, C. F. D., *Worship in the New Testament* (Richmond: John Knox, 1961).

Old, H. O., *Worship* (Atlanta: John Knox, 1984).

Richardson, C. C., IDB 4.883-894.

Rowley, H. H., *Worship in Ancient Israel: Its Forms and Meaning* (Philadelphia: Fortress, 1967).

Schönweiss, H. and Brown, C., NIDNTT 2.875-879.

Smart, N., *The Concept of Worship* (New York: Macmillan, 1972).

Webber, R. E., *Worship: Old and New* (Grand Rapids: Zondervan, 1982).

HOMILETICAL SUGGESTIONS

"Putting on" Virtues (3:12-17)

1. Put on the attire of the Christian (vv. 12-13) as God's chosen, dedicated, and dearly loved people (v. 12a): viz.
   (a) tenderheartedness (v. 12b)
   (b) kindness—humility (v. 12b)
   (c) gentleness—patience (v. 12b)
   (d) toleration (v. 13a), and
   (e) forgiveness (v. 13b, c).
2. Put on the robe of love (v. 14),
   (a) the final, outer garment (ἐπὶ πᾶσιν . . . τούτοις, v. 14a), which
   (b) binds together (σύνδεσμος) and
   (c) perfects (τῆς τελειότητος) all the other virtues (v. 14b).
3. The peace of Christ should act as arbitrator (v. 15)
   (a) in the decision-making of Christians (ἐν ταῖς καρδίαις ὑμῶν, v. 15a)

  (b) in the light of God's calling (v. 15b).
4. The message of Christ will indwell and enrich us (v. 16)
    (a) by our teaching and admonishing one another with all wisdom (v. 16a) and
    (b) as we sing to God with gratitude (v. 16b).
5. The name of the Lord Jesus should be the touchstone of behavior (v. 17),
    (a) whether words or deeds (v. 17a),
    (b) with constant praise of God (v. 17b).

Forgiveness (3:13b, c)

1. The need: any grievance against a neighbor (v. 13b)
2. The model: the Lord's ready forgiveness of us (v. 13c)

Christian Worship (3:16-17) involves:

1. mutual teaching of "the message of Christ" and
2. mutual admonition, both with all possible wisdom (v. 16a)
3. singing to God with gratitude and enthusiasm (v. 16b)
4. Christ-honoring words and deeds (v. 17a; cf. Heb. 13:16)
5. the expression of gratitude to God through Christ (v. 17b; cf. Heb. 13:15)

C. HOUSEHOLD RELATIONSHIPS (3:18–4:1)

18 Αἱ γυναῖκες, ὑποτάσσεσθε τοῖς ἀνδράσιν, ὡς ἀνῆκεν ἐν κυρίῳ. 19 Οἱ ἄνδρες, ἀγαπᾶτε τὰς γυναῖκας καὶ μὴ πικραίνεσθε πρὸς αὐτάς. 20 Τὰ τέκνα, ὑπακούετε τοῖς γονεῦσιν κατὰ πάντα, τοῦτο γὰρ εὐάρεστόν ἐστιν ἐν κυρίῳ. 21 Οἱ πατέρες, μὴ ἐρεθίζετε τὰ τέκνα ὑμῶν, ἵνα μὴ ἀθυμῶσιν. 22 Οἱ δοῦλοι, ὑπακούετε κατὰ πάντα τοῖς κατὰ σάρκα κυρίοις, μὴ ἐν ὀφθαλμοδουλίᾳ ὡς ἀνθρωπάρεσκοι, ἀλλ᾽ ἐν ἁπλότητι καρδίας, φοβούμενοι τὸν κύριον. 23 ὃ ἐὰν ποιῆτε, ἐκ ψυχῆς ἐργάζεσθε, ὡς τῷ κυρίῳ καὶ οὐκ ἀνθρώποις, 24 εἰδότες ὅτι ἀπὸ κυρίου ἀπολήμψεσθε τὴν ἀνταπόδοσιν τῆς κληρονομίας. τῷ κυρίῳ Χριστῷ δουλεύετε· 25 ὁ γὰρ ἀδικῶν κομίσεται ὃ ἠδίκησεν, καὶ οὐκ ἔστιν προσωπολημψία. 1 Οἱ κύριοι, τὸ δίκαιον καὶ τὴν ἰσότητα τοῖς δούλοις παρέχεσθε, εἰδότες ὅτι καὶ ὑμεῖς ἔχετε κύριον ἐν οὐρανῷ.

STRUCTURE

Addressees and Injunction			Motivation		
3:18	Αἱ γυναῖκες,	ὑποτάσσεσθε	ὡς ἀνῆκεν	ἐν	κυρίῳ
19	Οἱ ἄνδρες,	ἀγαπᾶτε			
		μὴ πικραίνεσθε			
20	Τὰ τέκνα,	ὑπακούετε	τοῦτο γὰρ . . . ἐν		κυρίῳ
21	Οἱ πατέρες,	μὴ ἐρεθίζετε			
22	Οἱ δοῦλοι,	ὑπακούετε	φοβούμενοι	τὸν	κύριον
23		ἐργάζεσθε	ὡς	τῷ	κυρίῳ
24			εἰδότες ὅτε	ἀπὸ	κυρίου
		δουλεύετε 25	ὁ γὰρ κτλ.		
			οὐκ ἔστιν κτλ.		
4:1	Οἱ κύριοι, . . .	παρέχεσθε	εἰδότες ὅτι . . .		κύριον

In these three pairs of "household" exhortations, listed in a natural order based on degree of intimacy, there is first an address, then an impv. vb. (in the first member of each pair, a ὑπο-compound), then the motivation for the action or attitude enjoined, except in the case of "husbands" (οἱ ἄνδρες, 3:19) and "fathers" (οἱ πατέρες, v. 21). In all four cases where the motivation is explicitly stated (viz. αἱ γυναῖκες, v. 18; τὰ τέκνα, v. 20; οἱ δοῦλοι, v. 22; οἱ κύριοι, 4:1), it is christological, for "the Lord" (κύριος) is invariably the point of reference. Christian conduct is motivated and determined by Christ.

This whole section shows that to pursue the realm above (3:1a) and to be preoccupied with its affairs (3:2a) does not prompt an ascetic otherworldliness, but rather a wholehearted commitment to the daily duties of this world for the sake of the Lord. See For Further Study 41, "Catalogs of Domestic Duties (*Haustafeln* = 'household tables')."

VERSE 18

Αἱ γυναῖκες, ὑποτάσσεσθε τοῖς ἀνδράσιν

2 pl. pres. mid./pass. impv. of ὑποτάσσω, (act.) subject/subordinate something (acc.) or someone (acc.) to someone (dat.; cf. BDF § 202); (mid.) subject/submit oneself; (pass.) subject oneself, be subjected, to someone (dat., here τοῖς ἀνδράσιν). Cf. BAGD 848, a, b, where mid. uses are subsumed under pass. Whether we classify ὑποτάσσεσθε *(1) as a direct (= refl.; cf. Z § 232) mid. (R 807, tentatively) or (2) as a refl. pass. (Moulton 163, apparently), it is refl. and the mid./pass. ambiguity can be suitably reflected in the Eng. tr. "be subject."

Αἱ γυναῖκες, "wives," "you married women" (Goodspeed), an art. nom. used in address (a "vocatival nom."; cf. BDF § 147[3]; Moulton 70; R 757; T 34; Z § 34). Since there is no voc. of the art., when the art. is required (as here, to indicate a class; cf. BDF § 252; R 757; T 180) the nom. of the art. and noun is used (cf. T 34). There are two voc. forms—e.g., θεέ (voc. proper, as in Matt. 27:46) and ὁ θεός ("vocatival nom.," always art., as in Mk. 15:34). In the present context, γυνή means "wife," not "woman," and ἀνήρ "husband," not "man."

This apostolic injunction does not imply the inferiority of the wife (see the comprehensive discussion in O'Brien 220-222); Eph. 5:21 enjoins mutual submission (ὑποτασσόμενοι ἀλλήλοις) within the church. It is a case of voluntary submission in recognition of the God-appointed leadership of the husband and the divinely ordained hierarchical order in creation (cf. 1 Cor. 11:3-9; Eph. 5:22-24). Tr.: "Wives, be subject to your (τοῖς denoting poss.; cf. R 769-770; T 173-174) husbands."

ὡς ἀνῆκεν ἐν κυρίῳ

3 sg. impf. act. indic. of ἀνήκει, an impers. vb., it is due, becoming, proper, fitting (cf. τὸ ἀνῆκον, what is proper, one's duty [Phlm. 8]). Ὡς is a comp. particle formed from the rel. pron. ὅς and expressing manner: "(in such a way) as is fitting" (BAGD 897a; sim. BDF § 358[2]; BAGD 66b). Various reasons have been suggested for the unexpected use of the impf.:

(1) It points to the period, now past, between one's conversion and the present: "ever since your conversion" (sim. Zerwick, *Analysis* 453; Vincent 916).

(2) It stands for the potential opt. of modest assertion (e.g., Acts 26:29; Zerwick, *Analysis* 453; cf. Z § 356): "as would be fitting."

(3) It expresses present time in an "unreal" condition without ἄν and with a protasis such as "if you did it" suppressed (cf. Zerwick, *Analysis* 453; Z §§ 313, 319).

*(4) It is an idiomatic use of the impf. indic. with a vb. expressing propriety in pres. time (Robertson, *Pictures* 506; sim. Burton § 32), a "potential" indic. (R 919; cf. 886-887, 920).

*(5) Behind the present fittingness ("as is fitting") lies a past determination of what was proper (cf. T 90-91; Lightfoot 225, "The past tense perhaps implies an essential *a priori* obligation"). The blurring of the distinction between present and past obligation is illustrated by the Eng. "ought" (Burton § 32), which may mean "is owing" (pres.) or "owed" (past). In the present case, there is no implication that the obligation of wives to be subject to their husbands was not being fulfilled; it is a matter of a previously existing obligation that still applies, not of an unfulfilled duty. Cf. NAB, "This is your duty"; sim. Goodspeed, Moffatt.

It seems antecedently probable that the phrase ἐν κυρίῳ, "in the Lord," has the same mng. at the end of vv. 18 and 20, for in each case it forms part of the justification (ὡς, v. 18; γάρ, v. 20) for an earlier impv., although in neither case should it be cstr. with that impv. The Lord (Jesus) is the yardstick for determining what is fitting (v. 18) or pleasing (v. 20). Accordingly the sense will be: "among Christians" (ZG 610, on v. 20), "for Christians" (Weymouth, v. 20), "as Christians" (Goodspeed, v. 18; GNB, v. 18), "for those who belong to the Lord" (sim. TCNT, vv. 18, 20); or, more generally, "as judged by a Christian standard" (Lightfoot 225, on v. 20), "according to the Christian way of life" (JB [study edition], note *i* on v. 18).

VERSE 19

Οἱ ἄνδρες, ἀγαπᾶτε τὰς γυναῖκας

2 pl. (after the voc. pl. οἱ ἄνδρες) pres. act. impv. of ἀγαπάω, love. "Maintain the habit of loving," "make it your practice to love." For the "vocatival nom." οἱ ἄνδρες see on v. 18a. Τάς is poss., "your (wives)."

καὶ μὴ πικραίνεσθε πρὸς αὐτάς

2 pl. pres. pass. impv. of πικραίνω, (act.) make bitter; (pass.) be(come) embittered (against someone, πρός τινα); foster bitter feelings; be harsh (πικρός, harsh, bitter, sharp); show bitterness (MH 402). Being a general directive in "household tables" unrelated to specific local circumstances, this prohibition (μή + pres. impv.—see on 2:16) is unlikely to mean "stop being embittered." Nor is it simply that habitual action is being forbidden (as if occasional

bitterness or harshness were permissible). Rather, this negative definition of love relates to action that must always be avoided: "do not be embittered against them" (NASB; Lohse 154, 158; sim. O'Brien 214), "never treat them harshly" (TCNT, sim. Weymouth), "do not be harsh with them" (RSV, NEB, GNB, NIV), "avoid any bitterness toward them" (NAB). Αὐτάς, acc. (after πρός) pl. fem. of αὐτός, -ή, -ό, he, she, it; -self, referring to γυναῖκας.

VERSE 20

Τὰ τέκνα, ὑπακούετε τοῖς γονεῦσιν κατὰ πάντα

2 pl. pres. act. impv. of ὑπακούω, obey, be subject to (cf. R 634), + dat., here τοῖς γονεῦσιν, dat. pl. of γονεύς, -έως, ὁ, parent; only pl. in NT: οἱ γονεῖς, -έων. The close relationship between ὑπακούω and ὑποτάσσομαι, both of which may mean "obey" or "be subject to," is well illustrated in 1 Pet. 3:5-6. In each of the three pairs of directives in these "household tables," the party that is to be submissive or is to obey is addressed first. Here, τὰ τέκνα, "children," male and female. On this "vocatival nom.," see v. 18a. Κατὰ πάντα means "in all respects" (BAGD 407d), "in everything" (ZG 610; Weymouth, NEB), "at every point" (Moffatt); rather than "always" (TCNT, Goodspeed, GNB, JB), although the resultant mng. is substantially the same.

τοῦτο γὰρ εὐάρεστόν ἐστιν ἐν κυρίῳ

Τοῦτο ("this") refers to children's obedience to parents in every respect. Εὐάρεστος, -ον, a two-termination adj., pleasing, acceptable (from ἀρέσκω, please). The implied dat. (of the person pleased) could be τῷ θεῷ (as in Rom. 12:1; 14:18; Phil. 4:18; so NEB, GNB here), but , given (1) the close conceptual link between εὐάρεστον and v. 24a (ἀπὸ κυρίου), (ii) the constant appeal throughout 3:18–4:1 to "the Lord (Christ)" as the motivation for action, and (iii) the parallels in Eph. 5:10 and 2 Cor. 5:8-9, it seems more appropriate to supply τῷ κυρίῳ (Χριστῷ; cf. v. 24b).

On ἐν κυρίῳ, see v. 18b. The sense is "for (γάρ, stating the ground for the impv.) such behavior pleases the Lord [τῷ κυρίῳ] and befits those who belong to him (ἐν κυρίῳ)." But some EVV take ἐν κυρίῳ as equivalent to τῷ κυρίῳ ("for this pleases the Lord," RSV, NIV; sim. Moffatt, NASB, JB; cf. Eph. 5:10; against this, see Moule 130), while Moule tentatively proposes that ἐν κυρίῳ represents a qualifying cond. clause—"provided that the children's obedience is . . . on a truly Christian level of motive" (130, citing 1 Cor. 7:39; Phil. 2:19), and Turner paraphrases "*in that state* of grace in which the Christian now lives" (T 263).

VERSE 21

Οἱ πατέρες, μὴ ἐρεθίζετε τὰ τέκνα ὑμῶν

2 pl. pres. act. impv. of ἐρεθίζω, arouse, excite; provoke, irritate, exasperate; (in a positive sense) stimulate (2 Cor. 9:2, the only other NT use). "Avoid irritating" (Moffatt), "do not exasperate" (NEB, NASB). A C D* F G *al* read μὴ παροργίζετε, 2 pl. pres. act. impv. of παροργίζω, make angry, a secondary variant from Eph. 6:4 (Lightfoot 225). On μή + pres. impv., see 3:19 and 2:16. Ὑμῶν is unnecessary to indicate poss. (cf. vv. 18a, 19a, 20a) and is therefore emphatic.

Οἱ πατέρες, a "vocatival nom." (see v. 18a), may signify *"fathers" (most EVV; G. Schrenk, TDNT 5.1004; Lohse 154, 159), or, by synecdoche, "parents" (BAGD 635b; GNB, JB; cf. τοῖς γονεῦσιν, v. 20a, and Heb. 11:23), or "parents, especially fathers" (O'Brien 234; cf. 225; 214, "fathers").

ἵνα μὴ ἀθυμῶσιν

3 pl. (referring to τὰ τέκνα ὑμῶν) pres. act. subjunc. (after ἵνα μή, expressing a neg. purpose) of ἀθυμέω, be discouraged, be despondent, lose heart, lack spirit. From ἄθυμος, spiritless = α- privative + θυμός, spirit. Thus, "lest they become dispirited" (Moffatt). The implication of ἵνα μή ("in order that . . . not") is "for, if you do (exasperate them), they will become disheartened and morose" (cf. ἀθυμία, moroseness), "or they will become discouraged" (GNB, NIV).

VERSE 22

Οἱ δοῦλοι, ὑπακούετε κατὰ πάντα τοῖς κατὰ σάρκα κυρίοις

2 pl. pres. act. impv. of ὑπακούω, obey, + dat. (here τοῖς . . . κυρίοις). On κατὰ πάντα see v. 20. "Obey . . . in every respect" could be rendered "give entire obedience to" (NEB; O'Brien 214). On the "vocatival nom." οἱ δοῦλοι see v. 18a.

Κατὰ σάρκα is an attrib. prep. phrase qualifying τοῖς κυρίοις (T 221-222) and functioning as an adj.; thus "earthly" (BAGD 407d, 408a; ZG 610; TCNT, Weymouth, Goodspeed, RSV, NEB, NIV) in contrast with κύριον ἐν οὐρανῷ (4:1), or "human" (GNB, NAB) in contrast with τῷ κυρίῳ Χριστῷ (v. 24b). Only in the earthly realm are slaveowners κύριοι. Alternatively, κατὰ σάρκα could mean "according to human standards" (BAGD 744a), denoting "the sphere in which the service-relation holds true" (BAGD 459b). The position of the prep. phrase between art. and noun is not unusual in Gk., being a variation of the word-order τοῖς κυρίοις τοῖς κατὰ σάρκα (cf. T 350).

μὴ ἐν ὀφθαλμοδουλίᾳ

Ὀφθαλμοδουλία, -ας, ἡ, lit. eyeservice (RV, RSV), formed from ὀφθαλμός and δουλεία, where the second element ("enslavement") is more closely defined by the first ("to the eye"; cf. BDF § 115[1]). This word, probably a Pauline coinage, describes (i) service that is concerned only with what the eye can see (i.e., external appearances), (ii) service that is rendered only under the master's eye (i.e., only when he is watching), or (iii) "service that is performed only to attract attention" (BAGD 599b, citing C. F. D. Moule, *ExpT* 59 [1947-48] 250). Ἐν denotes attendant circumstances ("with," "when"). Thus, corresponding to the possible mngs. of ὀφθαλμοδουλία outlined above: *(i) "not with external service" (NASB; sim. Goodspeed, NEB); (ii) "not only when their eyes are on you" (TCNT; sim. Moffatt, GNB, JB, Barclay, NIV); (iii) "not with the purpose of attracting attention" (NAB). The pl. ὀφθαλμοδουλίαις (read by ℵ C Ψ TR, and preferred by Lohse 160 and n. 44; Moule 130) either is a generalizing pl. (thus "eyeservice" or an equivalent tr.) or refers to "acts of eye service" (Weymouth).

　　　The neg. particle οὐ normally negates individual words or phrases (cf. BDF § 426; v. 23b); perhaps μή is used here because it negates two phrases—ἐν ὀφθαλμοδουλίᾳ and ὡς ἀνθρωπάρεσκοι. As often in an οὐ/μή—ἀλλά antithesis in Paul (e.g., 1 Cor. 1:17), μόνον ("only") needs to be supplied with the neg., at least in some translations—thus TCNT, GNB, JB, Barclay, NIV with the ἐν phrase (sim. Moffatt, NEB); Weymouth, Goodspeed, JB, Barclay with the ὡς phrase (sim. TCNT, NASB).

ὡς ἀνθρωπάρεσκοι

Ἀνθρωπάρεσκος, -ον, a two-termination adj. (see MH 271 on its formation) used here as a subst., a person who tries to please people (cf. εὐάρεστον, v. 20b) "at the sacrifice of principle" (BAGD 67d), "one currying favour" (ZG 610; see further Turner, *Words* 221-222). Ὡς is a comparative particle, depicting the manner in which something proceeds, here with an ellipsis (BAGD 897a, b): "as those who merely please people [are accustomed to serve]." Without the ellipsis the sense would be "as those who want to please people," which becomes simply "in order to please people" (Lohse 154, 160; O'Brien 214, 227; sim. NEB, NIV). *Alternatively, ὡς may introduce a hypothetical situation (cf. BAGD 898 b, c): "as if you were merely pleasing people" (sim. Zerwick, *Analysis* 453; TCNT, Goodspeed). A variation of this second view reduces "as if you were aiming only to please people" to "as aiming only to please [people]" (Weymouth).

ἀλλ' ἐν ἁπλότητι καρδίας

The second α of ἀλλά is not always elided, but is commonly before arts., prons., and particles, but rarely before nouns and vbs. (R 207, citing F. J. A. Hort). As in the parallel phrase ἐν ὀφθαλμοδουλίᾳ, the prep. ἐν indicates attendant circumstances: "but [serve them] with . . ." (cf. Moffatt). Ἁπλότης -ητος, ἡ, simplicity, sincerity, uprightness. Καρδία, "heart," here denotes the disposition (BAGD 404b). The gen. καρδίας, which is anar. after an anar. prep. phrase (in accordance with the canon of Apollonius; cf. BDF § 255; T 179-180), may be adj. ("with heartfelt sincerity") but is more probably a gen. of ref. or relation: "with sincerity in relation to the heart," "with sincerity of heart" (Goodspeed, NASB, NIV; O'Brien 214, 227), "with a sincere heart" (GNB; Zerwick, *Analysis* 453; cf. BAGD 85d); or "in singleness of heart" (RV, RSV; Moule 130, "i.e. 'in honesty,' 'with no ulterior motives'"; sim. Lohse 154, 160), "with a single heart" (Moffatt), "with singlemindedness" (NEB).

φοβούμενοι τὸν κύριον

Nom. pl. masc. (agreeing with the implied subj. of ὑπακούετε, viz. οἱ δοῦλοι) of the pres. pass. ptc. of φοβέω; only pass. in NT (BAGD 862b): be afraid, fear; reverence. The ptc. could be circumstantial, "as you reverence the Lord" (O'Brien 214, 234; sim. NIV), but most rightly take it as causal: "because you fear the Lord" (Weymouth, Goodspeed; sim. GNB) or "out of reverence for the Lord" (NEB, NAB; sim. Moffatt, JB). It should be cstr. with ὑπακούετε κτλ. (thus most EVV) rather than with ἐν ἁπλότητι καρδίας alone (GNB).

In this context the κύριος is Christ (BAGD 863b; Lohse 160; O'Brien 227, 228) rather than God (see v. 24b and Eph. 6:5). The art. distinguishes ὁ κύριος Χριστός (v. 24b) from οἱ κατὰ σάρκα κύριοι (v. 22a). The motive for the slave's wholehearted, obedient service is not to be cringing servility before an earthly master but reverential fear before the heavenly Lord. See For Further Study 48, "Slavery in the New Testament" (Phlm. 16).

VERSE 23

ὃ ἐὰν ποιῆτε, ἐκ ψυχῆς ἐργάζεσθε

2 pl. pres. act. subjunc. (in an indef. rel. clause) of ποιέω, do. Ὅ is acc. sg. neut. of the rel. pron. ὅς, ἥ, ὅ. Ἐάν is a variant of ἄν after rels. (BAGD 211d; BDF § 107), so that ὃ ἐάν = ὃ ἄν, whatever. This rel. clause is virtually the protasis of a condition (BAGD 48c; BDF § 380[1]): "whatever you do" = "if you do anything." Given the ambiguity in Eng. idiom of the tr. "whatever you do" (TCNT, GNB, Barclay, NAB, NIV) or "whatever you have to do" (BAGD

898a), it is better to render "whatever you are doing" (Weymouth, NEB) or "whatever your task" (RSV; sim. Moffatt, JB).

2 pl. pres. mid. impv. of dep. ἐργάζομαι, (intrans.) work, be active; (trans.) carry out, do. This vb. is probably simply a stylistic alternative to ποιέω. Its implied object is the whole rel. clause that precedes: "work at it" (viz. whatever you are doing). Ἐκ ψυχῆς, lit. "from (the) soul," is adv. (cf. R 550), "gladly" (BAGD 893c), "heartily" (Moffatt, RSV, NASB), "with enthusiasm," "with all your heart" (O'Brien 214; sim. ZG 611). Tr.: "Whatever your task, work at it with enthusiasm," "Whatever you are doing, put your whole heart into it" (NEB).

ὡς τῷ κυρίῳ καὶ οὐκ ἀνθρώποις

Τῷ κυρίῳ and ἀνθρώποις may be classified as dats. of "advantage" or "interest" (cf. BDF § 188; R 538-539; T 238; Z § 55), "for (the honor of) the Lord," "for (the benefit of) people." Individual words (here ἀνθρώποις) are negated by οὐ, not μή; and οὐ is preferred over μή in contrasting statements (here τῷ κυρίῳ— οὐκ ἀνθρώποις; BDF § 426). Moreover, καὶ οὐ is customary when a positive statement is followed by a neg. (cf. 2:8, 19; R 1164). Οὐκ is found before vowels and diphthongs that have a smooth breathing. This neg. relates solely to the contrast with τῷ κυρίῳ; it is not implied that slaves are not to work "for people."

Unlike ὡς in v. 22, which is virtually negated (μή), ὡς here does not introduce an unreal situation or hypothetical case—"as if it were for the Lord" (JB; sim. TCNT, NEB, GNB, Barclay). Rather, ὡς expresses subjective motivation, "with the thought that" (cf. BDF § 425[3]; T 158), before an ellipsis, ἐργαζόμενοι αὐτό, "doing it" (BDF § 425[4]; cf. R 1140; T 158 n. 1): "whatever be your task, work at it heartily, with the thought that you are actually doing it for the Lord and not only for people." Cf. Goodspeed: "Work at everything you do with all your hearts, as work done not for men only but for the Lord" (sim., with regard to ὡς, Weymouth, Moffatt, RSV, NIV; O'Brien 214, 228, 234). As with the μή— ἀλλά antithesis in v. 22, so here with the ὡς —καὶ οὐκ contrast, it is permissible—and in some renderings necessary—to supply μόνον ("only") with the neg.

VERSE 24

εἰδότες ὅτι ἀπὸ κυρίου ἀπολήμψεσθε

Nom. pl. masc. (agreeing with the implied subj. of ἐργάζεσθε) of the pf. act. ptc. of οἶδα, know, a pf.-pres. vb. (BAGD 555d; MH 220-221; R 881; T 82). The ptc. is causal: "since you know" (TCNT, NAB, NIV; sim. Weymouth,

Goodspeed). In Paul's letters, εἰδότες ὅτι often introduces a well-known fact that forms the basis (causal εἰδότες) of an exhortation or affirmation (e.g., 4:1; Rom. 5:3; 6:8-9; 2 Cor. 4:13-14; 5:6, 8).

2 pl. fut. mid. indic. of ἀπολαμβάνω, receive as due; get back (ἀπό; cf. MH 298). The pref. of this compound vb. is repeated with κυρίου (cf. R 559), "from (ἀπο + gen.) the Lord." In prep. phrases κύριος is often anar. (BAGD 460a; BDF § 254[1]; T 174); here it may also be anar. to stress the exalted status of the One who will reward his slaves (the qualitative force of an anar. noun; cf. Moulton 82-83).

τὴν ἀνταπόδοσιν τῆς κληρονομίας

Originally ἀνταπόδοσις (-εως, ἡ) was an abstract noun meaning "a giving (δόσις) in return"; then it came to mean "something given (where δόσις = δόμα, gift; cf. ἀνταπόδομα, repayment [Lk. 14:12; Rom. 11:9]) back (ἀπό) in return (ἀντί)," "exact recompense." Τῆς κληρονομίας is an epex./appos./defining gen. (see on 1:5), "the recompense that consists of your inheritance" (sim. RV, NASB; R 498; ZG 611; Lightfoot 227; Lohse 161), and thus "your inheritance as a reward" (sim. BAGD 73b; Weymouth, RSV, NEB, NAB, NIV; cf. Turner, *Words* 367). After τὴν ἀνταπόδοσιν the art. is expected (because of the canon of Apollonius) before the dependent gen. κληρονομίας; but in addition τῆς may denote poss. ("your inheritance") or may point to "that well-known" inheritance of God's children (= eternal life, ZG 611; or salvation, BAGD 435a). Paul is highlighting the paradox of slaves owned by humans becoming God's heirs (cf. Rom. 8:17; Gal. 4:7). See For Further Study 13, "The Concept of Inheritance in Paul" (1:12), and 42, "Recompense and Reward" (below).

τῷ κυρίῳ Χριστῷ δουλεύετε

2 pl. pres. act. indic./*impv. of δουλεύω, serve (+ dat., here τῷ κυρίῳ). Χριστῷ is in appos. to τῷ κυρίῳ and is therefore dat. Generally a noun in appos. is art. (T 206), but on the art. with Χριστός, see on 2:17. Χριστῷ is added, giving the unique NT combination ὁ κύριος Χριστός, "the Lord Christ," in order to specify which κύριος ultimately is worthy of service (cf. Lohse 161 n. 65).

Many EVV have followed the lead of Lightfoot (227) in taking δουλεύετε as indic. (thus RV, TCNT, Weymouth, RSV, NASB, GNB, JB, NIV): "You are serving the Lord Christ" (RSV), "Christ is the Master whose bondservants you are" (Weymouth). Two main arguments are adduced in favor of this view (cf. Lightfoot 227):

(1) The indic. explains v. 24a, esp. ἀπὸ κυρίου. Thus GNB, "For Christ is the real Master you serve"; cf. RV, RSV (D² Ψ TR actually add γάρ).

(2) If δουλεύετε were impv., we would expect ὡς τῷ κυρίῳ, as in Eph. 6:7 (after δουλεύοντες, "rendering service as to the Lord").

Δουλεύετε is cstr. as impv. by Moffatt, NEB, Barclay, NAB; Robertson, *Pictures* 507 (with hesitation); Lohse 154, 161 and n. 63; Moule 131; O'Brien 214, 229. These arguments support the choice of impv.:

(1) An impv. δουλεύετε resumes the impv. ἐργάζεσθε (v. 23a). Ἐργάζεσθε, ὡς τῷ κυρίῳ ("work, as for the Lord") becomes τῷ κυρίῳ Χριστῷ δουλεύετε ("serve the Lord Christ"; note the chiasmus, A-B-B-A). But the second clause is more than resumptive: work becomes service as slaves; the beneficiary becomes the Lord Christ.

(2) The γάρ of v. 25a is more easily explained by a preceding impv. than a preceding indic. Lohse suggests that the "inviolable law" of v. 25 is added ("for") lest a slave should regard lightly the injunction to serve Christ (161). "For the person who [does not serve Christ but who] does wrong. . . ." On ellipses with γάρ, see BAGD 152a. Only if γάρ bears an unusual adversative sense ("but," which is possible: see BAGD 152c; Z § 473) is the connection between an indic. δουλεύετε and v. 25 easily comprehensible. For the main NT uses of γάρ, see on Phlm. 7.

(3) "*Therefore* serve the Lord Christ" accords with v. 24a just as well as the sense "*For* you are serving the Lord Christ." Cf. (1) above.

(4) Rom. 12:11 has τῷ κυρίῳ δουλεύοντες (an impv. ptc.), "serve the Lord." Cf. (2) above.

VERSE 25

ὁ γὰρ ἀδικῶν

Nom. sg. masc. pres. act. ptc. of ἀδικέω, do wrong (in violation of either human or divine law, BAGD 17c). With the art., this ptc. becomes a subst. (cf. BDF § 413; R 764-765; T 150-151) that may be both timeless and indef. (cf. Burton § 123), "the wrongdoer," or it may denote a person who habitually does wrong (cf. Burton § 124). The primary ref. is probably to the slave guilty of dishonest action (cf. Lohse 161; O'Brien 230-231), but it is possible that the master who metes out injustice (cf. 4:1) to his slaves is principally in mind, or that both slaves and masters are in view (Lightfoot 227, citing Eph. 6:8).

κομίσεται ὃ ἠδίκησεν

3 sg. fut. mid. indic. of κομίζω, (act.) bring; (mid.) get for oneself, obtain; get back, be requited for. Ὅ is acc. sg. neut. of the rel. pron. ὅς, ἥ, ὅ. 3 sg. (+ movable ν) aor. act. indic. of ἀδικέω, do wrong. Lit. "he will get back that

which he did wrong." That is, "he will reap the reward of his wrongdoing" (BAGD 17c) or "he . . . will receive the consequences of the wrong which he has done" (NASB). It is a case of receiving from God due recompense for evil done. The fut. κομίσεται is a true fut., alluding to recompense received at the Great Assize, not a gnomic fut., portraying a general truth that is repeatedly fulfilled. Although the aor. ἠδίκησεν could conceivably be gnomic (". . . the wrong things he does," GNB), it is much more probably constative, viewing past actions (whether single, repeated, or continuous) unitarily: "For the wrong-doer will be repaid for the wrong he did."

καὶ οὐκ ἔστιν προσωπολημψία

This is, in effect, a second ground for the impv. δουλεύετε. Ἔστι(ν) retains its accent after οὐκ (MH 203). Either παρὰ τῷ θεῷ ("with God," cf. Rom. 2:11) or παρὰ τῷ κυρίῳ ("with the Lord") needs to be supplied. The latter is preferable, given v. 24a and the parallel in Eph. 6:9b. Προσωπολημψία, -ας, ἡ, partiality; (lit.) acceptance (cf. λῆμψις) of one's face (πρόσωπον), reflecting the Heb. idiom "to raise (= accept) the face of a humble suppliant" = "to show partiality" (see further E. Lohse, TDNT 6.779-780; Moule 132; Turner, *Words* 366-367). When Christ exercises his God-given role as judge (1 Cor. 4:4-5; 2 Tim. 4:1, 8; cf. Acts 17:31) there will be no favoritism. In determining and dispensing rewards (cf. v. 24a) and punishments (cf. v. 25a), he will apply the same standard of judgment to all (cf. GNB), ignoring externals ("one's face"), so that neither the slave nor the master will receive preferential treatment. Οὐκ ἔστιν may be a futuristic pres. ("there will be," TCNT) or a timeless pres. ("there is," most EVV), describing what is and always will be true. See further J. M. Bassler, *Divine Impartiality: Paul and a Theological Axiom* (Chico, CA: Scholars, 1981).

VERSE 1

Οἱ κύριοι, τὸ δίκαιον καὶ τὴν ἰσότητα τοῖς δούλοις παρέχεσθε

2 pl. (after the voc. pl. οἱ κύριοι) pres. mid. impv. of παρέχω, show, afford, grant (+ dat. of the recipient, here τοῖς δούλοις, "your slaves," the art. denoting poss.). The mid. stresses the required involvement and initiative of the masters: they were to act voluntarily, from their own resources (Zerwick, *Analysis* 453-454). Or the mid. may point to the slaveowners' reciprocal obligation: "exhibit on your part" (Lightfoot 228). On the "vocatival nom." οἱ κύριοι, see v. 18a.

Τὸ δίκαιον, "what is just" (BAGD 626d), "justice" (NASB; ZG 611). As here, the neut. art. may convert a neut. adj. into an abstract noun; cf. τὸ χρηστόν

(Rom. 2:4), "kindness" (BAGD 551b). Ἰσότης, -ητος, ἡ, equality; fairness (of treatment). The art. may be repeated with this second subst. because of the change in gender from neut. (τό) to fem. (τήν; R 788-789); but it may also point to concrete instances of fairness, acts that are equitable rather than equity as an abstract principle. Paul is not enjoining social equality through the emancipation of slaves, but rather even-handedness of treatment. "Grant to your slaves justice and fairness" (NASB). "Treat your slaves justly and fairly" (RSV; Lohse 154, 162; O'Brien 214). See For Further Study 48, "Slavery in the New Testament" (Phlm. 16).

εἰδότες ὅτι καὶ ὑμεῖς ἔχετε κύριον ἐν οὐρανῷ

Nom. pl. masc. (agreeing with the implied subj. of παρέχεσθε) of the pf. act. ptc. of οἶδα, know, a pf. (form)-pres. (mng.) vb. (see on 3:24). The ptc. is causal, as in 3:24, "because you know" (NIV; sim. TCNT). With ὑμεῖς, καί is adjunctive ("too," "for your part"). "You *have* a master" means "you are under a master's control" (BAGD 332b) or "you are accountable to a master." Κύριον is anar. because qualitative. The qualifying prep. phrase that follows has the effect of making κύριον definite and excluding ambiguity as to whom the κύριοι are accountable.

TRANSLATION

18 Wives, be subject to your husbands, as is appropriate in the Lord. 19 Husbands, love your wives and do not be harsh with them. 20 Children, obey your parents in everything, for this is pleasing in the Lord. 21 Fathers, do not provoke your children, lest they become disheartened. 22 Slaves, obey your earthly masters in everything, not with external service as if you were merely pleasing humans, but with sincerity of heart and out of reverence for the Lord. 23 Whatever your task, work at it with enthusiasm, as service for the Lord and not for humans, 24 because you know that from the Lord you will receive your inheritance as a reward. Serve the Lord Christ. 25 For the wrongdoer will be repaid for the wrong he did, and there is no favoritism. 4:1 Masters, treat your slaves justly and fairly, because you know that you too have a Master—in heaven.

EXPANDED PARAPHRASE

18 You wives, submit yourselves to the leadership of your husbands, for this is fitting behavior for those who belong to the Lord. 19 You husbands, show love to your wives constantly—never be harsh with them or foster bitter feelings against them. 20 You children, be obedient to your parents in every respect, for

such behavior pleases the Lord and befits those who belong to him. [21] You fathers, avoid exasperating your children by over-correcting them or scorning their efforts; for if you do provoke them, they will become disheartened and sullen. [22] You slaves, be totally obedient to your earthly masters. Serve them well, but not with concern only for external appearances, as though it were your responsibility simply to serve humans. Rather, serve them with heartfelt sincerity and out of your reverent fear of the Lord. [23] Perform any task you may have enthusiastically and as a service rendered to the Lord and not to humans, [24] since you well know that it is from this same Lord and Master that you will receive the glorious inheritance of believers as your full recompense, whatever dues you may or may not now receive from humans. So then, serve your heavenly Master who is Christ. [25] For everyone who does not serve the Lord Christ but engages in wrongdoing will be duly requited for all the wrong he has done, and this Master shows no favoritism in dispensing rewards and punishments or in treating masters and slaves. [4:1] And finally, you masters, give your slaves just and even-handed treatment, since you are well aware that you, like your slaves, have a Master in heaven—a heavenly employer to whom you are accountable.

FOR FURTHER STUDY

41. Catalogs of Domestic Duties (Haustafeln = "household tables") (3:18–4:1)

Balch, D. L., *Let Wives Be Submissive: The Domestic Code in 1 Peter* (Chico, CA: Scholars, 1981), esp. 1-20.

Cannon 95-131.

Crouch, J. E., *The Origin and Intention of the Colossian Haustafel* (Göttingen: Vandenhoeck & Ruprecht, 1972).

Hinson, E. G., "The Christian Household in Colossians 3:18–4:1," *Review and Expositor* 70 (1973) 495-506.

Lillie, W., "The Pauline House-tables," *ExpT* 86 (1974-75) 179-183.

Lohse 154-157.

Martin, R. P., NIDNTT 3.928-932.

*O'Brien, 214-219.

Schroeder, D., IDB 5.546-547.

Schweizer, E., "Traditional Ethical Patterns in the Pauline and post-Pauline Letters and their Development (Lists of Vices and House-tables)," *Text and Interpretation,* ed. E. Best and R. McL. Wilson (Cambridge: Cambridge University, 1979) 195-209.

42. Recompense and Reward (3:24-25)

Bassler, J. M., *Divine Impartiality: Paul and a Theological Axiom* (Chico, CA: Scholars, 1981).

Böttger, P. C., *et al.*, NIDNTT 3.134-145.

Büchsel, F., TDNT 2.167-169.

Buis, H., ZPEB 5.83-85.

Davies, P. E., IDB 4.71-74.

de Ru, G., "The Conception of Reward in the Teaching of Jesus," *NovT* 8 (1966) 202-222.

Dozeman, T. B., ISBE 4.179-180.

Filson, F. V., *St. Paul's Conception of Recompense* (Leipzig: Hinrichs, 1931).

Herion, G. A., ISBE 4.154-159.

Preisker, H., TDNT 4.714-728.

Towner, W. S., IDB 5.742-744.

*Travis, S. H., *Christ and the Judgement of God* (New York: Nelson, 1986)

HOMILETICAL SUGGESTIONS

Household Relationships (3:18–4:1)

1. Wives and Husbands (3:18-19)
   (a) Wives must be subject to their husbands (v. 18a)
   (b) Husbands must:
       (i) love their wives (v. 19a)
       (ii) not treat them harshly (v. 19b)
2. Children and Parents (vv. 20-21)
   (a) Children must obey their parents (v. 20a)
   (b) Fathers/parents must not provoke their children (v. 21a)
3. Servants and Masters (3:22–4:1)
   (a) Servants must:
       (i) obey their masters (3:22a)
       (ii) work with enthusiasm (3:23a)
       (iii) serve the Lord Christ (3:24b)
   (b) Masters must treat their slaves justly and fairly (4:1a)

Christian Motivation (3:18–4:1)

1. For wives:

your obligation to behave fittingly as those in the Lord (3:18b)
2. For children:
    your desire to please the Lord, which is fitting for those in the Lord
    (v. 20b)
3. For employees:
    reverence for the Lord (v. 22c)
    the Lord is your real employer (v. 23b)
    knowledge of your heavenly reward (v. 24a)
    wrongdoers will be recompensed for their evil (v. 25a)
    the Lord shows no favoritism (v. 25b)
4. For employers:
    knowledge that your real employer is in heaven (4:1b)

D. PRAYER AND WITNESS (4:2-6)

2 Τῇ προσευχῇ προσκαρτερεῖτε, γρηγοροῦντες ἐν αὐτῇ ἐν εὐχαριστίᾳ, 3 προσευχόμενοι ἅμα καὶ περὶ ἡμῶν, ἵνα ὁ θεὸς ἀνοίξῃ ἡμῖν θύραν τοῦ λόγου, λαλῆσαι
τὸ μυστήριον τοῦ Χριστοῦ, δι᾽ ὃ καὶ δέδεμαι, 4 ἵνα φανερώσω αὐτὸ ὡς δεῖ με
λαλῆσαι. 5 Ἐν σοφίᾳ περιπατεῖτε πρὸς τοὺς ἔξω, τὸν καιρὸν ἐξαγοραζόμενοι.
6 Ὁ λόγος ὑμῶν πάντοτε ἐν χάριτι, ἅλατι ἠρτυμένος, εἰδέναι πῶς δεῖ ὑμᾶς ἑνὶ
ἑκάστῳ ἀποκρίνεσθαι.

STRUCTURE

2	Τῇ προσευχῇ	προσκαρτερεῖτε,		
	γρηγοροῦντες ἐν αὐτῇ ἐν εὐχαριστίᾳ,			
3	*προσευχόμενοι* . . .	ἵνα ὁ θεὸς	ἀνοίξῃ . . .	λαλῆσαι
4		ἵνα	φανερώσω . . . ὡς δεῖ με	λαλῆσαι
5	Ἐν σοφίᾳ	περιπατεῖτε πρὸς	τοὺς ἔξω,	
			τὸν καιρὸν *ἐξαγοραζόμενοι*	
6	ὁ λόγος ὑμῶν	[ἔστω] πάντοτε	ἐν χάριτι,	
			ἅλατι *ἠρτύμενος*	
			εἰδέναι πῶς δεῖ ὑμᾶς . . . ἀποκρίνεσθαι	

Three impvs. (one implied: "be persistent," v. 2; "behave," v. 5; ["let it be,"
v. 6]) are followed by ptcs. (italicized above), the first three of which are impv.
in function ("be vigilant," v. 2b; "pray," v. 3a; buy up, v. 5b). The content of
the prayer (προσευχόμενοι) is indicated in two ἵνα clauses (vv. 3b, 4).

VERSE 2

Τῇ προσευχῇ προσκαρτερεῖτε

2 pl. pres. act. impv. of προσκαρτερέω, adhere to, persist in, be busily engaged
in, be devoted to (+ dat., here τῇ προσευχῇ; the dat. is common with προσ-
compound vbs., BDF § 202). "Devote yourselves to prayer" (NIV), "persist in
the practice of prayer," "pray perseveringly" (NAB).

γρηγοροῦντες ἐν αὐτῇ

Nom. pl. masc. (agreeing with the pl. subj. of προσκαρτερεῖτε) of the pres. act.
ptc. of γρηγορέω, be awake; be watchful, be on the alert. The ptc. is either
circumstantial ("as you watch," O'Brien 235, 237; "with mind awake," NEB)
or *impv., under the influence of the preceding vb. ("be wide awake," BAGD
167c; "be watchful," Lohse 164 and n. 4). Ἐν αὐτῇ, "in it" (= τῇ προσευχῇ;
locat. ἐν, cf. T 265, "occupied in") or possibly "as you pray" (GNB; cf. Moule

132, "while at prayer"; temp. ἐν). Paul is encouraging mental and spiritual alertness in prayer (cf. 1 Pet. 4:7b), perhaps even watchfulness against temptation (cf. Mk. 14:37-38) or for the Advent (O'Brien 235, 237-238, 243).

ἐν εὐχαριστίᾳ

Sociative ἐν, expressing attendant circumstances (ZG 611): "with thanksgiving" (RV, RSV), "with *an attitude of* thanksgiving" (NASB; sim. NEB, NAB). But possibly the phrase could be cstr. as a separate impv. ("and be thankful," O'Brien 235), or ἐν could be taken as locat., along with ἐν αὐτῷ ("being on the alert in it and in your giving of thanks," Weymouth), or even as instr. ("maintain your zest for prayer by thanksgiving," Moffatt).

VERSE 3

προσευχόμενοι ἅμα καὶ περὶ ἡμῶν

Nom. pl. masc. (agreeing with the pl. subj. of προσκαρτερεῖτε) of pres. mid. ptc. of dep. προσεύχομαι, pray. The adv. ἅμα, "at the same time," makes precise the temporal coincidence of two actions (cf. BDF § 425[2]; R 1139-1140); here, persistence or alertness in prayer, and intercession (προσεύχομαι here = intercede; cf. O'Brien 238).

With ἅμα, the ptc. will be either circumstantial ("praying," RV, NASB) or, better, impv., under the influence of προσκαρτερεῖτε (thus most EVV; Lohse 164 and n. 8): "At the same time pray for us too" (adjunctive καί; see 3:4). Περί here does not mean "concerning," but "for" = "on behalf of": it is equivalent to ὑπέρ (cf. BDF § 229[1]; Zerwick, *Analysis* 454; Z § 96) and introduces the person in whose interest the petition is being made (BAGD 644d). Ἡμῶν may refer to Paul himself (see on 1:3 for the epistolary pl.) but more probably includes his coworkers, such as Timothy (1:1) and Epaphras (4:12-13). Yet his own situation is principally in mind (note the sgs. δέδεμαι and φανερώσω in vv. 3-4).

ἵνα ὁ θεὸς ἀνοίξῃ ἡμῖν θύραν τοῦ λόγου

3 sg. aor. act. subjunc. of ἀνοίγω, open. Ἵνα introduces not the purpose ("so that," GNB) but the content of the prayer (O'Brien 238; cf. 1:9): "that God may open up for us (ἡμῖν, dat. of advantage or interest; cf. 3:23) a door" = ". . . may afford us opportunities" (cf. BAGD 366a) or ". . . may provide us with an opening" (NAB; sim. Goodspeed).

Λόγος may mean (a) "word" = "message" of the gospel or (b) "preaching" of the gospel. With θύραν the gen. τοῦ λόγου may be:

(1) subj.: a door "where the word enters" (BDF § 166); or

(2) obj.:

    *(a) "a door for our message" (NIV; sim. TCNT, Goodspeed),
        "opportunities for announcing the message" (JB; sim. GNB),
        "a door *of admission* for the word," "i.e., 'an opportunity of preach-
        ing the Gospel' " (Lightfoot 229; sim. RV, RSV, NASB),
        "a door which allows the word to pass through" (Zerwick, *Analysis*
        454),

    (b) "a door for preaching" (Weymouth; Robertson, *Pictures* 509),
        "an opening for preaching" (NEB).

Actually, it is only in a loose sense that this gen. may be classified as subj. or obj. Perhaps it is preferable to classify it more broadly as a gen. of relation (the basic connotation of the gen.) and to determine the nature of the relation between θύρα and λόγος by examining the context and parallel passages (such as 2 Cor. 2:12).

    In formulating this prayer request, Paul may possibly be alluding to a desired release from imprisonment (cf. Phlm. 22). Certainly he is soliciting prayer for special opportunities for evangelism (cf. 2 Cor. 2:12; 2 Thess. 3:1) and, by implication, the unimpeded progress of the gospel (cf. Acts 28:31).

λαλῆσαι τὸ μυστήριον τοῦ Χριστοῦ

Aor. act. infin. of λαλέω, speak. This infin. may be:

    (1) a definition of τοῦ λογοῦ: ". . . opportunities for preaching, that is, to proclaim the mystery of Christ" (sim. Weymouth, NAB; apparently also Moffatt, NEB);

    (2) ecbatic, expressing a result that is hypothetical rather than actual (R 1089-1090; cf. Lightfoot 229, "the infinitive of the consequence, like εἰδέναι ver. 6"): "so that we proclaim the mystery of Christ"; or

  *(3) telic: "so that we may speak of the truths hidden in the Christ" (TCNT; sim. NASB, NIV; cf. R 1086, 1087: an epex. infin. subsidiary to a preceding ἵνα clause and expressing a secondary purpose [as in 1:10]).

Τοῦ Χριστοῦ is an epex. gen. (cf. 1:27; 2:2; Robertson, *Pictures* 509; Zerwick, *Analysis* 454): Christ *is* the mystery. On the term μυστήριον, see 1:26, and also see above For Further Study 22, " 'Mystery' (μυστήριον) in Paul" (1:26-27).

δι' ὃ καὶ δέδεμαι

1 sg. pf. pass. indic. of δέω, bind. The pf. emphasizes the pres. consequences of the past act of being bound. Thus "I am in chains" (of literal binding: TCNT, JB, NIV; sim. RV), or, by metonymy, "I am in prison" (RSV; sim. Moffatt,

Goodspeed, NEB, GNB), "I am a prisomer" (NAB; cf. δεδεμένος, Acts 24:27), rather than "I have . . . been imprisoned" (NASB). Ὅ is acc. (after διά meaning "because of," "on account of") sg. neut. (agreeing with μυστήριον) of the rel. pron. ὅς. The final α of διά is elided before the rough breathing of ὅ. Καί may be emphatic ("because of which I am, *in fact*, in prison") or else strengthens the rel. and either remains untranslated or has the sense, "because of this *very* mystery."

VERSE 4

ἵνα φανερώσω αὐτό

1 sg. aor. act. subjunc. of φανερόω, reveal, make known, show. Αὐτό is acc. (as dir. obj.) sg. neut. (agreeing with μυστήριον) of αὐτός, -ή, -ό, he, she, it; -self. Ἵνα could be ecbatic/resultative ("Then I shall proclaim it fully," Weymouth; sim. TCNT), but more probably it introduces:

(1) a second purpose of the opened door: first, proclamation (λαλῆσαι, v. 3), second, open or bold proclamation (ἵνα φανερώσω); or
*(2) a second aspect of the content of the prayer, προσευχόμενοι (v. 3a) being understood before ἵνα: first, prayer for an open door to proclaim the message (v. 3b, c), second, prayer that Paul may proclaim it openly or fully or boldly (Lightfoot 230; cf. Eph. 6:19) or clearly (RSV, NEB, NASB, GNB, JB, NAB): "Pray that I may proclaim it clearly" (NIV).

ὡς δεῖ με λαλῆσαι

The impers. vb. δεῖ (3 sg. pres. act., "it is necessary," "one must"; "it is a duty," "one ought") is usually followed, as here, by the acc. (here με) and infin. (λαλῆσαι, aor. act. infin. of λαλέω, speak). "It is necessary for me to speak" = "I must speak"; or "it is a duty for me to speak" = "I ought to speak." The compulsion implied by δεῖ ranges from that of divine necessity or divine appointment (as here) to that of human custom or a human sense of fitness (see further W. Grundmann, TDNT 2.21-25). Ὡς may express manner ("in the way I ought to speak," NASB; cf. BAGD 897a) or possibly cause (where ὡς = ὅτι or ἐπεί; see LSJ s.v. ὡς B. IV; "because I must speak it" [viz. the mystery of Christ]; cf. Acts 23:11; 1 Cor. 9:16; cf. Moule 133).

VERSE 5

ἐν σοφίᾳ περιπατεῖτε πρὸς τοὺς ἔξω

2 pl. pres. act. impv. of περιπατέω, walk; (in a moral sense) live, behave,

conduct oneself. Ἐν σοφίᾳ expresses manner or an accompanying circumstance: "with wisdom," "wisely," "tactfully." Used as here of personal interrelationships (cf. R 625), πρός + acc. means "in dealing with," "towards." Ἔξω
is an adv. of place, "outside." With the art. it becomes subst. (cf. BAGD 552a
and see above on 3:1): οἱ ἔξω means "the outside ones" = "those outside [the
Church]," i.e., unbelievers, non-Christians, "outsiders" (Goodspeed, RSV,
NASB, NAB, NIV). Possibly the sense may be more general, "the outside
world" (TCNT, Weymouth, Moffatt), or more specific, "those outside your own
number" (NEB). Tr.: "Behave wisely towards outsiders," "Be prudent in dealing with outsiders" (NAB).

τὸν καιρὸν ἐξαγοραζόμενοι

Nom. pl. masc. (agreeing with the pl. subj. of περιπατεῖτε) of the pres. mid.
ptc. of ἐξαγοράζω, buy up, redeem. As well as referring to "time" in general,
καιρός often denotes critical or unique time, a moment of destiny, a fitting
season. Here it refers to each opportunity or all the opportunities afforded by
time (cf. F. Büchsel, TDNT 1.128; Lohse 168).

The ptc. is an indir. mid., where the subj. acts "for, to or by himself"
(R 809); thus, "buying up opportunities for yourselves" (sim. R 810; Lightfoot
230). The sense of the pref. ἐκ- (here ἐξ- before the initial vowel of ἀγοράζω,
buy in the marketplace [ἀγορά]) in the compound vb. ἐξαγοράζομαι may be:

(1) intensive: "I buy *eagerly* for myself" = "I make use of," "I take advantage
     of" (*utor;* Zerwick, *Analysis* 454, "perhaps");
(2) local/metaphorical:
     (a) "I ransom (*from* bondage)" (MH 309, citing J. A. Robinson), i.e., I
          redeem (= save from being lost) what has fallen, so to speak, into
          the wrong hands;
   *(b) "I buy *up*" every opportunity (sim. Weymouth, Barclay; Lightfoot
          230), where "buy up" means "use rightly" (Robertson, *Pictures*
          410), or "exploit" in the sense of "make the most of" (NAB, NIV;
          sim. TCNT, Moffatt, Goodspeed, RSV, NASB, JB; BAGD 395a [cf.
          271c]; Lohse 164, 167) or "use . . . to the full" (NEB; sim. GNB);
          or
(3) perfective: "I buy *out*" the whole stock of opportunity.

Given the close relation between v. 5a and v. 5b, the ptc. could be modal
("Be wise in your behavior toward outsiders *by snapping up* every opportunity
that comes," O'Brien 235, 241 [italics added]), but since v. 5b specifies merely
one application of the principle stated in v. 5a, it would seem better to cstr. the
ptc. as temp. ("*as* you buy up . . .") or *impv., under the influence of the
preceding impv. ("buy up every opportunity"; "make the most of the time,"

Lohse 164, 168 n. 28). In the open market where the commodity of καιρός is on sale, Christians are to make a "timely" purchase for themselves. In other words, they are to seize eagerly and use wisely every opportunity afforded them by time to promote the kingdom of God (cf. 4:11).

VERSE 6

ὁ λόγος ὑμῶν πάντοτε ἐν χάριτι

In v. 3 λόγος means "message" or "preaching"; here it means "speech" (RV, RSV, NASB, GNB, NAB; BAGD 35a, 111a) or "conversation" (TCNT, NEB, NIV), although it is possible that in vv. 5b-6 the verbal witness of evangelism is principally in view (cf. Goodspeed, "Always put your message attractively," v. 6a). A vb. such as ἔστω ("let it be"; 3 sg. impv. of εἰμί) is to be supplied (R 396). The prep. phrase ἐν χάριτι may express manner or circumstance ("with grace," RV, NASB; "with gracious charm," Barclay) or may be equivalent to an adj. ("gracious," RSV, NEB, NAB; "courteous," "amiable," ZG 611) or adj. phrase ("full of grace," NIV; "full of graciousness," Lohse 164). It is not necessary to supply ἐνδεδυμένος with ἐν, "clothed in graciousness" (as Zerwick, *Analysis* 454, proposes).

ἅλατι ἠρτυμένος

Nom. sg. masc. (agreeing with λόγος) of the pf. pass. ptc. of ἀρτύω, prepare; season (of food). Again ἔστω should be supplied (BAGD 35a). Dat. sg. of ἅλας, -ατος, τό, salt, instr. in sense (BDF § 195[1]): "seasoned with salt" (most EVV), referring to pungency and wittiness of speech (see Lightfoot 230-231). If this phrase is epex. of ἐν χάριτι, it would be legitimate to tr. "seasoned with the salt of grace" (Weymouth).

εἰδέναι πῶς δεῖ ὑμᾶς ἑνὶ ἑκάστῳ ἀποκρίνεσθαι

Pf. act. infin. of οἶδα, know. 3 sg. pres. act. of the impers. vb. δεῖ, it is necessary (+ acc. and infin., ὑμᾶς . . . ἀποκρίνεσθαι). Pres. mid. infin. of the dep. vb. ἀποκρίνομαι, answer (+ dat., here ἑνὶ ἑκάστῳ). Ἑνί is dat. sg. masc. of the cardinal numeral εἷς, μία, ἕν, gen. ἑνός, μιᾶς, ἑνός, one. Ἑκάστῳ is dat. sg. masc. of ἕκαστος, -η, -ον, each, every.

Εἰδέναι may be *telic ("so that you may know," Weymouth, RSV, NIV; sim. RV, TCNT, NASB) or ecbatic ("and so you will know"; sim. R 1090, hypothetical rather than actual result; Lightfoot 229, 231). But several EVV treat this infin. as an "absolute (imperatival) infinitive" (see R 1092-1093 for this usage; "and *learn* how to answer," Moffatt [italics added]; sim. Goodspeed, NEB, GNB). The interr. particle πῶς ("how?" "in what way?") here introduces an indir. question (BAGD 556b, 732c). Πῶς δεῖ ὑμᾶς may mean "how you should/ought" or "how you must" (see on v. 4 for δεῖ). Tr.: "so that you may know how you should answer [in a fitting manner] each individual." Ἑνὶ ἑκάστῳ is not simply "everyone" (= παντί) but "each separate person," the emphasis being on perceptive answers that have that delicate blend of pungency and graciousness suited to the varying needs of individuals.

TRANSLATION

2 Be persistent and vigilant in prayer, with thanksgiving. 3 At the same time pray for us, too, that God may open up for us a door for our message, so that we may proclaim the mystery of Christ, because of which I am in chains. 4 Pray that I may declare it boldly, as I ought. 5 Behave wisely toward outsiders; buy up every opportunity. 6 Let your conversation always be gracious, seasoned with salt, so that you may know how you should answer each individual.

EXPANDED PARAPHRASE

2 Always maintain the practice of prayer, and while you pray be alert in mind and heart. Also let thanksgiving always be a part of your prayer. 3 At the same time intercede for us too—that God may provide us with a wide, open door for the preaching of our message, so that we may proclaim Christ as God's open secret. It is, in fact, because of this open secret that I am now a prisoner in chains. 4 Pray, then, that I may declare this message openly and boldly, which is the way I ought to proclaim it. 5 Be tactful and wise in all your relations with unbelievers; buy up every possible opportunity to influence them for the kingdom of God. 6 Let your conversation always be graciously winsome and seasoned with the salt of wit and pungency, so that you may know how you should give an answer suitable for each occasion and each need to each separate individual.

HOMILETICAL SUGGESTIONS

Prayer and Witness (4:2-6)

1. The Ingredients in Effective Prayer (vv. 2-4):
   (a) Persistence: we need to be devoted to a habit (προσκαρτερεῖτε, v. 2a).
   (b) Vigilance: we need to be mentally and spiritually alert (γρηγοροῦντες, v. 2b).
   (c) Thanksgiving: we need to be grateful in all circumstances (ἐν εὐχαριστίᾳ, v. 2c; 1 Thess. 5:18).

(d) Petition: we need to ask for (προσευχόμενοι)

(i) unique opportunities to proclaim Christ (θύραν τοῦ λόγου, λαλῆσαι τὸ μυστήριον τοῦ Χριστοῦ, v. 3) and

(ii) appropriate boldness in proclaiming Christ (ἵνα φανερώσω αὐτό, v. 4).

2. The Ingredients in Powerful Witness (vv. 5-6):

(a) Behavior (περιπατεῖτε):

we need to be tactful (ἐν σοφίᾳ, v. 5a) and

we need to be resourceful in using opportunities (τὸν καιρὸν ἐξ-αγοραζόμενοι, v. 5b).

(b) Conversation (ὁ λόγος):

needs to be invariably winsome (πάντοτε ἐν χάριτι) and pungent (ἅλατι ἠρτυμένος, v. 6a)

needs to be tailored to each individual (εἰδέναι πῶς δεῖ ὑμᾶς ἑνὶ ἑκάστῳ ἀποκρίνεσθαι, v. 6b).

V. Personal Notes (4:7-18)

A. PAUL'S TWO REPRESENTATIVES (4:7-9)

7 Τὰ κατ' ἐμὲ πάντα γνωρίσει ὑμῖν Τύχικος ὁ ἀγαπητὸς ἀδελφὸς καὶ πιστὸς διάκονος καὶ σύνδουλος ἐν κυρίῳ, 8 ὃν ἔπεμψα πρὸς ὑμᾶς εἰς αὐτὸ τοῦτο, ἵνα γνῶτε τὰ περὶ ἡμῶν καὶ παρακαλέσῃ τὰς καρδίας ὑμῶν, 9 σὺν Ὀνησίμῳ τῷ πιστῷ καὶ ἀγαπητῷ ἀδελφῷ, ὅς ἐστιν ἐξ ὑμῶν· πάντα ὑμῖν γνωρίσουσιν τὰ ὧδε.

STRUCTURE

(1) Paul gives the credentials of his two messengers who will deliver the present letter (this is implied by the epistolary aor. ἔπεμψα, v. 8) to the Colossians. Each is ὁ ἀγαπητὸς ἀδελφός, "our dearly loved brother." Each is also πιστός ("trustworthy," "faithful"), Onesimus as an ἀδελφός, Tychicus as a διάκονος ("helper") and σύνδουλος ("fellow slave") ἐν κυρίῳ ("in the Lord's service"; vv. 7, 9).

(2) These two Gk. sentences contain three references to the information that Tychicus and Onesimus will give (γνωρίσει, v. 7; γνωρίσουσιν, v. 9) to the Colossians:

τὰ κατ' ἐμὲ πάντα (v. 7)	"all my circumstances"
τὰ περὶ ἡμῶν (v. 8)	"our situation," "how we are faring"
πάντα . . . τὰ ὧδε (v. 9)	"all that is happening here"

VERSE 7

Τὰ κατ' ἐμὲ πάντα γνωρίσει ὑμῖν Τύχικος

3 sg. fut. act. indic. of γνωρίζω, make known, reveal. The final α of κατά is elided before the initial vowel of ἐμέ. Τὰ κατ' ἐμέ, lit. "the things with respect

200

to me," i.e., "my circumstances" (BAGD 552a; ZG 611), although T 15 suggests that "what concerns me" may here (and in Phil. 1:12) mean "my lawsuit." Apparently the more informal and personal information about Paul was known to Tychicus alone (cf. the pl. γνωρίσουσιν in v. 9).

ὁ ἀγαπητὸς ἀδελφὸς καὶ πιστὸς διάκονος καὶ σύνδουλος ἐν κυρίῳ

On this art. subst., ὁ . . . ἀδελφός, in appos. to an anar. proper name (Τύχικος), see v. 9. The single art. with three coordinated nouns of the same gender and number indicates here that only one person is being referred to (cf. BDF § 276; R 785-786; T 181-182; Z § 184). Correspondingly, ἐν κυρίῳ (anar. because it is a formulaic phrase) may modify all three nouns; on the other hand, like πιστός (trustworthy, faithful, loyal), it may qualify only διάκονος and σύνδουλος (cf. Lightfoot 232). Certainly the parallel in Eph. 6:21 shows that ἐν κυρίῳ may be cstr. with διάκονος. "In the Lord" = "in the Lord's service" (sim. Weymouth, Goodspeed, NEB, JB) or possibly (see on 3:18) "as a Christian." Πιστὸς διάκονος means either "faithful minister" of Christ, or "trustworthy helper" (NEB; cf. BAGD 184d), "trusty assistant" (Weymouth) of Paul. Σύνδουλος, -ου, ὁ, "fellow slave" (NAB), "fellow servant" of Christ along with (σύν-) Paul. See For Further Study 43, "Paul and His Coworkers."

VERSE 8

ὃν ἔπεμψα πρὸς ὑμᾶς εἰς αὐτὸ τοῦτο, ἵνα γνῶτε τὰ περὶ ἡμῶν καὶ παρακαλέσῃ τὰς καρδίας ὑμῶν

1 sg. aor. act. indic. of πέμπω, send. Epistolary aor. (Burton § 44; Moule, *Idiom Book* 12; R 846; T 73; ZG 611), "whom I am sending [with this letter, Zerwick, *Analysis* 454]," where the writer projects himself into the situation of the recipients of the letter, for whom the "sending" will be in the past. Εἰς αὐτὸ τοῦτο, lit. "for this itself," thus "for just this" (cf. BAGD 123a), "for this very reason" (BAGD 229d), with the following ἵνα clause defining the purpose, "namely that" (BAGD 377b). Τοῦτο is therefore prospective, not retrospective (cf. Z § 213).

2 pl. second aor. act. subjunc. (after ἵνα) of γινώσκω, know, come to know. 3 sg. aor. act. subjunc. (after ἵνα) of παρακαλέω, exhort; comfort, encourage. Both aors. are constative, viewing the knowledge or acquisition of knowledge ("that you may know") and the encouragement ("that he may cheer your hearts," Weymouth) unitarily, without reference to the type of action involved (whether linear, momentary, or repeated). Τὰ περὶ ἡμῶν, lit. "the things concerning us," i.e., "our situation" (BAGD 161a; cf. 645a), "our circumstances" (TCNT, NASB, NIV), "how we are faring" (Weymouth).

On both external and internal evidence, the rdg. ἵνα γνῶτε τὰ περὶ ἡμῶν (accorded a "C" rating in all three UBS edd.) is to be preferred. It has strong and diversified support (incl. A B D* F G P 33 it *al*); it most easily explains the rise of other rdgs. (viz. ὑμῶν instead of ἡμῶν; γνῷ [3 sg. second aor. act. subjunc.] instead of γνῶτε; and the resultant ἵνα γνῷ τὰ περὶ ὑμῶν, "that *he* may know how *you* are faring"); it accords with vv. 7 and 9 regarding the purpose of Tychicus's visit; and it is supported by Eph. 6:22. See Lightfoot 233, 253; Metzger 626.

VERSE 9

σὺν Ὀνησίμῳ τῷ πιστῷ καὶ ἀγαπητῷ ἀδελφῷ, ὅς ἐστιν ἐξ ὑμῶν·

"I am sending him [Tychicus] (v. 8a) . . . along with (σύν) Onesimus." To make this connection with v. 8 clear, σὺν Ὀνησίμῳ may be tr. "With him I am sending Onesimus" (JB; sim. Weymouth) or "With him comes Onesimus" (NEB; sim. TCNT) or "He is coming with Onesimus" (NIV; sim. Moffatt). Ὀνήσιμος, -ου, ὁ, Onesimus; as a two-termination adj., ὀνήσιμος, -ον, means "useful," "profitable" (see the play on the word in Phlm. 10-11). It was a common slave name (see A. L. Connolly in Horsley 4.179-181). Ὀνησίμῳ (dat. after σύν) is anar., being a proper noun in a prep. phrase and being the first mention of this proper name (which in itself is def. and therefore does not require the art., R 759; cf. BDF § 260; T 165-166).

Substs. (here τῷ . . . ἀδελφῷ) in appos. to anar. proper names often have the art. (cf. BDF § 268; R 760; T 206) since such substs. serve to identify the person(s) named (cf. 4:7, 10; Phlm. 1, 2, 23, 24). Here τῷ anticipates ὅς: "that trustworthy and dear brother who is one of you." The rel. pron. ὅς is masc. sg. in agreement with Ὀνησίμῳ, but is nom. as the subj. of ἐστίν. Ἐξ ὑμῶν (ἐκ becomes ἐξ before vowels), lit. "[one] from you" (cf. εἷς ἐξ ὑμῶν, Matt. 26:21), a partitive use of ἐκ (cf. BDF § 164; R 599): "who is one of your own number" (Goodspeed), "who belongs to your group" (GNB), "who is a fellow-countryman of yours" (BAGD 225b). Paul adds this rel. clause not as a reproach to the Colossians but to highlight the radical nature of the conversion of one of their own: Onesimus, known to them as a dishonest, runaway slave, had become a reliable and dearly loved Christian brother.

πάντα ὑμῖν γνωρίσουσιν τὰ ὧδε

3 pl. (referring to Tychicus and Onesimus) fut. act. indic. of γνωρίζω, make known, reveal. Ὧδε, adv. of place: here, in this place. Πάντα . . . τὰ ὧδε, lit. "all the things here," the art. converting an adv. into a subst. (see on 3:1, τὰ ἄνω). Tr.: "the whole situation here" (NASB), "all the news here" (NEB; sim.

ZG 611), "everything that is happening here" (GNB, JB, NIV). The expression is wider in mng. than the comparable earlier phrases, τὰ κατ' ἐμὲ πάντα (v. 7) and τὰ περὶ ἡμῶν (v. 8), which refer to Paul in particular and the specialized knowledge of Tychicus. If Paul was imprisoned in Rome, the information that Tychicus and Onesimus would bring would include news of the church in Rome.

TRANSLATION

[7] Tychicus will let you know about all my circumstances. He is our dear brother, a trustworthy helper and fellow slave in the Lord. [8] I am sending him to you for this express purpose, that you may know how we are faring and that he may encourage your hearts. [9] With him I am sending Onesimus, that trustworthy and dear brother who is one of you. They will inform you about all that is happening here.

EXPANDED PARAPHRASE

[7] You will be told all the news about me by Tychicus, our dearly loved brother who has been a trustworthy helper and loyal fellow slave in the Lord's service. [8] There is a particular reason I am sending him to you: that you may find out how matters stand with us and have your hearts encouraged by the news he brings. [9] Along with him I am sending Onesimus, that trustworthy and dearly loved brother who is one of your own number. These two brothers will tell you everything that has been happening here in Rome.

FOR FURTHER STUDY

43. Paul and His Coworkers (4:7)

*Bruce, F. F., *The Pauline Circle* (Grand Rapids: Eerdmans, 1985).

*Ellis, E. E., "Paul and his Co-Workers," *NTS* 17 (1970-71) 437-452, reprinted in his *Prophecy and Hermeneutics in Early Christianity. New Testament Essays* (Tübingen: Mohr, 1978; Grand Rapids: Eerdmans, 1980, reprint) 3-22.

Filson, F. V., *Pioneers of the Primitive Church* (New York: Abingdon, 1940).

Hiebert, D. E., *Personalities around Paul* (Chicago: Moody, 1973).

Howson, J. S., *The Companions of St. Paul* (Boston: American Tract Society, 1872).

LaSor, W. S., *Great Personalities of the New Testament* (Westwood, NJ: Revell, 1961).

Lees, H. C., *St. Paul's Friends* (London: Religious Tract Society, 1917).

Robertson, A. T., *Some Minor Characters in the New Testament* (Garden City, NY: Doubleday, 1928).

Seekings, H. S., *The Men of the Pauline Circle* (London: Kelly, 1914).

HOMILETICAL SUGGESTIONS

Paul's Two Representatives (4:7-9)

1. Their credentials
   (a) Tychicus:
      (i) a dearly loved Christian brother
      (ii) a trustworthy helper and
      (iii) fellow slave in the Lord's service (ἐν κυρίῳ, v. 7b)
   (b) Onesimus: a Christian brother who is
      (i) trustworthy
      (ii) dearly loved
      (iii) a resident of Colossae (v. 9a)
2. Their mission
   (a) Tychicus:
      (i) to inform the Colossians of Paul's situation (vv. 7a, 8a)
      (ii) to cheer their hearts (v. 8b)
   (b) Tychicus and Onesimus: to inform the Colossians of the wider situation in Rome (v. 9b)

B. GREETINGS AND FINAL INSTRUCTIONS (4:10-18)

10 Ἀσπάζεται ὑμᾶς Ἀρίσταρχος ὁ συναιχμάλωτός μου, καὶ Μᾶρκος ὁ ἀνεψιὸς
Βαρναβᾶ (περὶ οὗ ἐλάβετε ἐντολάς, ἐὰν ἔλθῃ πρὸς ὑμᾶς δέξασθε αὐτόν), 11 καὶ
Ἰησοῦς ὁ λεγόμενος Ἰοῦστος, οἱ ὄντες ἐκ περιτομῆς οὗτοι μόνοι συνεργοὶ εἰς
τὴν βασιλείαν τοῦ θεοῦ, οἵτινες ἐγενήθησάν μοι παρηγορία. 12 ἀσπάζεται ὑμᾶς
Ἐπαφρᾶς ὁ ἐξ ὑμῶν, δοῦλος Χριστοῦ Ἰησοῦ, πάντοτε ἀγωνιζόμενος ὑπὲρ ὑμῶν
ἐν ταῖς προσευχαῖς, ἵνα σταθῆτε τέλειοι καὶ πεπληροφορημένοι ἐν παντὶ θελήματι
τοῦ θεοῦ. 13 μαρτυρῶ γὰρ αὐτῷ ὅτι ἔχει πολὺν πόνον ὑπὲρ ὑμῶν καὶ τῶν ἐν
Λαοδικείᾳ καὶ τῶν ἐν Ἱεραπόλει. 14 ἀσπάζεται ὑμᾶς Λουκᾶς ὁ ἰατρὸς ὁ ἀγαπητὸς
καὶ Δημᾶς. 15 Ἀσπάσασθε τοὺς ἐν Λαοδικείᾳ ἀδελφοὺς καὶ Νύμφαν καὶ τὴν κατ᾽
οἶκον αὐτῆς ἐκκλησίαν. 16 καὶ ὅταν ἀναγνωσθῇ παρ᾽ ὑμῖν ἡ ἐπιστολή, ποιήσατε
ἵνα καὶ ἐν τῇ Λαοδικέων ἐκκλησίᾳ ἀναγνωσθῇ, καὶ τὴν ἐκ Λαοδικείας ἵνα καὶ
ὑμεῖς ἀναγνῶτε. 17 καὶ εἴπατε Ἀρχίππῳ, Βλέπε τὴν διακονίαν ἣν παρέλαβες ἐν
κυρίῳ, ἵνα αὐτὴν πληροῖς.

18 Ὁ ἀσπασμὸς τῇ ἐμῇ χειρὶ Παύλου. μνημονεύετέ μου τῶν δεσμῶν. ἡ
χάρις μεθ᾽ ὑμῶν.

STRUCTURE

10 Ἀσπάζεται	ὑμᾶς	Ἀρίσταρχος	ὁ συναιχμάλωτός μου, καὶ
		Μᾶρκος	ὁ ἀνεψιὸς Βαρναβᾶ. . . , καὶ
11		Ἰησοῦς	ὁ λεγόμενος Ἰοῦστος,
		οἱ ὄντες	
		οὗτοι	
		οἵτινες	
12 ἀσπάζεται	ὑμᾶς	Ἐπαφρᾶς	ὁ ἐξ ὑμῶν, δοῦλος Χριστοῦ Ἰησοῦ,
			πάντοτε ἀγωνιζόμενος ὑπὲρ ὑμῶν
13			ἔχει πολὺν πόνον ὑπὲρ ὑμῶν
14 ἀσπάζεται	ὑμᾶς	Λουκᾶς	ὁ ἰατρὸς ὁ ἀγαπητὸς καὶ
		Δημᾶς.	
15 Ἀσπάσασθε	τοὺς . . . ἀδελφοὺς καὶ		
	Νύμφαν καὶ τὴν . . . ἐκκλησίαν		
16 ποιήσατε			ἵνα . . . ἀναγνωσθῇ, καὶ . . .
[βλέπετε]			ἵνα . . . ἀναγνῶτε. καὶ
17 εἴπατε	Ἀρχίππῳ, Βλέπε. . . ,		ἵνα αὐτὴν πληροῖς.
18 μνημονεύετέ μου τῶν δεσμῶν.			

(1) Paul records greetings (ἀσπάζεται ὑμᾶς, v. 10) from three Jewish Christians (Aristarchus, Mark, and Jesus Justus), each of whom is briefly
identified (ὁ . . . , ὁ . . . , ὁ . . .) before they are corporately described in

three clauses (οἱ ὄντες . . . , οὗτοι . . . , οἵτινες . . .). Then follow greetings (ἀσπάζεται ὑμᾶς, vv. 12, 14) from three Gentile believers, one of
whom is identified and described at some length (Epaphras), one briefly
identified (Luke), and one simply named (Demas).

(2) Final instructions are issued in four impvs. (vv. 15, 16, 17, 18), with two
more impvs. implied (viz. βλέπετε before ἵνα in v. 16c and ἀναγνῶτε
["read"] implied in the ὅταν clause in v. 16a).

VERSE 10

Ἀσπάζεται ὑμᾶς Ἀρίσταρχος ὁ συναιχμάλωτός μου, καὶ Μᾶρκος ὁ
ἀνεψιὸς Βαρναβᾶ

3 sg. pres. mid. indic. of dep. ἀσπάζομαι, greet. In expressing greetings at the
end of a letter, this vb. (whether in the indic., as here, or in the impv., as in
v. 15) regularly stands first in the sentence, and where more than one person
gives greetings (here, Ἀρίσταρχος, Μᾶρκος, Ἰησοῦς), it agrees with the number of the first noun (here sg.; cf. Rom. 16:3-16, impvs.; 16:21-23, indics.). In
the indic. we find this fixed order: ἀσπάζεται, then the obj. (the person[s]
greeted), then the subj. (the person greeting). The subj. is generally anar. (a
proper noun being already def.), while substs. in appos. are usually art.—thus
Ἀρίσταρχος ὁ συναιχμάλωτός μου . . . Μᾶρκος ὁ ἀνεψιός (v. 10), Λουκᾶς ὁ
ἰατρός (v. 14; see on 4:9 above; cf. Rom. 16:21-23).

Συναιχμάλωτος, -ου, ὁ, fellow prisoner (formed from σύν + αἰχμή [war]
+ ἀλίσκομαι [be captured]). It is possible that Aristarchus had actually been
imprisoned with Paul or that he was voluntarily sharing his imprisonment (cf.
JB, "who is here in prison with me"; sim. GNB, NAB). But since Paul was
not technically an αἰχμάλωτος, "prisoner *of war*," and the customary term for
a literal "fellow prisoner" is either (ὁ) συνδέσμιος (cf. δέσμιος, "prisoner,"
Phlm. 1, 9) or (ὁ) συνδεδεμένος (cf. Heb. 13:3) or συνδεσμώτης, it is perhaps
more likely that συναιχμάλωτος is fig. not lit., describing Aristarchus as a
voluntary bondslave of Christ, along with Paul ("Christ's captive like myself,"
NEB; sim. G. Kittel, TDNT 1.196-197; Zerwick, *Analysis* 454; Moule 136-
137). For a defense of the lit. mng., see Lightfoot 234; Lohse 172 n. 20;
O'Brien 249-250). Ἀνεψιός, -οῦ, ὁ, cousin. Βαρναβᾶ, gen. sg. of Βαρναβᾶς,
Barnabas.

περὶ οὗ ἐλάβετε ἐντολάς, ἐὰν ἔλθῃ πρὸς ὑμᾶς δέξασθε αὐτόν

WH, UBS, and most EVV rightly cstr. this whole statement as parenthetical.
Moreover, the ἐὰν clause defines ἐντολάς by reproducing the dir. speech of the
original instructions (cf. Lightfoot 236). Thus RSV: ". . . Mark the cousin of

Barnabas (concerning whom you have received instructions—if he comes to you, receive him) . . ." (sim. NASB, GNB, NAB).

2 pl. second aor. act. indic. of λαμβάνω, receive; take. The antecedent of οὗ (gen. [after περί, with regard to; BAGD 644d] sg. masc. of the rel. pron.) is Μᾶρκος, not the dependent gen. Βαρναβᾶ.

3 sg. (referring to Μᾶρκος) second aor. act. subjunc. (after ἐάν) of dep. ἔρχομαι, come; go. 2 pl. aor. mid. impv. of dep. δέχομαι, receive, welcome. Ἐάν (= εἰ + ἄν) followed by the aor. subjunc. in the protasis of a cond. sentence portrays some fut. event as a unitary action (constative aor.) occurring prior to the action of the vb. in the prot. (cf. BDF § 373[3]; Moule, *Idiom Book* 148-149; R 1016-1020; T 114-115). In this so-called "third class" cond., the aor. subjunc. generally expresses a higher degree of probability of fulfillment than does the pres. subjunc. Indeed, on occasion ἐάν + aor. subjunc. approaches the mng. of ὅταν ("when," "whenever"; T 114; Z § 322 and n. 8, where the German antecedent of BAGD [cf. 211b] is cited, which lists 4:10 as an instance of this phenomenon). In the present case, a single visit (ἔλθῃ) is envisaged, and, correspondingly, a single welcome (δέξασθε, also constative aor.).

VERSE 11

καὶ Ἰησοῦς ὁ λεγόμενος Ἰοῦστος

Nom. sg. masc. (agreeing with Ἰησοῦς) of the pres. pass. ptc. of λέγω, speak, name; (pass.) be called. This art. ptc., which here identifies rather than describes Ἰησοῦς (cf. Burton §§ 295, 426), is equivalent to a rel. clause (cf. BDF § 412; R 764; T 152): "who is called Justus" (TCNT, Moffatt, Goodspeed, RSV, NASB, NIV), "whose surname is" Justus (BAGD 470a; sim. Lightfoot 233). NEB and JB render this by "Jesus Justus." On "the use of a double name," see Horsley 1.89-96, esp. 93, 95. On the anar. Ἰησοῦς, see v. 10.

οἱ ὄντες ἐκ περιτομῆς οὗτοι μόνοι συνεργοὶ εἰς τὴν βασιλείαν τοῦ θεοῦ

Nom. pl. masc. of the pres. ptc. of εἰμί, be. Οἱ ὄντες may be an art. ptc. (a) that is equivalent to a nonrestrictive/explanatory rel. clause (cf. Burton § 295), "who are," or (b) that is a "hanging nom.": "As for those who." Or the words may be accented οἵ, ὄντες, "who, being . . ." (οἵ, nom. pl. masc. of the rel. pron.; cf. Moule 137). Ἐκ περιτομῆς, lit. "from the circumcision" (NASB; sim. RV), means either "of Jewish birth," "Jews" (Moule 137), or "[converts] from Judaism" (sim. TCNT, Goodspeed; cf. Lightfoot 236), "Jewish converts" (GNB). On E. E. Ellis's distinctive view of the mng. of οἱ ὄντες ἐκ περιτομῆς, see O'Brien 251-252, 256.

Οὗτοι is nom. pl. masc. of the demonstrative adj. and pron. οὗτος, αὕτη, τοῦτο, this. Συνεργός, -όν (two-termination adj.), working together with; (subst.) helper, coworker. Tr.: "these only [of the Jews, τῆς περιτομῆς; cf. Robertson, *Pictures* 511] are [εἰσίν] my coworkers for [the promotion of] the kingdom of God (τοῦ θεοῦ, poss. gen.)." Alternative renderings of the εἰς phrase would be "in the work of God's realm" (Moffatt; referential εἰς, "with respect to"), "for the reign of God" (Goodspeed).

With regard to the punctuation of the Gk., there are four options (cf. Moule 137; Moule, *Idiom Book* 31):

(1) . . . Ἰοῦστος, οἱ ὄντες ἐκ περιτομῆς. οὗτοι μόνοι . . . : ". . . who are Jewish converts. These alone . . ." (sim. RV, Barclay)

(2) . . . Ἰοῦστος, οἵ, ὄντες ἐκ περιτομῆς, οὗτοι μόνοι . . . : ". . . who, being Jewish converts, are in fact the only ones . . ."

(3) . . . Ἰοῦστος. οἱ ὄντες ἐκ περιτομῆς, οὗτοι μόνοι . . . : "As for those who are Jewish converts, only these . . ." (sim. NEB)

*(4) . . . Ἰοῦστος, οἱ ὄντες ἐκ περιτομῆς οὗτοι μόνοι συνεργοί . . . (UBS; WH adds a comma after περιτομῆς): "These are the only Jewish converts among my coworkers . . ." (sim. most EVV).

According to (1) and (2), Aristarchus, Mark, and Jesus Justus were Paul's only coworkers at the time of writing or previously; according to (3) and (4), they were his only current or previous *Jewish* coworkers. Most EVV reflect the latter interpretation, which is supported by the implication of vv. 12-14 that Epaphras and probably Luke and Demas were also currently Paul's fellow workers.

οἵτινες ἐγενήθησάν μοι παρηγορία

3 pl. aor. pass. indic. of dep. γίνομαι, become, be. In HGk. not only the second aor. mid. ἐγενόμην but also the aor. pass. ἐγενήθην meant "I became," "I was." (On the tendency in HGk. for some dep. vbs. to prefer aor. pass. over aor. mid. forms, see BDF § 78; T 54; Z §§ 229-230.) Οἵτινες is nom. pl. masc. (referring to Aristarchus, Mark, and Jesus Justus) of the compound indef. rel. pron. ὅστις, ἥτις, ὅ τι, who(ever); such a one who. This may be a stylistic variant of οἵ (the rel. pron.) after οἱ ὄντες, or may be qualitative, "who, being the kind of men they were. . . ." Μοι is the encl. form of the dat. sg. of the first pers. personal pron.; here a dat. of advantage or interest, or an ethical dat. (see on 3:23). In the obl. cases the encl. forms με, μου, μοι are used when the emphasis falls on the noun or vb. rather than the pron. (BAGD 217b, c). For this reason and because of its position, παρηγορία (-ας, ἡ, solace, comfort) is emphatic. Tr.: "and they have been (aor. tr. as pf.) a comfort to me" (RSV), "and they have proved to be an encouragement to me" (NASB; sim. NIV, "—they are men who (οἵτινες) have been a comfort to me" (Weymouth; sim. RV).

VERSE 12

ἀσπάζεται ὑμᾶς Ἐπαφρᾶς ὁ ἐξ ὑμῶν, δοῦλος Χριστοῦ Ἰησοῦ

On the vb., the word-order, and the anar. proper noun Ἐπαφρᾶς (see 1:7), see on v. 10. Used with the prep. phrase ἐξ ὑμῶν (on which see v. 9), the art. functions as a rel. pron. (cf. ὅς ἐστιν ἐξ ὑμῶν [v. 9], of Onesimus; BAGD 551d, 552a): "Epaphras, who is one of you." Χριστοῦ Ἰησοῦ is poss. gen. (but possibly obj., "one who serves Christ Jesus").

πάντοτε ἀγωνιζόμενος ὑπὲρ ὑμῶν ἐν ταῖς προσευχαῖς

Nom. sg. masc. (agreeing with Ἐπαφρᾶς) of the pres. mid. ptc. of dep. ἀγωνίζομαι, strive, contend; take part in a contest ("here as it were w. God," ZG 612). It is difficult to relate this ptc. to the finite vb. ἀσπάζεται, for while the greeting is single and unrepeated the wrestling in prayer is constant (πάντοτε, "always"). Either the ptc. is used abs. ("He is always wrestling in prayer for you," NIV; sim. TCNT, Goodspeed, NEB, GNB) or it is descriptive of δοῦλος ("a servant of Christ Jesus who is always earnest in prayer for you," Moffatt; sim. JB, NAB). In the phrase ἐν ταῖς προσευχαῖς, the prep. is locat. ("in") rather than instr. ("by"), the art. may be poss. ("in his prayers"), and προσευχαῖς could be a generalizing pl. ("in prayer"). Ἀγωνιζόμενος . . . ἐν ταῖς προσευχαῖς may be rendered "He . . . prays fervently" (GNB; sim. NEB).

ἵνα σταθῆτε τέλειοι καὶ πεπληροφορημένοι

2 pl. (referring to ὑμῶν) aor. pass. subjunc. (after ἵνα) of ἵστημι, cause to stand; stand. The aor. pass. of ἵστημι is intrans. in mng. (BAGD 382b; BDF § 97[1]) so that ἵνα σταθῆτε is identical in sense with ἵνα στῆτε (2 pl. second aor. act. subjunc.; T 57; Z § 231), the rdg. actually found in ℵ² A C D F G Ψ al. ("that you may stand"). It is therefore inappropriate to look for an implied agent behind the pass., as if the mng. were "that you may be upheld." As the opposite of "fall" (πίπτω), "stand" may here mean "stand firm" (TCNT, Weymouth, Moffatt, GNB, NAB, NIV; sim. Goodspeed, NEB; cf. BAGD 382d), or even "stand forth" (Lohse 170, 173; O'Brien 245, 253).

Τέλειοι may mean "perfect" (RV, NASB, NAB; BAGD 809c) in the sense of "complete," or *"mature" (RSV, GNB, Barclay, NIV; G. Delling, TDNT 6.310), "with a matured faith" (TCNT). See above For Further Study 23, "Christian Perfection" (1:28).

Nom. pl. masc. (agreeing with the subj. of σταθῆτε) of the pf. pass. ptc. of πληροφορέω, fill (completely) + gen. or (in the pass.) ἐν + dat. to denote that which fills (cf. BDF § 172); convince fully; fulfill; (pass.) be absolutely convinced, be fully assured. Accordingly, this ptc. may mean:

(1) "full" (BAGD 670b), "filled" (Lohse 170, 173; O'Brien 245, 253, 254), "brought to full measure" (G. Delling, TDNT 6.310), where the vb. is a synonym for πληρόω; 𝔭⁴⁶ TR in fact read πεπληρωμένοι, the pf. pass ptc. of πληρόω (cf. 2:10);

*(2) "fully assured" (RV, RSV, NASB, NIV; BAGD 670c), "fully persuaded" (Lightfoot 238), "convinced" (Moule 138; sim. Moffatt, GNB), "with a sure conviction" (TCNT); or

(3) if τέλειοι καὶ πεπληροφορημένοι forms a hendiadys, "ripe in conviction" (NEB), "fully mature," "(like persons of) mature conviction" (Goodspeed).

ἐν παντὶ θελήματι τοῦ θεοῦ

With the anar. θελήματι, παντί means "every aspect of" (see 1:9). Τοῦ θεοῦ is either a poss. gen., "all of God's will," or subj. gen., "everything willed by God" (Lightfoot 238). This phrase may be cstr. in four ways:

*(1) With σταθῆτε (cf. Rom. 5:2; 1 Cor. 15:1), so that τέλειοι and πεπληροφορημένοι are used abs. and denote attendant circumstances: "that you may stand firm in all the will of God, mature and fully assured" (NIV, locat. ἐν; sim. G. Delling, TDNT 6.310; G. Schrenk, TDNT 3.59).

(2) With πεπληροφορημένοι: "and have full conviction about whatever pertains to God's will" (NAB, ἐν meaning "with respect to," "about"; sim. TCNT, Weymouth; Lohse 170, 173; O'Brien 245, 253-254; for both Lohse and O'Brien ἐν παντὶ κτλ. denotes "[filled] with everything that is God's will"; instr. ἐν).

(3) With both τέλειοι and πεπληροφορημένοι: "that you may stand mature and fully assured in all the will of God" (RSV, locat. ἐν; sim. RV, NASB, JB; Lightfoot 233, 238: ἐν denotes "the atmosphere, the surroundings, of the conviction").

(4) Independently, with ἐν describing attendant circumstances: "engaged in doing all the will of God" (Moule 138; sim. GNB, Barclay), "whatever be the will of God for you" (Moffatt, followed by R 772; sim. Goodspeed).

VERSE 13

μαρτυρῶ γὰρ αὐτῷ ὅτι ἔχει πολὺν πόνον

1 sg. pres. act. indic. of μαρτυρέω, bear witness, testify. Αὐτῷ is dat. of advantage (see 3:23) of the person in whose favor the testimony is given (cf. BAGD 492d). Ὅτι introduces the content or substance of the testimony. Tr.: "For I bear him witness that. . . ," "For I can vouch for him that. . . ." Πόνος, -ου, ὁ,

labor, hard work. Πολύν is acc. sg. masc. (agreeing with πόνον) of πολύς, πολλή, πολύ, gen. πολλοῦ, -ῆς, -οῦ, as an adj., (sg.) much, large, (pl.) many, large; as a subst., (pl.) many. Whether we render ἔχει πολὺν πόνον by "he has toiled greatly" (Barclay) or "he works tirelessly" (NEB), the pres. tense implies Epaphras's habit of toiling strenuously in prayer.

ὑπὲρ ὑμῶν καὶ τῶν ἐν Λαοδικείᾳ καὶ τῶν ἐν Ἱεραπόλει

The single prep. ὑπέρ ("for," "on behalf of") governs each of the three gens. Οἱ ἐν + dat. = "those in—," "the people at—" (cf. BAGD 551d, 552a). Λαοδίκεια, -ας, ἡ, Laodicea. Ἱεράπολις, -εως, ἡ, Hierapolis. BDF § 115(2); R 257; Robertson, *Pictures* 512; WH 1.450 believe that Ἱεραπόλει should be written Ἱερᾷ Πόλει (but cf. MH 151, 278).

VERSE 14

ἀσπάζεται ὑμᾶς Λουκᾶς ὁ ἰατρὸς ὁ ἀγαπητὸς καὶ Δημᾶς

On the sg. vb., the word-order, the anar. proper nouns (Λουκᾶς, -ᾶ, ὁ, Luke; Δημᾶς, -ᾶ, ὁ, Demas), and the art. appos. noun ἰατρός, see on v. 10. It is possible that the art. with ἰατρός could signify "*our* dear doctor" (TCNT, GNB; sim. NAB), with or without the implication that Luke served as physician for Paul and his coworkers. The adj. ἀγαπητός is in the alternative attrib. position where both subst. and adj. are emphatic (R 776-777; but cf. BDF § 270).

VERSE 15

Ἀσπάσασθε τοὺς ἐν Λαοδικείᾳ ἀδελφούς

2 pl. aor. mid. impv. of dep. ἀσπάζομαι, greet. A constative/complexive aor. (see on 1:7), usual in greetings (BDF § 337[4]).

καὶ Νύμφαν καὶ τὴν κατ' οἶκον αὐτῆς ἐκκλησίαν

There are two problems here—one relating to accentuation, the other (resultant) problem relating to the text. The issues will become clear if we set out the options in tr.:

*(1) "Nympha and the church in her house" (RSV, NIV; O'Brien 245 [cf. 245-246, 256]; sim. TCNT, Moffatt, Goodspeed, NEB, NASB, GNB, JB; Lohse 170, 174 and n. 44). This presupposes:
  (a) the accentuation Νύμφαν, from Νύμφα, -ας, ἡ (= Attic Νύμφη, -ης, ἡ [BAGD 545a]; TCNT has Nymphe; see Moulton 48 and his article "Nympha," *ExpT* 5 [1893-94] 66-67);

(b) the rdg. αὐτῆς (gen. sg. fem. of αὐτός, -ή, -ό, he, she, it), found in B 1739 syrʰ copˢᵃ Origen, and preferred by BAGD 241a; WH 1.450-451; all three UBS edd. (with a "C" rating; see Metzger 627); Moulton 48.

(2) "Nymphas and the church in his house" (sim. NAB; Moule 28 and n. 1). This presupposes:
   (a) the accentuation Νυμφᾶν, from Νυμφᾶς, -ᾶ, ὁ;
   (b) the rdg. αὐτοῦ (gen. sg. masc.), found in D G K L Ψ Byz Lect syrᵖ goth.

(3) "Nymphas, and the church in their house" (sim. RV, Weymouth, Barclay; Lightfoot 240). This presupposes:
   (a) the accentuation Νυμφᾶν (as in 2[a] above);
   (b) the rdg. αὐτῶν (gen. pl. masc.), found in ℵ A C P 33 copᵇᵒ, and preferred by Lightfoot 240-241, 254. This αὐτῶν would include ἀδελφούς with Νυμφᾶν, or conceivably refers to Nymphas and his wife or friends.

Καὶ . . . καί does not here mean "both . . . and." If the house church associated with Nympha(s) was part of the larger Laodicean church (vv. 15a, 16), the first καί could mean "especially" (Weymouth; Lightfoot 240); on the other hand, if the church linked with Nympha(s) met elsewhere than in Laodicea (e.g., at Hierapolis, v. 13), the first καί could mean "also" (Moffatt; sim. NASB).

In κατ' οἶκον the final α of κατά has been elided before an initial diphthong. In the NT elision regularly occurs before prons. and particles and before nouns in frequently used combinations, such as κατ' οἶκον, κατ' ἐμέ (v. 7), or ἀπ' ἀρχῆς (R 207-208; cf. BDF § 17). Κατά + acc. here denotes location (cf. R 608), "in her house." This attrib. prep. phrase κατ' οἶκον αὐτῆς (see R 656; and esp. T 221-222) functions as a rel. clause: "(the church) that meets in her house." Ἐκκλησία is here explicitly used of a house church. See For Further Study 45, "The House Church in the NT" (Phlm. 2).

VERSE 16

καὶ ὅταν ἀναγνωσθῇ παρ' ὑμῖν ἡ ἐπιστολή

3 sg. aor. pass. subjunc. of ἀναγινώσκω, read; here, read aloud in public (BAGD 51d). Ὅταν (= ὅτε + ἄν, "when," "whenever") + aor. subjunc. regularly specifies a fut. action whose accomplishment precedes the action of the principal vb. (R 972; T 112); in such cases ὅταν could be rendered "after" (GNB, JB, NIV) or "once" (NAB). This ὅταν clause implies an impv., ἀναγνῶτε, "read." Παρ' ὑμῖν (on the elision see the previous note) may be rendered "at your

gathering" or "in your hearing" (Weymouth mg.), as well as by the rather stilted "among you" (several EVV). The art. ἡ with ἐπιστολή (-ῆς, ἡ, letter) is anaphoric: "this letter" (most EVV), i.e., "the letter I have just written." Tr.: "When this letter has been read (a constative aor. rendered by an Eng. pf.) at your gathering. . . ."

ποιήσατε ἵνα καὶ ἐν τῇ Λαοδικέων ἐκκλησίᾳ ἀναγνωσθῇ

2 pl. aor. act. impv. of ποιέω, do, make. 3 sg. aor. pass. subjunc. (after ἵνα) of ἀναγινώσκω, read (with ἡ ἐπιστολή from v. 16a as the implied subj.). When, as here, the vb. ποιέω means "cause," "bring about," the result of the action is regularly expressed by the acc. and infin. construction (e.g., Mk. 1:17; BAGD 681d). Here the ἵνα clause replaces that construction and the telic force of ἵνα is lost (cf. BAGD 377c, d; 681d). Tr.: "arrange that it be read," "have it read" (Goodspeed, RSV; sim. RV, NASB). Burton (§ 205) classifies this ἵνα clause as an object clause after a vb. of effecting.

Λαοδικέων is gen. pl. of Λαοδικεύς, -έως, ὁ, Laodicean. Being def. by nature, proper names are regularly anar. Basically the gen. case limits a noun by specifying the particular category or class (Lat. *genus,* Gk. γένος) to which it belongs (cf. R 493-494): "the church—that is composed of Laodiceans," virtually "the Laodicean church." This broadest use of the gen. may be termed the gen. of relation or ref. Καί is adjunctive: "*also* in the church of the Laodiceans."

καὶ τὴν ἐκ Λαοδικείας ἵνα καὶ ὑμεῖς ἀναγνῶτε

2 pl. second aor. act. subjunc. (after ἵνα) of ἀναγινώσκω, read. As a subordinating conj. ἵνα usually stands at the beginning of its dependent clause. Its irregular position here emphasizes the preceding words (BAGD 378c; BDF § 475[1]). Lightfoot (242) is probably right to regard this ἵνα as independent and elliptical, with βλέπετε to be supplied ("see that you also read . . ."; sim. Goodspeed, RSV). He notes that ellipses are frequent before ἵνα (e.g., Jn. 9:3; 2 Cor. 8:13; 2 Thess. 3:9; 1 Jn. 2:19). On the other hand, if ποιήσατε in v. 16b is given a general mng. ("see that . . .") rather than a strictly causative sense ("bring it about that . . ."), it is possible that this second ἵνα clause in v. 16 is also dependent on ποιήσατε (thus TCNT, Moffatt, NEB, NAB, NIV). Alternatively, ἵνα could be impv. (see 2:4): "you are to read" (GNB; sim. NASB). Καί probably denotes correspondence: "you in turn" (Weymouth, NIV), "you, for your part" (NASB), "you in return" (NEB).

With τήν we must understand ἐπιστολήν, from v. 16a. "The letter from (ἐκ) Laodicea" means "the letter that will be forwarded to you from Laodicea" (sim. TCNT, Goodspeed, Moffatt, NASB, Barclay, NAB), not "the letter written by the Laodiceans and sent from Laodicea." In a piece of typical brachylogy (cf. R 1204), Paul directs that the letter he had written (τήν is probably poss., "my letter" [NASB]) to the Laodiceans should be read by the Colossians after its arrival "from Laodicea." See For Further Study 44, "The Letter from Laodicea."

VERSE 17

καὶ εἴπατε ᾿Αρχίππῳ, Βλέπε τὴν διακονίαν ἣν παρέλαβες ἐν κυρίῳ

2 pl. second aor. act. impv. of λέγω, say, speak. In HGk. the endings of the weak (or first) aor. are used on strong (or second) aor. stems much more frequently than in CGk. (Z § 489; cf. BDF § 80; MH 183). Here εἴπατε = εἴπετε (cf. BDF § 81[1]). The person to whom something is said is expressed by the dat. (as here) or by πρός + acc. (BAGD 468c). ῎Αρχιππος, -ου, ὁ, Archippus.

2 sg. (referring to Archippus) pres. act. impv. of βλέπω, see; direct one's attention to, attend to. The message that the Colossians were to pass on to Archippus from Paul is recorded in direct speech. "And say to Archippus: 'Attend to the ministry which you have received in the Lord.' " Τὴν διακονίαν ("ministry") might refer to some temporary responsibility ("the piece of Christian service"; cf. Goodspeed, Barclay; Acts 12:25) or some unspecified formal and permanent function.

῾Ην is acc. sg. fem. (referring to διακονίαν) of the rel. pron. Παρέλαβες is 2 sg. second aor. act. indic. of παραλαμβάνω, receive. The special responsibility of Archippus, whatever its nature, may have been received directly from Paul but ultimately Archippus had received it ἐν κυρίῳ, "as a servant of the Lord" (Weymouth), "in the Lord's service" (NEB, GNB), or possibly "at the Lord's bidding," "from and for the glory of the Lord."

ἵνα αὐτὴν πληροῖς

2 sg. pres. act. subjunc. of πληρόω, fill; fulfill, accomplish. ᾿Αυτήν is acc. sg. fem. of αὐτός, -ή, -ό, referring to διακονίαν. Many EVV (TCNT, Weymouth, Goodspeed, RSV, GNB, NAB, NIV; also Burton §§ 205, 209 ["probably"]; Lohse 170; O'Brien 245, 259) cstr. this ἵνα clause directly with the impv. βλέπε (cf. 1 Cor. 16:10; 2 Jn. 8)—e.g., "See that you fulfil the ministry which you have received in the Lord" (RSV), "Take care to discharge the ministry you have received in the Lord" (NAB). But this is to overlook the position of τὴν διακονίαν and the presence of αὐτήν and would accord better with βλέπε ἵνα τὴν διακονίαν ἣν παρέλαβες ἐν κυρίῳ πληροῖς. Significantly, WH (1.451) and all three UBS edd. print a comma after κυρίῳ, which makes it difficult to cstr. ἵνα directly with βλέπε ("See that . . ."). There are three alternative ways to cstr. the ἵνα clause:

(1) as independent and impv.: " 'Attend to the duty entrusted to you in the Lord's service, and discharge it to the full' " (NEB; sim. BAGD 671d);

(2) as independent and elliptical, with βλέπε supplied: "Attend to the ministry. . . ; see that you fulfil it" (Moffatt; sim. JB); or

*(3) as final: "Take heed to the ministry. . . , that you may fulfill it" (NASB; cf. Burton § 209 ["possibly"]).

For J. Knox's distinctive interpretation of vv. 16-17, see the Introduction to Philemon.

VERSE 18

Ὁ ἀσπασμὸς τῇ ἐμῇ χειρὶ Παύλου

With ἀσπασμός (-οῦ, ὁ, greeting) we must supply γέγραπται (3 sg. pf. pass. indic. of γράφω, write; cf. BAGD 880a): "this greeting [has been written = is written] with my own hand." The art. ὁ is demonstrative (cf. BDF § 249; R 755; T 36; Z § 165). Τῇ . . . χειρί is an instr. dat. (BAGD 880a; Robertson, *Pictures* 513). Χείρ, χειρός, ἡ, hand; here, handwriting (BAGD 880a; TCNT). The poss. adj. ἐμός, -ή, -όν, my, mine (often called a poss. pron.) is art. unless it is pred. ("mine"; R 770; cf. 685), and although it sometimes is indistinguishable from μου (gen. sg. of pers. pron. ἐγώ), here it is emphatic, "with my own hand" (BAGD 255c; cf. BDF § 285[1]; T 191).

The gen. Παύλου may be cstr.:

(1) as subj. gen. dependent on ὁ ἀσπασμός: "This greeting is from Paul" (NAB; sim. Goodspeed, Moffatt, GNB);

(2) as poss. gen. dependent on a second χειρί that is to be supplied: ". . . with my own hand—the hand of Paul"; or

(3) in appos. to the gen. idea in the poss. adj. ἐμῇ, "with the hand of me, Paul" (R 685; Robertson, *Pictures* 513).

μνημονεύετέ μου τῶν δεσμῶν

2 pl. pres. act. impv. of μνημονεύω, remember, keep in mind; mention (+ gen., here τῶν δεσμῶν; or sometimes + acc.). Δεσμός, -οῦ, ὁ; pl. δεσμά (neut.) and δεσμοί (masc., BDF § 49[3]; MH 121-122), bond, fetter; by metonymy, prison; imprisonment. The gen. pl. here, τῶν δεσμῶν, could be neut. or masc. Μου is poss. gen. ("my bonds") rather than obj. gen. ("remember me"). Thus, "Remember my bonds" (BAGD 525a; RV), "remember my imprisonment" (NASB), "remember I am in prison" (NEB; sim. Goodspeed). It is possible (as O'Brien [260] argues) that Paul is here requesting continued intercession for

himself. The sense would then be, "Keep on remembering before God in prayer my imprisonment for the gospel" (cf. 4:3-4).

ἡ χάρις μεθ' ὑμῶν

Before a rough breathing, the final α of μετά is elided and τ becomes θ. "The grace" is that of the Lord Jesus (as in 1 Cor. 16:23; 2 Cor. 13:13; Gal. 6:18; Phil. 4:23; 1 Thess. 5:28; 2 Thess. 3:18; Phlm. 25). The vb. understood with ἡ χάρις may be indic. (ἐστίν or ἔσται [2 Cor. 13:11; 2 Jn. 3]), impv. (ἔστω), or opt. (εἴη). "With you" means "with your spirit" (Gal. 6:18; Phil. 4:23; Phlm. 25). This abbreviated benediction is also found in 1 Tim. 6:21; 2 Tim. 4:22.

TRANSLATION

[10] My fellow prisoner Aristarchus sends you his greetings, as does Mark, the cousin of Barnabas. (You received instructions about him: if he comes to you, welcome him.) [11] And Jesus, who is called Justus, also sends his greetings. These are the only Jewish converts among my coworkers for the kingdom of God, and they have proved a comfort to me. [12] Epaphras, who is one of you and a slave of Christ Jesus, sends you his greetings. He is always wrestling for you in his prayers, that with maturity and conviction you may stand firm in doing all the will of God. [13] For I can vouch for his strenuous toil for you and for the people at Laodicea and Hierapolis. [14] Luke, the dearly loved physician, sends you his greetings, and so does Demas. [15] Give my greetings to the brothers at Laodicea and to Nympha and the church in her house. [16] When this letter has been read at your gathering, have it read also in the church of the Laodiceans; and see that you in turn read the letter from Laodicea. [17] And say to Archippus: "Attend to the Christian service that you have received in the Lord, so that you may discharge it fully."

[18] This greeting comes from Paul—in my own hand. Remember my bonds. Grace be with you.

EXPANDED PARAPHRASE

[10] I pass on greetings from Aristarchus, a fellow prisoner of Christ; from Mark, the cousin of Barnabas (let me remind you of the directions you have already received about him—"if he pays you a visit, you are to give him a warm, hospitable welcome"); [11] and from Jesus, who is known as Justus. All three are Jewish converts and at present they are the only Jewish coworkers I have in the task of spreading the kingdom of God. They have, these men, been a source of real comfort to me. [12] Greetings also from Epaphras, one of your own number, a devoted bond-slave of Christ Jesus who is always praying for

you with great intensity that you may stand firm in every aspect of God's will as mature and convinced Christians. [13] For I can certainly testify how strenuously he toils for you in intercessory prayer—for you and for Christians at Laodicea and Hierapolis. [14] Greetings, too, from our dear friend, Luke the physician, and from Demas. [15] Please convey my own greetings to the brothers at Laodicea, and to Nympha and the church that meets in her home. [16] When this present letter has been read at your gathering, ensure that it is read in the church of the Laodiceans as well and that in turn you read the letter that I have sent to Laodicea, which you will get from them. [17] Finally, give Archippus this message from me: "Pay special attention to the responsibility you have received and undertaken as a servant of the Lord, so that you may discharge it to the full."

[18] And now I add this final greeting in my own handwriting—from me, PAUL. Remember the chains I wear. (I am writing with a manacled hand!) May the grace of Jesus Christ continue to be your portion.

FOR FURTHER STUDY

44. The Letter from Laodicea (4:16)

Anderson, C. P., "Who Wrote 'the Epistle from Laodicea'?" *JBL* 85 (1966) 436-440.

Bacon, B. W., "St. Paul to the Laodiceans," *Expositor,* eighth series, 17 (1919) 19-36.

*Hendriksen, W., *New Testament Commentary. Exposition of Colossians and Philemon* (Grand Rapids: Baker, 1964) 194-197.

Knox, J., *Philemon among the Letters of Paul. A New View of its Place and Importance* (New York: Abingdon, 1959[2], 1960[2]) 38-47.

Lightfoot 272-298.

O'Brien 257-258.

Rutherford, J., "St. Paul's Epistle to the Laodiceans," *ExpT* 19 (1907-08) 311-314.

Schneemelcher, W., "The Epistle to the Laodiceans," in E. Hennecke and W. Schneemelcher, *New Testament Apocrypha,* Vol. 2 (Philadelphia: Westminster, 1965) 128-132.

HOMILETICAL SUGGESTIONS

Greetings and Final Instructions (4:10-18)

1. Greetings to the Colossians from Paul's friends (vv. 10-14)
   (a) From three Jewish Christians (οἱ ὄντες ἐκ περιτομῆς, v. 11b) who were Paul's coworkers (συνεργοί) in promoting the Kingdom of God

(v. 11c) and who had been a source of encouragement (παρηγορία) to him (v. 11d):

(i) Aristarchus, who, like Paul, was Christ's captive (συναιχμάλωτος, v. 10a)

(ii) Mark, the cousin of Barnabas (v. 10b, c; cf. Acts 15:36-40; 2 Tim. 4:11)

(iii) Jesus Justus (v. 11a).

(b) From three Gentile Christians (vv. 12-14):

(i) Epaphras, a Colossian and a slave of Christ Jesus (v. 12a; cf. 1:7-8)

(ii) Luke, the dearly loved physician (v. 14a)

(iii) Demas (v. 14b; interestingly, no description of Demas is added; cf. 2 Tim. 4:10).

2. Final instructions to the Colossians from Paul (vv. 15-18)

(a) Convey my greetings

(i) to the Laodicean Christians (v. 15a)

(ii) to Nympha and her house church (v. 15b)

(b) Read the present letter at your gathering (v. 16a)

(c) Ensure that it is also read at Laodicea (v. 16b) and that you read my letter to Laodicea (v. 16c)

(d) Exhort Archippus to fulfill his special responsibility (v. 17)

(e) Remember my imprisonment for the gospel (v. 18b; cf. 4:3).

Prayer (4:12-13)

1. It should be persistent (πάντοτε ἀγωνιζόμενος, v. 12b)
2. It involves strenuous toil (ἀγωνιζόμενος, v. 12b; πολὺν πόνον, v. 13a)
3. It petitions God for:
   stability in doing every part of his will (ἵνα σταθῆτε ... ἐν παντὶ θελήματι τοῦ θεοῦ, v. 12c)
   maturity of outlook and experience (τέλειοι, v. 12c)
   full assurance of faith (πεπληροφορημένοι, v. 12c)
4. It is specific but not parochial (ὑπὲρ ὑμῶν καὶ τῶν κτλ., v. 13c).

Translation

1 ¹ Paul, an apostle of Christ Jesus by the will of God, and Timothy our brother, ² to the people of God in Colossae, faithful brothers in Christ. Grace and peace to you from God our Father.

³ We always give thanks to God, the Father of our Lord Jesus Christ, when we pray for you, ⁴ because we have heard of your faith in Christ Jesus and of the love you show to all God's people. ⁵ Both stem from the hope stored up for you in heaven. You heard about this hope previously through the message of truth, the good news ⁶ that has come to you just as it is also constantly producing fruit and growing all over the world in the same way that it has been among you ever since you heard about and came to know the grace of God in reality. ⁷ You learned this from Ephaphras, our dear fellow slave, who is a faithful minister of Christ on our behalf. ⁸ He it was who informed us of your love in the Spirit.

⁹ That is why, ever since we heard this, we also have not ceased praying for you, asking that you may be filled with the knowledge of God's will by having all spiritual wisdom and discernment. ¹⁰ You will then lead a life that is worthy of the Lord and that seeks to please him in everything, bearing fruit in every kind of good deed and growing in the knowledge of God, ¹¹ being empowered with all power through his glorious strength for endurance and patience of every kind, and joyfully ¹² giving thanks to the Father who has qualified you to share the inheritance of his people in the kingdom of light. ¹³ He has rescued us from the dominion of darkness and transferred us into the kingdom of his dearly loved Son, ¹⁴ in whom we have redemption, the forgiveness of sins.

¹⁵ He is the image of the invisible God, the firstborn over all creation, ¹⁶ for in him all things in heaven and on earth were created, things visible and things invisible, whether thrones or dominions or principalities or powers—all things have been created through him and for him. ¹⁷ And he himself is before

everything, and in him all things hold together. [18] And he himself is the head of the Body, the Church. He is the beginning, the firstborn from the dead, so that in everything he alone became preeminent, [19] for in him God in all his fullness was pleased to dwell [20] and through him to reconcile all things to himself by making peace through his blood shed on the cross—through him, whether things on earth or things in heaven.

[21] Although you were at one time estranged from God and enemies in your minds because of your evil deeds, you also [22] he has now reconciled through Christ's death in his physical body. He did this in order to present you holy and without blemish or reproach in his sight—[23] provided that you persist in faith, established, steadfast, and not shifting from the hope generated by the gospel which you heard. This gospel has been proclaimed to every creature under heaven, and I, Paul, have become its servant.

[24] I rejoice now in the midst of my sufferings for your sake, and for my part I am filling up in my own person what is still lacking with regard to the afflictions of Christ, for the sake of his Body, which is the Church. [25] I have become a servant of the Church by virtue of the commission God gave me with regard to you, to declare fully the word of God— [26] the mystery kept secret for ages and generations past but now disclosed to God's people. [27] For God chose to divulge to his people how great are the glorious riches of this mystery displayed among the Gentiles, which is Christ within you, your hope of glory. [28] It is this Christ that we proclaim as we admonish and teach everyone with all wisdom, so that we may present everyone mature in Christ. [29] To achieve this I toil and strive with the energy that Christ powerfully generates within me.

2 [1]For I want you to know how strenuously I am striving for you, for those at Laodicea and all who have not seen me personally, [2] that they may be welded together in love and their hearts may be encouraged, also that they may gain the full wealth of conviction that is brought by understanding and come to a deeper knowledge of God's mystery, which is Christ. [3] For in him all God's treasures of wisdom and knowledge are stored up.

[4] I am telling you this so that no one may delude you by persuasive argument. [5] For though I am physically absent, yet I am spiritually present with you and delighted to see your orderliness and the stability of your faith in Christ. [6] So just as you received the Messiah, Jesus the Lord, continue to walk in him, [7] now rooted and being built up in him, becoming established in the faith, as you have been taught, and overflowing with gratitude. [8] Take care that no one carries you off as spoil by an empty, deceptive philosophy derived from human tradition and centered on the elemental spirits of the universe, but not based on Christ.

⁹ For in him there dwells the whole fullness of deity in bodily form. ¹⁰ And you have your completeness in him, who is the head over every power and authority. ¹¹ Also in him you were circumcised with a circumcision not performed by human hands, when you stripped off your fleshly nature in Christ's circumcision. ¹² You were buried with him in baptism, and in baptism you were raised with him through your faith in the action of God who raised him from the dead. ¹³ And when you were dead because of your trespasses and your uncircumcised flesh, God brought you to life together with Christ. He forgave us all our trespasses, ¹⁴ cancelled the bond, along with its decrees, that stood against us and threatened us, and has set it aside by nailing it to the cross. ¹⁵ And after disarming the powers and authorities, he boldly displayed them in public by leading them in triumphal procession through Christ.

¹⁶ Let no one therefore sit in judgment on you regarding food and drink, or concerning a festival, a new moon, or a sabbath day. ¹⁷ These things are a shadow of what was to come; the reality, however, belongs to Christ. ¹⁸ Let no one disqualify you by insisting on self-humiliation and angel-worship, taking his stand on his visions and inflated with futile notions by his sensuous mind. ¹⁹ He does not hold firmly to the Head, in dependence on whom the whole Body, nourished and fitted together by its joints and sinews, grows with a growth stimulated by God.

²⁰ You died with Christ and were thus freed from the elemental spirits of the universe. Why, then, as though your life were worldly, do you submit to regulations such as ²¹ "Do not handle this!" "Do not taste that!" "Do not touch this!" ²² —things that are all destined to perish with use—in compliance with man-made injunctions and teachings? ²³ Such rules indeed appear wise by reason of their self-imposed worship, flaunted humility, and severe treatment of the body, but they lack any value in combating fleshly gratification.

3 ¹ If, then, you were raised with Christ, seek the realm above where Christ is, seated at God's right hand. ² Fix your thoughts on the realm above, not on earthly things. ³ For you died, and so your life is now hidden with Christ in God. ⁴ When Christ, who is your life, appears, then you too will appear with him in glory.

⁵ Therefore put to death your limbs as used for earthly purposes—immorality, impurity, lust, evil craving, and especially ruthless greed, which is idolatry. ⁶ These sins incur God's wrath. ⁷ You also once practiced these sins when you used to live that way. ⁸ But now you are in fact to put all these off—anger, rage, spite, slander, foul-mouthed language. ⁹ Do not lie to one another, for you have stripped off the old nature with its practices ¹⁰ and have put on the new nature which is being renewed after the image of its Creator until it reaches full knowledge of him. ¹¹ Here no distinction exists between Greek and Jew,

circumcision and uncircumcision, barbarian, Scythian, slave and freeman, but Christ is everything and in all.

[12] Therefore, as God's chosen people, who are holy and loved by him, put on heartfelt compassion, kindness, humility, gentleness, and patience. [13] You are to bear with one another, and if anyone has a grievance against someone else, you are to forgive one another. Just as the Lord forgave you, so you also must forgive. [14] And in addition to all these garments, put on love, which is the bond that perfects them all. [15] And let the peace that Christ gives rule in your hearts, for you were actually called to experience this peace as members of one Body. Also be thankful. [16] Let the message of Christ dwell in you richly by your teaching and admonishing one another in all wisdom, as you sing to God gratefully with all your heart, using psalms, hymns, and spiritual songs. [17] And whatever you are doing, whether in word or in deed, do everything in the name of the Lord Jesus, giving thanks to God the Father through him.

[18] Wives, be subject to your husbands, as is appropriate in the Lord. [19] Husbands, love your wives and do not be harsh with them. [20] Children, obey your parents in everything, for this is pleasing in the Lord. [21] Fathers, do not provoke your children, lest they become disheartened. [22] Slaves, obey your earthly masters in everything, not with external service as if you were merely pleasing humans, but with sincerity of heart and out of reverence for the Lord. [23] Whatever your task, work at it with enthusiasm, as service for the Lord and not for humans, [24] because you know that from the Lord you will receive your inheritance as a reward. Serve the Lord Christ. [25] For the wrongdoer will be repaid for the wrong he did, and there is no favoritism.

4 [1] Masters, treat your slaves justly and fairly, because you know that you too have a Master—in heaven.

[2] Be persistent and vigilant in prayer, with thanksgiving. [3] At the same time pray for us, too, that God may open up for us a door for our message, so that we may proclaim the mystery of Christ, because of which I am in chains. [4] Pray that I may declare it boldly, as I ought. [5] Behave wisely toward outsiders; buy up every opportunity. [6] Let your conversation always be gracious, seasoned with salt, so that you may know how you should answer each individual.

[7] Tychicus will let you know about all my circumstances. He is our dear brother, a trustworthy helper and fellow slave in the Lord. [8] I am sending him to you for this express purpose, that you may know how we are faring and that he may encourage your hearts. [9] With him I am sending Onesimus, that trustworthy and dear brother who is one of you. They will inform you about all that is happening here.

[10] My fellow prisoner Aristarchus sends you his greetings, as does Mark, the cousin of Barnabas. (You received instructions about him: if he comes to you,

welcome him.) [11] And Jesus, who is called Justus, also sends his greetings. These are the only Jewish converts among my coworkers for the kingdom of God, and they have proved a comfort to me. [12] Epaphras, who is one of you and a slave of Christ Jesus, sends you his greetings. He is always wrestling for you in his prayers, that with maturity and conviction you may stand firm in doing all the will of God. [13] For I can vouch for his strenuous toil for you and for the people at Laodicea and Hierapolis. [14] Luke, the dearly loved physician, sends you his greetings, and so does Demas. [15] Give my greetings to the brothers at Laodicea and to Nympha and the church in her house. [16] When this letter has been read at your gathering, have it read also in the church of the Laodiceans; and see that you in turn read the letter from Laodicea. [17] And say to Archippus: "Attend to the Christian service that you have received in the Lord, so that you may discharge it fully."

[18] This greeting comes from Paul—in my own hand. Remember my bonds. Grace be with you.

Expanded Paraphrase

1 ¹ This letter comes from Paul, the special envoy of Christ Jesus commissioned by the will of God, and from our brother and colleague Timothy, ² to the people of God in Colossae, who are brothers in the fellowship of Christ and faithful to God. May the grace and peace that come from God our heavenly Father be your portion.

³ Whenever we pray for you, without fail we give thanks to God, the Father of our Lord Jesus Christ, ⁴ because we have heard of your faith as those who are in Christ Jesus and also of the love you show toward all God's people. ⁵ Both of these qualities are stimulated by the hope that is reserved for you in heaven. You came to hear about this hope previously when you heard the message that has the stamp of truth on it—the message that is the good news ⁶ that has come to you. In the same way this gospel continues to produce throughout the whole world the same kind of harvest and increase it has been yielding in you from the very first day that you heard about and came to appreciate God's undeserved favor for what it truly is. ⁷ That was the way you learned it from Epaphras, our dearly loved fellow slave, who has been faithfully serving Christ as our representative. ⁸ It was he, in fact, who informed us of your love—love that is produced by God's Spirit.

⁹ Because of this encouraging news about you, from the very day we heard it we also have never stopped praying for you. Our request to God is that he may fill you with a knowledge of what his will is by giving you every form of spiritual wisdom and discernment. ¹⁰ Once you have this you will lead a life that is worthy of the Lord Jesus and that aims to give him complete satisfaction in every respect. Your life will then be marked by perennial fruit-bearing in every kind of good deed, by continuous growth in your knowledge of God, ¹¹ by a constant supply of strength generated by his glorious power for every form of endurance and patience, ¹² and by continual and joyful thanksgiving

to God the Father, the one who has entitled you to receive a share in the heritage that belongs to his people in the kingdom of light. [13] Yes, in the kingdom of light, for he has rescued us from the dominion that is characterized by darkness and has transferred us as free colonists into the kingdom of the Son whom he loves so dearly. [14] In union with this Son we have gained and now enjoy release from bondage, namely the forgiveness of our sins.

[15] This one who redeemed us is the exact and visible Expression of the God whom no one can see. Being the image of God, he is also the Firstborn—prior to all creation and supreme over it, [16] because it was in his person that all things in heaven and on earth were once created, things that can be seen by the human eye, and those things that cannot be seen, whether they be the angelic occupants of heavenly thrones or supernatural beings who exercise dominion or rule or authority—all these things were created, and now exist, through him and for him. [17] He—and no one else—is before everything in time and rank, and it is in his person and by his agency that all things hold together and are sustained. [18] What is more, he himself is the Head of his body, which is the Church. This is because he is its cause and the source of its life, and also because as the Firstborn he was the first person to rise from the dead to immortality, and as a result he himself became preeminent and peerless in every realm. [19] All this is true of Jesus because it was God's choice and pleasure to have all divine attributes and powers reside in Jesus [20] and to reconcile the whole universe to himself through him by making peace through the blood Jesus shed on the cross—to reconcile all things through him alone, whether they be things on earth or things in heaven.

[21] This universal reconciliation includes you Colossians, although you were at one time in a state of alienation from God and were his inveterate enemies in thought and attitude because of your evil actions. [22] But as things now stand, God has reconciled you to himself by means of Christ's death in his physical body. God's purpose in all this was to present you in his own presence at the End as people who will then be without any sin, without blemish, and beyond accusation. [23] But this will occur only if you continue to exercise faith, the faith in which you were once firmly founded and now should be steadfast, refusing to shift from the hope that is held out to you in the good news which you heard. This good news has been proclaimed to every person beneath heaven's orb. And I, Paul, have been entrusted with the task of communicating the good news.

[24] Now, when I recognize the privilege of my apostolic vocation, I rejoice even in the midst of all that I am suffering for your sake. In fact, through this personal suffering of mine I am making my distinctive contribution toward filling up whatever remains to be endured of "the afflictions of Christ." All this is for

the sake of his body, the universal Church, 25 whose servant I have become as a result of the commission entrusted to me by God with regard to you, the task of fully proclaiming to you Gentiles the message of God. 26 This message is none other than the sacred secret of God's plan of salvation that was hidden during all the past ages and generations but has now been disclosed to the new and holy people of God. 27 For in his eternal counsel God had chosen to divulge this mystery to his people in all its glory and richness displayed in the Gentile mission. What is this mystery or sacred secret? Christ indwelling you Gentiles (and all believers), which is your assurance of a share in his glory. 28 And this is the Christ we proclaim when we warn every unbeliever and teach every believer with all possible wisdom, our aim being to present every believer mature and perfect as a member of Christ's body who is in personal union with Christ. 29 In my eager desire to achieve all this, I toil and earnestly strive, energized by the power of the indwelling Christ that is so mightily at work in my life.

2 1 Indeed, I want you to be fully aware of my ongoing and intense wrestling in prayer for the spiritual welfare of you and the Laodicean believers and all others in the Lycus Valley who have yet to meet me in person. 2 The aim of this spiritual wrestling of mine is multiple: that they all may be welded together and established in mutual love and that their hearts and yours may be encouraged and strengthened; that they may gain assured conviction in its full richness, a conviction that comes from spiritual insight and an understanding mind, and may have an enriched appreciation and knowledge of God's mystery, which is nothing other than Christ himself. 3 For it is in Christ—and Christ alone—that the full treasury of God's wisdom and knowledge is stored up.

4 My aim in telling you all this is that none of the false teachers talk you into error and delude you by the use of persuasive language or plausible argument. 5 For even if I may be absent from you in body, I am certainly present with you in spirit, and I am delighted to see how orderly your Christian life is and how solid and stable your faith in Christ. 6 You personally embraced the Christian tradition that recognizes the Messiah to be Jesus the Lord. So then, continue living in him, 7 for at the time of your conversion you were first rooted in him and remain so but now you need to be progressively built up on him and established in the faith, in keeping with the instruction that you have received from Epaphras and others. Also see to it that you always overflow with gratitude. 8 Maintain a constant watch lest anyone take you captive through a seductive type of "philosophy" that is hollow and deceptive and that comes from mere human tradition and whose focus is on the elemental spirits of the universe and not on the one source of divine revelation and depository of divine truth—Christ himself.

[9] For it is in Christ, and Christ alone, that all the fullness of God's being now has its permanent abode in bodily form. [10] And therefore it is in him who is completely God that you have come to completeness, the satisfaction of every spiritual need—in Christ, who is the sovereign head over every cosmic power and authority, whether conceivable or real. [11] Furthermore, it is also in Christ that you were circumcised, but this circumcision was no external rite performed by human hands on actual flesh. Rather, it involved the stripping off of your fleshly nature in a heart-circumcision characteristic of the followers of Christ. [12] This heart-circumcision took place at the time of your baptism, when you were identified with Christ not only in burial but also in resurrection, for you were spiritually raised with him through your faith in the powerful activity of God, the God who demonstrated that power by raising Jesus from the dead. [13] Indeed! For when you were spiritually dead because of your trespasses and because you were rank pagans without knowledge of the true God, God raised you to spiritual life in union with Christ whom he raised. And not only so: At that time he also forgave us all our trespasses; [14] he completely cancelled the certificate of indebtedness—broken decrees and all—that stood as a testimony against us and was an ominous threat to us; in fact he has removed it altogether from sight by nailing it to the cross; [15] what is more, after he had rendered the powers and authorities helpless, he boldly exposed them to public display when, through Christ's death, he led them in his triumphal procession as his enemy captives.

[16] In the light of all this, do not allow anyone to take you to task about what you eat and what you drink, or in the matter of observing yearly religious festivals or monthly new moons or weekly sabbaths. [17] These things are merely a shadow cast by a reality to come; now that reality has in fact arrived, and it is none other than the gospel of Christ. [18] Do not allow anyone who indulges and delights in self-abasement and the cultic worship of angels to declare you disqualified and thus rob you of your prize of the benefits of salvation. Such a person presumes to parade his visionary experiences, and his fleshly thought and outlook have filled him with futile ideas and conceit. [19] Moreover, he fails to adhere to Christ, the Head, although it is in dependence on him alone that the whole Body experiences growth that is stimulated by God, as it is nourished and fitted together into one by means of its joints and ligaments.

[20] When you died with Christ you were freed from the control of the elemental spirits of the universe. Why, then, do you live as if you still belonged to the world and were not citizens of heaven? And why do you allow yourselves to be subjected to pointless regulations such as [21] "Do not handle this thing here!" "Do not taste that food there!" "Do not even touch that item!"? [22] Purely material things, such as food and drink, are all destined to pass out of existence

as they are used! In any case, why should you be bound by merely human precepts and instructions? [23] What is more, although these regulations at first glance might appear to be wise and beneficial with their self-imposed devotion, their affected humility, and their ascetic ill-treatment of the body, they are in fact without any value at all in the very area of their apparent value, namely, in curbing sensual indulgence.

3 [1] In your baptism, then, you came to share in Christ's resurrection. In light of this, always seek whatever belongs to that heavenly realm above, where the risen Christ now reigns, seated at God's right hand in the place of unrivaled honor and authority. [2] Focus your attention and your thoughts exclusively and constantly on the heavenly realm above, not on the earthly realm below. [3] This is appropriate and necessary, for in baptism you died with Christ to sin and the world and now your new, spiritual life, enjoyed in union with Christ, is concealed in the safekeeping of God in heaven. [4] Although your life is now hidden, when this Christ, who is your very Life, appears at his second Advent and his glory is manifested, then you too will fully share in his appearance and in the open display of his glory.

[5] So then, give evidence of your death to the world: regard your bodily limbs as completely dead with respect to their former earthly actions—immorality and impurity of any and every type, sensual craving and debased passion, and especially covetousness, which makes the desire to get and to have into a god. [6] Never forget that it is these very sins that bring God's wrath. [7] There was a time when you yourselves also indulged in these sins, when your life was given over to such action. [8] But as things now stand, you must put off all sins of any kind, including chronic anger, sudden rage, malicious spite, slanderous talk, and foul-mouthed language. [9] Do not lie to one another in either word or deed; remember that you have stripped off forever the old Adamic nature, the old Humanity, together with the actions that expressed it, [10] and have put on the new nature you have in Christ, the new Humanity, which is being renewed day by day in conformity with Christ, who is the image of the God who created this new nature, until it finally attains full knowledge of God and his will. [11] In this new Humanity, the Church, all personal distinctions are eradicated—between Greek and Jew, the circumcised and the uncircumcised, barbarian, Scythian, the slave and the freeman. On the contrary, Christ himself amounts to everything and he is in all of you.

[12] So then, since you are God's chosen people, his Elect, dedicated to his service and the objects of his special love, clothe yourselves appropriately—with tenderhearted compassion, kindness, humility, gentleness of spirit, and patient endurance. [13] You must patiently bear with one another and readily forgive one another if anyone has a complaint against his neighbor. The Lord

readily forgave you; so you, for your part, ought to follow his example and readily forgive. [14] And in addition to all these garments just mentioned, clothe yourselves with the robe of love, for when this final, outer garment is put on, it binds together and perfects all the other virtues. [15] And let the preservation of the peace that Christ gives be the determinative factor in your decision-making, for in reality your Christian calling as fellow members of the one Body of Christ is to share in that peace. And always remember to be grateful. [16] Let the message of Christ be operative in your hearts and in your midst and enrich you with all its wealth through your teaching and admonishing one another with all possible wisdom, as you sing to God with thanksgiving and with your whole heart—not simply with your lips—using psalms, hymns, and spiritual songs. [17] To sum up: whatever you are doing, whether it be speech or action, do everything in the name of the Lord Jesus, at the same time giving thanks to God the Father on the basis of the mediatorial work of Christ.

[18] You wives, submit yourselves to the leadership of your husbands, for this is fitting behavior for those who belong to the Lord. [19] You husbands, show love to your wives constantly—never be harsh with them or foster bitter feelings against them. [20] You children, be obedient to your parents in every respect, for such behavior pleases the Lord and befits those who belong to him. [21] You fathers, avoid exasperating your children by over-correcting them or scorning their efforts; for if you do provoke them, they will become disheartened and sullen. [22] You slaves, be totally obedient to your earthly masters. Serve them well, but not with concern only for external appearances, as though it were your responsibility simply to serve humans. Rather, serve them with heartfelt sincerity and out of your reverent fear of the Lord. [23] Perform any task you may have enthusiastically and as a service rendered to the Lord and not to humans, [24] since you well know that it is from this same Lord and Master that you will receive the glorious inheritance of believers as your full recompense, whatever dues you may or may not now receive from humans. So then, serve your heavenly Master who is Christ. [25] For everyone who does not serve the Lord Christ but engages in wrongdoing will be duly requited for all the wrong he has done, and this Master shows no favoritism in dispensing rewards and punishments or in treating masters and slaves.

4 [1] And finally, you masters, give your slaves just and even-handed treatment, since you are well aware that you, like your slaves, have a Master in heaven—a heavenly employer to whom you are accountable.

[2] Always maintain the practice of prayer, and while you pray be alert in mind and heart. Also let thanksgiving always be a part of your prayer. [3] At the same time intercede for us too—that God may provide us with a wide, open door for the preaching of our message, so that we may proclaim Christ as God's

open secret. It is, in fact, because of this open secret that I am now a prisoner in chains. ⁴ Pray, then, that I may declare this message openly and boldly, which is the way I ought to proclaim it. ⁵ Be tactful and wise in all your relations with unbelievers; buy up every possible opportunity to influence them for the kingdom of God. ⁶ Let your conversation always be graciously winsome and seasoned with the salt of wit and pungency, so that you may know how you should give an answer suitable for each occasion and each need to each separate individual.

⁷ You will be told all the news about me by Tychicus, our dearly loved brother who has been a trustworthy helper and loyal fellow slave in the Lord's service. ⁸ There is a particular reason I am sending him to you: that you may find out how matters stand with us and have your hearts encouraged by the news he brings. ⁹ Along with him I am sending Onesimus, that trustworthy and dearly loved brother who is one of your own number. These two brothers will tell you everything that has been happening here in Rome.

¹⁰ I pass on greetings from Aristarchus, a fellow prisoner of Christ; from Mark, the cousin of Barnabas (let me remind you of the directions you have already received about him—"if he pays you a visit, you are to give him a warm, hospitable welcome"); ¹¹ and from Jesus, who is known as Justus. All three are Jewish converts and at present they are the only Jewish coworkers I have in the task of spreading the kingdom of God. They have, these men, been a source of real comfort to me. ¹² Greetings also from Epaphras, one of your own number, a devoted bond-slave of Christ Jesus who is always praying for you with great intensity that you may stand firm in every aspect of God's will as mature and convinced Christians. ¹³ For I can certainly testify how strenuously he toils for you in intercessory prayer—for you and for Christians at Laodicea and Hierapolis. ¹⁴ Greetings, too, from our dear friend, Luke the physician, and from Demas. ¹⁵ Please convey my own greetings to the brothers at Laodicea, and to Nympha and the church that meets in her home. ¹⁶ When this present letter has been read at your gathering, ensure that it is read in the church of the Laodiceans as well and that in turn you read the letter that I have sent to Laodicea, which you will get from them. ¹⁷ Finally, give Archippus this message from me: "Pay special attention to the responsibility you have received and undertaken as a servant of the Lord, so that you may discharge it to the full."

¹⁸ And now I add this final greeting in my own handwriting—from me, PAUL. Remember the chains I wear. (I am writing with a manacled hand!) May the grace of Jesus Christ continue to be your portion.

Exegetical Outline

For the correlation between these outlines and the Greek text, see the first entry under "Homiletical Suggestions" for each section.

I. Introduction (1:1-14)
  A. Introductory Greeting (1:1-2)
    1. The writers: Paul (and Timothy) (v. 1)
    2. The addressees: the Colossians (v. 2a)
    3. The greeting: grace and peace (v. 2b)
  B. Paul's Thanksgiving for the Colossians (1:3-8)
    1. The reason for thanksgiving (vv. 3-4)
    2. The stimulus afforded by hope (v. 5a)
    3. The content and potency of the gospel (vv. 5b-6)
    4. The ministry of Epaphras (vv. 7-8)
  C. Paul's Intercession for the Colossians (1:9-14)
    1. Its commencement and frequency (v. 9a)
    2. Its principal content (v. 9b): a request for wisdom and discernment and thus knowledge of God's will
    3. Its intended results (vv. 10-14): a life that is:
      (a) worthy of the Lord (v. 10a)
      (b) pleasing to the Lord (v. 10a)
      (c) marked by:
        (i) fruitfulness of action (v. 10b)
        (ii) growth in knowledge (v. 10b)
        (iii) power for endurance (v. 11)
        (iv) gratitude to God (v. 12a)
            for qualification (v. 12b)
                deliverance (vv. 13a, 14)
                transference (v. 13b)
II. Christ's Work and Paul's Mission (1:15–2:3)

231

A. The Supremacy of Christ in Creation and Redemption (1:15-20)
  1. Supremacy in Creation (vv. 15-17)
     As the Image of the invisible God (v. 15a)
     As the Firstborn over all creation (v. 15b)
     As the Creator of all things (v. 16a, b)
     As the Goal of all things (v. 16c)
     As the One "before" everything (v. 17a)
     As the Sustainer of all things (v. 17b)
  2. Supremacy in Redemption (vv. 18-20)
     As the Head of the Body, the Church (v. 18a)
     As the Beginning (v. 18b)
     As the Firstborn from the dead (v. 18c)
     As the Possessor of all God's fullness (v. 19)
     As the Agent of God's reconciliation (v. 20)
B. Reconciliation and the Colossians (1:21-23)
  1. Their previous state: alienated and enemies (v. 21)
  2. Their present condition: reconciled through Christ (v. 22a)
  3. Their future destiny: presented blameless before God (v. 22b)
  4. Their present duty: persisting in faith and maintaining hope (v. 23)
C. Paul's Stewardship of God's Mystery (1:24-29)
  1. Paul's sufferings for the sake of the Church (v. 24)
  2. Paul's stewardship as servant of the Church (v. 25)
  3. God's mystery, once hidden but now revealed (vv. 26-27)
  4. Paul's proclamation of the mystery of the indwelling Christ (v. 28)
  5. Paul's toil, empowered by Christ (v. 29)
D. Paul's Spiritual Struggle (2:1-3)
  1. Its nature (v. 1a)
  2. Its beneficiaries (v. 1b)
  3. Its objectives (v. 2):
     (a) encouragement of heart (v. 2a)
     (b) unity in love (v. 2b)
     (c) full assurance through understanding (v. 2c)
     (d) more profound penetration of God's mystery (v. 2d)
  4. The justification of this fourth, comprehensive objective (3.d.): Christ is the Reservoir of God's wisdom and knowledge (v. 3)
III. Error and Its Remedy (2:4–3:4)
  A. Warning against Specious Philosophy (2:4-8)

1. The danger of being talked into error by specious argument (vv. 4-7)
   (a) evidence of Paul's concern for the Colossians' welfare: his joy in their orderliness and stability (v. 5)
   (b) protection against this danger:
       (i) recalling Christian tradition (v. 6a)
       (ii) life in union with Christ (v. 6b), marked by:
           (α) rootage in Christ (v. 7a)
           (β) building on Christ (v. 7a)
           (γ) stability in the faith (v. 7b)
           (δ) overflow of thanksgiving (v. 7c)
2. The danger of being carried off as spoil by hollow deceptive philosophy (v. 8)
   (a) origin (κατά) of this philosophy: human tradition
   (b) content (κατά) of this philosophy: the elemental spirits of the universe
   (c) protection against this danger: Christ, who is neither the source nor the substance (οὐ κατά) of this philosophy
B. Christ, the Remedy against Error (2:9-15)
   1. Why is Christ the remedy against error and the standard of truth (cf. v. 8c)? (vv. 9-10)
      (a) Because the fullness of deity resides in him (v. 9) and
      (b) because Christians have completeness in him, the universal Head (v. 10).
   2. How were Christians brought to this completeness? (vv. 11-13b)
      (a) By circumcision of the heart, as followers of Christ (v. 11),
      (b) by being buried with Christ (v. 12a), and
      (c) by being raised with Christ when spiritually dead (vv. 12b-13b).
   3. What did God achieve through Christ's death? (vv. 13c-15)
      (a) The forgiveness of trespasses (v. 13c),
      (b) the cancellation of indebtedness (v. 14), and
      (c) the disarming of opposition (v. 15).
C. Warning against Mystical Legalism (2:16-19)
   1. The danger of succumbing to groundless accusations regarding:
      (a) diet (food and drink)
      (b) religious festivals
      (c) calendrical observances

       (d) sabbatarianism (v. 16),
           all of which are shadows in comparison with the reality
           of Christ (v. 17).
   2. The danger of succumbing to unjustifiable disqualification by
       another's insistence on:
       (a) self-humiliation and
       (b) angel-worship,
           while he himself
       (a) parades his visions,
       (b) is filled with futile notions (v. 18), and
       (c) fails to adhere to Christ, the source of the Church's
           growth (v. 19).
D. Consequences of Death with Christ (2:20-23)
  Freedom from (ἀπό):
   1. control by the elemental spirits of the universe (v. 20a)
   2. the old world-order (v. 20b)
   3. restrictive regulations (v. 20b)
       —that prohibit touching or eating certain things (v. 21), all of
         which are destined to perish when used (v. 22a)
   4. bondage to merely human precepts and doctrines (v. 22b)
   5. enforced ascetic disciplines (v. 23)
       —that involve self-imposed devotion, flaunted humility, and
         harsh treatment of the body (v. 23b),
       —that, in popular estimation, appear advantageous (v. 23a),
       —and that, in reality, are totally ineffective in restraining self-
         gratification (v. 23c).
E. Consequences of Resurrection with Christ (3:1-4)
   1. Pursuit of the realm above (v. 1a), because of:
       (a) resurrection with Christ (v. 1a)
       (b) the session of Christ (v. 1b)
   2. Preoccupation with the realm above (v. 2a), because of:
       (a) death with Christ (v. 3a),
       (b) identification with Christ in life (vv. 3b, 4a) and glory
         (v. 4b).
IV. Exhortation to Holiness (3:5–4:6)
  A. "Putting off" Vices (3:5-11)
      1. Put to death your bodily limbs as used for earthly purposes
        (v. 5a):
        immorality—impurity
        lust—evil craving, and

ruthless greed, which is idolatry (v. 5b)

because:

  (a) you have died (with Christ, 2:20) to the world and its sin (vv. 3, 5)

  (b) such sins incur God's wrath (v. 6)

  (c) such conduct belongs to your past (v. 7).

2. Put off all the following vices (v. 8a):

anger—rage

spite—slander

foul language from your mouth.

3. Put an end to lying to one another (v. 9a) because:

  (a) you have put off the old Humanity, your Adamic nature, along with its characteristic conduct (v. 9b)

  (b) you have put on the new Humanity, your new nature in Christ, which is being constantly renewed (v. 10b) and in which all traditional barriers are abolished and Christ is central (v. 11).

B. "Putting on" Virtues (3:12-17)

1. Put on the attire of the Christian (vv. 12-13) as God's chosen, dedicated, and dearly loved people (v. 12a): viz.

  (a) tenderheartedness (v. 12b)

  (b) kindness—humility (v. 12b)

  (c) gentleness—patience (v. 12b)

  (d) toleration (v. 13a), and

  (e) forgiveness (v. 13b, c).

2. Put on the robe of love (v. 14),

  (a) the final, outer garment (v. 14a), which

  (b) binds together and

  (c) perfects all the other virtues (v. 14b).

3. The peace of Christ should act as arbitrator (v. 15)

  (a) in the decision-making of Christians (v. 15a)

  (b) in the light of God's calling (v. 15b).

4. The message of Christ will indwell and enrich us (v. 16)

  (a) by our teaching and admonishing one another with all wisdom (v. 16a) and

  (b) as we sing to God with gratitude (v. 16b).

5. The name of the Lord Jesus should be the touchstone of behavior (v. 17),

  (a) whether words or deeds (v. 17a),

  (b) with constant praise of God (v. 17b).

C. Household Relationships (3:18–4:1)
1. Wives and Husbands (3:18-19)
(a) Wives must be subject to their husbands (v. 18a)
(b) Husbands must:
(i) love their wives (v. 19a)
(ii) not treat them harshly (v. 19b)
2. Children and Parents (vv. 20-21)
(a) Children must obey their parents (v. 20a)
(b) Fathers/parents must not provoke their children (v. 21a)
3. Servants and Masters (3:22–4:1)
(a) Servants must:
(i) obey their masters (3:22a)
(ii) work with enthusiasm (3:23a)
(iii) serve the Lord Christ (3:24b)
(b) Masters must treat their slaves justly and fairly (4:1a)
D. Prayer and Witness (4:2-6)
1. The Ingredients in Effective Prayer (vv. 2-4):
(a) Persistence: we need to be devoted to a habit (v. 2a).
(b) Vigilance: we need to be mentally and spiritually alert (v. 2b).
(c) Thanksgiving: we need to be grateful in all circumstances (v. 2c).
(d) Petition: we need to ask for
(i) unique opportunities to proclaim Christ (v. 3) and
(ii) appropriate boldness in proclaiming Christ (v. 4).
2. The Ingredients in Powerful Witness (vv. 5-6):
(a) Behavior: we need to be tactful (v. 5a) and
we need to be resourceful in using opportunities (v. 5b).
(b) Conversation: needs to be invariably winsome and pungent (v. 6a)
needs to be tailored to each individual (v. 6b).
V. Personal Notes (4:7-18)
A. Paul's Two Representatives (4:7-9)
1. Their credentials
(a) Tychicus:
(i) a dearly loved Christian brother
(ii) a trustworthy helper and
(iii) a fellow slave in the Lord's service (v. 7b)
(b) Onesimus: a Christian brother who is

             (i) trustworthy
            (ii) dearly loved
          (iii) a resident of Colossae (v. 9a)

2. Their mission
   (a) Tychicus:
       (i) to inform the Colossians of Paul's situation (vv. 7a, 8a)
      (ii) to cheer their hearts (v. 8b)
   (b) Tychicus and Onesimus: to inform the Colossians of the wider situation in Rome (v. 9b)

B. Greetings and Final Instructions (4:10-18)
   1. Greetings to the Colossians from Paul's friends (vv. 10-14)
     (a) From three Jewish Christians (v. 11b) who were Paul's coworkers in promoting the kingdom of God (v. 11c) and who had been a source of encouragement to him (v. 11d):
       (i) Aristarchus, who, like Paul, was Christ's captive (v. 10a)
      (ii) Mark, the cousin of Barnabas (v. 10b, c)
     (iii) Jesus Justus (v. 11a).
     (b) From three Gentile Christians (vv. 12-14):
       (i) Epaphras, a Colossian and a slave of Christ Jesus (v. 12a; cf. 1:7-8)
      (ii) Luke, the dearly loved physician (v. 14a)
     (iii) Demas (v. 14b).
   2. Final instructions to the Colossians from Paul (vv. 15-18)
     (a) Convey my greetings
       (i) to the Laodicean Christians (v. 15a)
      (ii) to Nympha and her house church (v. 15b)
     (b) Read the present letter at your gathering (v. 16a)
     (c) Ensure that it is also read at Laodicea (v. 16b) and that you read my letter to Laodicea (v. 16c)
     (d) Exhort Archippus to fulfill his special responsibility (v. 17)
     (e) Remember my imprisonment for the gospel (v. 18b; cf. 4:3).

Philemon

Introduction

AUTHORSHIP AND DATE

Hardly any modern commentator doubts that Paul wrote Philemon. It displays all the formal characteristics of a short personal letter of the early Christian era, its tone reflects the pastoral skill and sensitivity of Paul (who is named in vv. 1, 9, and 19), and its style and vocabulary betray the hand of the apostle. In the Introduction to Colossians we listed the features that Philemon and Colossians have in common, similarities that lead us to assume that these two letters belong to the same period, viz. A.D. 60-61.

OCCASION AND PURPOSE

Onesimus was a slave of Philemon in Colossae (cf. Col. 4:9) who had not only run away from his master (Phlm. 15-16) but had also absconded with some of Philemon's money or possessions (vv. 18-19). Attracted by the anonymity and excitement of a large metropolis, he traveled furtively to Rome (some say Ephesus, e.g., L 84), where somehow he met the imprisoned Paul, possibly through Epaphras. Paul led Onesimus to faith in Christ (v. 10) and soon discovered him to be an able and willing helper as well as a Christian companion (vv. 11-13, 16-17).

Other considerations apart, Paul would have kept Onesimus at his side (v. 13), but he felt compelled to send him back to Colossae so that Philemon, the legal owner of Onesimus (v. 16), might himself have the opportunity of receiving him back as a Christian brother (v. 16) and of releasing him for further service to Paul (vv. 14, 20-21). Accordingly, Onesimus returned to Philemon with this letter (v. 12) in the company of

Tychicus, the bearer of Colossians and Ephesians (Col. 4:7-9; Eph. 6:21-22).

The main alternative to this traditional understanding of the background of Philemon is the fascinating reconstruction of events put forward by J. Knox in *Philemon among the Letters of Paul* (Chicago: University of Chicago, 1935; New York: Abingdon, 1959[2]). The essential features of his view can be stated thus:

1. Philemon, who succeeded Epaphras as overseer of the Lycus Valley churches, probably lived at Laodicea, not Colossae.
2. Archippus lived at Colossae, hosted the Colossian church (Phlm. 2), and owned the slave Onesimus, but was unknown to Paul.
3. The letter that we call "Philemon" was sent with Onesimus first to Philemon in Laodicea (so that Paul's appeal might gain Philemon's support), then to Archippus in Colossae, who, as the owner of Onesimus, was the principal addressee of the letter.
4. "Philemon" is in fact "the letter from Laodicea" (Col. 4:16) and the "service" that Paul, through the Colossians, asked Archippus to fulfill (Col. 4:17) was the release of Onesimus for Christian ministry.

For all its ingenuity this hypothesis faces some insuperable difficulties (see G 636-638; Moule 15-18), so that it has not gained widespread acceptance. First, the singular "your" (σου) in the phrase "in your house" (κατ' οἶκόν σου, Phlm. 2) refers naturally to the addressee named first as the principal recipient of the letter (viz. Philemon), rather than to the nearest antecedent (viz. Archippus). If so, the owner of Onesimus was Philemon, who was Paul's convert (v. 19) and, along with Archippus (cf. Col. 4:17), was a resident of Colossae. Second, Col. 4:16 envisages an exchange of letters between Colossae and Laodicea: Paul's letter addressed to the Colossians was to be read in the church of the Laodiceans and his letter addressed to the Laodiceans was to be read to the Colossian congregation. But on Knox's view, "Philemon" was addressed principally to Archippus at Colossae and it came to Colossae merely by way of Laodicea. Third, in Colossians 4:17 διακονία ("ministry," "service") describes an active and ongoing ministry (note the present tense vbs. βλέπε and πληροῖς) that was fulfilled (πληροῖς) in the church and was "received" from Paul or by revelation (παρέλαβες), rather than the passive, individual, and one-time action of surrendering the slave Onesimus for Christian work. Finally, in "Philemon" Paul makes his plea on behalf of Onesimus with exquisitely delicate touches. It would have been totally out of keeping and insensitive for him then to put additional pressure on the owner of Onesimus by the public reading of Col. 4:17, where, on Knox's hypothesis, the master is named and indirectly requested to release his own runaway slave.

Was the letter successful? Did Philemon pardon Onesimus on his return, welcome him as a Christian brother and as though he were Paul (vv. 12, 16-17), and then set him free so that he could continue to serve as Paul's aide (vv. 11, 13, 16, 20-21)? With a high degree of confidence, we can answer Yes. The very preservation of the letter, so intensely personal and specific in its references, as well as its inclusion in the canon of the NT, lead us to believe that Philemon complied with Paul's requests. If Philemon, as the principal recipient of the letter, had remained unmoved by Paul's appeal, he and other Christians would doubtless have opposed the circulation of the letter, for it would then have testified to his hardheartedness and to Paul's failure in this matter.

OUTLINE

A. Introductory Greeting (vv. 1-3)
B. Thanksgiving and Intercession for Philemon (vv. 4-7)
C. Paul's General Appeal on Behalf of Onesimus (vv. 8-16)
D. Paul's Specific Requests regarding Onesimus (vv. 17-20)
E. Final Remarks, Greetings, and Benediction (vv. 21-25)

RECOMMENDED COMMENTARIES

Each of the four commentaries listed in the Introduction to Colossians also contains a commentary and a bibliography on Philemon. As with Colossians, so here with Philemon, reference will be made to Lightfoot, Lohse, Moule, and O'Brien.

A. INTRODUCTORY GREETING (VV. 1-3)

1 Παῦλος δέσμιος Χριστοῦ Ἰησοῦ καὶ Τιμόθεος ὁ ἀδελφὸς Φιλήμονι τῷ ἀγαπητῷ καὶ συνεργῷ ἡμῶν 2 καὶ Ἀπφίᾳ τῇ ἀδελφῇ καὶ Ἀρχίππῳ τῷ συστρατιώτῃ ἡμῶν καὶ τῇ κατ' οἶκόν σου ἐκκλησίᾳ· 3 χάρις ὑμῖν καὶ εἰρήνη ἀπὸ θεοῦ πατρὸς ἡμῶν καὶ κυρίου Ἰησοῦ Χριστοῦ.

STRUCTURE

1	Παῦλος	δέσμιος		Χριστοῦ Ἰησοῦ
	καὶ Τιμόθεος ὁ ἀδελφός			
		Φιλήμονι ...	καὶ	
2		Ἀπφίᾳ ...	καὶ	
		Ἀρχίππῳ ...	καὶ	
		τῇ ... ἐκκλησίᾳ ...		
3	χάρις	ὑμῖν		
	καὶ εἰρήνη	ἀπὸ θεοῦ ... καὶ		
		κυρίου Ἰησοῦ	Χριστοῦ	

VERSE 1

Παῦλος δέσμιος Χριστοῦ Ἰησοῦ

In introductory greetings in letters, proper names are regularly anarthrous. Δέσμιος (-ου, ὁ, prisoner) is in appos. to Παῦλος and is therefore in the same case (nom.), but exceptionally (see v. 1b), has no article (cf. T 206). Usually Paul begins his letters with ἀπόστολος (e.g., 2 Cor. 1:1) or δοῦλος (cf. Phil. 1:1) or both terms (Rom. 1:1; Tit. 1:1) after his name. This letter derives much of its potency from the fact that Paul appeals, directly or indirectly, (a) to his friendship with Philemon, rather than to his apostolic authority (vv. 7-9, 14, 17, 19, 20; but cf. v. 21); and (b) to his present circumstances as a prisoner (vv. 1, 9, 10, 13, 23).

After δέσμιος the gens. Χριστοῦ Ἰησοῦ (see Col. 1:1 for this name) express a multiple relationship: possession ("belonging to"), purpose ("for the sake of," GNB; sim. TCNT, Weymouth), and cause ("because of [my service for]"). The Eng. tr. "of Christ Jesus" retains the multiple sense of the Gk.

καὶ Τιμόθεος ὁ ἀδελφός

See on Col. 1:1. Timothy is here associated with Paul not as a coauthor (the sg. is used from v. 4 onward, apart from v. 6, and Paul's name alone appears in vv. 9, 19) but because he is known to Philemon and the Colossian church (cf. Acts 19:22; thus most EVV have "our brother" here; the art. points to a well-known person). On ἀδελφός, see Moule 147.

Φιλήμονι τῷ ἀγαπητῷ καὶ συνεργῷ ἡμῶν

Φιλήμονι is dat. of Φιλήμων, -ονος, ὁ, Philemon, specifying the first addressee of the letter. Philemon is therefore the principal addressee: a form of sg. σύ is used twenty times, sg. σεαυτόν once, and sg. σός once. Συνεργός, -οῦ, ὁ, coworker, helper. Paul uses this term of his associates in the tasks of evangelism and pastoral care; but the association (συν-) does not amount to an unqualified equality (cf. G. Bertram, TDNT 7.874). The emphasis rests on shared toil rather than on parity of status or shared fellowship. See above For Further Study 43, "Paul and His Coworkers" (Col. 4:7).

Because ἀγαπητῷ is followed by the coordinative καί, it is not an adj. qualifying συνεργῷ. With the art. (τῷ) the adj. ἀγαπητός is a subst., "dear friend" (NEB, NIV), "beloved *brother*" (NASB), or simply "friend" (GNB; see further Turner, *Words* 266-268). Moreover, a subst. in appos. to an anar. proper name (here Φιλήμονι) often has the art. (cf. BDF § 268; R 760; and vv. 2, 23; Col. 4:7, 9-11). The coordinated substs. ἀγαπητῷ and συνεργῷ are shown to refer to the same person by the single art. τῷ (Granville Sharp's rule), and the poss. ἡμῶν qualifies both terms: "(Philemon) our dear friend and coworker." It is just conceivable that this is a case of hendiadys, "our dear fellow worker" (JB).

VERSE 2

καὶ Ἀπφίᾳ τῇ ἀδελφῇ καὶ Ἀρχίππῳ τῷ συστρατιώτῃ ἡμῶν

Ἀπφία, -ας, ἡ, Apphia; probably the wife of Philemon (BAGD 103b; Lightfoot 304; Lohse 190). If so, Paul's injunctions regarding Onesimus would have particular relevance to her. Either τῇ denotes poss. or ἡμῶν is to be understood from the preceding or following phrase ("*our* sister," thus most EVV).

Ἀρχίππος, -ου, ὁ, Archippus (Col. 4:17); perhaps the son of Philemon (Lightfoot 306-307). Συστρατιώτης, -ου, ὁ, "fellow-soldier" (Moffatt, GNB; sim. RSV, JB, NAB), "comrade-in-arms" (NEB; ZG 652), "fellow-campaigner" (Moule 140), "fellow combatant" (Lohse 190); used of devotion to the service of the gospel (BAGD 795c).

καὶ τῇ κατ' οἶκόν σου ἐκκλησίᾳ

The fourth addressee expressed by the dat. is "the church [that meets] in your house." Since the prep. phrase κατ' οἶκόν σου (on which see Col. 4:15) functions as an adj., it has the position of an adj., viz. it is placed between the art. and the noun (the other possible word-order would have been τῇ ἐκκλησίᾳ τῇ κατ' οἶκόν σου). The sg. pron. σου, a poss. gen., refers back to Philemon, the addressee named first as the principal recipient of the letter, not to Archippus, the nearest antecedent (for the latter view, see the Introduction to Philemon). Some EVV make the ref. to Philemon clear with "at Philemon's house" (TCNT), by treating the second and third addressees parenthetically ("To Philemon . . .—and to our sister Apphia and our comrade Archippus—as well as to the Church in your house," Weymouth), or by inserting v. 2c after v. 1 ("To . . . Philemon, and the church that meets in your house," GNB).

There is no evidence of special buildings for church activities until the third century A.D. NT refs. or allusions to house churches and their hosts are: Gaius at Corinth (Rom. 16:23), Aquila and Priscilla at Ephesus (1 Cor. 16:19) and at Rome (Rom. 16:3, 5), Lydia at Philippi (Acts 16:15, 40), Nympha at Laodicea (Col. 4:15), Philemon at Colossae (Phlm. 2), and probably Mary at Jerusalem (Acts 12:12) and Jason at Thessalonica (Acts 17:5-6). See For Further Study 45, "The House Church in the NT."

VERSE 3

χάρις ὑμῖν καὶ εἰρήνη ἀπὸ θεοῦ πατρὸς ἡμῶν καὶ κυρίου Ἰησοῦ Χριστοῦ.

For χάρις . . . ἡμῶν see on Col. 1:2b (which has identical wording, and where ℵ A C F G it add καὶ κυρίου Ἰησοῦ Χριστοῦ). The absence of ἀπό before κυρίου, which ἀπό also governs, indicates not that God and Jesus are one and the same person (as though καί were epex.) but that they jointly form a single source of divine grace and peace. Of no mere human being could it be said that, together with God, he was a fount of spiritual blessing; the deity of Christ is thus implicitly affirmed. See above For Further Study 4, "NT Benedictions" (Col. 1:2).

TRANSLATION

[1] Paul, a prisoner of Christ Jesus, and Timothy our brother, to Philemon our dear friend and coworker, [2] to Apphia our sister, to Archippus our fellow soldier, and to the church in your house. [3] Grace and peace to you from God our Father and the Lord Jesus Christ.

EXPANDED PARAPHRASE

[1] This letter comes from Paul, now the prisoner of Christ Jesus, and from our brother and colleague Timothy, to Philemon our dear friend and coworker in the gospel, [2] to our sister Apphia, to our fellow soldier Archippus, and to the

church that meets in Philemon's home. [3] May the grace and peace that come from God our heavenly Father and the Lord Jesus Christ be your portion.

FOR FURTHER STUDY

45. The House Church in the NT (v. 2)

*Banks, R., *Paul's Idea of Community. The Early House Churches in their Historical Setting* (Grand Rapids: Eerdmans, 1980), esp. 33-42.

Filson, F. V., "The Significance of the Early House Churches," *JBL* 58 (1939) 105-112.

Green, E. M. B., *Evangelism in the Early Church* (Grand Rapids: Eerdmans, 1970), esp. 207-223.

Malherbe, A. J., "House Churches and their Problems," in *Social Aspects of Early Christianity* (Baton Rouge: Louisiana State University, 1977) 60-91.

Peterson, J. M., "House-Churches in Rome," *Vigiliae Christianae* 23 (1969) 264-272.

Verner, D. C., *The Household of God: The Social World of the Pastoral Epistles* (Chico, CA: Scholars, 1983).

HOMILETICAL SUGGESTIONS

Introductory Greeting (vv. 1-3)

1. The writers—Paul (and Timothy; v. 1a)
2. The addressees—
   Philemon (v. 1b)
   Apphia
   Archippus
   the church in Philemon's house (v. 2)
3. The greeting—grace and peace (v. 3)

B. THANKSGIVING AND INTERCESSION FOR PHILEMON (VV. 4-7)

4 Εὐχαριστῶ τῷ θεῷ μου πάντοτε μνείαν σου ποιούμενος ἐπὶ τῶν προσευχῶν μου,
5 ἀκούων σου τὴν ἀγάπην καὶ τὴν πίστιν ἣν ἔχεις πρὸς τὸν κύριον Ἰησοῦν καὶ
εἰς πάντας τοὺς ἁγίους, 6 ὅπως ἡ κοινωνία τῆς πίστεώς σου ἐνεργὴς γένηται ἐν
ἐπιγνώσει παντὸς ἀγαθοῦ τοῦ ἐν ἡμῖν εἰς Χριστόν· 7 χαρὰν γὰρ πολλὴν ἔσχον
καὶ παράκλησιν ἐπὶ τῇ ἀγάπῃ σου, ὅτι τὰ σπλάγχνα τῶν ἁγίων ἀναπέπαυται διὰ
σοῦ, ἀδελφέ.

STRUCTURE

4   *Εὐχαριστῶ* . . . πάντοτε
         μνείαν . . . ποιούμενος
5   ἀκούων . . . τὴν ἀγάπην ——— καὶ ——— τὴν πίστιν
         πρὸς τὸν Κ. Ἰ. ——— καὶ ——— εἰς πάντας τ. ἁγ.
6   *[προσευχόμενος]*
         ὅπως ἡ κοινωνία . . . ἐνεργὴς γένηται
                                          ἐν ἐπιγνώσει
7 χαρὰν . . . *ἔσχον* καὶ παράκλησιν
         ἐπὶ τῇ ἀγάπῃ σου,
         ὅτι τὰ σπλάγχνα . . . ἀναπέπαυται

4 I always give thanks	Thanksgiving
when I mention	—frequency
5 because I hear . . .	—cause
6 I pray	Intercession
that the generosity . . .	—content
7 I have gained . . .	Joy and Comfort
from your love	—cause
because . . .	—cause further defined

VERSE 4

Εὐχαριστῶ τῷ θεῷ μου πάντοτε μνείαν σου ποιούμενος ἐπὶ τῶν προσευχῶν μου

1 sg. pres. act. indic. of εὐχαριστέω, give thanks (+ dat., τῷ θεῷ, "to God").
Nom. sg. masc. (agreeing with the sg. subj. of εὐχαριστῶ) of the pres. mid. ptc.
of ποιέω, do make; (mid.) do (something) for oneself/on one's own initiative.
Μνεία, -ας, ἡ, remembrance, mention. The phrase μνείαν ποιοῦμαι (+ gen.)
means (lit.) "I make mention of (someone)," that is, "I mention (someone)" in

prayer (BAGD 524b, c; sim. NEB; Moule 140-141), but it is also possible that the phrase is simply a periphrasis for "remember" (μιμνῄσκομαι; so RSV, NIV), as in CGk (Z § 227; cf. BAGD § 683a) or for "pray" (προσεύχομαι; cf. Burton § 203). Σου is obj. gen. after the verbal notion implied in μνεία (viz. "remembering you"). See above For Further Study 6, "PaulineThanksgivings" (Col. 1:3).

The adv. πάντοτε is probably to be cstr. with εὐχαριστῶ (see on Col. 1:3), rather than with μνείαν . . . ποιούμενος: "I always give thanks" (sim. most EVV). But since the following temp. ptc. ποιούμενος restricts the mng. of πάντοτε ("always . . . when I mention"), the sense is "I give thanks . . . whenever I mention" or "I never mention you in my prayers without thanking . . ." (Goodspeed).

In the phrase ἐπὶ τῶν προσευχῶν μου, ἐπί + gen. has the same sense as ἐν + dat. (cf. Col. 4:12; BAGD 713b, c; 286d): "in my prayers" (thus most EVV). But alternatively ἐπί could mean "upon the occasion of" here (Robertson, *Pictures* 465). See above For Further Study 11, "Prayer in Paul" (Col. 1:9-12).

VERSE 5

ἀκούων σου τὴν ἀγάπην καὶ τὴν πίστιν ἣν ἔχεις

Nom. sg. masc. (agreeing with the subj. of εὐχαριστῶ) of the pres. act. ptc. of ἀκούω, hear. As in Col. 1:3-4 (εὐχαριστοῦμεν . . . ἀκούσαντες), the ptc. is causal (most EVV; Lightfoot 332; Lohse 192, 193; O'Brien 276, 277); but whereas there it is aor. ("because we [have] heard"), here it is pres. ("[I give thanks . . .] because I continue to hear"; "for I keep hearing," NAB). Σου is not gen. of the person after ἀκούω, but a poss. gen. qualifying τὴν ἀγάπην (acc. of the thing heard about) and standing in the emphatic position (pers. prons. denoting poss. more often follow the noun they qualify: T 189). It is indistinguishable in mng. from ἣν ἔχεις ("which you have"), which qualifies τὴν πίστιν alone (a second acc. after ἀκούων). Ἥν is acc. sg. fem. of the rel. pron. ὅς, ἥ, ὅ. See above For Further Study 39, "Love" (Col. 3:14).

πρὸς τὸν κύριον Ἰησοῦν καὶ εἰς πάντας τοὺς ἁγίους

These two coordinated prep. phrases can be related to the two preceding nouns (τὴν ἀγάπην and τὴν πίστιν) in three basic ways:

(1) Both phrases may modify each noun:
    "the love and faith which you show, not only to the Lord Jesus, but also to all his people" (TCNT; sim. Moffatt ["your love and loyalty to . . ."], Goodspeed, NEB, JB, NAB).

(2) Both phrases may modify τὴν πίστιν only:
"I hear of your love and of the faith which you have toward the Lord
Jesus and all the saints" (RSV; sim. Weymouth).
*(3) The εἰς phrase may modify τὴν ἀγάπην and the πρός phrase τὴν πίστιν,
in an instance of chiasmus (A-B-B-A):
"your love for all God's people and the faith which you have in the Lord
Jesus" (GNB; sim. NIV [but with the order "faith . . . love"]; BDF
§ 477[2]; R 1200; Turner, *Style* 97; Vincent 920; ZG 652; Lightfoot
332-333; Lohse 193 and nn. 15, 16; Moule 141-142; O'Brien 275,
278-279; R. Bultmann, TDNT 6.212 n. 277 ["probably"]).
The following considerations may be urged in favor of alternative (3).
(a) That ἀγάπην and πίστιν should be cstr. separately seems indicated
by the repeated article τήν and by the repeated qualification "which
you have" (assuming σου = ἣν ἔχεις—see above).
(b) The rel. clause ἣν ἔχεις refers exclusively to τὴν πίστιν. This suggests
that the πρός phrase, which completes the sense of the rel. clause,
also applies solely to τὴν πίστιν.
(c) In a parallel passage (Col. 1:4), εἰς πάντας τοὺς ἁγίους qualifies τὴν
ἀγάπην ἣν ἔχετε, while Phlm. 7 refers again to Philemon's love for
God's people.
(d) If τὴν πίστιν is cstr. with εἰς κτλ. as well as with πρός κτλ., it becomes
necessary to understand πίστις in two different senses (viz. "faith"
in the Lord Jesus, "faithfulness" toward all God's people) or as
meaning "faithfulness"/"loyalty" (Moffatt) in both cases. But, as
Lohse notes (193 n. 15), πίστις always means "faith" when it is
associated with ἀγάπη.
(e) There are Pauline parallels for ἀγάπη followed by εἰς (Eph. 1:15;
Col. 1:4; 1 Thess. 3:12) and for πρός with πίστις (1 Thess. 1:8), but
none for πρός with ἀγάπη.
See For Further Study 46, "Chiasmus in the NT." On the phrase εἰς πάντας
τοὺς ἁγίους, see Col. 1:4.

VERSE 6

ὅπως ἡ κοινωνία τῆς πίστεώς σου

The conj. ὅπως + subjunc. (usually aor., as in this verse) often indicates purpose
(= ἵνα, in order that), occasionally result (= ὥστε, so that), but here specifies
the content of Paul's prayer (so also ZG 652; Lohse 193 n. 18; Moule 142;
O'Brien 276, 279). This whole clause (v. 6) could depend on μνείαν σου
ποιούμενος (v. 4) understood as meaning "when I intercede for you" (O'Brien

279), but, with almost all EVV (cf. BAGD 577a; Lohse 192 n. 3), it is perhaps easier to supply the pres. ptc. προσευχόμενος from τῶν προσευχῶν μου in v. 4 ("praying that," "I pray that," "my prayer is that"). Alternatively, αἰτούμενος could be supplied ("asking that," "my request [to God] is that"; cf. Col. 1:9) .

Κοινωνία, -ας, ἡ, has three basic meanings—(1) participation or sharing in; (2) (spiritual) fellowship or partnership; (3) the sharing of something, a charitable gift, contributory help. See further F. Hauck, TDNT 3.797-809, who treats the κοινων- root in the NT under three heads: (1) "to share with someone in something" (participation); (2) "to give someone a share in something" (impartation); (3) fellowship. See also For Further Study 47, "Κοινωνία in the NT."

Σου may apply solely to τῆς πίστεως ("your faith") or may qualify the whole phrase ἡ κοινωνία τῆς πίστεως (see the tr. options below). Πίστις may refer to personal faith in the Lord Jesus (v. 5) or to the Christian profession and way of life as "the Faith." The gen. τῆς πίστεως may be:

(1) qualitative: "your fellowship [with Christ] that is characterized by faith" = "your faith-communion with Christ";
(2) obj.:
    (a) "your sharing in the faith" (Lohse 192, 193-194; sim. BAGD 439b; TCNT ["the Faith"], NEB),
    (b) "their participation in your faith" (Weymouth; "their" refers to "all the saints"; sim. Moffatt, Goodspeed),
    (c) "our fellowship with you as believers" (GNB),
    (d) "your sharing of the faith with others" (NAB; sim. NIV); or
(3) subj.:
    (a) "your fellowship [with Christ]/[with other believers] that arises from your faith"; "your faith, that enables you to share in Christ,"
    *(b) "your generosity, which arises from your faith" (O'Brien 275, 280; sim. Vincent 920; Lightfoot 333, "your kindly deeds of charity . . ."; Barclay). For κοινωνία = "generosity," "altruism" (a sense derived from meaning 3 listed above), see BAGD 439b, and note Rom. 15:26; 2 Cor. 8:4; 9:13; Heb. 13:16, where κοινωνία refers to charitable contributions, almsgiving.

ἐνεργὴς γένηται ἐν ἐπιγνώσει

3 sg. second aor. mid. subjunc. (after ὅπως) of γίνομαι, become, be; prove to be. Ἐνεργής, -ές (a two-termination adj.), effective, active, powerful. After ἐν-εργής, the locat. ἐν denotes the sphere of operation: "that your generosity . . . may become effective in [promoting] deeper understanding . . ." Less probably ἐν could be telic or ecbatic (= εἰς; "so that you will have," NIV),

instr. ("through [coming to know]," Goodspeed; sim. NASB), or circumstantial ("as you come to. . . ," TCNT). On ἐπίγνωσις, -εως, ἡ, "(full) knowledge," see Col. 1:9; 3:10; here, both understanding and experience are involved (O'Brien 280-281). In the context it seems more likely that it is Philemon's "knowledge" that is being spoken about, rather than that of other Christians or of unbelievers.

παντὸς ἀγαθοῦ τοῦ ἐν ἡμῖν εἰς Χριστόν

Being anar., παντὸς ἀγαθοῦ (obj. gen. after ἐν ἐπιγνώσει, denoting the thing known; cf. BAGD 291b) probably means "every blessing" (GNB; O'Brien 275, 280; sim. NASB, Barclay, NIV), but occasionally the anar. πᾶς can mean "the whole of," "all the" (thus "all the good," RSV, NAB; Lohse 192, 194; on this view ἀγαθοῦ may be anar. because the noun on which it is dependent [ἐπιγνώσει] is anar.). On the uses of (ὁ) πᾶς, see on Col. 1:4, 9, 23.

In spite of the strong and geographically diversified evidence supporting ἐν ὑμῖν (𝔭61 ℵ G P 33 1739 Byz vg syrp, h copsa, bo arm), the rdg. ἐν ἡμῖν (supported by A C D K Ψ al) is to be preferred because: (1) scribes would be more likely to have altered ἡμῖν to ὑμῖν than vice versa, given (a) the two uses of the 2 sg. σου in the preceding vv. 5-6a (also note ἔχεις) and in the following v. 7 (also note ἀδελφέ), and (b) a scribal desire to apply Paul's statement specifically to Philemon and his household (Lightfoot 334 for this latter point); and (2) if παντὸς ἀγαθοῦ refers to spiritual blessings to which all Christians are heir, the inclusive ἡμῖν is more appropriate than ὑμῖν. The rdg. ἐν ἡμῖν is defended by Metzger 657; Lightfoot 334; Lohse 194 and n. 23; O'Brien 275.

In the art. prep. phrase τοῦ ἐν ἡμῖν, τοῦ agrees with ἀγαθοῦ (gen. sg. neut.) and functions as a rel. pron. introducing a restrictive rel. clause: "that is in us," "that is ours" (RSV; sim. NAB), "that we have" (sim. NIV). Because (τὸ) ἀγαθόν often denotes a good deed performed, the whole expression could mean "(all) the good which is done and must be done among you" (Zerwick, *Analysis* 490), but this seems unlikely.

Although εἰς Χριστόν could be cstr. with either ἐνεργὴς γένηται or ἐν ἐπιγνώσει, it seems preferable to connect it with the phrase that immediately precedes, viz. παντὸς ἀγαθοῦ τοῦ ἐν ἡμῖν. This εἰς could express:

(1) direction: "with Christ as the goal" (cf. Lightfoot's paraphrase [332]: "looking unto and striving after Christ"; sim. RV, Weymouth),

(2) purpose: "for the glory of Christ" (Lohse 192, 194, 195), "for Christ's sake" (NASB; sim. JB),

(3) result: "that brings us ever closer to Christ" (Barclay; sim. Moule 142; NEB mg.),

(4) location: "in Christ" (where εἰς Χριστόν is virtually equivalent to ἐν Χριστῷ; RSV, NAB, NIV; O'Brien [275, 281] paraphrases "as fellow-

members in the body of Christ" and suggests that εἰς Χριστόν is a stylistic variation for ἐν Χριστῷ to avoid three prep. phrases introduced by ἐν [281]), or

*(5) relation: "in our relation to Christ," "in our life in union with Christ" (GNB; sim. NEB); "as Christians" (Goodspeed; sim. Moffatt).

Paul's prayer was that Philemon's faith would prompt his generosity, and that his generous act of welcoming Onesimus (v. 17) and then of releasing him for the work of the gospel (cf. vv. 13-14, 20-21) would prove effective in deepening his understanding and experience of every spiritual blessing that is the Christian's heritage through being related to Christ (cf. 2 Cor. 9:11a).

VERSE 7

χαρὰν γὰρ πολλὴν ἔσχον καὶ παράκλησιν ἐπὶ τῇ ἀγάπῃ σου

1 sg. second aor. act. indic. of ἔχω, have. This aor. could conceivably be classified as epistolary ("I have/derive"; Moule 144, "probably"), gnomic ("I find," NAB), or ingressive (Robertson, *Pictures* 465; "I came to have," "I had"), but it is probably simply preterit ("I derived/got," ZG 652; often rendered by the Eng. pf., "I have had," Moffatt; "I have derived," RSV). Γάρ may introduce a further ground (after the causal ptc. ἀκούων, v. 5) for Paul's thanksgiving (Vincent 920; Lightfoot 334; O'Brien 282) or may introduce a confirmation ("indeed," TCNT) of v. 5a. The main NT uses of the postpositive conj. γάρ are (1) explanatory ("for," "now," "for instance," "you see"), (2) causal ("for," "because"), and (3) confirmatory/emphatic ("indeed," "certainly"). Less common uses are (4) resumptive ("then") and (5) connective (= δέ; "and," "but"). Πολλήν (acc. sg. fem. of πολύς, πολλή, πολύ, much, many) modifies both χαράν and παράκλησιν.

’Επί defines the basis of a state or action, esp. after an expression of feeling, "because of," "from" (cf. BAGD 5c, 287b, c; Z § 126; ZG 652): "I have derived much joy and comfort from your love" (RSV), or "Your love . . . has brought me great joy and much encouragement!" (GNB; sim. NIV).

ὅτι τὰ σπλάγχνα τῶν ἁγίων ἀναπέπαυται διὰ σοῦ, ἀδελφέ

3 sg. (after a neut. pl. subj.—see of Col. 1:16) pf. pass. indic. of ἀναπαύω, (trans.) give rest to, refresh; (mid.) rest. This ὅτι clause elucidates ἐπὶ τῇ ἀγάπῃ σου, alluding to instances of Philemon's love for God's people (cf. v. 5a): ". . . from your love, because through you (διά + gen. expressing agency), my brother, the hearts of God's people have been refreshed," ". . . over your love,

my brother, over the way you have refreshed the hearts of the saints" (Moffatt).
The pf. tense either points to repeated acts of love that still occur at the time
of writing or emphasizes the present effect of some dramatic display of love
that brought refreshment. Weymouth's rendering reflects this ambiguity: "(the
hearts of God's people) have been, and are, refreshed."

Σπλάγχνον, -ου, τό, always pl. in the NT: entrails, inward parts; heart(s),
"inmost feelings" (Moule 144; cf. vv. 12, 20; Col. 3:12). Here τὰ σπλάγχνα
refers to the whole person (by synecdoche) as having experienced refreshment
at the deepest emotional level (cf. H. Köster, TDNT 7.555). The voc. sg. ἀδελφέ
is emphatic by position (see v. 20 for the more usual position); thus "my
brother" (Weymouth, Goodspeed, Moffatt, RSV, NEB; all these EVV have a
simple "brother" in v. 20).

This verse forms the transition from the thanksgiving and petition (vv.
4-6) addressed to God (τῷ θεῷ μου, v. 4) to the heart of the letter (vv. 8-20)
addressed to Philemon (ἀδελφέ, v. 7). Accordingly there are verbal links with
what precedes (ἀγάπη, ἅγιοι, vv. 5, 7) and with what follows (ἀγάπη, vv. 7, 9;
σπλάγχνα, vv. 7, 12, 20; ἀναπαύω, vv. 7, 20; ἀδελφέ, vv. 7, 20; παρακαλ-, vv.
7, 9, 10).

TRANSLATION

[4] I always give thanks to my God when I mention you in my prayers, [5] because
I hear of your love for all God's people and the faith you have in the Lord
Jesus. [6] I pray that the generosity which your faith prompts may effectively
increase your knowledge of every blessing we have in our relation to Christ.
[7] From your love I have derived much joy and comfort, because through you,
my brother, the hearts of God's people have been refreshed.

EXPANDED PARAPHRASE

[4] Whenever I mention you in my prayers, Philemon, without fail I give
thanks to my God, [5] because I continue to hear of your love and faith—the
faith you have in the Lord Jesus and the love you show to all God's people.
[6] It is my prayer that your Christian generosity, prompted as it is by your
faith, may prove effective in increasing your appreciation and experience of
all the spiritual blessings that are ours to enjoy because of our relationship
with Christ. [7] Your love has brought deep joy and great comfort to me,
because through that love of yours, my brother, the hearts of God's people
have been refreshed.

FOR FURTHER STUDY

46. Chiasmus in the NT (v. 5)

BDF § 477[2].

Bligh, J., *Galatians in Greek* (Detroit: University of Detroit, 1966).

————, *Galatians: A Discussion of St. Paul's Epistle* (London: St. Paul, 1969) 37-42.

Collins, J. J., "Chiasmus, the 'ABA' Pattern and the Text of Paul," *Studiorum Paulinorum Congressus Internationalis Catholicus 1961* (Rome: Pontifical Biblical Institute, 1963), 2.575-583.

Lund, N. W., *Chiasmus in the New Testament* (Chapel Hill: University of North Carolina, 1942).

————, "The Presence of Chiasmus in the New Testament," *Journal of Religion* 10 (1930) 74-93.

Moule, *Idiom Book* 193-194.

*T 345-347.

Turner, *Style* 97-99.

47. Κοινωνία in the NT (v. 6)

Campbell, J. Y., "ΚΟΙΝΩΝΙΑ and its Cognates in the New Testament," *JBL* 51 (1932) 352-380, reprinted in his *Three New Testament Studies* (Leiden: Brill, 1965), 1-28.

George, A. R., *Communion with God in the New Testament* (London: Epworth, 1953).

Hauck, F., TDNT 3.789-809.

Koch, E. W., "A Cameo of Koinonia. The Letter to Philemon," *Interpretation* 17 (1963) 183-187.

McDermott, M., "The Biblical Doctrine of κοινωνία," *Biblische Zeitschrift*, new series, 19 (1975) 64-77, 219-233.

Panikulam, G., *Koinōnia in the New Testament: A Dynamic Expression of Christian Life* (Rome: Pontifical Biblical Institute, 1979).

*Schattenmann, J., NIDNTT 1.639-644.

HOMILETICAL SUGGESTIONS

Thanksgiving and Intercession for Philemon (vv. 4-7)

1. Thanksgiving for Philemon (vv. 4-5)
   (a) its frequency (μνείαν σου ποιούμενος, v. 4)

    (b) its cause (ἀκούων κτλ., v. 5)
2. Intercession for Philemon (v. 6)
       its content (ὅπως κτλ., v. 6)
3. Joy and comfort from Philemon (v. 7)
    (a) their cause (ἐπί)—love shown by Philemon
    (b) their cause further defined (ὅτι)—refreshment given by Philemon

Christian Generosity (κοινωνία, v. 6)

1. Arises from faith (v. 6a)
2. Increases understanding and experience (ἐπίγνωσις) of spiritual blessings
    (v. 6b; cf. 2 Cor. 9:6b, 8, 11)

C. PAUL'S GENERAL APPEAL ON BEHALF OF
ONESIMUS (VV. 8-16)

8 Διό, πολλὴν ἐν Χριστῷ παρρησίαν ἔχων ἐπιτάσσειν σοι τὸ ἀνῆκον, 9 διὰ τὴν ἀγάπην μᾶλλον παρακαλῶ, ποιοῦτος ὢν ὡς Παῦλος πρεσβύτης, νυνὶ δὲ καὶ δέσμιος Χριστοῦ Ἰησοῦ— 10 παρακαλῶ σε περὶ τοῦ ἐμοῦ τέκνου, ὃν ἐγέννησα ἐν τοῖς δεσμοῖς Ὀνήσιμον, 11 τόν ποτέ σοι ἄχρηστον νυνὶ δὲ καὶ σοὶ καὶ ἐμοὶ εὔχρηστον, 12 ὃν ἀνέπεμψά σοι, αὐτόν, τοῦτ᾽ ἔστιν τὰ ἐμὰ σπλάγχνα· 13 ὃν ἐγὼ ἐβουλόμην πρὸς ἐμαυτὸν κατέχειν, ἵνα ὑπὲρ σοῦ μοι διακονῇ ἐν τοῖς δεσμοῖς τοῦ εὐαγγελίου, 14 χωρὶς δὲ τῆς σῆς γνώμης οὐδὲν ἠθέλησα ποιῆσαι, ἵνα μὴ ὡς κατὰ ἀνάγκην τὸ ἀγαθόν σου ᾖ ἀλλὰ κατὰ ἑκούσιον. 15 τάχα γὰρ διὰ τοῦτο ἐχωρίσθη πρὸς ὥραν ἵνα αἰώνιον αὐτὸν ἀπέχῃς, 16 οὐκέτι ὡς δοῦλον ἀλλ᾽ ὑπὲρ δοῦλον, ἀδελφὸν ἀγαπητόν, μάλιστα ἐμοί, πόσῳ δὲ μᾶλλον σοὶ καὶ ἐν σαρκὶ καὶ ἐν κυρίῳ.

STRUCTURE

8	... παρρησίαν	ἔχων ἐπιτάσσειν	σοι ...
9	μᾶλλον παρακαλῶ, ...ὢν ...	Παῦλος πρεσβύτης	
		... καὶ δέσμιος ...	
10	—παρακαλῶ σε περὶ τοῦ		ἐμοῦ τέκνου,
		ὃν ἐγέννησα ...	
		Ὀνήσιμον,	
11		τόν ποτέ	σοι ἄχρηστον
		νυνὶ δὲ καὶ	σοὶ
		καὶ	ἐμοὶ εὔχρηστον,
12		ὃν ἀνέπεμψά	σοι,
		αὐτόν, ... τὰ	ἐμὰ σπλάγχνα
13	ὃν ... ἐβουλόμην ...	κατέχειν, ἵνα ...	διακονῇ
14	... οὐδὲν ἠθέλησα	ποιῆσαι, ἵνα μὴ ὡς κατὰ ἀνάγκην ... ᾖ	
		ἀλλὰ κατὰ ἑκούσιον	
15	... ἐχωρίσθη πρὸς ὥραν ἵνα		
		αἰώνιον αὐτὸν ἀπέχῃς,	
16		οὐκέτι ὡς δοῦλον	
		ἀλλ᾽ ὑπὲρ δοῦλον,	
		ἀδελφὸν ἀγαπητόν, μάλιστα	ἐμά,
		πόσῳ δὲ μᾶλλον σοί	

Structurally, this paragraph falls into three sections corresponding to the three sentences in Greek (vv. 8-12, 13-14, and 15-16):

(1) At the heart of vv. 8-12 lies Paul's appeal to Philemon on behalf of
     Onesimus (παρακαλῶ occurs twice in vv. 9-10), while the distinctive
     features of these verses are Paul's vivid description of himself
     (πρεσβύτης, δέσμιος, ἐγέννησα, vv. 9-10), his colorful portrait of Ones-
     imus (τοῦ ἐμοῦ τέκνου, ἄχρηστον, εὔχρηστον, τὰ ἐμὰ σπλάγχνα, vv. 10-12),
     and the intensely personal nature of his appeal to Philemon (σοι appears
     four times; ἐμοῦ, ἐμοί, ἐμά, vv. 8, 10-12).
(2) Verses 13 and 14 both have a verb of wishing followed by a complemen-
     tary inf. and a purpose clause.
(3) In vv. 15-16 we find a series of contrasts: ἐχωρίσθη—ἀπέχης, πρὸς
     ὥραν—αἰώνιον, ὡς δοῦλον—ὑπὲρ δοῦλον, μάλιστα—πόσῳ δὲ μᾶλλον,
     ἐμοί—σοί.

VERSE 8

Διό, πολλὴν ἐν Χριστῷ παρρησίαν ἔχων

Nom. sg. masc. (agreeing with the subj. of παρακαλῶ, v. 9a) of the pres. act.
ptc. of ἔχω, have. This ptc. is concessive (most EVV; Moule, *Idiom Book* 102;
Robertson, *Pictures* 466; T 157; ZG 652): "although I have." Διό ("so then";
"accordingly," NEB; "for this reason," GNB) bases Paul's appeal "in the name
of love" (v. 9a) on Philemon's evident possession of this virtue (vv. 5, 7).
Πολλῆς (acc. sg. fem. of πολύς, πολλή, πολύ, much, many) qualifies παρρησίαν
("boldness"; on this term see O'Brien 287-288). Ἐν Χριστῷ may mean simply
"as a Christian" (Goodspeed; cf. ἐν κυρίῳ in Col. 3:18) or may be brachylogy
for "as your brother in Christ" (GNB) or "because of your union with Christ"
(sim. TCNT; cf. 2 Cor. 13:4) or "in the name of Christ." See above For Further
Study 3, "The 'In Christ' Formula" (Col. 1:2).

ἐπιτάσσειν σοι τὸ ἀνῆκον

Pres. act. infin. of ἐπιτάσσω, order, command (+ dat.; here σοι). This is an
adnominal and epex. inf. that defines (πολλὴν . . .) παρρησίαν: lit. "having
much boldness to order you"; "though I am bold enough . . . to command you"
(RSV; sim. O'Brien 284). Acc. sg. neut. of the pres. act. ptc. of ἀνῆκει, an
impers. vb., it is due, becoming, proper, fitting. The neut. art. with the neut.
(sg. or pl.) of an adj. or (as here) of a ptc. used adjectivally creates an abstract
noun (cf. BDF § 263[2]; R 762-763; T 13-14). Thus τὸ μωρόν (1 Cor. 1:25) =
ἡ μωρία (1 Cor. 1:21), "foolishness"; τὸ ἀνῆκον (here) = "what is proper,"
"one's duty" (BAGD 66b; cf. 302b; H. Schlier, TDNT 1.360), "what should
be done" (GNB; sim. Goodspeed, NAB). Τὸ ἀνῆκον is either an acc. of respect

("with respect to your duty," "as to where your duty lies," Barclay) or a dir.
obj. after an implied ποιῆσαι (". . . to order you [to do] what is fitting"; sim.
BAGD 66b; most EVV; Lohse 196; O'Brien 284).

VERSE 9

διὰ τὴν ἀγάπην μᾶλλον παρακαλῶ

1 sg. pres. act. indic. of παρακαλέω, summon; exhort, comfort; request, appeal
to (with acc. σε understood; cf. v. 10a). Μᾶλλον ("rather" = "instead," following a neg. that may be supplied from the context, viz. "I do not order," BAGD
489c) modifies παρακαλῶ and highlights the contrast between issuing a command (v. 8) and making an appeal: "I make a request instead" (GNB), "I would
rather appeal to you" (NEB; sim. NASB; ZG 652), "I prefer to appeal to you"
(Goodspeed, Moffatt, RSV; sim. NAB). Διά + acc. specifies a reason: "because
of love," "on the basis of love" (NIV), "for love's sake" (BAGD 5c; RV, RSV,
NASB). The art. with ἀγάπην is anaphoric, referring back to what is familiar:
either Philemon's well-known love for all God's people (vv. 5, 7; "because of
that same love," NEB), or, less probably, Paul's own love for Philemon ("because I love you," GNB) or Christian love as an ethical touchstone.

τοιοῦτος ὢν ὡς Παῦλος πρεσβύτης

Nom. sg. masc. (agreeing with the subj. of παρακασλῶ in v. 9a or v. 10a) of
the pres. ptc. of εἰμί, be. This ptc. is either *concessive ("although I am,"
Weymouth; sim. TCNT, GNB; Moule 144; O'Brien 284, 290) or causal ("since
I am," NASB; BAGD 821c). Nom. sg. masc. of τοιοῦτος, τοιαύτη, τοιοῦτον, of
such a kind. This adj. may refer back to Paul's preference for brotherly appeal
over apostolic command (vv. 8-9a), in which case ὡς . . . Ἰησοῦ qualifies
παρακαλῶ σε (v. 10a; so Moffatt, NAB). *Alternatively, τοιοῦτος may point
forward to Paul's description of himself (ὡς Παῦλος κτλ., v. 9b, c), in which
case τοιοῦτος . . . ὡς are correlatives ("such a one as," RV; sim. NASB, Barclay;
ZG 652; Lightfoot 335-336).

   Πρεσβύτης, -ου, ὁ, has been rendered three main ways:

(1) "an old man" (RSV mg., GNB mg., JB, Barclay, NIV; cf. G. Bornkamm,
     TDNT 6.683; Lohse 196, 199),
(2) "the aged man" = "the aged" (RV, Weymouth, NASB), or
*(3) "an ambassador" (RV mg., TCNT, RSV; R 201-202; O'Brien 284, 290;
     sim. NEB, NAB; GNB and Moule [144], "the ambassador"; Goodspeed,
     "an envoy").

(2) is a possible tr. of anar. πρεσβύτης, but Παῦλος ὁ πρεσβύτης might have
been expected in this case (note the similar cstr. in v. 23 and Col. 4:7, 10, 14;

cf. Moule, *Idiom Book* 113). "The aged Paul" would normally require ὁ Παῦλος ὁ πρεσβύτης. (3) assumes either that πρεσβύτης is a spelling variant for πρεσβευτής, -οῦ, ὁ ("ambassador," from πρεσβεύω, be an ambassador, 2 Cor. 5:20; Eph. 6:20; thus Lightfoot 336-337; WH 1.499; 2[Appendix].136) or that the rdg. πρεσβευτής was original (F. J. A. Hort in WH 2[Appendix].136). See further MH 86-87. In connection with view (3), Χριστοῦ Ἰησοῦ is usually cstr. with πρεσβύτης as well as with δέσμιος—"an ambassador of/for Christ Jesus." Various ways of tr. this whole clause will be discussed below.

νυνὶ δὲ καὶ δέσμιος Χριστοῦ Ἰησοῦ

Νυνί, an intensive form of νῦν with the same mng. (BDF § 64[2]; BAGD 546b), is often linked, as here, with an adversative δέ: "but now a prisoner (δέσμιος, -ου, ὁ) of Christ Jesus (see v. 1 for these gens.) as well (adjunctive καί; see on Col. 3:4)," i.e., in addition to being his ambassador.

With respect to the punctuation of the Gk. text of v. 9, there are several options:

(1) τοιοῦτος . . . Ἰησοῦ forming a parenthesis, with the παρακαλῶ of v. 10 being resumptive (reflected in RSV, NASB),

(2) a period after παρακαλῶ (v. 9a), with a comma or a dash (sim. NEB, NIV) after Ἰησοῦ, or

*(3) a comma after παρακαλῶ (v. 9a), with a comma, a dash (WH 1.499; UBS[1, 2, 3]), a colon (RV), or *a period (Goodspeed, JB, Barclay; Lightfoot 335, 336) after Ἰησοῦ.

Given all these exegetical and punctuation options, it is not surprising that the EVV all differ. However, three representative trs. of v. 9 may be cited:

NASB: ". . . , [9] yet for love's sake I rather appeal *to you*—since I am such a person as Paul, the aged, and now also a prisoner of Christ Jesus— [10] I appeal . . ."

NEB: ". . . , [9] yet, because of that same love, I would rather appeal to you. Yes, I, Paul, ambassador as I am of Christ Jesus—and now his prisoner— [10] appeal . . ."

* ". . . , [9] I prefer to appeal to you on the basis of your love, though I am none other than Paul, an ambassador of Christ Jesus but now his prisoner as well. [10] I appeal. . . ."

VERSE 10

παρακαλῶ σε περὶ τοῦ ἐμοῦ τέκνου

Παρακαλῶ (see v. 9a) is resumptive after the lengthy concessive clause, τοιοῦτος ὢν κτλ. (v. 9b, c). Here περί (+ gen.) does not merely mean "concern-ing" but "for" (RV, TCNT, RSV, NIV) = ὑπέρ, "on behalf of" (Weymouth, Moffatt, GNB; ZG 652; Lohse 199 n. 23; on the interchange of περί and ὑπέρ see above on Col. 1:3; 4:3; Harris 1174); not "I entreat you about," but "I appeal to you on behalf of." The poss. adj. ἐμός, -ή, -όν, my, mine (often called a poss. pron.) is art. unless it is pred. ("mine," R 770). In the expression τῇ ἐμῇ χειρί (v. 19; Col. 4:18) it is emphatic ("with my own hand," BAGD 255c), as it probably is here also ("my own child," Weymouth; sim. GNB; "this child of mine," sim. TCNT, JB), given the clause that follows.

ὃν ἐγέννησα ἐν τοῖς δεσμοῖς Ὀνήσιμον

1 sg. aor. act. indic. of γεννάω, (of men) become the father of, beget; (of women) give birth to, bear (+ acc.). Paul views the process of bringing Ones-imus to spiritual birth (cf. 1 Cor. 4:15, 17) in a comprehensive glance (summary aor.). Ὅν, acc. sg. masc. of the rel. pron. ὅς, ἥ, ὅ, agrees with the real gender (masc.) rather than the grammatical gender (neut.) of its antecedent (τέκνου, neut., referring to Onesimus; cf. Col. 2:19; BAGD 583d, 584a; R 713). Tr.: "whose father I became/have become."

Δεσμός, -οῦ, ὁ; pl. δεσμά (neut.) and δεσμοί (masc.; BDF § 49[3]; MH 121-122), bond, fetter; by metonymy, prison; imprisonment. The dat. pl. here (after ἐν) could be neut. or masc. Τοῖς is either anaphoric or poss. Ἐν is either local or circumstantial. Thus "in this prison" (NEB), "while in my chains" (Weymouth), "during my imprisonment" (NAB).

We might have expected Paul to write περὶ τοῦ ἐμοῦ τέκνου Ὀνησίμου (gen. in appos. to τέκνου) ὃν ἐγέννησα. But, in a delicate touch, Paul makes clear to Philemon the new status of Onesimus as a Christian *before* he mentions his name. Standing after ὅν, Ὀνήσιμου is attracted to the case of this rel. pron. (viz. acc., Ὀνήσιμον, from Ὀνήσιμος, -ου, ὁ, Onesimus; see Col. 4:9) and stands in appos. to it (cf. Zerwick, *Analysis* 490). Some EVV reflect this emphatic position of Ὀνήσιμον by using a dash or starting a new sentence: "—I mean Onesimus" (Barclay; sim. Weymouth, NEB, JB), "It is Onesimus!" (sim. Moffatt).

VERSE 11

τόν ποτέ σοι ἄχρηστον νυνὶ δὲ καὶ σοὶ καὶ ἐμοὶ εὔχρηστον

The art. τόν agrees with Ὀνήσιμον (acc. sg. masc.) and modifies both ἄχρηστον and εὔχρηστον, functioning as a rel. pron. (as if Paul had written ὅς ποτέ σοι ἄχρηστον ἦν νυνὶ δὲ κτλ.; cf. Col. 1:23): "Who was (or, He was) at one time useless to you but now [he is/has become/will be] useful. . . ." Ποτέ, an enclitic particle (BAGD 695a), refers not to a single, particular occasion but to a former period of uselessness ("at one time," "formerly") and anticipates νυνὶ δέ (on which see v. 9 above and cf. Col. 1:21-22). Ἄχρηστος, -ον (useless, worthless) and εὔχρηστος, -ον (useful, serviceable), both two-termination adjs., form a play on words (paronomasia) that is esp. appropriate, since the adj. ὀνήσιμος, -ον means "useful," "profitable," "beneficial." This paronomasia can be reproduced in Eng. by "useless—useful" (many EVV), "unprofitable—profitable" (RV), or "a worthless character—'worth' something" (Moffatt). Εὔχρηστον may mean "really useful," i.e., not useful (ὀνήσιμος) only in name (ZG 652). Καὶ . . . καί means "both . . . and."

VERSE 12

ὃν ἀνέπεμψά σοι, αὐτόν

1 sg. aor. act. indic. of ἀναπέμπω, send back (+ acc. [ὅν] and dat. [σοι]), used of a lit. returning or of referring a case to or back to some other tribunal (Moule 145). Epistolary aor. (BDF § 334; Burton § 44; Moule, *Idiom Book* 12; Moule 145; Robertson 846; *Pictures* 467; ZG 652): "I am sending him back to you [with this letter]." Ὅν agrees with its antecedent Ὀνήσιμον (v. 10) in number (sg.) and gender (masc.) but its case (acc.) is determined by its function (dir. obj.) in its own clause. The RSV places v. 11 in a parenthesis; this associates ὅν with Ὀνήσιμον more clearly and highlights the parallelism of ὃν ἐγέννησα (v. 10b) and ὃν ἀνέπεμψα (v. 12a).

Αὐτόν is acc. sg. masc. (agreeing with ὅν, to which it is appos.) of the intensive pron. αὐτός, -ή, -ό, self. This use is probably not a Heb. (where an indecl. rel. pron. is followed by a pron. or pronominal suf.) but is either a redundant resumption of the rel. ὅν, as a prelude to τοῦτο κτλ. (Moule 145-146: "whom I am sending. . . ; and when I say [I am sending] him, I mean my very self," 146), or, more probably, simply emphatic (MH 434-435): "in his own person" (RV), "in person" (NASB). Scribes sought to ameliorate this text (read by ℵ* A 33) by adding the impv. προσλαβοῦ ("receive") from v. 17 and subsequently by inserting σὺ δέ ("and you") as the subj. of προσλαβοῦ. See Metzger 657-658 for further details.

τοῦτ᾽ ἔστιν τὰ ἐμὰ σπλάγχνα

Τοῦτ᾽ ἔστιν ("this/that means," "that is to say," BAGD 223d, 224a, 597b) is a formulaic phrase in the NT (the o of τοῦτο is lost by elision, BDF § 17), the nom. sg. neut. τοῦτο being used without regard to the number, gender, or case of the word(s) explained or of the words that provide the explanation (cf. BDF § 132[2]; R 399, 705). At this point the sentence (vv. 8-12 or vv. 10-12)

becomes anacoluthic, for αὐτόν, in appos. to ὅν, is acc., while τοῦτ(ο) and the
pred. τὰ ἐμὰ σπλάγχνα (after ἔστιν) are nom. On σπλάγχνα, see v. 7b. On the
poss. adj. ἐμά, which is here emphatic, see v. 10a. Tr.: "my very heart" (most
EVV; BAGD 763a), "my own self" (JB). This whole explanatory clause may
be rendered, "that is to say, (I am sending) my own heart," or more vividly,
"(I am sending him back to you), sending my very heart" (RSV).

VERSE 13

ὃν ἐγὼ ἐβουλόμην πρὸς ἐμαυτὸν κατέχειν

1 sg. impf. mid. indic. of dep. βούλομαι, wish, desire. This impf. has been tr.
in three basic ways:

(1) "I wished" (BAGD 422c), "It was my wish" (Weymouth), denoting the
    mere existence in the past of a state of desire, with no implication in the
    tense concerning the fulfillment of the desire.
(2) "I would like" (GNB; Moule 146 ["perhaps"]; cf. *Idiom Book* 9), "I
    should like" (TCNT). Here the tense is explained as "epistolary" (so
    Moule), i.e., written from the standpoint of Philemon after the arrival of
    Onesimus (Robertson, *Pictures* 467), or as a courteous use of the impf.
    indic. to express present time (R 919; but cf. 886 and ἐβουλόμην in Acts
    25:22).
*(3) "I would have liked" (Goodspeed, Moffatt, NIV; Lohse 196, 201;
    O'Brien 284, 293; sim. RV, RSV; BAGD 146b; Lightfoot 335), "I should
    have liked" (NEB, JB, BDF § 359[2]; ZG 653; cf. Burton § 33), express-
    ing a personal preference of the past that was put aside ("the desire
    awakened but arrested," Vincent 922) or a wish that was unfulfilled
    (T 91; but cf. 65). Cf. ἠθέλησα (aor.), "I determined," "I resolved," in
    v. 14, of an actual decision in the past.

Κατέχειν is the pres. act. infin. of κατέχω, hold back, hold down, hold
fast; retain, detain. Complementary infin. after ἐβουλόμην. Ὅν is acc. sg. masc.
of the rel. pron., referring to Ὀνήσιμον (v. 10). Ἐμαυτόν is acc. of the refl.
pron. of the first pers. sg., ἐμαυτοῦ, -ῆς, which is found only in gen., dat., and
acc. Πρὸς ἐμαυτόν, "with me," "at my side." In HGk πρός + acc. sometimes
expresses position (= παρά + dat.) as opposed to motion (BAGD 254a, 711a;
Moule, *Idiom Book* 53; Harris 1204-1205; cf. MH 467).

ἵνα ὑπὲρ σοῦ μοι διακονῇ ἐν τοῖς δεσμοῖς τοῦ εὐαγγελίου

3 sg. pres. act. subjunc. (after telic ἵνα) of διακονέω, serve, care for, help (+ dat.,
here the encl. μοι, dat. sg. of ἐγώ, with emphasis on the vb.; cf. BAGD 217b).

'Υπέρ here expresses substitution (= ἀντί, Harris 1174, 1196; ZG 653; cf. BAGD 838d-839a; R 631; Z § 91), "in your place" (Goodspeed, GNB, NAB; sim. Robertson, *Pictures* 467), "as your proxy" (Harris 1196; sim. Moffatt): Paul assumes that Philemon would have wished to attend to Paul's needs personally if such had been possible (Lightfoot 339). Σοῦ is accented thus, because after preps. (except πρός) only the accented forms of σύ and ἐγώ are used (BDF § 279; MH 180). Tr.: "so that he could continue helping (pres. tense) me in your place." On ἐν τοῖς δεσμοῖς, see v. 10b.

The gen. τοῦ εὐαγγελίου (art. according to the canon of Apollonius) may be:

(1) subj.:
"(in the bonds) which the gospel has brought to me" (Barclay; sim. JB), "(in these bonds) with which the Gospel has invested me" (Lightfoot's paraphrase, 335) as "a decoration of honour" (339) or
(2) a gen. of ref. or relation: "(while I am in prison) for the gospel" (NAB; sim. most EVV), "for the gospel's sake" (GNB; Zerwick, *Analysis* 491; sim. Lohse 202) = both "because of" and "in the interests of" the gospel.

VERSE 14

χωρὶς δὲ τῆς σῆς γνώμης οὐδὲν ἠθέλησα ποιῆσαι

1 sg. aor. act. indic. of θέλω, wish. For the aug. ἠ- instead of ἐ- and the relation of θέλω to the CGk vb. ἐθέλω, see BDF §§ 66(3), 101 (s.v. θέλειν); MH 188; R 205-206. The aor. could refer to a settled desire of the past, viewed unitarily ("I wanted"), but, in contrast to the impf. ἐβουλόμην ("I would have liked"), it rather points to a specific past decision ("But [adversative δέ] I resolved," "But I determined"); as Lightfoot (339) expresses it, "The will stepped in and put an end to the inclinations of the mind."

Ποιῆσαι is aor. act. infin. of ποιέω, do. Complementary infin. after ἠθέλησα. Οὐδέν is acc. sg. neut. of the adj./noun οὐδείς, οὐδεμία, οὐδέν, no; no one, nothing. Tr.: "I resolved to do nothing," "I refused to do anything"; "I did not want to do anything" (Moffatt, JB, NAB, NIV; sim. Barclay). Χωρίς is an adv. meaning "separately" but in the NT is usually an improper prep. (+ gen., here γνώμης) meaning "apart from," "without making use of/possessing something."

Γνώμη, -ης, ἡ, opinion, purpose, consent. Σῆς is gen. sg. fem. of the poss. adj. of second pers. sg. σός, σή, σόν, your(s), more emphatic than σοῦ or σεαυτοῦ (BAGD 759b). Tr.: "without your consent" (most EVV; BAGD 163b), "without having obtained/possessing your consent" (BAGD 890d).

ἵνα μὴ ὡς κατὰ ἀνάγκην τὸ ἀγαθόν σου ᾖ ἀλλὰ κατὰ ἑκούσιον

3 sg. pres. subjunc. (after telic ἵνα) of εἰμί, be. The neut. art. with the neut. (sg. or pl.) of an adj. creates a noun, τὸ ἀγαθόν, which may be specific and concrete ("good deed," "act of kindness"), generic ("good things" [Lk. 6:45], "a favor"), or abstract ("goodness," "kindness," "generosity"; cf. BDF § 263; R 762-763; T 13-14). The gen. σου may be poss. ("your") or subj. ("done by you"). Thus "your generosity" (TCNT), "this (anaphoric art.) kind action of yours" (Wey-mouth), "any favor you do" (NIV; O'Brien 284, 294). The allusion is to Philemon's "generous act" (κοινωνία, v. 6), not yet specified, of welcoming Onesimus back into his household—without punishment—as though he were welcoming Paul himself (v. 17) and then of manumitting him for service in the company of Paul (cf. vv. 13, 20-21).

Μή can be cstr. either with ἵνα ("in order that . . . not"), or, in a μὴ . . . ἀλλά contrast (cf. 1 Pet. 5:2-3), with ὡς κατὰ ἀνάγκην; the resulting mng. is not significantly different. Ὡς ("as") has here the sense of "having the appearance of" (sim. Goodspeed, Moffatt; Lightfoot 340), i.e., "seeming to be," or is equivalent to ὡσεί, "as if," or ὡσάν, "as it were" (TCNT, NASB; BAGD 52c), "so to speak" (cf. BDF § 453[3]). In each prep. phrase κατά specifies the cause, origin, or basis (BAGD 407b): "because of/from necessity" (ἀνάγκη, -ης, ἡ, necessity, compulsion) and "on the basis of/from [your own] free will." Ἑκούσιον is acc. sg. masc. or neut. of ἑκούσιος, -ία, ιον, voluntary, as a volunteer; willing, acting from free will. If ἑκούσιον is masc., τρόπον ("man-ner") is to be supplied (Lightfoot 340; Robertson, *Pictures* 467 ["perhaps"]); if it is neut., [τὸ] ἑκούσιον = willingness, free will. Either way, κατὰ ἑκούσιον = ἑκουσίως (adv.), willingly, voluntarily. Tr.: "so that your act of kindness should not appear to be forced but might be voluntary."

VERSE 15

τάχα γὰρ διὰ τοῦτο ἐχωρίσθη πρὸς ὥραν

3 sg. aor. pass. indic. of χωρίζω (act.), divide, separate; (pass.) be separated, be taken away; go away. "He went away" may be merely a euphemism for "he ran away" (ἔφυγεν; cf. ZG 653), but more probably this is a "theological passive" (cf. Z § 236), "he was separated [from you]" "by God," i.e., in the providential and hidden outworking of God's will (cf. Lightfoot 335; Lohse 202-203; O'Brien 286, 295). Here and in Rom. 5:7, the adv. τάχα ("perhaps," most EVV; "it may be," TCNT, GNB, Barclay) is used simply with the indic. instead of τάχ' ἄν + opt., usual in CGk (BAGD 806d; BDF § 385[1]). On the significance of γάρ, see above on v. 7. Διὰ τοῦτο ("on account of this") is prospective, pointing forward to ἵνα: "for this reason, (namely) that" (BAGD

597a; sim. 377b and most EVV). Πρὸς ὥραν (lit. "for an hour") is idiomatic, "for a short time" (GNB; cf. BAGD 710a), "for a while" (BAGD 896b).

ἵνα αἰώνιον αὐτὸν ἀπέχῃς

2 sg. pres. act. subjunc. (after telic ἵνα) of ἀπέχω, (act.) receive (payment) in full; (intrans.) be distant; (mid.) abstain. In this context the pref. ἀπ(ο)- signifies either (a) "in full/completely" (as in Phil. 4:18) or (b) "back." Thus, (a) "that you might possess him" (NAB), "that you might have him as your own/to yourself"; or (b) "that you might have him back" (sim. most EVV; Lightfoot 335, "regain him"). Weymouth combines both senses: "that you might receive him back wholly (and for ever) yours." Just as "from you" is implied with ἐχωρίσθη, so "with you" is to be understood with the antithetical ἀπέχῃς.

Αἰώνιον may be parsed in two ways: (a) acc. (of extent of time) sg. neut. of the subst. form (τὸ) αἰώνιον used adv. (on the analogy of μικρόν, "for a moment") or (b) acc. sg. masc. (agreeing with αὐτόν) of the two-termination adj. (but see MH 157) αἰώνιος, -ον, "eternal," used adv. Either way, it is adv. in mng. In general Gk. usage, the adj. αἰώνιον means "lasting for an age (αἰών)," and thus "eternal," "lifelong," "perpetual." Here, then, standing in contrast to πρὸς ὥραν, αἰώνιον may mean either of the following:

(1) "For ever/forever" (most EVV; Lohse 196, 202 n. 58, 203; cf. O'Brien 284, 296, who also has "permanently"). Lightfoot explains "for ever" (335) as " 'for all time and for eternity.' . . . Since he left, Onesimus had obtained eternal life, and eternal life involves eternal interchange of friendship" (340). On this view, Paul is gently suggesting (cf. τάχα) that in the divine providence the final result and therefore the ultimate purpose of Onesimus's flight was that he should become Philemon's "beloved brother" (v. 16) eternally, whether or not he resided in Philemon's household.

*(2) "Permanently" (Moule 146), "for good" (Moffatt, NEB, NIV; Moule 146), "for all time" (GNB). H. Sasse (TDNT 1.209) compares the expression οἰκέτης εἰς τὸν αἰῶνα, "slave for life," in Deut. 15:17 (cf. Exod. 21:6), and BAGD 28c refers to Job 40:28 (LXX; EVV 41:4), δοῦλον αἰώνιον, "permanent slave" (although both these authorities render αἰώνιον here by "for ever," apparently in the sense of "permanently"). In this case, Paul is envisaging the real possibility (cf. τάχα) that, as a result of Philemon's decision, Onesimus might always remain a slave in Philemon's household, albeit as a "beloved brother" (v. 16). Both τάχα and γάρ (see below) support this view.

Verses 14 and 15 state two reasons that Paul decided (ἠθέλησα, v. 14) not to follow his personal inclinations (ἐβουλόμην, v. 13) and keep Onesimus at his side as Philemon's proxy (v. 13): first, in order that (ἵνα, v. 14b) Philemon's "act of kindness" toward Onesimus and Paul should be voluntary; second, because (γάρ, "for," v. 15b) it was possible that the divine purpose behind Onesimus's flight was that Philemon should regain Onesimus in a permanent reunion.

VERSE 16

οὐκέτι ὡς δοῦλον ἀλλ᾽ ὑπὲρ δοῦλον, ἀδελφὸν ἀγαπητόν

Ὡς points to a subjective appraisal: "no longer regarded as a slave." A simple οὐκέτι δοῦλον would mean "no longer a slave," implying manumission. The final α of ἀλλά is elided before the initial vowel of ὑπέρ (cf. Col. 3:22). Ὑπέρ + acc., "over," "above," is used metaphorically of what excels or surpasses: "as one who is more than a slave" (BDF § 230; cf. R 632). After ὡς, ὑπέρ functions as a correlative: "no longer viewed as a mere slave but as more than a slave—as a dearly loved brother" (sim. Moffatt, GNB). Both instances of δοῦλον are in appos. to the preceding αὐτόν (v. 15b), and ἀδελφὸν ἀγαπητόν is in epex. appos. to the phrase ὑπὲρ δοῦλον. If Philemon decided to retain the services of Onesimus, the outward master-slave relation would remain unaltered, but a new inward relation would obtain—that of brothers in Christ (cf. vv. 7, 20, where Paul addresses Philemon as his ἀδελφός).

μάλιστα ἐμοί, πόσῳ δὲ μᾶλλον σοὶ καὶ ἐν σαρκὶ καὶ ἐν κυρίῳ

If μάλιστα (superl. of the adv. μάλα, very, very much) is a true superl., Paul is speaking hyperbolically (rather than illogically): "most of all to me, but . . . more so (μᾶλλον, comp. of μάλα) to you" (sim. Barclay; Lightfoot 341). But if μάλιστα is elative in mng. ("above all," "particularly"; "especially so," ZG 653), μᾶλλον can retain a strictly logical, comp. mng.: "dear especially to me, but how much dearer to you" (Goodspeed; sim. Moffatt, RSV, NEB, NASB, JB, NAB, NIV). This μάλιστα . . . δὲ μᾶλλον contrast (adversative δέ) relates to the preceding phrase ἀδελφὸν ἀγαπητόν. Onesimus was particularly dear to Paul as his son in the faith (v. 10).

Πόσῳ, dat. sg. neut. of πόσος, -η, -ον, how great/much/many, is dat. of measure or degree of difference (cf. Moule, *Idiom Book* 44; R 532): lit., "by how much (more to you)!" In contrasts such as ἐμοί, . . . δὲ . . . σοί the accented forms of the sg. obl. cases of ἐγώ and σύ are used (BDF § 279; BAGD 772b). Καὶ . . . καί means "both . . . and." Ἐν σαρκί and ἐν κυρίῳ are anar. as common, stereotyped prep. phrases. They delineate the two realms (locat. ἐν) in which Onesimus was related to Philemon as a "dear brother": first, "in the flesh" = on the outward and human level, "as a man" (Goodspeed, Moffatt, Barclay,

NAB, NIV; sim. TCNT, NEB), or (better) "as a slave" (GNB; sim. Weymouth); second, "in the Lord" = on the inward and spiritual level, "as a Christian" (Goodspeed, Moffatt, Barclay; BAGD 744b; ZG 653; sim. TCNT, Weymouth), "as a brother in the Lord" (GNB, JB, NIV). Onesimus would be an even dearer brother to Philemon than to Paul (πόσῳ . . . μᾶλλον σοί), perhaps because their dual relation as slave and master (ἐν σαρκί) and as Christian brothers (ἐν κυρίῳ) would be experienced within the intimacy of a single household.

Throughout vv. 15-16 Paul is entertaining the possibility that, having forgiven and reinstated Onesimus, Philemon will retain him as a slave. Nowhere in the letter does Paul demand the release of Onesimus or even assume that Philemon will set him free. But although the apostle accepts slavery as a social condition and as a legal fact (he returns Onesimus to his rightful owner with a promissory note to cover any indebtedness), he indirectly undermines the institution of slavery by setting the master-slave relation on a new footing when he highlights Onesimus's true status as a dearly loved Christian brother. See For Further Study 48, "Slavery in the NT."

TRANSLATION

[8] So then, although I have enough boldness in Christ to command you to do what should be done, [9] I prefer to appeal to you on the basis of your love, though I am none other than Paul, an ambassador of Christ Jesus but now his prisoner as well. [10] I appeal to you on behalf of my own child whose father I have become while in prison—I mean Onesimus. [11] At one time he was useless to you but now he has become "useful" both to you and to me. [12] I am sending him back to you, sending my very heart. [13] I would have liked to keep him with me, so that he could continue helping me in your place while I am imprisoned for the gospel. [14] But I decided to do nothing without your consent, so that your act of kindness should not appear to be forced but might be voluntary. [15] Moreover, it may be that he was separated from you for a short time precisely so that you might have him back permanently, [16] no longer as a slave but as more than a slave—as a dear brother, particularly to me but how much more to you, both as a slave and as a Christian.

EXPANDED PARAPHRASE

[8] So then, although I could quite appropriately issue you a bold command in the name of Christ to do what your Christian duty dictates in the present circumstances, [9] I prefer to make an appeal to you on the basis of your demonstrated love. Do I not have the right to command—I, Paul, an ambassador commissioned by Christ Jesus as his representative but now, in addition,

serving him as his prisoner? [10] My appeal to you is on behalf of my own child in the faith, someone whose father I became while here in prison. I am referring, of course, to Onesimus, [11] whom you have found to be virtually useless in the past, but now he lives up to his name and has thus become "useful" to both of us, to you and to me. [12] Now that I am sending him back to you with this letter, it is my very heart I am sending. [13] My own preference would have been to keep him here at my side so that he could continue to take your place, Philemon, in attending to all my needs during this imprisonment that I am suffering for the gospel's sake. [14] But I drew back from that course of action, for I did not wish to make any decision or take any action without having obtained your express consent, so that your kind action might come about of your own free will and not have the appearance of being forced. [15] It may well be, in God's providence, that you and he were separated from one another for a short time for the very purpose that you might have him back with you on a permanent basis, [16] no longer regarded by you as merely a slave but as something far better than a slave—as a dearly loved brother in Christ, especially dear to me but how much more so to you since he is now related to you by spiritual ties as a fellow Christian, as well as by human ties as a slave in your household.

FOR FURTHER STUDY

48. Slavery in the NT (v. 16)

Barrow, R. H., *Slavery in the Roman Empire* (New York: Barnes and Noble, 1968 reprint of 1928 ed.).

Bartchy, S. S., ΜΑΛΛΟΝ ΧΡΗΣΑΙ: First-Century Slavery and the Interpretation of I Corinthians 7:21 (Missoula, MT: University of Montana, 1973).

*———, ISBE 4.543-546.

Finley, M. I., ed., *Slavery in Classical Antiquity* (New York: Cambridge University, 1968[2]), esp. 229-236 ("Bibliographical Essay").

Judge, E. A., *The Social Pattern of Christian Groups in the First Century* (London: Tyndale, 1960).

Kittel, G., TDNT 2.43.

Lyall, F., "Roman Law in the Writings of Paul: the Slave and the Freedman," *NTS* 17 (1970-71) 73-79.

———, *Slaves, Citizens, Sons: Legal Metaphors in the Epistles* (Grand Rapids: Zondervan, 1984) 27-46.

Peterson, N. R., *Rediscovering Paul: Philemon and the Sociology of Paul's Narrative World* (Philadelphia: Fortress, 1985), esp. 240-257.

Rengstorf, K. H., TDNT 2.261-280.

Rollins, W. G., IDB 5.830-832.

Rupprecht, A. A., "Attitudes on Slavery among the Church Fathers," *New Dimensions in New Testament Studies,* ed. R. N. Longenecker and M. C. Tenney (Grand Rapids: Zondervan, 1974) 261-277.

*———, ZPEB 5.453-460.

Tuente, R., NIDNTT 3.589-598.

Westermann, W. L., *The Slave Systems of Greek and Roman Antiquity* (Philadelphia: American Philosophical Society, 1955).

Wiedemann, T., *Greek and Roman Slavery* (Baltimore: Johns Hopkins, 1981).

Wolff, H. W., "Masters and Slaves," *Interpretation* 27 (1973) 259-272.

HOMILETICAL SUGGESTIONS

Paul's General Appeal on Behalf of Onesimus (vv. 8-16)

1. Paul's choice not to command Philemon (v. 8)
2. Paul's appeal on behalf of Onesimus (vv. 9-10)
   (a) on the basis of Philemon's love (v. 9a; cf. vv. 5, 7)
   (b) as an ambassador of Christ Jesus (v. 9b)
   (c) as a prisoner of Christ Jesus (v. 9c)
   (d) as Onesimus's spiritual father (v. 10)
3. Paul's dispatch of Onesimus (vv. 10-12)
   (a) who was once useless (v. 11a)
   (b) who is now useful (v. 11b)
   (c) who is Paul's very heart (v. 12b)
4. Paul's decision not to detain Onesimus (vv. 13-16)
   (a) his personal preference (v. 13)
   (b) his considered decision, based on:
      (i) the need for Philemon's voluntary consent (v. 14)
      (ii) the possibility of Philemon's permanent gain (vv. 15-16)

Wishing and Willing (vv. 12-14; cf. Mk. 14:36; Phil. 2:4)

1. Paul's personal wish (v. 13)
   —to keep Onesimus at his side to attend to his needs as Philemon's deputy
2. Paul's decisive will (vv. 12, 14)
   —to return Onesimus to his master (v. 12) so that Philemon's "kindness" (v. 14) in welcoming Onesimus (v. 17) and then releasing him for service to Paul (cf. vv. 20-21) might be voluntary, not enforced.

D. PAUL'S SPECIFIC REQUESTS REGARDING ONESIMUS (VV. 17-20)

17 Εἰ οὖν με ἔχεις κοινωνόν, προσλαβοῦ αὐτὸν ὡς ἐμέ. 18 εἰ δέ τι ἠδίκησέν σε ἢ ὀφείλει, τοῦτο ἐμοὶ ἐλλόγα· 19 ἐγὼ Παῦλος ἔγραψα τῇ ἐμῇ χειρί, ἐγὼ ἀποτίσω· ἵνα μὴ λέγω σοι ὅτι καὶ σεαυτόν μοι προσοφείλεις. 20 ναί, ἀδελφέ, ἐγώ σου ὀναίμην ἐν κυρίῳ· ἀνάπαυσόν μου τὰ σπλάγχνα ἐν Χριστῷ.

STRUCTURE

17   εἰ οὖν *με ἔχεις* κοινωνόν,   προσλαβοῦ αὐτόν
18   εἰ δέ τι   ἠδίκησέν σε
         ἢ ὀφείλει, τοῦτο *ἐμοὶ*   *ἐλλόγα*
19   ἐγὼ Παῦλος ,   ἔγραψα
     ἐγὼ   ἀποτίσω
          ἵνα μὴ   *λέγω σοι* ὅτι καὶ *σεαυτόν μοι προσοφείλεις*
20   *ἐγώ σου*   *ὀναίμην* ἐν κυρίῳ
                      ἀνάπαυσόν μου τὰ σπλάγχνα·
                 ἐν Χριστῷ

(1) Note the high incidence of pers. prons., and the six instances (italicized) where first and second pers. forms are juxtaposed. Since this paragraph is the heart of the letter, it is not surprising that personal interrelationships feature so prominently.

(2) Paul makes three specific requests of Philemon, each expressed by an impv.: προσλαβοῦ (v. 17), ἐλλόγα (v. 18), ἀνάπαυσον (v. 20). The first of these three indicates the actual content of the request referred to in vv. 9-10 (παρακαλῶ . . . παρακαλῶ σε περὶ τοῦ ἐμοῦ τέκνου): "welcome him as you would me" (v. 17).

(3) Προσοφείλεις ("you owe [me] in addition [προσ-] [your very self]," v. 20) clearly echoes ὀφείλει ("[if] he owes [you anything]," v. 18).

VERSE 17

Εἰ οὖν με ἔχεις κοινωνόν

2 sg. pres. act. indic. of ἔχω, have, hold. When ἔχω is used with a double acc.—a dir. obj. (here με) and a pred. acc. (here κοινωνόν) with or without εἰς, ὡς, or ὅτι—it means "consider," "regard," "take to be" (cf. BAGD 333b; 440a; BDF § 157[1, 3]; R 480-481; T 246-247). Postpositive οὖν here is not inferential ("therefore") but transitional or resumptive ("so then"), reverting to the main theme of the letter, viz. Paul's request on behalf of Onesimus (vv. 9-10;

on οὖν see BDF § 451[1]; R 1191-1192). Εἰ = "if, as is true": the condition is assumed to be a reality (cf. Col. 2:20).

Κοινωνός, -οῦ, ὁ and ἡ, partner. In a Christian context this term implies more than mere friendship or similarity of outlook. It betokens spiritual unity in Christ and common loyalty to Christ, partnership in believing and working for the gospel (thus "partner in the faith," NEB; sim. ZG 653; F. Hauck, TDNT 3.807). Κοινωνόν is anar. because it is pred. and because emphasis is being placed on the qualities of the partnership (cf. Moulton 82-83); thus "a partner" (RV, NASB, Barclay), rather than "your partner" (RSV, GNB).

προσλαβοῦ αὐτὸν ὡς ἐμέ

2 sg. second aor. mid. impv. of προσλαμβάνω, (mid.) take aside/along; receive, welcome. It is likely that the vb. has here the technical mng. "receive into one's home/household" (cf. BAGD 717b) and that Paul is thereby (indirectly) requesting not only the forgiveness of Onesimus but also his reinstatement into the household of Philemon. Such a view does not exclude the possibility of his subsequent release by Philemon for service with Paul. But Robertson (*Pictures* 468) classifies this mid. as indirect: "take him to yourself as myself."

Ὡς ἐμέ means either (a) "as [you would receive/welcome] me" (sim. most EVV), where ὡς = καθώς, "in just the same way as"; (b) "as if he were I myself" (Weymouth; sim. RV; Lightfoot 335), where ὡς = ὡσεί or ὡσάν, "as if." Either way, v. 12 supplies the conceptual background; and ἐμέ is acc. under the influence of αὐτόν. When, as here, the emphasis falls on the pron., the longer, accented forms of the obl. cases of sg. ἐγώ are used (BAGD 217b; BDF § 279).

VERSE 18

εἰ δέ τι ἠδίκησέν σε ἢ ὀφείλει

3 sg. aor. act. indic. of ἀδικέω, (intrans.) do wrong; (trans.) treat unjustly; injure (+ double acc., τι . . . σε), lit. "if he has injured you anything" (= "in any way," NASB, JB). If Paul is alluding to poor service, the sense will be "if he has wronged you in any way" or "if he was ever dishonest"; if to theft, the sense is "if he has cheated you of any money" (Moffatt) or "if he has caused you any loss" (BAGD 17d; Goodspeed). Although Paul may actually have known of the loss incurred by Philemon and of the debt owed to him, with tact he describes the situation hypothetically in an open condition.

3 sg. pres. act. indic. of ὀφείλω, owe (something to someone [τινί τι]). With ὀφείλει we must therefore understand εἴ τι σοί, "if he owes you anything." The disjunctive particle ἢ ("or") here separates related terms (cf. BAGD 342a);

the financial debt (BAGD 598d) may have arisen from the "injury" or may define the nature of the "injury." Since Onesimus must have stolen from Philemon at least his fare to Rome, ὀφείλει may be a euphemism for theft. But neither the "injury" nor the "debt" can be specified with certainty (see O'Brien's discussion, 299-300).

τοῦτο ἐμοὶ ἐλλόγα

2 sg. pres. act. impv. of ἐλλογέω, charge something (acc., here τοῦτο) to someone's account (dat., here ἐμοί). Ἐλλόγα is an example of an -έω form (viz. ἐλλόγει, found in TR) being assimilated to an -άω form (MH 196; R 342). In HGk there is sometimes a confusion (in both directions) of the paradigms of -έω and -άω vbs. (BDF § 90). Τοῦτο refers to the debt implied by ὀφείλει and the compensatory damages (cf. ἀποτίσω, v. 19a) related to the "injury." On ἐμοί, see v. 17 on ἐμέ. Tr.: "charge it to me" (NAB, NIV), "put that down to my account" (Moffatt, NEB; sim. Barclay), "debit me with the amount" (Weymouth).

VERSE 19

ἐγὼ Παῦλος ἔγραψα τῇ ἐμῇ χειρί

1 sg. aor. act. indic. of γράφω, write. Epistolary aor. (cf. ἀνέπεμψα in v. 12; BDF § 334; Moule 148; Robertson, *Pictures* 468; ZG 653), "I am writing," referring not to the letter just finished (as R 845-846) but forward to the formal fiscal commitment of ἐγὼ ἀποτίσω. As in Col. 1:23, the ἐγώ with Παῦλος is probably emphatic (cf. 2 Cor. 10:1; Gal. 5:2). On τῇ ἐμῇ χειρί, see Col. 4:18a. Tr.: "I, Paul, am writing [this] with my own hand/in my own handwriting."

ἐγὼ ἀποτίσω

1 sg. fut. act. indic. of ἀποτίνω, make compensation; pay the damages (a legal term; see MM 71). The prefix ἀπο- signifies "back" (MH 298), thus "to pay back/repay" (most EVV); or it may signify "in full" (perfective ἀπο: "I will pay you in full," Weymouth). Tr.: "I will repay [you] myself" (emphatic ἐγώ), "I will make compensation for it" (Lohse 196).

This whole verse is "Paul's promissory note" (Robertson, *Pictures* 468), a χειρόγραφον (cf. Col. 2:14), a signed statement of indebtedness by which he formally and legally assumes all the indebtedness of Onesimus toward Philemon. The fact that Paul's autograph occurs here, and not, as usual, at the end of the letter (cf. 1 Cor. 16:21; Col. 4:18; 2 Thess. 3:17), does not prove that the whole letter was written in Paul's own hand. But such a view can scarcely be dismissed as implausible if we recall that the letter is relatively short and intensely personal and that it contains a formal promissory note.

ἵνα μὴ λέγω σοι ὅτι καὶ σεαυτόν μοι προσοφείλεις

1 sg. pres. act. subjunc. (after ἵνα) of λέγω, speak. This ἵνα could be impv. (T 95): "Let me not mention to you that (ὅτι). . . ." But it is better to take ἵνα here in its usual final sense and assume a preceding ellipsis (cf. Moule, *Idiom Book* 145) which may be marked in tr. by a dash (thus most EVV, although Weymouth, NASB, GNB, and Lohse [196, 204] make this whole sentence, ἵνα . . . προσοφείλεις, a parenthesis). This ellipsis may be "[I have thus become indebted to you]—not to mention to you that. . . ," or "[Accept this guarantee]/[You cannot really demand repayment from me], lest I remind you that . . ." Whatever the content of the ellipsis, ἵνα μὴ λέγω κτλ. is an instance of paralipsis (παράλειψις, a passing over), where the writer pretends to pass over (παραλείπω) a matter he actually mentions (cf. R 1199; Turner, *Style* 83).

Far less plausible is the proposal of an alternative punctuation: τοῦτο ἐμοὶ ἐλλόγα (. . .), ἵνα μὴ λέγω· σοί, ὅτι κτλ. "Charge this to *me* (. . .), not to say: to *you*, because . . ." (a case of epidiorthosis; cf. BDF § 495[1]). It is artificial and arbitrary to cstr. σοί with a distant or an implied ἐλλόγα and to render ὅτι "because," when λέγω + dat. + ὅτι is such a common NT cstr.

Προσοφείλεις is 2 sg. pres. act. indic. of προσοφείλω, owe (besides) something (acc.) to someone (dat.). Σεαυτόν is acc. masc. of the second pers. sg. refl. pron. σεαυτοῦ, -ῆς, yourself (used only in gen., dat., and acc.). Μοί is the encl. and unemphatic form of the dat. sg. of the first pers. personal pron. Given the HGk preference for compound forms even when they have the same sense as simple forms (Z § 484), προσοφείλω may not differ in mng. from ὀφείλω, owe (Zerwick, *Analysis* 491, ["perhaps"]). But here the prefix προσ- means "in addition" (MH 324) or "besides" (R 623) and corresponds to the adjunctive ("also," "as well") or ascensive ("even") καί. "In addition to your owing me any amount I might repay, you owe me your self as well" (or, "even your self" = "your very self" [NEB, GNB, Barclay, NAB, NIV; BAGD 717d], i.e., your Christian existence). Evidently Philemon was converted through Paul—not at Colossae (cf. Col. 2:1) but perhaps at Ephesus (cf. Acts 19:10; 20:31) or when Paul was on his way to Ephesus (cf. Acts 19:1; Lightfoot 303).

This addition in v. 19b to Paul's promissory note in v. 19a shows that he is not really envisaging a precise monetary debt or an actual legal obligation. He says, in effect: "If 'debts' are under review, you owe infinitely more to me than Onesimus does to you! I have not 'charged' you who are my son in the faith; you should not 'charge' Onesimus who is now your Christian brother. But if you choose to, I will pay on his behalf."

VERSE 20

ναί, ἀδελφέ, ἐγώ σου ὀναίμην ἐν κυρίῳ

1 sg. second aor. mid. opt. of ὀνίνημι, (mid.) derive benefit/joy/profit from, +
gen. denoting the source of the joy (here σου; BAGD 570d). This is a volitive
opt. (an "optative of wishing," Burton §§ 175-177), the only NT instance in
the first pers.; the other thirty-seven examples are in the third pers., fifteen of
them being μὴ γένοιτο ("may it never be!" R 939-940; cf. Moule, *Idiom Book*
23; Moule 149). Tr.: "Let me have some benefit from you in the Lord" (BAGD
570d; sim. Moule, *Idiom Book* 136).

Ναί ("yes") introduces an emphatic repetition (BAGD 533a): the "benefit" Paul hopes to derive from Philemon is Philemon's warm reception of
Onesimus back into his household (v. 17). Conceivably it could also include
the cancelling of Onesimus's debt now debited to Paul's account (v. 19) and
the release of Onesimus for further service to and with Paul (see v. 21). On
ἀδελφέ, see v. 7. As in vv. 13 and 19, ἐγώ is emphatic: Philemon's generosity
toward Onesimus would bring as much pleasure and benefit to Paul as it would
to Onesimus himself. If ἐν κυρίῳ is cstr. with ἀδελφέ or σου, it may mean "as
a Christian" (NEB; cf. Col. 3:18) or "because of your union with the Lord"
(TCNT); if with ὀναίμην, it means "for the Lord's sake" (Weymouth, GNB) or
"in a Christian sense" (Goodspeed; cf. Barclay, "some Christian profit").

ἀνάπαυσόν μου τὰ σπλάγχνα ἐν Χριστῷ

2 sg. aor. act. impv. of ἀναπαύω, (trans.) give rest to, refresh; (mid.) rest. On
τὰ σπλάγχνα, see v. 7b. The poss. μου is emphatic by position and because it
corresponds to τῶν ἁγίων in v. 7: "What you have done for others, now do for
me. Refresh this heart of mine." Ἐν Χριστῷ is not instr. ("by your Christlike
spirit," TCNT); the means of the refreshment is expressed by v. 20a, viz. by
Paul's deriving some profit from Philemon. The phrase belongs with the impv.:
"Cheer my heart as a Christian" (Goodspeed; cf. ἐν κυρίῳ in v. 20a), "as a
brother in Christ, cheer me up!" (GNB).

TRANSLATION

[17] So if you regard me as a partner, welcome him as you would me. [18] And if
he has caused you any loss or owes you anything, charge it to me. [19] I, Paul,
am writing this with my own hand: I will repay you myself—not to mention
that you owe me in addition your very self. [20] Yes, brother, let me derive some
profit from you in the Lord. Refresh my heart in Christ!

EXPANDED PARAPHRASE

[17] So then, since you consider me a partner in the faith, give Onesimus, my partner in the faith, the same ready welcome on his arrival that you would afford me. [18] Has he caused you any loss? Does he owe you anything? Charge any such debts to my account. [19] I, Paul, am giving this guarantee, this IOU, in my own handwriting: I myself will repay all his debts. I have thus become indebted to you for some trifling amount—to say nothing about the immeasurably greater debt that you owe me, your very self! [20] Yes, dear brother, let me gain some benefit from you such as your father in the faith might rightly expect. Refresh this heart of mine as a brother in Christ!

HOMILETICAL SUGGESTIONS

Paul's Specific Requests regarding Onesimus (vv. 17-20)

1. Welcome (προσλαβοῦ) Onesimus as you would me (v. 17b),
   since (εἰ) you consider me your partner in the faith (v. 17a).
2. Charge Onesimus's debts to my account (ἐλλόγα, v. 18b),
   if (εἰ) he has caused you loss or owes you anything (v. 18a).
   I give you this written guarantee of repayment (v. 19a),
   but remember that you owe your spiritual life to me! (v. 19b)
3. Refresh (ἀνάπαυσον) my heart in Christ (v. 20b)
   by letting me gain some benefit from you (v. 20a).

The Gospel in a Mirror (vv. 17-19a)

1. When we come to God in repentance and faith, he welcomes us as if we were Christ (v. 17).
2. What we owe God, he has debited to Christ's account (v. 18).
3. Christ assumed personal responsibility for the full repayment of our debt to God (v. 19).

E. FINAL REMARKS, GREETINGS, AND BENEDICTION
(VV. 21-25)

21 Πεποιθὼς τῇ ὑπακοῇ σου ἔγραψά σοι, εἰδὼς ὅτι καὶ ὑπὲρ ἃ λέγω ποιήσεις. 22 ἅμα δὲ καὶ ἑτοίμαζέ μοι ξενίαν, ἐλπίζω γὰρ ὅτι διὰ τῶν προσευχῶν ὑμῶν χαρισθήσομαι ὑμῖν. 23 Ἀσπάζεταί σε Ἐπαφρᾶς ὁ συναιχμάλωτός μου ἐν Χριστῷ Ἰησοῦ, 24 Μᾶρκος, Ἀρίσταρχος, Δημᾶς, Λουκᾶς, οἱ συνεργοί μου. 25 Ἡ χάρις τοῦ κυρίου Ἰησοῦ Χριστοῦ μετὰ τοῦ πνεύματος ὑμῶν.

STRUCTURE

21	Πεποιθὼς ...	ἔγραψά		σοι,
	εἰδὼς ... ὑπὲρ ἃ	λέγω	ποιήσεις	
22			ἑτοίμαζε	
		ἐλπίζω ... διὰ τῶν προσευχῶν		ὑμῶν
		χαρισθήσομαι		ὑμῖν
23	Ἀσπάζεταί σε	Ἐπαφρᾶς ὁ συναιχμάλωτός		μου. . . ,
24		Μᾶρκος,		
		Ἀρίσταρχος,		
		Δημᾶς,		
		Λουκᾶς,	οἱ συνεργοί	μου
25	Ἡ χάρις ...	μετὰ τοῦ πνεύματος		ὑμῶν

VERSE 21

Πεποιθὼς τῇ ὑπακοῇ σου ἔγραψά σοι

Nom. sg. masc. (agreeing with the subj. of ἔγραψα) of the second pf. act. ptc. of πείθω, (act.) persuade, convince; (pass.) be persuaded; believe; obey. The second pf. has a pres. mng., "rely on," "trust in," "put one's confidence in" + dat. (here, τῇ ὑπακοῇ; BAGD 639c; BDF § 341; T 82; R 881). The reliance or confidence is contemporaneous with the writing (ἔγραψα).

ㅤㅤὙπακοή, -ῆς, ἡ, may mean:

(1) "obedience":
ㅤㅤto God's will (O'Brien 305, 308),
ㅤㅤto Paul (as God's representative; cf. BAGD 837a, citing 2 Cor. 7:15; 10:6),
ㅤㅤto the word of Paul (Lohse 206 and n. 2),
ㅤㅤto Philemon's duty/what should be done (τὸ ἀνῆκον, v. 8), or
ㅤㅤto what Philemon's conscience indicated was right; or

*(2) "compliance":
      with Paul's wishes/requests.

Tr.: either "relying on your obedience" (Moffatt; sim. Goodspeed, RSV, NASB,
NIV) or "confident of your compliance" (NAB; sim. TCNT, Weymouth, NEB,
JB; ZG 653; Lightfoot 341; Robertson, *Pictures* 469). In light of Paul's decision
not to issue commands (for obedience; vv. 8-9) but to seek Philemon's express
and willing consent (γνώμη, v. 14), "compliance" seems more in keeping with
the delicate tact of the letter.

Ἔγραψα is 1 sg. aor. act. indic. of γράφω, write, probably an epistolary
aor., "I am writing" (as in v. 19; Robertson, *Pictures* 469; BDF § 334 [cited
with ?]; most EVV), but it could be preterit and refer to the letter, in its essence,
as already written (viz. "I have written").

εἰδὼς ὅτι καὶ ὑπὲρ ἃ λέγω ποιήσεις

Nom. sg. masc. (agreeing with the subj. of ἔγραψα) of the pf. act. ptc. of οἶδα,
know, a pf.-pres. vb. (see on Col. 3:24; 4:1). The ptc. is causal, "for I know"
(Weymouth; sim. NASB, Barclay), qualifying πεποιθώς. Ποιήσεις is 2 sg. fut.
act. indic. of ποιέω, do. Ὑπέρ + acc., "over," "above," is used metaphorically
(as in v. 16) of what surpasses, "more than." This prep. governs the rel. pron.
ἃ (acc. pl. neut., the obj. of λέγω) but in reality it belongs to an omitted
demonstrative pron. (BAGD 583b, c), viz. ταῦτα: "more than [these things] that
I say," "beyond what I am asking" (i.e., in this written communication; BAGD
469d). Καί is probably ascensive ("even," BAGD 393b; sim. most EVV) and
qualifies ὑπέρ, although NEB takes it as emphatic and qualifying ποιήσεις ("I
know that you will in fact do better than I ask").

There are several possible identifications of this undefined and climactic
"more":

(1) an even more generous reception for Onesimus than Paul has proposed
    (in v. 17), or, more specifically,
(2) forgiveness and reinstatement of Onesimus in Philemon's household, or
*(3) manumission of Onesimus for Christian service either at Colossae or at
    Rome with Paul. Lightfoot comments: "The word 'emancipation' seems
    to be trembling on his [Paul's] lips, and yet he does not once utter it"
    (321; cf. 343). See the discussion in Lohse 206; O'Brien 267, 305-306.

That the "more" is not defined, is significant. When Paul appeals to his
position as Philemon's Christian brother (vv. 7, 20) and spiritual father (v. 19),
when he mentions Philemon's widely attested love (vv. 5, 7, 9) and his faith
that prompts generosity (v. 6a), when he calls himself an imprisoned ambassador of Christ (vv. 1, 9, 10, 13), when he foregoes his apostolic right to give

commands (vv. 8-9) and chooses to request Philemon's voluntary consent (v. 14), when he issues a promissory note to cover Onesimus's debts (vv. 18, 19a), when he expresses confidence in Philemon's compliance (v. 21) and intimates that he plans to visit Philemon after his anticipated release (and can thus personally reassure himself that Philemon has done his Christian duty, vv. 8, 22), then he is putting considerable psychological or spiritual pressure on Philemon to comply with his basic request (v. 17) and extend to Onesimus a ready welcome on his return to Colossae. Yet although he assumes Philemon's compliance with this basic request (v. 21), he leaves him free, beyond this, to follow the dictates of his Christian conscience in determining how his ἀγάπη (vv. 5, 7) should be expressed, and seriously entertains the possibility that Philemon might decide to retain the services of Onesimus as a slave permanently (vv. 15-16).

VERSE 22

ἄμα δὲ καὶ ἑτοίμαζέ μοι ξενίαν

2 sg. pres. act. impv. of ἑτοιμάζω, prepare; put/keep in readiness (of preparations for receiving and entertaining someone; BAGD 316b). Ξενία, -ας, ἡ, hospitality; guest room (either in an inn or in a private house). The pres. impv. may be rendered "keep a guest room ready," "be getting a room ready" (ZG 653 ["perhaps"]), "have a room ready" (NEB). Μοι, dat. of advantage or interest (cf. Col. 4:11). The adv. ἄμα, "at the same time," makes precise the temporal coincidence of two actions (BAGD 42a; BDF § 425[2]), here, compliance with Paul's requests (v. 21) and keeping quarters ready for Paul's visit (v. 22a). Δέ, if tr., is conj. ("and"), while καί is adjunctive (["at the same time] also").

This Pauline injunction represents a change in the apostle's travel plans (see Rom. 15:23-24, 28), possibly prompted by the seriousness of the situation at Colossae and generally in the Lycus Valley.

ἐλπίζω γὰρ ὅτι διὰ τῶν προσευχῶν ὑμῶν χαρισθήσομαι ὑμῖν

1 sg. fut. pass. indic. of dep. χαρίζομαι, graciously confer; grant as a favor; forgive; grant somebody (acc.) to someone (dat.). Here the dir. obj. of the mid. voice (act. in Eng.; "[God] will grant me to you") has become the subj. in the pass. ("I shall be [granted =] restored to you [by God]," a "theological pass."; cf. Z § 236). Γάρ introduces the reason for the request ἑτοίμαζε κτλ. Whether διά (+ gen.) is thought to express means ("through") or to denote the occasion (BAGD 180c; "as a consequence of"), the sense is "through/as a consequence of [God's answering] your prayers" = "in answer to your prayers" (TCNT,

Goodspeed, NEB, NIV; O'Brien 304). Second pers. pl. (ὑμῶν . . . ὑμῖν) is seen here for the first time since v. 3; to indicate this, TCNT has ". . . given back to you all," and GNB, ". . . the prayers of all of you." Paul assumes that Philemon and his household and the whole Colossian church (vv. 1-2) are praying for his release from prison and an early visit.

VERSE 23

Ἀσπάζεταί σε Ἐπαφρᾶς ὁ συναιχμάλωτός μου ἐν Χριστῷ Ἰησοῦ

3 sg. pres. mid. indic. of dep. ἀσπάζομαι, greet. On the position and sg. number of this vb. (pedantically, TR has the pl. ἀσπάζονται) and on the anar. Ἐπαφρᾶς and art. συναιχμάλωτος, see Col. 4:10. On Epaphras, see Col. 1:7-8; 4:12-13. Ὁ συναιχμάλωτός μου ("my fellow prisoner") means either "who is in prison with me" (GNB; sim. JB; Lohse 207 and n. 15; O'Brien 307) or "(Christ's) captive like myself" (NEB; sim. Moule 136-137; Robertson, *Pictures* 469, who cites the vb. αἰχμαλωτίζω, "take captive" [2 Cor. 10:5] as also being fig.). For a defense of the latter, the fig. mng., see on Col. 4:10. Ἐν Χριστῷ Ἰησοῦ, "for the sake of Christ Jesus" (Weymouth, GNB; sim. TCNT, Goodspeed) or "in the cause/service of Christ Jesus." It is quite unnecessary to follow Lohse (172 n. 26, 176 n. 54, 206, 207 n. 16) and others in the conjecture that the final letter of Ἰησοῦς was accidentally omitted in the course of scribal transmission and that in reality Ἰησοῦς (= Ἰησοῦς ὁ λεγόμενος Ἰοῦστος, Col. 4:11) is the first of five persons mentioned in vv. 23-24 as Paul's coworkers (cf. Col. 4:10-14). The Χριστὸς Ἰησοῦς combination is also found in vv. 1, 9.

VERSE 24

Μᾶρκος, Ἀρίσταρχος, Δημᾶς, Λουκᾶς, οἱ συνεργοί μου

For these names, see Col. 4:10, 14. Along with Epaphras (v. 23), each of these men sends his greetings to Philemon (ἀσπάζεταί σε, from v. 23a). Συνεργός, -όν (a two-termination adj.), working together with, helping; (subst.) helper, coworker. Cf. v. 1 and Col. 4:11. Συνεργοί is nom. pl. in appos. to the four preceding proper names. Μου refers to Paul, not Timothy (cf. v. 1). See above For Further Study 43, "Paul and His Coworkers" (Col. 4:7).

VERSE 25

Ἡ χάρις τοῦ κυρίου Ἰησοῦ Χριστοῦ μετὰ τοῦ πνεύματος ὑμῶν

Εἴη ("may it be," 3 sg. opt. of εἰμί) may be understood with χάρις. The gens.

τοῦ κυρίου ᾽Ιησοῦ Χριστοῦ are either poss. ("belonging to") or subj. ("given by"; cf. v. 3). The addition of ἡμῶν after κυρίου (A C D K Ψ it vg syrᵖ copˢᵃ, ᵇᵒ eth *al*) is clearly a secondary rdg.; the shorter rdg., simply κυρίου, read by ℵ P 33 1739 syrʰ, ᵖᵃˡ arm, is to be preferred (cf. Metzger 658).

Τοῦ πνεύματος (gen. after μετά) is a distributive sg. (cf. BDF § 140; R 409; T 23-25; Goodspeed, "your spirits"). As in Gal. 6:18; Phil. 4:23, μετὰ τοῦ πνεύματος ὑμῶν ("with your spirit") is simply a variation of μεθ᾽ ὑμῶν ("with you," 1 Thess. 5:28), i.e., τὸ πνεῦμα ὑμῶν ("your spirit") = ὑμεῖς ("you"; cf. E. Schweizer, TDNT 6.435). Although numerous authorities add the customary concluding ἀμήν after ὑμῶν, it is a secondary addition; important Alexandrian (A 33 81 copˢᵃ *al*) and Western (D* itᵈ *al*) witnesses omit it.

TRANSLATION

²¹ I am writing this to you confident of your compliance, for I know that you will do even more than I am asking. ²² At the same time also, keep a guest room ready for me, for I hope to be restored to you through your prayers. ²³ Epaphras, my fellow prisoner in Christ Jesus, sends you his greetings. ²⁴ So do my coworkers, Mark, Aristarchus, Demas, and Luke. ²⁵ The grace of the Lord Jesus Christ be with your spirit.

EXPANDED PARAPHRASE

²¹ It is because I am confident that you will accede to my requests and do what I ask that I am writing to you like this. In fact I know that you will go beyond my actual requests. ²² At the same time also, please prepare a guest room and keep it ready for me, for I am hoping that I shall shortly be set free and restored to all of you in answer to your prayers for me.
²³ I pass on greetings to you, Philemon, from Epaphras, my fellow prisoner for the sake of Christ Jesus, ²⁴ and from my coworkers, Mark, Aristarchus, Demas, and Luke. ²⁵ May the grace given by the Lord Jesus Christ be with you, your household, and the whole church, sanctifying the spirit of each of you.

HOMILETICAL SUGGESTIONS

Final Remarks, Greetings, and Benediction (vv. 21-25)

1. Final Remarks (vv. 21-22)
   (a) Paul's confident expectation (πεποιθὼς . . . εἰδώς . . .) of:
       (i) Philemon's compliance (v. 21a)

(ii) Philemon's exceeding (ὑπέρ) Paul's requests (v. 21b)
  (b) Philemon's preparation for Paul's anticipated visit (v. 22)
2. Greetings (vv. 23-24)
  (a) from a fellow (συν-) prisoner: Epaphras (v. 23)
  (b) from four co- (συν-) workers: Mark, Aristarchus, Demas, and Luke (v. 24)
3. Benediction (v. 25)

Translation

¹ Paul, a prisoner of Christ Jesus, and Timothy our brother, to Philemon our dear friend and coworker, ² to Apphia our sister, to Archippus our fellow soldier, and to the church in your house. ³ Grace and peace to you from God our Father and the Lord Jesus Christ.

⁴ I always give thanks to my God when I mention you in my prayers, ⁵ because I hear of your love for all God's people and the faith you have in the Lord Jesus. ⁶ I pray that the generosity which your faith prompts may effectively increase your knowledge of every blessing we have in our relation to Christ. ⁷ From your love I have derived much joy and comfort, because through you, my brother, the hearts of God's people have been refreshed.

⁸ So then, although I have enough boldness in Christ to command you to do what should be done, ⁹ I prefer to appeal to you on the basis of your love, though I am none other than Paul, an ambassador of Christ Jesus but now his prisoner as well. ¹⁰ I appeal to you on behalf of my own child whose father I have become while in prison—I mean Onesimus. ¹¹ At one time he was useless to you but now he has become "useful" both to you and to me. ¹² I am sending him back to you, sending my very heart. ¹³ I would have liked to keep him with me, so that he could continue helping me in your place while I am imprisoned for the gospel. ¹⁴ But I decided to do nothing without your consent, so that your act of kindness should not appear to be forced but might be voluntary. ¹⁵ Moreover, it may be that he was separated from you for a short time precisely so that you might have him back permanently, ¹⁶ no longer as a slave but as more than a slave—as a dear brother, particularly to me but how much more to you, both as a slave and as a Christian.

¹⁷ So if you regard me as a partner, welcome him as you would me. ¹⁸ And if he has caused you any loss or owes you anything, charge it to me. ¹⁹ I, Paul, am writing this with my own hand: I will repay you myself—not to mention

that you owe me in addition your very self. [20] Yes, brother, let me derive some profit from you in the Lord. Refresh my heart in Christ!

[21] I am writing this to you confident of your compliance, for I know that you will do even more than I am asking. [22] At the same time also, keep a guest room ready for me, for I hope to be restored to you through your prayers.

[23] Epaphras, my fellow prisoner in Christ Jesus, sends you his greetings. [24] So do my coworkers, Mark, Aristarchus, Demas, and Luke. [25] The grace of the Lord Jesus Christ be with your spirit.

Expanded Paraphrase

¹ This letter comes from Paul, now the prisoner of Christ Jesus, and from our brother and colleague Timothy, to Philemon our dear friend and coworker in the gospel, ² to our sister Apphia, to our fellow soldier Archippus, and to the church that meets in Philemon's home. ³ May the grace and peace that come from God our heavenly Father and the Lord Jesus Christ be your portion.

⁴ Whenever I mention you in my prayers, Philemon, without fail I give thanks to my God, ⁵ because I continue to hear of your love and faith—the faith you have in the Lord Jesus and the love you show to all God's people. ⁶ It is my prayer that your Christian generosity, prompted as it is by your faith, may prove effective in increasing your appreciation and experience of all the spiritual blessings that are ours to enjoy because of our relationship with Christ. ⁷ Your love has brought deep joy and great comfort to me, because through that love of yours, my brother, the hearts of God's people have been refreshed.

⁸ So then, although I could quite appropriately issue you a bold command in the name of Christ to do what your Christian duty dictates in the present circumstances, ⁹ I prefer to make an appeal to you on the basis of your demonstrated love. Do I not have the right to command—I, Paul, an ambassador commissioned by Christ Jesus as his representative but now, in addition, serving him as his prisoner? ¹⁰ My appeal to you is on behalf of my own child in the faith, someone whose father I became while here in prison. I am referring, of course, to Onesimus, ¹¹ whom you have found to be virtually useless in the past, but now he lives up to his name and has thus become "useful" to both of us, to you and to me. ¹² Now that I am sending him back to you with this letter, it is my very heart I am sending. ¹³ My own preference would have been to keep him here at my side so that he could continue to take your place, Philemon, in attending to all my needs during this imprisonment that I am suffering for the gospel's sake. ¹⁴ But I drew back from that course of action, for I did not wish to make any decision or take any action without having obtained your

express consent, so that your kind action might come about of your own free will and not have the appearance of being forced. [15] It may well be, in God's providence, that you and he were separated from one another for a short time for the very purpose that you might have him back with you on a permanent basis, [16] no longer regarded by you as merely a slave but as something far better than a slave—as a dearly loved brother in Christ, especially dear to me but how much more so to you since he is now related to you by spiritual ties as a fellow Christian, as well as by human ties as a slave in your household. [17] So then, since you consider me a partner in the faith, give Onesimus, my partner in the faith, the same ready welcome on his arrival that you would afford me. [18] Has he caused you any loss? Does he owe you anything? Charge any such debts to my account. [19] I, Paul, am giving this guarantee, this IOU, in my own handwriting: I myself will repay all his debts. I have thus become indebted to you for some trifling amount—to say nothing about the immeasurably greater debt that you owe me, your very self! [20] Yes, dear brother, let me gain some benefit from you such as your father in the faith might rightly expect. Refresh this heart of mine as a brother in Christ!

[21] It is because I am confident that you will accede to my requests and do what I ask that I am writing to you like this. In fact I know that you will go beyond my actual requests. [22] At the same time also, please prepare a guest room and keep it ready for me, for I am hoping that I shall shortly be set free and restored to all of you in answer to your prayers for me.

[23] I pass on greetings to you, Philemon, from Epaphras, my fellow prisoner for the sake of Christ Jesus, [24] and from my coworkers, Mark, Aristarchus, Demas, and Luke. [25] May the grace given by the Lord Jesus Christ be with you, your household, and the whole church, sanctifying the spirit of each of you.

Exegetical Outline

For the correlation between these outlines and the Greek text, see the first entry under "Homiletical Suggestions" for each section.

A. Introductory Greeting (vv. 1-3)
    1. The writers—Paul (and Timothy; v. 1a)
    2. The addressees—
       Philemon (v. 1b)
       Apphia
       Archippus
       the church in Philemon's house (v. 2)
    3. The greeting—grace and peace (v. 3)
B. Thanksgiving and Intercession for Philemon (vv. 4-7)
    1. Thanksgiving for Philemon (vv. 4-5)
      (a) its frequency (v. 4)
      (b) its cause (v. 5)
    2. Intercession for Philemon (v. 6)
       its content (v. 6)
    3. Joy and comfort from Philemon (v. 7)
      (a) their cause—love shown by Philemon
      (b) their cause further defined—refreshment given by Philemon
C. Paul's General Appeal on Behalf of Onesimus (vv. 8-16)
    1. Paul's choice not to command Philemon (v. 8)
    2. Paul's appeal on behalf of Onesimus (vv. 9-10)
      (a) on the basis of Philemon's love (v. 9a; cf. vv. 5, 7)
      (b) as an ambassador of Christ Jesus (v. 9b)
      (c) as a prisoner of Christ Jesus (v. 9c)
      (d) as Onesimus's spiritual father (v. 10)
    3. Paul's dispatch of Onesimus (vv. 10-12)
      (a) who was once useless (v. 11a)

        (b) who is now useful (v. 11b)

        (c) who is Paul's very heart (v. 12b)

    4. Paul's decision not to detain Onesimus (vv. 13-16)

        (a) his personal preference (v. 13)

        (b) his considered decision, based on:

             (i) the need for Philemon's voluntary consent (v. 14)

           (ii) the possibility of Philemon's permanent gain (vv. 15-16)

D. Paul's Specific Requests regarding Onesimus (vv. 17-20)

    1. Welcome Onesimus as you would me (v. 17b),
        since you consider me your partner in the faith (v. 17a).

    2. Charge Onesimus's debts to my account (v. 18b),
        if he has caused you loss or owes you anything (v. 18a).
        I give you this written guarantee of repayment (v. 19a),
        but remember that you owe your spiritual life to me! (v. 19b)

    3. Refresh my heart in Christ (v. 20b)
        by letting me gain some benefit from you (v. 20a).

E. Final Remarks, Greetings, and Benediction (vv. 21-25)

    1. Final Remarks (vv. 21-22)

        (a) Paul's confident expectation of:

             (i) Philemon's compliance (v. 21a)

           (ii) Philemon's exceeding Paul's requests (v. 21b)

        (b) Philemon's preparation for Paul's anticipated visit (v. 22)

    2. Greetings (vv. 23-24)

        (a) from a fellow prisoner: Epaphras (v. 23)

        (b) from four coworkers: Mark, Aristarchus, Demas, and Luke
            (v. 24)

    3. Benediction (v. 25)

Glossary of Grammatical
and Rhetorical Terms

This is not a comprehensive list. For items not listed, or for further details on the terms discussed, consult the indices of the larger grammars. Where possible or needed, examples are drawn from Colossians or Philemon, so that the reader can refer to the relevant discussion in the text. These examples are sometimes merely possible or proposed instances of the usage in question but references to the grammars or other literature are often listed there. A diagonal line (/) is used between different terms for the same item of grammar or rhetoric, or to indicate variant translations.

Absolute (from Lat. *absolutus,* independent)
When a word is "standing alone," it is said to be absolute; e.g., a noun without syntactical relation to its sentence (Col. 3:17) or a verb without its usual object (Matt. 7:7). When a subject (noun or pronoun) and a participle both stand in the genitive, usually at the beginning of a sentence or clause, and are grammatically unrelated to the rest of the sentence, they form a *genitive absolute* clause (2 Cor. 2:12). A nominative or accusative substantive or participle that is syntactically unrelated to the sentence in which it stands is termed a nominative absolute (= "hanging nominative" = *nominativus pendens;* Col. 3:16, 17) or an accusative absolute (Eph. 1:18a).

Accusative
Basically, as the adverbial case, the accusative limits the application of a verb (or adjective or noun) with regard to extent, just as the genitive limits the application of a noun with regard to kind. The accusative denotes the direct object of a transitive verb, extent of time or space, or the subject of an infinitive. Other uses include the cognate accusative, the double accusative, and the accusative of respect (Col. 1:9).

Active
See **Voice.**

Adjectival Genitive
See **Genitive.**

Adnominal
Related to a noun.

Adverbial
Functioning as an adverb; related to another word, especially a verb.

Agent
The person performing or responsible for an action. When something impersonal performs or is responsible for an action, we speak of the instrument rather than the agent.

Anacoluthon (adj.: anacoluthic; from negating α(ν)- + ἀκόλουθος, following on; thus "[a construction] not following on")
A change of construction in the course of a sentence leading to a grammatical breach in continuity (Col. 2:2).

Anaphora (adj.: anaphoric; ἀνα-φορά, a reference back)
Repetition of one or more words in successive statements (οὐκ εἰμί in 1 Cor. 9:1). In addition, the article is anaphoric when it points back to a previous use of the same noun (2 Cor. 5:4, ἐν τῷ σκήνει, "in *this* tent" [cf. 5:1]) or points to someone or something familiar to the writer (and readers) (Col. 1:1; 3:5; 4:16).

Anarthrous (ἄν-αρθρος)
Without the article. An anarthrous noun may be indefinite (Col. 1:23, διάκονος), definite (Col. 1:15), qualitative (Heb. 1:2, υἱῷ); or may indicate the predicate (Col. 1:15) or a nonreciprocating proposition (1 Jn. 4:8).

Antecedent
Any word(s) to which reference is made later in the sentence. In particular, the substantive to which a relative pronoun refers is called the antecedent of that pronoun (in Col. 1:7 the antecedent of ὅς is Ἐπαφρᾶ).

Aorist
In all moods the aorist tense represents action as being conceived of as a whole ("punctiliar"). The action is presented simply as occurring, there being no indication in this tense itself whether the action is single (·), continuous (——), or repeated (·····). That is, with regard to the type of action involved, this tense is ἀ-όριστος, "undefined," "undetermined" (negating α-privative + ὁρίζω, define, determine). As a "punctiliar" tense that views action unitarily, the aorist

denotes "point" action (cf. Lat. *punctum,* point, dot), which either may be single, momentary action or may be continuous or repeated action that is telescoped into a point by perspective.

Most commonly the aorist denotes the *point of occurrence,* bare facticity; this use is termed constative/summary/complexive/global (Zerwick)/historical (Burton) (Col. 1:7). On occasion the aorist may also denote (a) the beginning or (b) the end of an action as: (a) the ingressive/inceptive (Burton)/incoha-tive/inchoative aorist (1:19), properly indicating the *point of entrance upon a state* (2 Cor. 8:9, ἐπτώχευσεν, "he became poor") but also loosely used of the *point of entry into an action* (e.g., T 74-75; = inceptive imperfect); (b) the effective/resultative/culminative/perfective aorist (Matt. 27:20; 2 Cor. 5:14, κρίναντας), indicating the *point of completion.* But these latter two categories (viz. ingressive, effective) are somewhat artificial and often reflect the meaning of the verb itself rather than a distinctive use of the aorist. Other uses include the epistolary aorist (Col. 4:8) and the gnomic aorist (1 Pet. 1:24).

Apodosis (ἀπό-δοσις, a giving back)
The clause in a conditional sentence that states the expected, actual, or neces-sary result of the fulfillment of the "if" clause (the protasis; see on Col. 4:10). See also **Conditional Sentence.**

Apollonius
See **Canon of Apollonius.**

Apposition
Placement of two nouns side by side, the second (which is "in apposition to" the first) elucidating or more specifically defining the first. They are usually in the same case (e.g., "the city, Jerusalem"; see also Col. 1:1, 25-26) but sometimes the second noun, the one in apposition, is in the genitive case ("the city *of* Jerusalem," an appositional/epexegetic/defining genitive; Rom. 4:11, σημεῖον . . . περιτομῆς; Col. 1:12).

Article
Greek has no indefinite article like English "a." Indefiniteness is shown by the absence of the article or by the indefinite pronoun or adjective, τις, τι, someone, something. A noun with the article (an articular noun) may be anaphoric (2 Cor. 5:4) or generic (Col. 3:18); it may denote possession (1:12) or may indicate that a proposition is reciprocating (1:18) or that a concrete application of an abstract noun is in view (3:14).

Articular
Any noun, adjective, participle, infinitive, adverb, prepositional phrase, etc.,

that is used with the article is said to be articular (or in a few grammars "arthrous"—the opposite of "anarthrous").

Articular participle
Used in agreement with an antecedent substantive, an articular participle (such as τοῦ παρόντος, Col. 1:6) is equivalent in meaning to a relative clause ("that has come," 1:6), and is either restrictive, specifically identifying the preceding substantive (1:26, "[the mystery] that was kept secret," τὸ ἀποκεκρυμμένον; not "[the mystery], which was kept secret"), or explanatory/nonrestrictive, describing the preceding substantive (2:12, "[God], who raised," τοῦ ἐγείραντος; not, "[the God] who raised").

Ascensive
Forming a climax (e.g., ascensive καί meaning "even").

Asyndeton (adj.: asyndetic; ἀ-σύν-δετος, not bound together, unconnected)
Omission of a conjunction, whether coordinating (Col. 1:10) or adversative (3:4; 1 Cor. 15:42b-44).

Attraction
Attraction occurs when a relative pronoun is "attracted" or drawn out of its proper case or gender by another word. The relative is attracted either to the case of its antecedent (Col. 1:6) or to the gender of its predicate (Gal. 3:16). When the antecedent assumes the case of the relative, *inverse attraction* has occurred.

Attributive (adj.)
"Attributive" can have the general meaning of "adjectival," or it can more particularly describe an adjective that directly modifies a substantive (Col. 1:7, ἀγαπητοῦ), as opposed to a predicative adjective, which modifies a substantive indirectly (πιστός in the same verse).

Augment
Usually the prefix ἐ- added to verbs in the indicative mood to signify past time. When a verb already begins with a vowel, the augment usually causes this initial vowel to be lengthened.

Brachylogy (βραχυ-λογία, brevity in speech or writing)
Conciseness or over-conciseness of expression (Col. 2:20). Sometimes this term is loosely used as a synonym for ellipsis; but, strictly speaking, ellipsis is a means of brachylogy. See **Ellipsis.**

Canon of Apollonius
The principle formulated by Apollonius Dyscolus, an Alexandrian grammarian of the second century A.D., that nouns in regimen (i.e., in a relation of syntac-

tical dependence) either both have the article or both lack it (cf. Moule, *Idiom Book* 114-115; T 180). Thus we find ἐν τῷ πνεύματι τοῦ θεοῦ (1 Cor. 6:11), but ἐν πνεύματι θεοῦ (1 Cor. 12:3), where πνεύματι is the "governing noun" *(nomen regens)* and θεοῦ the "governed noun" *(nomen rectum)*. See also Col. 1:5; 2:2. Apparent exceptions to the canon may often be accounted for by reference to other grammatical principles.

Cases
See **Nominative.**

Catachresis (κατάχρησις, misuse, misapplication)
Use of a term or expression in an alien, surprising, or incorrect sense (Col. 3:5; Gal. 3:8).

Causal
Stating or introducing the cause of an action. Used especially of a clause, conjunction (Col. 2:9), or participle (3:24).

Causative
Expressing a cause. Used of a verb (e.g., δουλόω, I cause to be a slave, enslave).

Chiasmus (adj.: chiastic; χιασμός, crosswise arrangement)
Arrangement of words or phrases so that they correspond to one another crosswise (A-B-B-A, etc.), like the Greek letter chi (X; see Col. 1:15-20, Structure; 3:11; Phlm. 5).

Circumlocution
See **Periphrasis.**

Circumstantial
Expressing the circumstances attendant on an action or situation (Col. 1:10).

Classical Greek
Broadly defined as the Age of Dialects (c. 1000-300 B.C.); or, *more narrowly, as the period c. 450-300 B.C.

Clause
Any section of a sentence that contains some verbal form.

Cognate
Having the same root or of the same derivation (Col. 1:11). When a verb is followed by the accusative case of a noun that is cognate with the verb, we have an instance of a cognate accusative (Matt. 2:10; 6:20).

Colwell's Rule
A set of rules formulated by E. C. Colwell in 1933 (*JBL* 52 [1933] 12-21)

regarding the use of the article with definite predicate nouns in sentences in which the verb occurs. The two most widely applicable rules are: (1) definite predicate nouns that follow the verb (as is customary) usually take the article, and (2) definite predicate nouns that precede the verb usually lack the article. See Moule, *Idiom Book* 115-116; T 183-184; Z § 175.

Comparative
The second degree of comparison of adjectives and adverbs (positive—comparative—superlative) is translated into English by "-er," "more——," "rather ———," or "somewhat ———." A comparative clause is introduced by a comparative conjunction and states a comparison (Col. 1:7, καθώς; Col. 3:13, καθὼς . . . οὕτως).

Complement (adj.: complementary)
A word or phrase that completes the meaning of another word (such as θέλω, Col. 2:1) or phrase.

Complexive
See **Aorist.**

Compound (adj.)
Consisting of two or more elements (ἀπ—ἐκ—δυσις in Col. 2:11). See also **Preposition.**

Conative
Describing action that is attempted (and usually unsuccessful). See **Present, Imperfect.**

Concessive
Stating or introducing a concession ("although. . . ," "even if . . ."). Used especially of a clause (Col. 2:5), participle (Col. 2:13), or conjunction.

Concomitant (= contemporaneous)
Accompanying, occurring at the same time; used of circumstances or actions (Col. 2:12).

Concord (adj.: concordant)
Agreement of one word with another with respect to number, gender, or case (ὅς in Col. 2:10).

Conditional Sentence
A sentence that posits a condition (the *protasis* or "if" clause) and the result of the fulfillment of the condition (the *apodosis* or "then" clause). There are many variations of this basic structure.
Traditionally, conditions have been divided into four classes:

1. real / factual / simple / first class/"determined as fulfilled" (R 1007), where the condition is assumed to be a reality (Col. 3:1);

2. unreal / contrary to fact / second class/"determined as unfulfilled" (R 1012), where the condition is assumed to be contrary to fact;

3. probable / slightly probable / more probable future / objectively possible / third class/"undetermined, but with prospect of determination" (R 1016), where the condition refers exclusively to the future, and ranges from slight possibility to virtual certainty (with regard to the expectation of fulfillment; Col. 3:13); and

4. improbable / less probable future / uncertain / potential / subjectively possible / fourth class/"remote prospect of determination" (R 1020), where the condition refers exclusively to the future, and states a remote possibility or a hypothesis that is, nevertheless, capable of being fulfilled.

Conjunction (adj.: conjunctive)
A word that connects a pair of elements, whether words, phrases, clauses, or sentences. Some conjunctions (such as καί or ἀλλά) serve to coordinate; others (such as ὅτε or ἵνα) serve to subordinate.

Consecutive (adj.)
Expressing a consequence or effect; = resultative/ecbatic (ἔκ-βασις, outcome). In HGk. the distinction between purpose and result tends to become blurred; in any case, a purpose is an intended result, and a result is an achieved purpose.

Constative
See **Aorist.**

Constructio ad sensum (Lat., "construction according to the sense")
Constructio ad sensum occurs when a construction neglects the strict requirements of grammar and follows the dictates of sense (Col. 2:15; 3:16).

Construction (vb.: construe)
Grammatical arrangement, the way in which the elements of a phrase or sentence are arranged by a writer or analyzed by a reader.

Contraction
Shortening of a word by the combination of vowels or diphthongs; the resulting shortened form. See also **Crasis, Elision.**

Coordination (= parataxis; adj.: coordinate)
Placement of clauses, etc., side by side through the use of a coordinating conjunction (Matt. 18:21), rather than subordinating one clause to another to indicate their logical relation (= subordination).

Copula (adj. [and sometimes noun]: copulative)
An intransitive verb (especially εἰμί) that connects subject and predicate. The adjective also means "linking," in a broad sense.

Correlative (noun)
The first or (esp.) the second element in a pair of words that are complementary (e.g., τοιοῦτος . . . οἷος, "of such a kind . . . as"; see Col. 2:1) or that are customarily found together.

Crasis (κρᾶσις, "mixing")
A union of the vowels of two syllables of two successive words, the former word being short (the article or καί) and closely associated with the latter word, the breathing mark of which is retained to mark the contraction. E.g., in the phrase καὶ ἐμοί, the ι of καί is omitted and the vowels (α, ε) thus juxtaposed contract to produce the fused form κἀμοί (1 Cor. 15:8). Greek often prevents the hiatus brought about by the meeting of final and initial vowels by (1) crasis, (2) elision, or (3) movable ν.

Dative
The case that denotes the person or thing to which something is given or for which something exists or is done. Thus the dative expresses the indirect or more remote object of a verb and the purpose or result of an action. Other uses include the dative of interest/advantage or disadvantage, of possession, of manner, of attendant circumstance, of cause, of reference, the locatival dative, the instrumental dative, and the sociative/associative/comitative dative (which subsumes the dative of manner and of attendant circumstance).

Deliberative
Involving the consideration of options. The deliberative subjunctive expresses a question that deliberates or weighs various courses of action (Acts 2:37, τί ποιήσωμεν; "what are we to do?").

Demonstrative (adj.; from Lat. *demonstro,* point out)
Pointing out. Αὐτός, οὗτος, and ἐκεῖνος are demonstrative pronouns, οὗτος and ἐκεῖνος also serving as demonstrative adjectives (this, that).

Dependent
In a relation of dependence; subordinate.

Deponent
Used to describe certain verbs that have middle or passive forms but active meanings. They seem to have laid aside (Lat. *depono,* lay aside) their active forms (rather than their middle or passive meanings).

Diaeresis (δι-αίρεσις, a division into parts)

Separation of two vowels that might otherwise be taken as a diphthong into two syllables, shown by a diacritical mark (··) placed over the second of the two vowels. Each vowel is then pronounced separately (Col. 3:12). Diaeresis is the opposite of contraction.

Diphthong
Two different vowels placed together and pronounced as a single vowel sound.

Direct Discourse
See **Direct Speech.**

Direct Object
The thing or person directly affected by the action of a verb.

Direct Question
A question in the precise form it was asked in direct discourse.

Direct Speech
Any communication recorded in the actual form in which it was given (Col. 4:10).

Distributive
Applying to each individual in a class but not to that class collectively (Col. 3:8; Phlm. 25).

Double Accusative
Occurs when two accusatives are dependent on a single verb (e.g., Mk. 4:2, ἐδίδασκεν αὐτοὺς . . . πολλά).

Ecbatic
See **Consecutive.**

Effective
See **Aorist.**

Elative Superlative
When the superlative degree of an adjective or adverb does not involve a comparison but is used absolutely, it has an elative sense (e.g., ἐλάχιστος, very/extremely small; ἥδιστα, very/most sweetly).

Elision
The cutting off of the final vowel of a word before an initial vowel or diphthong of the next word. The removal of the vowel is marked by an apostrophe (Col. 1:16; 4:15).

Ellipsis/Ellipse (from adj. ἐλλιπής, lacking)
Omission of words that are necessary to the sense and can be readily supplied

either from the context or from linguistic usage (Col. 4:16, τὴν ἐκ Λαοδικείας [ἐπιστολήν], "the [letter] from Laodicea"; 3:1, ἐν [τῇ] δεξιᾷ [χειρί], "at the right [hand]").

Enallage (ἐν-αλλαγή, interchange)
Use of one number, mood, tense, case, etc., in the place of another (Col. 3:18). This terminology is simply a convenient way of explaining apparent "exceptions" to "rules" (1 Thess. 3:11, κατευθύναι, singular verb after plural subject).

Enclitic (from ἐγκλίνομαι, lean on)
A word that "leans on" the preceding word to make its significance clear and that gives its accent to that word if it can receive it (there cannot be two acute accents on successive syllables).

Epexegetic (from ἐπ-εξ-ήγησις, explanation)
Defining, explanatory. Used, e.g., of the genitive (Col. 1:5), an infinitive (1:25), or καί (2:8).

Epidiorthosis (ἐπιδιόρθωσις)
Correction of a previous expression or impression; an apology added (ἐπι-) in retrospect (Phlm. 19; 2 Cor. 12:11). See also **Prodiorthosis.**

Epistolary Plural (= literary plural/editorial "we")
Occurs when, according to literary or epistolary custom, a single writer speaks of himself or herself using the plural number (Col. 1:3).

Final
Expressing purpose; = telic.

Finite Verb
Any verbal form that limits the action or state being expressed to a specific subject in the nominative case, whether expressed or understood.

Frequentative
See **Imperfect.**

Future
This tense expresses linear (————), iterative (·····), or most commonly punctiliar (·) action in future time relative to the writer or speaker. Apart from this basic usage to denote progressive, repeated, or single action in the future, this tense may express a command (imperatival/imperative/volitive/declarative future) or a real or rhetorical question (deliberative future). When a writer or speaker wishes to emphasize future linear action, the periphrastic future is often used.

Futuristic Present
See **Present.**

Generalizing Plural (= categorical/categoric/allusive plural)
Occurs when the plural actually refers to a specific singular subject (e.g., Matt. 2:20, οἱ ζητοῦντες = Herod; Matt. 2:23, τῶν προφητῶν = Hosea). The opposite is the generic singular.

Generic
Relating to a particular class or category (γένος, Lat. *genus*). An articular noun may be generic (e.g., ὁ ἄνθρωπος, mankind; οἱ νεκροί, the deceased; Col. 3:18, αἱ γυναῖκες, wives).

Generic Singular
Occurs when a singular noun in reality denotes a class or multiple examples (Col. 1:10). The opposite is the generalizing/categorical plural.

Genitive
Basically, as the adjectival/descriptive or adnominal case, the genitive limits the application of a noun with regard to kind, by indicating the class or category (γένος) to which it belongs, just as the accusative limits the application of a verb with regard to extent. Exegetically it is the richest of the cases. Uses include possessive (Col. 1:5), objective (the same verse), subjective/genitive of author (v. 6), epexegetic/defining/appositional (v. 5), qualitative/adjectival/descriptive/attributive/Semitic/Hebrew (v. 5), and partitive (v. 12). There is also the genitive of origin/source (1:13; 2:19), of comparison (1:15), and of relation/relationship/reference/"general genitive" (vv. 1, 15). This latter broad, basic classification ("genitive of relation, etc.") is simply a convenient way of grouping together those genitives that do not readily fit into one of the other major categories of genitival use. Such a procedure avoids the proliferation of categories (e.g., genitive of purpose, of direction, of advantage, "verbal" genitive) to cover all the unusual or unique uses and allows the exegete to determine from the context the precise nature of the "relation" (e.g., Jn. 5:29, ἀνάστασιν ζωῆς, "a resurrection that results in [eternal] life"; Col. 1:24).

Genitive Absolute
See **Absolute.**

Gnomic
Expressing a general truth (γνώμη, maxim). See **Present, Aorist.**

Granville Sharp's Rule
A rule regarding the repetition or nonrepetition of the article with coordinated substantives, formulated by Sharp in 1798. In essence the rule (as simplified

and abbreviated from pages 4-5 [Rule I] of *Remarks on the Uses of the Definitive Article in the Greek Text of the New Testament* [London: Vernor and Hood, 1798]) states:

> When καί connects two personal nouns of the same case, if the article in any of its cases precedes the first and is not repeated before the second, then the second always relates to the same person as that expressed or described by the first noun; that is, it is a further description of the first named person.

Following Zerwick's lead (Z § 184), we may simplify and extend the rule as follows:

> With two (or more) coordinated nouns, the repetition of the article distinguishes, while a single article associates the notions in a conceptual unity (or sometimes an identity). (See on Col. 2:8; 4:7.)

This restatement goes beyond Sharp's formulation in two regards—it applies the rule to more than persons and it explains the significance of the repeated article (not simply the significance of the nonrepetition).

Hapax Legomenon (pl. hapax legomena)
A word, phrase, or construction used only once in a specified body of literature (e.g., συλαγωγέω [Col. 2:8] is a *hapax legomenon* in the New Testament).

Hellenistic Greek
The Greek of the period c. 300 B.C.–A.D. 550, also known as *Koine* Greek.

Hendiadys (ἓν διὰ δυοῖν, one by means of two)
Expression of a single idea through two separate words coordinated by καί (Col. 1:9). Whereas epexegetic καί indicates a precise equation of two elements (X = Y), the καί used in hendiadys points to a relation, not to an identity, the second idea being subordinate to the first (Col. 2:5, χαίρων καὶ βλέπων, "rejoicing to see"), or, sometimes, the first to the second (in the same verse, "viewing with joy").

Historic Present
See **Present**.

Hortatory (= hortative/cohortative/exhortative/exhortatory/volitive)
Giving encouragement or an exhortation. The hortatory subjunctive replaces the imperative in the first person singular and plural (Heb. 12:1, τρέχωμεν, "let us run").

Hyperbaton (from adj. ὑπερβατός, transposed)
Inversion of normal word-order, usually for emphasis.

Hyperbole (adj. hyperbolic; ὑπερβολή, a throwing beyond, extravagance)

Intentional exaggeration of a fact for dramatic effect. The writer or speaker does not intend the statement to be taken literally (Col. 1:23; Phlm. 16; Jn. 21:25).

Hypotaxis (adj. hypotactic; from ὑπο-τάσσω, place under)
See **Subordination.**

Imperative
The mood of coercion or volition; a command.

Imperfect
This tense, which occurs only in the indicative mood, regularly expresses linear action (————) in past time (as indicated by the augment). Apart from this basic usage to denote action in progress in past time, the principal customary classifications of the imperfect are: iterative/habitual/customary/frequentative, conative/tendential/desiderative/of attempted action, inceptive/ingressive, and voluntative/volitive/deliberative/potential/of hesitant wish.

Impersonal Verb
A verb (such as δεῖ, "it is necessary," Col. 4:5; or ἀνῆκει, "it is fitting," cf. 3:18) without an expressed subject, rendered in English with the impersonal subject "it."

Improper Preposition
See **Preposition.**

Inceptive
Denoting the commencement of an action. See **Imperfect, Aorist.**

Indeclinable
Having only one form; not capable of being inflected.

Indefinite
Not referring to a specific thing or person. E.g., the enclitic τις may be an indefinite pronoun ("anyone," Col. 2:8) or an indefinite adjective ("any," v. 23).

Indicative
The mood of factuality or reality.

Indirect Command
A command that is not given in its original form but is reported indirectly (Lk. 18:40).

Indirect Object
The thing or person indirectly affected by the action of the verb; the thing or person to or for whom or which an action is carried out. It is never expressed by the accusative case (= the case of the direct object) but generally by the dative case, sometimes by the genitive, and is often preceded by a preposition.

Indirect Question
A question that is not given in its original form but is reported indirectly (Col. 1:27).

Indirect Speech
Any form of discourse in which statements, commands, or questions are recorded without the original words being quoted.

Ingressive
Denoting entrance upon a state or commencement of an action. See **Aorist.**

Inflection
The addition of endings to the stem of a word to indicate grammatical relationships.

Instrument (adj.: instrumental)
The personal or impersonal means by or through which an action is performed (Col. 1:10). When a person performs or is responsible for an action, we usually speak of the agent rather than the instrument.

Intensive
Having greater force or heightened significance; emphatic.

Interest
See **Dative.**

Interjection
An exclamatory word that usually expresses emotion (Gal. 3:1, ˀΩ).

Interrogative (adj.)
Related to the asking of a question; introducing a direct or indirect question (Col. 4:6). As a noun, "interrogative" refers to the word that marks and introduces a direct or indirect question.

Intransitive
Used of a verb (e.g., αὔξω, Col. 2:19) whose action ends with the subject and does not "go over" (Lat. *transeo,* go over) to a direct object. Thus intransitive verbs are verbs incapable of governing a direct object. See **Transitive.**

Inverse Attraction
See **Attraction.**

Irony (adj. ironic[al]; εἰρωνεία, dissimulation)
The expression of meaning by saying the opposite of what is intended (Mk. 7:9; 1 Cor. 4:8; 2 Cor. 11:20-21; 12:13).

Irregular Verb
Any verb whose forms deviate from the normal patterns of inflection.

Itacism
The displacement of vowels or diphthongs by an iota in pronunciation and spelling; more generally, the substitution of certain vowels or diphthongs (η, ι, υ, ῃ, ει, οι, υι) for one another as a result of their identical pronunciation (viz. "ee" as in "feet") in Hellenistic Greek.

Iterative
Denoting repeated or habitual action. See **Present, Imperfect.**

Koine
See **Hellenistic Greek.**

Linear
Denotes action that is continuous or durative (————). It is the opposite of one sense of punctiliar (viz. instantaneous, [·]).

Litotes (= meiosis; λιτότης, frugality)
Understatement, as when an affirmative statement is made by negating its opposite (Acts 15:2, "no small dissension" = a great dissension).

Locative (adj.: locatival/local)
A grammatical case expressing location, whether literal or figurative.

Meiosis (μείωσις, diminution)
See **Litotes.**

Metonymy (μετ-ωνυμία, from μετά + ὄνομα, change of name)
The substitution of the name of an attribute or characteristic for the name of the person or thing meant; or, more generally, the substitution of one term for another with which it is associated ("the pen is mightier than the sword" = "writing is more powerful than warfare"; see Col. 1:16; 4:18).

Middle
The middle voice represents the subject as intimately affected by its own action, or more specifically, as acting for its own advantage. See **Voice.** Originally the passive was one of the uses of the middle (the only purely

passive verbal forms are the aorists in -θην and -ην, and the future forms derived therefrom, -θήσομαι and -ήσομαι). In Modern Greek there are only two voices, active and passive-deponent. The beginning of this ultimate eclipse of the middle voice is apparent in Hellenistic Greek, where active or passive forms are not infrequently substituted for the middle. Four uses of the middle voice in the NT may be distinguished: (1) direct/reflexive (Col. 2:20; rare in NT), (2) indirect (4:5), (3) causative/permissive (Lk. 2:5), and (4) reciprocal (Matt. 26:4; very rare).

Modal
Indicating manner; sometimes used to denote attendant circumstances or even means.

Modern Greek
Broadly defined as the Greek of the period from A.D. 1450 to present; or, *more narrowly, the Greek written or spoken at the present day.

Modifier (vb.: modify)
A word or expression that qualifies or restricts the sense of another word or expression.

Moods
Categories of the finite verb that indicate the way or mode in which the action or state denoted by the verb is regarded by the writer or speaker—whether actual (indicative) or potential (imperative, subjunctive, optative); whether fact (indicative), command (imperative), idea (subjunctive), or wish (optative). In broad terms, the indicative is the mood of factuality or reality ("I did"); the imperative, the mood of coercion or volition ("you must"; "you should"); the subjunctive, the mood of contingency or probability ("I may"; "I well may"); and the optative, the mood of possibility or hope ("I might"; "O that I might!"). Some grammarians associate the subjunctive and optative as categories of a "conjunctive" mood. Again, some grammarians include the infinitive, the participle, and the verbal adjective as moods—moods that belong to the "infinite verb."

Nominative
The case of the subject. Historically, the nominative was regarded as the normative or "upright" case, with other cases being "oblique" (Lat. *obliquus,* slanting, deviating from the upright) as deviations or "fallings-away" (πτώσεις; Lat. *casus,* cases) from the norm. For the "nominative absolute" or "hanging nominative," see **Absolute.** On the "vocatival nominative," the articular nominative used for the vocative in an *enallage* of case, see Col. 3:18.

Object
The thing or person to which or whom the action of a verb is directed. See **Direct Object, Indirect Object.**

Objective Genitive
See **Genitive.**

Oblique Cases
See **Nominative.**

Optative
The mood of possibility or hope. In independent clauses, the optative may express a wish or prayer (voluntative/volitive optative) or may indicate what would happen if a supposed condition (a suppressed protasis) were fulfilled (potential optative).

Oratio Obliqua
See **Indirect Speech.**

Oratio Recta
See **Direct Speech.**

Parataxis (adj.: paratactic; παρά-ταξις, placement side by side)
See **Coordination.**

Paronomasia (παρ-ονομασία, a pun)
A play on words that sound alike (Lk. 21:11; Heb. 5:8) or that belong to the same word-stem (2 Cor. 9:8).

Particle
A word, usually short and always indeclinable, that expresses subtle shades of meaning and sometimes indicates syntactical relationships (e.g., ἄρα, γε, δέ, μέν, δή). The term is sufficiently broad to include conjunctions (e.g., ἀλλά) and negatives (οὐ, μή). Particles are often found in combinations (e.g., εἰ δὲ μή γε).

Partitive
See **Genitive.**

Passive
See **Voice, Theological Passive.**

Perfect
This tense represents an action as complete and as having abiding results at the time of writing or speaking. Sometimes the emphasis falls on the past action; more often it falls on the resulting present state (Col. 2:7, 14; 3:3; 4:3).

Periphrasis (= circumlocution; περί-φρασις)

A roundabout way of speaking; a circumlocutory expression. E.g., "to see someone's face" for "to see someone" (Col. 2:1); "harsh treatment of the body" for "asceticism" (v. 23).

Periphrastic Tenses
Five tenses in Greek that are formed by combining the present participle (in the present, imperfect, and future periphrastic tenses) or the perfect participle (in the perfect [Col. 2:10] and pluperfect periphrastic tenses) with the present, imperfect, or future tense of εἰμί. The action thus denoted is linear/durative/progressive. Sometimes, however, the participle is virtually equivalent to an adjective (1:21).

Permissive
Giving permission (e.g., the permissive use of the passive, Col. 2:20).

Pleonasm (adj.: pleonastic; πλεον-ασμός, superfluity; the use of redundant words)
See **Tautology.**

Pluperfect
This tense represents an action as complete and as having abiding results at a point of past time in relation to the writer or speaker. A comparison with the perfect tense (see **Perfect**) shows that the pluperfect is simply the perfect in retrospect.

Positive
The simple form of an adjective or adverb, expressing no comparison (in contrast with the comparative and superlative degrees of comparison) or no particular intensity (in contrast with the elative superlative).

Possessive
See **Genitive, Dative.**

Postpositive
Placed after another word; never occurring first in a clause or sentence. For example, γάρ is a postpositive conjunction.

Predicate (adj.: predicative)
That part of a clause or sentence which affirms (or denies) a certain fact as being true of the subject of the clause or sentence. E.g., in Matt. 5:13 ὑμεῖς is the subject, ἐστὲ τὸ ἅλας τῆς γῆς is the predicate (the copula is regarded as part of the predicate). A predicative adjective is one that modifies a substantive indirectly through the use of a copula (Col. 1:7, ὅς ἐστιν πιστός).

Pregnant Construction (Lat. *constructio praegnans*)

Occurs when one expression contains within itself an implied expression (Lk. 6:8, στῆθι εἰς τὸ μέσον, lit. "stand into the center," i.e., "come *into the center* and *stand* here," "stand in the center."

Preposition

A word placed before a noun or pronoun to show the syntactical relationship of this substantive to other parts of the sentence. Originally prepositions were adjuncts to verbs, "ad-verbs." This being so, prepositions have traditionally been divided into two categories: those that can be prefixed to verbs to form compound verbs (e.g., ἀπό in ἀπολύω) are called "proper" prepositions (eighteen are used in the NT); those that cannot (e.g., κατενώπιον, Col. 1:22) are termed "improper" prepositions (forty-two are used in the NT), all but two of which (ἅμα and ἐγγύς, + dative) govern the genitive case.

Present

This tense regularly expresses linear (——) action in present time. Apart from this basic usage to denote action in progress in present time, the principal customary classifications of the present are: historic(al)/dramatic, durative/progressive/of past action still in progress, aoristic/punctiliar, iterative, conative/tendential, gnomic, and futuristic.

Preterit

Expressing an action or state occurring in the past.

Privative

"'A-privative" is the prefix α, used in negating a word (Col. 1:22, ἄ-μωμος, un-blemished). Before a vowel the ἀ- becomes ἀν- (in the same verse, ἀν-έγκλη-τος, ir-reproachable).

Proclitic

A word that has no accent of its own since it derives its meaning or significance from what follows (e.g., ὁ, εἰς, εἰ, ὡς, οὐ). It "leans forward" (προκλίνω, lean forward) to the following word and forms an accentual unit with it.

Prodiorthosis (προδιόρθωσις)

Anticipatory correction of an expression or impression; an apology given in advance (προ-; 2 Cor. 11:1, 21). See also **Epidiorthosis.**

Prohibition

A negative command.

Proleptic (from πρό-ληψις, anticipation)

Anticipatory. When a tense is used proleptically, it depicts a future event as having already occurred, because it is so certain that it will happen (Jn. 15:6, ἐβλήθη, proleptic aorist).

Pronoun
A word that stands in the place of a noun. There are eight types of pronouns: personal (ἐγώ, I), relative (ὅς, who), demonstrative (οὗτος, this; ἐκεῖνος, that), possessive (ἐμός, -ή, -όν, my; more properly called the possessive adjective), indefinite (τις, someone, anyone), interrogative (τίς, who?), reflexive (ἐμαυτόν, myself), and reciprocal (ἀλλήλους, one another).

Proper Preposition
See **Preposition.**

Prospective
Pointing forward (Phlm. 15).

Protasis (πρό-τασις, a placing in front)
The clause in a conditional sentence that states the condition or hypothesis ("If . . . , [then] . . ."; Greek εἰ or ἐάν). See also **Conditional Sentence.**

Punctiliar (from Lat. *punctum,* point)
This term is used by grammarians in two distinct senses. With regard to action in itself, it denotes instantaneous, momentary, or "once and for all" action, the opposite of "linear" action. With regard to "aspect," i.e., how an action is regarded by a writer, it denotes action conceived of as a point, the actual nature of that action (whether single, continuous, or repeated) being undefined. In a particular instance the aorist tense *may be* punctiliar in the former sense (Col. 4:4), whereas the aorist tense itself *is* punctiliar in the latter sense (1:7, 10).

Recitative ὅτι
This redundant ὅτι, not rendered in translation, is a marker of the direct speech that follows and is the equivalent of quotation marks (Col. 2:9).

Reduplication
Usually the prefixing of the initial consonant of a verb's stem with the intervening vowel ε to indicate completed action in all moods of the perfect and pluperfect tenses. See **Augment.**

Reflexive
"Bending back" on the subject; implying that the subject acts on himself or itself. See **Pronoun, Middle.**

Relative
See **Pronoun.** A subordinate clause introduced by a relative pronoun is called a relative clause.

Reported Speech
See **Indirect Speech.**

Respect
See **Accusative, Genitive, Dative.**

Retrospective
Pointing back (Col. 2:4).

Semitism (adj.: Semitic)
Any linguistic feature in Greek that shows the influence of Hebrew or Aramaic or of both languages.

Sociative
See **Dative.**

Solecism (from σολοικισμός, incorrectness in the use of language)
An offensive blunder in grammar or idiom (Col. 3:14; but see discussion there).

Subjunctive
The mood of contingency or probability.

Subordination (adj.: subordinate; = hypotaxis, adj.: hypotactic)
The placing of one clause in a relation of dependence on another clause, especially through the use of a subordinating conjunction (such as ὅτε or ἵνα).

Subjective Genitive
See **Genitive.**

Substantive
A noun or any word or group of words that functions as a noun.

Superlative
The third degree of comparison of adjectives and adverbs (positive—comparative—superlative), translated into English by "-est" or "most ———" (e.g., swiftest, most beautiful), or, if no comparison is involved, by "very ———" or "extremely ———" (see **Elative Superlative**).

Synecdoche (συν-εκ-δοχή, from σύν + ἐκδέχομαι, receive from; thus, understanding and associating one thing with another)

Designation of the whole by means of the part (Col. 3:15, 21), or (less
frequently) the part by means of the whole (2 Cor. 9:2).

Tautology (= pleonasm; adj.: tautologous, tautological; ταὐτο-λογία)
Repetition of words or thoughts that adds nothing to the sense.

Telic (from τέλος, the end proposed)
See **Final.**

Temporal
Relating to time.

Theological Passive
Use of the passive voice with God as the implied agent (Phlm. 22), sometimes
to avoid a direct naming of God (perhaps v. 15).

Transitive
Used of a verb whose action does not end with the subject but "goes over"
(Lat. *transeo,* go over) to a direct object. Thus transitive verbs are verbs capable
of governing a direct object. See **Intransitive.**

Vocative
The case indicating the person directly addressed, used with (Acts 1:1) or
without (Jn. 2:4) the interjection ὦ.

Voice
A category of the verb showing the relation of the subject to the action or state
denoted by the verb. The *active* voice portrays the subject as performing the
action expressed by the verb. The *middle* voice represents the subject as
intimately affected by its own action, or more specifically, as acting for its own
advantage. The *passive* voice represents the subject as the recipient of action
carried out by someone or something else.

Volitive
See **Voluntative.**

Voluntative (= volitive)
Expressing a wish or prayer. See **Imperfect, Optative.**

Zeugma (ζεῦγμα, bond; that which is joined together)
Two nouns or clauses joined together by a single verb which, strictly speaking,
suits only one of them (1 Cor. 3:2, "I gave you milk to drink [ἐπότισα], not
solid food"; but cf. RSV, "I fed you with milk, not solid food"; Lk. 1:64; 1 Tim.
4:3).